Russian Imperialism
The Interaction of Domestic and Foreign Policy 1860–1914

Dietrich Geyer

Russian Imperialism

The Interaction of Domestic and
Foreign Policy 1860–1914

Translated from the German by
Bruce Little

Yale University Press
New Haven & London

Originally published as *Der russische Imperialismus*
Translated from the German by permission of the publisher,
Vandenhoeck & Ruprecht, Göttingen.
© Vandenhoeck & Ruprecht, Göttingen, 1977

English translation first published in Great Britain 1987 by Berg Publishers
English translation first published in the United States 1987 by Yale University
Press

English translation © Berg Publishers 1987

Printed in Great Britain

Library of Congress Cataloging-in-Publication Data
Geyer, Dietrich.
  Russian imperialism.

  Translation of: Der russische Imperialismus.
  Bibliography: p.
  Includes index.
  1. Soviet Union—Politics and government—19th
century. 2. Soviet Union—Economic conditions—
1861–1917. 3. Soviet Union—Foreign relations—
19th century. I. Title.
DK189.G4713   1987   327.47   86–26732
ISBN 0–300–03796–1

10 9 8 7 6 5 4 3 2 1

Contents

Tables

*Thankfully dedicated to Waldemar Besson
(1929–1971)*

My unforgotten friend from our years together as
Assistenten

Preface

This history of Russian imperialism originally appeared in German ten years ago. The international response of specialists was exceedingly flattering for the author; only in the Soviet Union did the book meet with silence, eliciting neither praise nor criticism. Several Western reviewers expressed the hope that the volume could be translated into English and thereby reach a larger audience. I am happy that this has now become possible.

Only minor changes have been made in the substance of this English version. Where necessary, I have added references in the notes and bibliography to more recent specialised literature, so that in this respect the volume reflects the current state of scholarship.

This English edition could not have been possible without the initiative of Dr Marion Berghahn, and I am grateful for her care and attention. Professor Gregory Freeze rendered assistance with the reading of the galley proofs, and I wish to express my sincere thanks to him as well.

Tübingen, November 1986   **D.G.**

Technical Note

Dates are given in accordance with the Julian calendar which prevailed in Russia until 1918. In the nineteenth century it lagged twelve days behind the Gregorian calendar customarily used in the West. In the twentieth century the difference became thirteen days. However, for clarity's sake I have given both dates, especially when referring to events of international significance.

Some Russian weights and measures were not converted:

1 desyatina	=	1.09 hectares
1 verst	=	1.06 kilometres
1 pood	=	16.3 kilograms

Introduction

The subject of this book is Russian imperialism between 1860 and 1914, between the emancipation of the serfs and the outbreak of the First World War. Of special concern is the connection between foreign and domestic policy — the internal workings of what we shall call 'Russian imperialism'. This is therefore not a history of diplomacy but an account of the internal background to foreign policy. We shall examine two different aspects of that background: firstly, the internal social and economic forces which influenced the great power policies of imperial Russia, and secondly the impact of Russia's international involvement on domestic tensions and problems of development.[1]

No strict division can be made between foreign and domestic policy. The venerable thesis of the 'primacy of foreign policy' (*Primat der Außenpolitik*) has not been replaced with a counter-proposal nailing the 'primacy of domestic policy' to its standard. The author would also like to keep his distance from a controversy which has recently broken out again and which can easily degenerate into shadow boxing, namely the academic dispute waged with typical Germanic thoroughness about 'modern political history'. The legitimacy of this field is not however really being challenged,[2] and in any case the effectiveness of various approaches is determined

1. The relationship of domestic and foreign policy in Russia has seldom been studied previously; cf. T. v. Laue, 'Problems of Modernization', in I.J. Lederer (ed.), *Russian Foreign Policy. Essays in Historical Perspective* (New Haven, 1966³), pp. 69–108; R. Pipes, 'Domestic Politics and Foreign Affairs' in ibid., pp. 145–70. There are also almost no recent presentations of the totality of Russian foreign policy over relatively long periods as treated in this book. Short overviews can be found in: N.S. Kinyapina, *Vneshnyaya politika Rossii vtoroi poloviny XIX veka* (Moscow, 1974); V.I. Bovykin, *Ocherki vneshnei politika Rossii, konets XIX–1917 g.* (Moscow, 1960); for an even briefer summary see: B. Jelavich, *St Petersburg and Moscow. Tsarist and Soviet Foreign Policy, 1814–1974* (Bloomington, Ind., 1974).
2. A. Hillgruber, 'Politische Geschichte in moderner Sicht', *HZ* 216 (1973), pp. 529–52; for a critical view on this see: H.-U. Wehler, 'Moderne Politikgeschichte oder "Große Politik der Kabinette"', *GuG* 1 (1975), pp. 344–69 and a reply from K.

in the end by the fruit of research and not by trench warfare conducted between historians, regardless of their debating skill.

There is however no reason to mask the fact that this book is much indebted to a kind of research that is beginning in the Federal Republic of Germany to view itself as *Historische Sozialwissenschaft* (historical social science). Its concern with introducing 'explicit and consistent conceptual and categorical systems' into historiography is shared by this author, although I cannot claim to have performed adequately in this respect.[3] This book might therefore seem somewhat old-fashioned. Nevertheless, many of the concepts and categories employed are related to the new directions in historical research. I do not claim as a result to have created an original theory, not least of all because of my inclination to trust in a scientific *lingua franca* that is understandable to modern historians but is not a rigid jargon.

My confidence that this can be done is based on the discussions in recent historical research. Most pertinent to this book is the fact that this research has succeeded in restoring the concept of imperialism (which had degenerated into a mere slogan) to such an extent that a useful basis has been created for a discussion of the problem, at least for the classical period of modern imperialism before 1914. The possibilities and difficulties inherent in international comparisons have been investigated, relevant questions raised and new fields of study staked out. In its most general sense, imperialism before 1914 refers to the direct (or formal) and indirect (or informal) rule which the developed, capitalist, industrial states exercised over less developed regions and peoples. This minimal consensus requires that we explain the political, socio-economic and psychological causes and conditions that prompted the imperialism of the 'metropoles'.[4]

The attempt to arrive at insights with broader significance is clearly much more difficult here than if one were comparing how the great powers operated and the various strategies for expansion in the international system. Even the European countries' methods

---

Hildebrand 'Geschichte oder "Gesellschaftsgeschichte". Die Notwendigkeit einer politischen Geschichtsschreibung von den Internationalen Beziehungen', *HZ* 223 (1976), pp. 328–57. Hildebrand even compares the controversy with the 'frenzied methodological quarrel' that raged around Karl Lamprecht pp. 329f.

3. H.-U. Wehler, *Geschichte als Historische Sozialwissenschaft* (Frankfurt, 1973); J. Kocka, 'Theorien in der Sozial- u. Gesellschaftsgeschichte', *GuG* 1 (1975), pp. 9–42.

4. W.J. Mommsen (ed.), *Moderner Imperialismus* (Stuttgart, 1971) with contributions from H. Böhme (Germany), K. Rohe (Great Britain), G. Ziebura (France), W. Schieder (Italy), H.-U. Wehler (USA); the impetus for this debate came from Wehler's book, *Bismarck und der Imperialismus* (Cologne, 1969).

of colonial rule[5] were more homogeneous than their internal reasons for conquering colonies and securing zones of influence. The comparatistic impulse in modern research into imperialism therefore makes us as much aware of how motivations differed as of the similarities in European imperialism.

This is especially true of 'economic imperialism', whose basic pattern has been described in classic theories.[6] Continuing expansion of industry, increasing interconnection of capital and markets, and internationalisation of economic cycles created a climate which doubtless affected even such backward empires as Russia or Austria-Hungary. However, it is impossible to rely on general answers without further qualification when it comes to judging the extent to which imperialist expansion was indeed prompted by over-production, dwindling markets, rising consumption of raw materials, or the need to export.

In view of subsequent developments, one may be tempted to understand imperialism as a reaction of political elites forced to do something to save their privileged position when the social basis of their power shrank or was even endangered as a result of socio-economic change. There is no doubt that the social consequences of advancing capitalism played an important role in the perceived danger. The 'democratic' tendency engendered by the transition to a bourgeois class society collided with outworn political systems. The ability of imperialistic states to reform themselves therefore took on new significance. Industrialisation acted as a catalyst in the disintegration of traditional social relations, and a great need arose for long-term management of the ensuing crisis. The mushrooming popular nationalisms of all kinds, the strain of Social Darwinism in imperialist thought, and the increasing attractiveness of a messianic mission to civilise the world can be understood in the context of internal strains and stresses.[7] This is why the classic theory of diversion (*Konfliktableitung*) has been so well received in recent

5. From the large amount of recent literature see: R. v. Albertini, *Kolonialherrschaft, 1880–1940* (Zurich, 1976).
6. M.B. Brown, *The Economics of Imperialism* (London, 1974); V.G. Kienan, *Marxism and Imperialism* (London, 1975); P. Hampe, *Die 'ökonomische Imperialismustheorie'. Kritische Untersuchungen* (Munich, 1976); H.C. Schröder, *Sozialistische Imperialismusdeutung* (Göttingen, 1973); W.J. Mommsen, *Imperialismustheorien* (Göttingen, 1977).
7. Wehler, 'Sozialdarwinismus im expandierenden Interventionsstaat', *Deutschland in der Weltpolitik des 19. und 20. Jhs. Festschrift für F. Fischer* (Düsseldorf, 1973), pp. 133–42; for an analysis of the relationship between nationalism and imperialism see: W.J. Mommsen, *Das Zeitalter des Imperialismus* (Frankfurt, 1969), pp. 152ff., 208ff.

3

research into imperialism: war and expansion are seen as methods to distract and integrate society and quell internal conflict.[8]

Despite all the controversies the heuristic quality of these hypotheses has been very beneficial, especially for attempts to highlight the multitude of factors which had an effect and the particular reasons within the general explanation. More specialised studies have also furthered the professional interest historians have in drawing distinctions and making differentiations. The results have elicited both support and opposition and have encouraged new questions — the discussion about 'social imperialism' for instance, as described by Hans-Ulrich Wehler using Bismarck as an example, or the debate about the relationship between imperial expansion and the vicissitudes of the economy, or the concept of 'organised capitalism' according to which the appearance of the modern interventionist state was a general characteristic of the era.[9]

The following study builds on what the author has learned from the aforementioned attempts to define categories. An effort is made to improve the methods used to assess Russian imperialism and thus to bring the history of this imperialism closer to the stages which have been reached in modern research into other imperialisms. It need not be emphasised that such an attempt is not intrinsically easy. The idea of comparing Russian imperialism with the imperialism of the advanced industrial powers might seem rather forced in view of the following facts: agrarian Russia remained economically backward right up to the First World War[10]; she suffered from a chronic lack of capital and a rising dependence on capital imports from abroad; her ability to develop an economic foreign policy was relatively limited; the development of a modern class system was weak in comparison with western Europe; when industrialisation

8. For the history of this concept since the time of Aristotle see: A.J. Mayer, 'Internal Causes and Purposes of War in Europe', *JMH* 41 (1969), pp. 291–303.

9. Wehler, *Bismarck*; Mommsen (ed.), *Moderner Imperialismus*; H.A. Winkler (ed.), *Organisierter Kapitalismus. Voraussetzungen u. Anfänge* (Göttingen, 1974); for an early Soviet debate on this concept of R. Hilferding see: 'Organizovannyi kapitalizm', *Diskussiya v Komakademii* (Moscow, 1930).

10. A. Gerschenkron introduced the concept of 'economic backwardness' into research on comparative industrialisation and based his Russian studies on it: *Economic Backwardness in Historical Perspective* (Cambridge Mass., 1962), especially pp. 5–30, 31–51; Gerschenkron, 'Agrarian Policies and Industrialization: Russia 1861–1917', *CEHE* 6, pp. 706–800; idem, *Continuity in History and Other Essays* (Cambridge, Mass., 1968), pp. 77–97; idem, *Europe in the Russian Mirror* (New York, 1970); for Soviet criticism of this concept see: I.N. Olegina, 'Kapitalisticheskava i sotsialisticheskaya industrializatsiya v traktovke A. Gershenkrona', *ISSSR* (1971–72), pp. 181–202, as well as Gerschenkron's reply, 'Criticism from Afar: A Reply', *SS* 25 (1973), pp. 170–95.

began, the autocracy's monopoly on power remained undiminished and society enjoyed very few opportunities to organise and participate.

There is indeed a great deal of confusion in specialised western studies when it comes to adequately describing the Russian variant of imperialism. The view is widespread that Russian imperialism 'was still in a preliminary stage as late as the first few years of the twentieth century' — roughly comparable with the stage passed by the United States in the mid-nineteenth century. Analyses which tie imperialism to highly developed industrialisation automatically lead to this result. Russia's peculiar position is usually explained by claiming (as some Soviet historians have also done) that 'from an economic point of view tsarist Russia was also a colonial dependency of European financial circles and therefore both a subject and an object of imperialism'.[11] Since there is a dearth of adequate discussions of the problem, the existing uncertainty has even made its way into specialised studies. Seldom is there much more to be found in the way of useful comparative insights than the uninformative statement that Russia played a part in the oligopolistic competition between states during the 'age of imperialism'. The actual social and economic conditions have not been adequately studied.[12]

This problem contributes to the stereotype, still found in western literature, that the expansionism of the tsarist empire was due to a natural law of Russian history. The problem of imperialism gets lost in the old cliché about the Russians' unbridled drive to expand and dominate the world. As part of the nineteenth-century confrontation between the autocratic Russian Empire and liberal public opinion in Europe, this belief was passed on from generation to generation in exaggerated forms which could at times become grotesque. It finally even entered the European working-class parties through Marx and Engels. Examples from three centuries abound. Count Miximilian Yorck von Wartenburg, for instance, calculated that since the time of Peter the Great 'the Russian Empire has grown by ninety square kilometres' per day. Historical research can apparently never get its fill of such suggestive data, as Reinhard Wittram quite rightly points out.[13]

11. Mommsen, *Moderner Imperialismus*, pp. 9f.
12. For an early outline of the problems see: E. Müller, 'Imperialismus [Rußland], Rückständigkeit, Großmacht', *Sowi* 1 (1972–4), pp. 27ff.; D. Geyer, 'Rußland als Problem der vergleichenden Imperialismusforschung', *Das Vergangene u. die Geschichte. Fs. f. R. Wittram* (Göttingen, 1973), pp. 337–68.
13. Y. v. Wartenburg, *Weltgeschichte in Umrissen* (Berlin, 1901), p. 495, cited in

It is not my intention to use new theories of imperialism to eliminate by definition the whole history of Russian expansion since the formation of the grand principality of Moscow in the Middle Ages. The Russian Empire developed by continually expanding the Tsar's domains, and this brought about great changes in the state after the might conquests of the seventeenth and eighteenth centuries. Non-Russian peoples were subjugated and a unique kind of colonial rule created. The Empire was involved in European affairs and in the Orient. With trading companies and settlements in 'Russian America' it made its presence felt on both sides of the Pacific.[14] When St Petersburg found itself confronting more advanced industrial nations in the nineteenth century, its policies remained tied to the traditions and consequences of the historical process of empire-building. In order to discover what 'modern imperialism' entailed in the Russian case, we need to study the *qualitative* changes which transformed the Empire and its policies between 1860 and 1914.[15] Only then can we see why this huge multinational empire did not lose its position as a great power — like the Ottoman Empire — when its economic and cultural backwardness became obvious.

If Soviet historiography is examined from this vantage point the difficulties quickly become evident. One is inevitably confronted with a theory of imperialism which continues to derive its axiomatic truth from an exegesis of Lenin's writings. Imperialism is seen as referring to a historical stage authenticated by the laws of history — it is the 'most recent step' or the 'highest stage of capitalism'.[16] Lurking behind this concept is the notion of the inevitable downfall of capitalism and, equally important, the development of the inter-

---

O. Hoetzsch, *Rußland in Asien. Geschichte einer Expansion* (Stuttgart, 1966), p. 29. For the continuity question see: R. Wittram, 'Das russische Imperium u. sein Gestaltwandel', *HZ* 187 (1959), pp. 568–93; D. Geyer, *Sowjetunion. Außenpolitik I, Osteuropa-Handbuch* (Cologne, 1973), pp. 1–18; for convincing arguments against geographically determined reasons for the history of Russian expansion see: C. Goehrke, 'Geographische Grundlagen der russischen Geschichte', *JGO* 18 (1970), pp. 161–202. Recent examples of the use of the concept 'imperialism' to describe expansionism since the fifteenth century include: H.R. Huttenbach, 'The Origins of Russian Imperialism' in T. Hunczak (ed.), *Russian Imperialism from Ivan the Great to the Revolution* (New Brunswick N.J., 1974), pp. 18–44. E. Sarkisyanz, 'Russian Imperialism Reconsidered' in ibid., pp. 45–81.

14. For the gradual building of the Empire see: C. Goehrke, 'Die geographischen Gegebenheiten Rußlands in ihrem historischen Beziehungsgeflecht', *Handbuch der Geschichte Rußlands*, vol. 1, pp. 8–72.

15. For an overview of recent approaches to research see the anthology: D. Geyer (ed.), *Wirtschaft und Gesellschaft im vorrevolutionären Rußland* (Cologne, 1975).

16. Lenin, 'Imperialism as the Highest Stage of Capitalism', *PSS* 27, pp. 299–429.

national class struggle under the hegemony of the proletariat and the leadership of the Communist Party. For imperialism to exist, tendencies toward 'monopoly capitalism' and 'state monopolies' have to be present, as well as domination by finance capital. The latter's historical role is to create all the material preconditions needed by socialism.

Soviet historians have therefore always ascribed prime importance to the socio-economic foundations of Russian imperialism. Their interest is focused on concentration in industry and banking. By demonstrating a continual process of monopolisation, Soviet historians try to prove that Russian capitalism had already entered its 'highest stage' around the turn of the century. By the time of the First World War at the latest, it had completed the transition to forms of state monopoly — which, according to Lenin, are the conditions that made the socialist revolution inevitable in Russia as well. For Soviet historians, Russian capitalism was therefore just as imperialistic in nature as that of the western powers and Russia cannot have been backward in any way which impinges on the preconditions required for socialism to emerge.[17]

From a chronological point of view, imperialism for the Soviets refers to the years after 1900 and thus coincides with the period leading up to 'Red October'. The concept of imperialism is therefore also useful for elucidating how this revolution followed the laws of history. However, this moulding of the concept around an end result should not blind us to the fact that Soviet research is far from producing unanimous conclusions about individual aspects of Russian imperialism. The controversies have a history of their own.[18] The debates are continually being renewed — not least because Lenin did not treat the imperialism of the Russian Empire systematically, nor did he consistently include it in his general theory. It seems that he wanted the syndrome of imperialism in Russia (and Japan) understood as a particular type or at least as a modification of classic imperialism. This distinction can be seen primarily where Lenin differentiates between 'monopolistic' or

17. Cf. K.N. Tarnovskii, *Sovetskaya istoriografiya rossiiskogo imperializma* (Moscow, 1964). For further discussion of Soviet research see: B. Bonwetsch, 'Oktoberrevolution. Legitimationsprobleme der sowjetischen Geschichtswissenschaft', *PVS* 17 (1976), pp. 149–85.

18. Besides Tarnovskii see the omnibus volume: *Ob osobennostyakh imperializma v Rossii* (Moscow, 1963); for the history of the imperialism debate in the Soviet Union see: K.H. Schlarp, *Ursachen u. Entstehung des Ersten Weltkrieges im Lichte der sowjetischen Geschichtsschreibung* (Hamburg, 1971), pp. 37–85.

'capitalist' imperialism and 'military-feudal' imperialism.[19] In any case, Soviet historians have had to make do with a scattering of remarks whose precise meaning cannot easily be determined even after persistent' attempts to do so. Judging by Lenin's dictum that in Russia during the First World War 'military-feudal imperialism' (*voennofeodal'nyi imperializm*) was still far more important than 'capitalist imperialism',[20] one would think that the compulsion apparently still felt by the heirs to the October Revolution to prove their historical legitimacy can be satisfied only by interpretations of Lenin which are extremely elaborate though still not free of inconsistency.

In view of this state of affairs, little is to be gained from recognising that the uniqueness of Russian imperialism must be discovered in the discrepancy between highly developed financial and industrial capitalism, a backward agricultural system still burdened by 'feudal remnants' and a system of internal colonies.[21] The same holds true for the view that the tsarist state continued to be closely allied with the landowning class and should therefore be considered as a decaying superstructure built by a feudal social order which had already outlived its time. It is not surprising that attempts to be specific soon led to controversy. In an effort to break the log-jam, Soviet historians have made a stimulating attempt to make their model more flexible by adding the concept of 'polymorphousness' (*mnogoukladnost'*) to the conventional historical stages when referring to Russian history before 1917.[22]

The comments bequeathed by Lenin offer an acceptable description of the problems posed by Russia's economic backwardness for the analysis of imperialism. However, Lenin did not solve those problems. Discussion continues to revolve around the extent to

19. A.L. Sidorov, 'V.I. Lenin o russkom voenno-feodal'nom imperializme', *Ob osobennostyakh*, pp. 11–52, as well as the contributions in the same volume from I.M. Brover (pp. 53–72), P.V. Volobuev (pp. 73–85), I.F. Gindin (pp. 86–123), A.P. Pogrebinskii (pp. 124–48) and others.
20. Cf. for example Lenin's articles in: *PSS* 26, pp. 209–65, 307–50, *PSS* 30, pp. 17–58.
21. Agrarian capitalism judged in the context of the discussion on imperialism: *Osobennosti agrarnogo stroya Rossii v period imperializma* (Moscow, 1962); K.N. Tarnovskii, 'Problemy agrarnoi istorii Rossii perioda imperializma v sovetskoi istoriografii' in *Problemy sotsial'no-ekonomicheskoi istorii Rossii* (Moscow, 1971), pp. 264–71; L.M. Goryushkin, 'Razvitie kapitalizma v shir i kharakter agrarno-kapitalisticheskoi evolyutsii v Rossii perioda imperializma', *ISSSR* (1974/2), pp. 49–70; P.G. Galuzo, 'Das Kolonialsystem des russischen Imperialismus am Vorabend der Oktoberrevolution', *ZfG* 15 (1967), pp. 997–1014.
22. *Voprosy istorii kapitalisticheskoi Rossii. Problema mnogoukladnosti* (Sverdlovsk, 1972).

which the tsarist regime which Lenin described as 'medieval', 'barbarous' and 'rapacious' had progressed by 1917 along the path toward 'bourgeois monarchy'. In view of the class character of the government, is it possible to speak of a 'merging' (*srashchivanie*) of capitalist and feudal interests? Or was their relationship already one of 'subordination' (*podchinenie*), in which the tsarist government could be characterised as an agent of Russia's industrial and financial bourgeoisie?[23] If one agrees with the theory of 'subordination', the generally accepted view that the Russian bourgeoisie did not finally seize power until the February revolution of 1917 is undermined. If one argues in favour of 'merging', the question arises of how quickly and to what extent the amalgamation of the landowning and middle classes had proceeded and how political power was distributed between them. What we lack are standards and criteria to judge the actual empirical research that has been completed. Further problems are posed by attempts to assess the degree of dependence which resulted from the flow of foreign capital into the Russian economy. Capital imports (not capital exports) were a peculiarity of Russian imperialism, in contrast with the general theory of imperialism. The thesis once advanced by Stalin, that the Russian Empire was a semi-colony, has been out of favour now for many years. However, the emphasis given by the Soviets to the relative independence of Russian foreign policy and finance capital speaks more for virulent patriotism in the Soviet Union than for increased confidence that the unchanging 'dependence' of the Empire can be squared with the Soviet theory of imperialism.[24]

One should not, however, overlook the valuable contributions made by Soviet historians to the study of Russian imperialism. This is especially true of the large quantity of recent research into economic and social history. The present book could not have been written without this essential work. Studies exploring the relationship between industrial, agricultural and financial policies were particularly helpful. Profitable use was also made of individual studies of military and naval rearmament and of research into the

23. K. Tarnovskii, 'Eshche raz o "srashchivanii" i "podchinenii"', *Ob osobennostyakh*, pp. 419–38; A. Ya. Avrekh, 'Russkii absolyutizm i ego rol' v utverzhdenii kapitalizma v Rossii', *ISSSR* (1968/2), pp. 82–104; the discussion on absolutism which Avrekh sparked off between 1968 and 1972 centred on the question of the evolution of Tsarism into a 'bourgeois monarchy'.

24. *Monopolii i inostrannyi kapital v Rossii* (Moscow, 1962); I.V. Bovykin, 'O nekotorykh voprosakh izucheniya inostrannogo kapitala v Rossii', *Ob osobennostyakh*, pp. 250–313; B. Bonwetsch, 'Das ausländische Kapital in Rußland. Bemerkungen zum Forschungsstand', *JGO* 22 (1974), pp. 412–25.

effect which political parties and economic interest groups had on the decision-making process.[25] Little systematic work has been done for a long time, however, on the impact of economic fluctuations and crises on Russia's international, great power policies.[26] Analysis of socio-psychological factors and collective mentalities would also be desirable. The latter are of course weak points of international historical research as well.

Some aspects of the theoretical discussion in the Soviet Union do deserve consideration when freed from their dogmatic armour. First and foremost is a recognition of the multifaceted social and economic nature of Russian imperialism. Lenin's distinction between 'military-feudal' and 'capitalist imperialism' in pre-revolutionary Russia implies the coexistence and at times fusion, of traditional interests based on pre-modern social and political structures and modern interests similar to those in the advanced industrial nations. The characteristic features of Russian imperialism will have to be found in the structure created by this overlapping and intertwining of the old with the new. We have to realise from the outset that in various regions and at various times imperial policy was influenced by very different combinations of factors. We shall make this clear using the examples of Russian policy in the Far East, involvement in European affairs, and expansion into Central Asia with the system of internal colonies to which it gave birth.

Even Soviet research indirectly implies that useful explanations of imperialism cannot focus exclusively on mature industrial capitalism. The processes of internal change that increasingly affected such backward countries as the Russian Empire or Japan after mid-century must also be considered.[27] It has long been a commonly accepted practice for research into the modernisation process to include structurally heterogeneous agricultural societies. Indeed they have even prompted the basic concepts of this kind of research.[28] Further study of Russian imperialism may well demonstrate that this approach produces more stimulating results for the analysis of

25. See the Soviet studies mentioned in the bibliography.
26. Theoretical studies of crisis and expansion in the economic history of the Russian Empire include: A.F. Yakovlev, *Ekonomicheskie krizisy v Rossii* (Moscow, 1955); L.A. Mendelson, *Teoriya i istoriya ekonomicheskikh krizisov i tsiklov* (Moscow, 1959), *passim*. For the older school of Russian theories of the economic cycle see: W.W. Rostow, 'Kondratieff, Schumpeter and Kuznets. Trend Periods Revisted', *JEH* 35 (1975), pp. 417–53.
27. C.E. Black et al., *The Modernization of Japan and Russia. A Comparative Study* (New York, 1975).
28. H.-U. Wehler, *Modernisierungstheorie u. Geschichte* (Göttingen, 1975).

imperialism than might be expected from a continual fixation on the stages of economic growth.[29]

The fruitfulness of such expansion and differentiation for social history has been pointed out by Barrington Moore in his studies of the role of landowners and peasants in the creation of the modern world.[30] Economic history also gained new insights from the model introduced by Alexander Gerschenkron into the history of industrialisation. It became clear that the complicated problem of industrial take-off could not be understood merely on the basis of the English experience,[31] and researchers have come to feel that differences must be noted if valid comparisons are to be drawn. Such observations also encourage us to investigate the particular features of imperialisms which were characterised by structural underdevelopment and economic dependence. Among them is Russian imperialism which has hitherto played only a very marginal role in the discussion among western historians.

The concept of imperialism on which this book is founded consequently includes the problems which ensued from a modernisation drive to catch up with the West — the crises produced by a process of socio-economic transformation which threatened the very existence of the system. The results were not unlike those experienced by the more developed industrial powers under pressure from the tensions of economic growth and rapid social change. We acknowledge that the long-term crises in Russia were related to the advance of capitalism, the destruction of the old social order based on agriculture, and the declining credibility of the old regime. The interdependence of expansionist strategies and more rapid socio-economic change also raise the question of the internal effects of imperialist behaviour. This book will attempt to discover how tsarist Russia actually fits these interpretations in the period between 1860 and 1914.

Given these opening remarks, there is no further need to justify the first part of the book which begins with the abolition of serfdom and the connection between liberal reforms and expansionism. Separate chapters outline the reform crisis (1); economic conditions under partial modernisation (2); and the impact of popular

29. W.W. Rostow, *The Stages of Economic Growth. A Non-Communist Manifesto* (Cambridge, 1960); idem (ed.), *The Economics of Take-off into Sustained Growth* (London, 1963).

30. B. Moore, *Social Origins of Dictatorship and Democracy* (Boston, 1966), also the controversy over this between S. Rothman and Moore in *APSR* 64 (1970), pp. 61–85.

31. Cf. Note 10.

nationalism on the autocracy's freedom of movement (3). Case studies are then offered for the two outstanding examples of offensive, expansionist policies between 1860 and 1885: the Balkan crisis (considered within the framework of the Eastern Question) and advances into Central Asia (4). Here we seek to show the part played by special interest groups in the development of imperialist strategies. A further chapter examines the internal limitations on Russian power — limitations that became highly visible during the 1880s (5).

In Part II, modernisation policies aiming at rapid industrial expansion are first discussed. These policies reached their extraordinary climax under Finance Minister Witte during the 1890s (6). The methods and costs of this attempt to overcome Russia's economic backwardness are elucidated in the ensuing chapters, which deal with the commercial and tariff policies that most disrupted Russia's relations with Germany (7), and touch on the link between the military alliance and dependence on foreign capital with regard to Russia's relations with France (8). Our attention turns next to St Petersburg's hazardous penetration of East Asia. This move was closely related to Witte's great industrial and railway projects which would determine the ability of the autocratic regime to withstand international and internal conflict (9). The catastrophe of the Russo-Japanese War and the revolutionary shocks of 1905 revealed the consequences of this 'borrowed imperialism' (10).

Part III discusses the problems of the period between 1905 and 1919 when the regime, decked out in constitutional garb, sought to re-establish its internal stability and international prestige. The internal connections between financial policies, rearmament and economic expansion are elucidated in chapter (11). The next chapter (12) delineates the tension between military planning and foreign policy which arose in Russia during the period of the international crises between 1908 and 1914 is then outlined. The following section describes the situation of internal conflict that ensued in the wake of political stagnation and apparent economic prosperity. Particular attention is paid to Russian nationalism and its role in the events leading up to the First World War (13). The final chapter describes Russia's colonial system and illustrates once again the distinctive aspects of imperialism as practised in pre-Revolutionary Russia (14).

It is not difficult to pinpoint the lacunae that remain. They are perhaps most obvious in the lack of detail to be found in the description of changing Russian society and the slow evolution of modern social classes.[32] Problems relating to the multinational structure of the Empire should also have been treated more fully. These failings are partly due to the underdeveloped state of the research but also to the author's own limited resources. A more serious deficiency is that the book does not include the period of the First World War although this would have been highly desirable in a work of this nature.[33] However, such an extension would have meant discussing the history of the Revolution of 1917, especially the connection between war and revolution which, unlike 1905, put a total end to the imperialism of the old regime. The author must crave indulgence for his inability to take on this intriguing task — a task which probably would have quickly evolved into an independent work.

---

32. For a research report see: M. Hildermeier, 'Sozialer Wandel im städtischen Rußland', *JGO* 25 (1977), pp. 525–66.

33. A Freiburg group is concentrating on comparative research into Russian history during the First World War. Cf. for the present G. Schramm, 'Die russische Armee als politischer Faktor vor der Februarrevolution (1914–1917)', *MGM* 18 (1975), pp. 33–62; Schramm, 'Militarisierung u. Demokratisierung. Typen der Massenintegration im Ersten Weltkrieg', *Francia* (1975); H. Haumann, *Kapitalismus im zaristischen Staat* 1906–1917 (Königstein 1980). H. Linke (Bonn) recently published a book on Russian foreign policy during the war *Das zarische Rußland und der Erste Weltkrieg. Diplomatie und Kriegsziele (1914–1917)* (Munich 1982): also important is the dissertation of B. Bonwetsch, *Kriegsallianz u. Wirtschaftsinteressen. Rußland in den Wirtschaftsplänen Englands u. Frankreichs 1914–1917* (Düsseldorf, 1973).

PART I

Reform and Expansion 1860–1885

1

Contours of the Reform Crisis

Modern imperialism, as understood by recent historians, cannot predate the development of modern bourgeois society. The formation of such a society requires the more or less rapid decline of traditional social and political structures based on 'feudalism'. As this occurs, and as capitalist economic relations flourish, a process of far-reaching transformation is unleashed. Any attempt to measure the extent to which this general model can be applied to Russia must begin with the effects of the emancipation of the serfs after 1861.

In the period between the Petrine reforms of the early eighteenth century and the revolutionary convulsions of 1917, nothing so profoundly altered the social, economic and political foundations of Russia as the emancipation of the serfs. This 'revolution from above' has always been portrayed by historians as the dawn of a new era.[1] According to Soviet historiography, the capitalist mode of social organisation, which had been gathering strength in the belly of the old feudal system now burst forth, propelling Russia into the age of capitalism. Non-Marxist historians find the reforms of the 1860s hardly less significant and they generally agree that the emancipation of the serfs represented a crucial step forward in the development of capitalism and new 'bourgeois' social relations.

In order to appreciate fully the degree of change, one must bear in mind that the old agricultural order, the *krepostnichestvo*, regulated more than just the peasant's relationship to the landowner. Serfdom

---

1. The historical literature on the 'liberation of the serfs' is immense. For an analysis with particular attention to Soviet studies see: P. Scheibert, *Die russische Agrarreform von 1861. Ihre Probleme und der Stand ihrer Forschung* (Cologne, 1973); in addition: L.G. Zakharova, 'Otechestvennaya istoriografiya o podgotovke krest'yanskoi reformy', *ISSSR* (1976/4), pp. 54–76; Zakharova, 'Pravitel'stvennaya programma otmeny krepostnogo prava', ibid. (1975/2), pp. 22–47. For government policy in relationship to the liberation of the serfs see: V.G Chernukha, *Krest'yanskii vopros v pravitel'stvennoi politike Rossii (60–70-e gody XIX v.)* (Leningrad 1972).

17

in Russia had created a tightly interwoven social, political and economic system with ramifications far beyond the realm of agriculture. The rights and duties of the various estates, the administrative, judicial and tax systems, the armed forces and the organisation of the economy were all bound up with *krepostnichestvo*. The 'emancipation of the serfs' therefore undermined the entire traditional political and social system.

For this reason, the process initiated by the Tsar's edict of 19 February (3 March) 1861 could not be confined to a simple restructuring of the peasants' legal status and it opened the door to profound and lasting changes in social relations, economic conditions and the administration of the Empire. The social evolution set in motion by emancipation had to be accommodated: communal lands needed to be separated and redeemed; institutions of self-government had to be established in the villages and rural districts and provinces; a court system had to be developed, municipalities reformed, universal conscription introduced, and the financial and tax systems gradually modernised. The inevitability of the process is indicated by the multitude of reforms introduced in only a few years by a handful of liberal senior bureaucrats and a not unwilling Emperor.[2] Measured by the notion of time which prevailed in old Russia they acted with remarkable dispatch.

Besides the institutional and social aspects of emancipation, there was a clear connection from the very beginning between domestic reform and foreign policy. Defeat in the Crimean War was certainly not the only reason for reforming Russia, but it was the unhappy outcome of that conflict that was directly responsible for forcing the government of Alexander II to pass from mere words to actual deeds. The Treaty of Paris (30 March 1856) deprived the Empire of the European hegemony it had won under Catherine II, consolidated at the time of Napoleon, and could demonstrate still most impressively under Nicholas I. The treaty seriously undermined Russia's imperial role and the prestige of its government by ending the Tsar's protectorate over the Danubian principalities and orthodox Christians in the Ottoman Empire, blocking Russia's access to the mouth of the Danube, demilitarising the shores of the Black Sea

2. For the internal connection between the reforms see: S.F. Starr, *Decentralization and Self-Government in Russia, 1830–1870* (Princeton, 1972); for individual reforms: F.B. Kaiser, *Die russische Justizreform von 1864* (Leiden, 1972); L.T. Hutton, 'The Reform of City Government in Russia, 1860–1870', PhD thesis, University of Illinois, 1972; for zemstvo reform see note 30 and for military reform see note 6.

and the Åland Islands, and obliging the imperial government to surrender Kars to the Porte.[3]

Defeat laid bare the discrepancy between Russia's traditional claim to great-power status and the backwardness of an Empire that had as yet scarcely felt the 'industrial revolution' sweeping through western Europe.[4] Within the ministries and among an influential minority of ruling aristocrats, the long acknowledged need for change was now perceived as urgent. The government recognised Russia's enormous underdevelopment and made its decision in favour of reform. The word 'progress', previously taboo, now began to appear in official statements: it would be needed, the government knew, if Russia was to be strengthened militarily and its endangered status as a great power recovered.[5] The outmoded armed forces could not be modernised without the emancipation of the serfs, and a flood of plain-spoken documents addressed to the Tsar's cabinet from the Ministries of War and the Navy left no doubt that Russia's ability to defend herself depended on a thorough reform of society, public finances and the administrative machinery.[6]

Agricultural conditions still dominated the economic planning of the reformers, and the regime was unlikely to concentrate on a programme of forced industrialisation immediately after the Treaty of Paris.[7] Economic planners felt they had first to deal with rescuing the ravaged public finances and then with strengthening the aristocracy's means of support and the ability of the peasantry to survive.

---

3. W. Baumgart, *Der Friede von Paris 1856. Studien zum Verhältnis von Kriegsführung, Politik u. Friedensbewahrung* (Munich, 1972), pp. 110ff.; P.W. Schroeder, *Austria, Great Britain and the Crimean War. The Destruction of the European Concert* (Ithaca, 1972).

4. W.L. Blackwell, *The Beginnings of Russian Industrialization 1800–1860* (Princeton, 1968); for critical remarks on this see A. Gerschenkron, *SS* 21 (1970), pp. 507–15.

5. On the attempt to keep 'progress' out of government papers (May 1858) see: M. Lemke, *Ocherki po istorii russkoi tsenzury i zhurnalistiki XIX stoletiya* (St Petersburg, 1904), p. 323.

6. A.J. Rieber (ed.), *The Politics of Autocracy. Letters of Alexander II to Prince A.I. Bariatinsky, 1857–1864* (Paris, 1966); Rieber, 'Alexander II. A Revisionist View', *JMH* 43 (1971), pp. 42–58. For a more balanced judgement of the motives for military reform see: D. Beyrau, *Militär und Gesellschaft im vorrevolutionären Rußland* (Cologne, 1984).The fundamental Soviet work on the military reforms is: P.A. Zayonchkovskii, *Voennye reformy 1860–1870 godov v Rossii* (Moscow, 1952); in addition, F.A. Miller, *Dmitrii Miliutin and the Reform Era in Russia* (Nashville, Tenn., 1968); J.W. Kipp, 'Consequences of Defeat: Modernizing the Russian Navy, 1856–1863', *JGO* 20 (1972), pp. 210–25.

7. For the economic prerequisites for the reform period see chap. 2; also A.A. Skerpan, 'The Russian National Economy and Emancipation', in A.D. Ferguson and A. Levin (eds.), *Essays in Russian History* (Hamden, Conn., 1964), pp. 161–229; N.A. Tsagolov, *Ocherki russkoi ekonomicheskoi mysli perioda padeniya krepostnogo prava* (Moscow, 1956).

Great significance was attached, even under the new conditions, to preserving the loyalty and good will of those social classes on whom the autocracy depended for its existence. At the same time, though, and despite a weak currency and low capital reserves, social progress was linked to a further initiative to which the government attached the highest priority: the development of Russia's stunted railway system.[8]

The creation of an expanded, far-reaching railway network was to be the first step on the road to overcoming Russia's economic backwardness and military inferiority. If the regime was to survive, agriculture, trade and commerce had to be encouraged, for only sustained economic growth could eradicate the danger of national bankruptcy which hung over the country like the sword of Damocles. In particular, grain exports had to be increased because a high trade surplus was needed to stabilise permanently a balance of payments that had been heavily weighed down by foreign loans. The best way to favour exports was to build a modern, effective transportation system that would permit freight rates to fall. To this extent it can be said that improvements in the transportation system were part of a political strategy for holding onto power.

Military strategists also thought that constructing railways was one of the most important tasks facing the government — even though the 'iron horse' had long been denounced as a foolish fad, a 'liberal swindle', and a threat to decency. Russia had paid dearly in the Crimean War for her neglect of railways. Besides branch lines to the royal palaces in Tsarskoe Selo, Pavlovsk and Peterhof, the only railways that existed when hostilities erupted were the Warsaw–Vienna line (1848) and the state-run Nicholas Railway (1852) by which travellers could speed from St Petersburg to Moscow in barely twenty-four hours. Since there was no line between central Russia and the south, guns and ammunition had to be transported to Sevastopol' by horse. French units from the Paris area arrived at the front four times faster than Russian troops from the more remote provinces.[9]

8. The Russian railway system before 1855: Blackwell, pp. 264–326. W. Pintner, *Russian Economic Policy under Nicholas I* (Cornell, 1967), pp. 131–52; N.S. Kinyapina, *Politika samoderzhaviya v oblasti promyshlennosti (20–50-e gody XIX v.)* (Moscow, 1968), pp. 150–96; A.M. Solovyeva, *Zheleznodorozhnyi transport Rossii vo vtoroi polovine XIX v.* (Moscow, 1975), pp. 11–60; R.M. Haywood, *The Beginnings of Railway Development in Russia in the Reign of Nicholas I 1835–1842* (Durham, N.C., 1969).

9. W. Baumgart, 'Eisenbahn und Kriegsführung in der Geschichte', *Technikgeschichte* 38 (1971) pp. 191–209, here p. 208.

The institutions governing Russia had therefore a number of military, fiscal and economic reasons for focusing on the railways as the heart of their financial and economic policy and strategic planning. Because of the perilous state of the treasury it was imperative that an attempt be made to entrust construction of the transportation system to private joint-stock companies which, the autocracy hoped, would be able to mobilise foreign capital. As a result, the loan business and speculation on the stock exchange experienced an initial, short boom in Russia as early as 1857 despite world depression. No thought was given at the time however to extensive industrialisation. It was only a decade later, after a preliminary look at the very meagre fruits of government policy, that the regime set out to use railway construction as a catalyst to stimulate the languishing heavy industry sector. This had been built up with serf labour, and now, after emancipation, was threatened with extinction.

This strategy for maintaining imperial power touched on all facets of life and it is important to realise how risky it was. The regime had to withstand a dangerous examination of its inner stability. Both autocracy and 'society' — the socially and economically privileged classes — experienced this era of rapid change initiated by government reform as a time of crisis. It was only after the turn of the century, when Russian liberals discovered their heroes in the 'social movement' of the 1860s that historians began to reinterpret the dark gloom characteristic of the age of 'great reforms' as the warm, optimistic sensation that comes from stretching for new horizons.[10]

Reasons are not hard to find for the grave misgivings felt at the time. One must bear in mind that up to and beyond mid-century traditional society and authority had gone largely unscathed; the self-image of the bureaucracy, the armed forces, and the land and serf-owning aristocracy was fully intact. However, the Crimean War blew the lid off this enclosed, secure world by exposing the rot in Nicholas' regime. Hopes were raised when the new government took power in 1855, but were permeated from the beginning by anxiety and doubt. These feelings only intensified as time progressed.

The government wrestled with the problem of how to manage reform without harming the institution of autocracy and the notion of unlimited authority. The landowning aristocracy for the most

10. Cf. for example the great jubilee edition: *Velikaya reforma (1861–1911). Russkoe obshchestvo i krest'yanskii vopros v proshlom i nastoyashchem* (6 vols., Moscow, 1911).

part resisted the impending loss of traditional privileges, and it could clearly not be allowed a decisive role in reform. However, the tsarist government was forced to try to persuade the ruling strata in the countryside to accord reform a certain degree of acceptance. The bureaucracy would not have been able to impose such a complicated modification of the terms governing rural labour and property ownership in the teeth of organised obstruction from the landowners.[11]

Besides the need to allow the nobility some limited, closely super-vised participation in designing and implementing reforms, the government faced other problems in implementing its programme. Graver than the concern about controlling the nobility were the anxieties that surrounded possible loss of control over the peasant population. The very poorly developed local police forces and the traditional loyalty of the rural gentry were both put to the test by continual outbreaks of local unrest sparked off by excited peasants carried away with unrealistic expectations.[12] Equally serious was the burden that fell on the constabulary and secret police because of the 'revolutionary activities' of 'nihilists' who, in urban intellectual circles, educational institutions and even scattered officer groups, had chosen to turn their backs on 'society'. In underground pam-phlets and proclamations they warned the government that the divine wrath of the people, its hunger for land and freedom, would sweep away the established order in a bloody revolt fuelled with the destructiveness of a new *pugachevshchina* — the rebellion of Cos-sacks and peasants in the reign of Catherine (1773–4).[13] It was the much feared conjunction of elemental peasant unrest with the calculated agitation of revolutionaries which made internal security seem the keystone of reform. The renewed outbreak in 1861 of a liberation movement in the Kingdom of Poland demonstrated with stunning clarity how easily the revolutionary danger could infect foreign affairs and embroil the government in serious international

11. D. Field, *The End of Serfdom. Nobility and Bureaucracy in Russia, 1855–1861* (Cambridge, Mass., 1976); Starr, *Decentralization, passim*; T. Emmons, *The Russian Landed Gentry and the Peasant Emancipation of 1861* (Cambridge, Mass., 1968).

12. Soviet documentation on the 'peasant movement': *Krest'yanskoe dvizhenie v Rossii. Sbornik dokumentov, 1857–1861 gg.* (Moscow, 1963); also the general discus-sion of D. Beyrau, 'Agrarstruktur und Bauernprotest. Zu den Determinanten der Russian Agrarreform von 1861', VSWG 64 (1977); T. Emmons, 'The Peasant and Emancipation', in W.S. Vucinich (ed.), *The Peasant in 19th-Century Russia* (Stan-ford, 1968), pp. 41–71.

13. P. Pétoux, 'L'ombre de Pougachev' in R. Portal (ed.), *Le statut des paysans libérés du servage, 1861–1961* (Paris, 1963), pp. 128–52.

conflicts. Within two years, not only Congress Poland but large areas of Russia's western provinces were in open revolt against St Petersburg.[14]

By now the government was plagued with other concerns besides peace and security. Most landowners were taking a dim view of events in Russia. Very few doubted that the nobility would be called upon to pay for reform, and many shuddered at the prospect of having to adapt their own operations, chronically deficient in capital, to a money-economy and hired labour. The liquidation of the old state-owned banks and the liberation of the 'souls' pledged there (about 66 per cent of all proprietary peasants in 1859!) revealed the enormous indebtedness of the gentry. Even the prospect of selling the land allotted to peasant communes had little effect. Most of the fixed-interest letters of credit advanced to the landowners by the finance minister as compensation for lost land went to pay off accumulated debts and were dissipated. It seemed likely that many estates would not be able to endure commercialisation and would be ruined.

The various elements of the nobility were of course affected very differently by the 'emancipation of the serfs' and general conclusions must be drawn with care. A glance at property holdings will show that the economic interests of aristocrats were not necessarily identical. Statistics on holdings of male serfs show that the majority of landed nobles (*pomeshchiki*) lived in modest and usually very constrained circumstances: 76.7 per cent of all landed aristocrats (79,068 people in 46 provinces of European Russia) held fewer than 100 male serfs each at the time of the tenth census (1857–8). This amounts to only about one-fifth of all male serfs. More than one-half of these petty nobles (42,959 people) had fewer than 21 'souls' on their lands, which could often scarcely be distinguished from impoverished peasant properties. Every fifth rural noble (19.5 per cent of the total) owned from 101 to 500 'souls' and can therefore be assigned to the middle stratum; the revenues of these 20,162 individuals were considered adequate, and collectively they possessed about 37 per cent of all serfs. Only 3.8 per cent of the landed gentry belonged to the category of large landowners with over 500 serfs each (or 43.7 per cent of the total).[15]

14. For the Polish rebellion, see chap. 3.
15. On the holdings of the Russian nobility see: A.P. Korelin, 'Dvoryanstvo v poreformennoi Rossii (1861–1904 gg.)', *IZ* 87 (1971), pp. 91–173, especially pp. 139ff. For a general work on population and social statistics in the pre-reform period

These data do not provide sufficient insight into the wealth of individual nobles or into their chances of adapting to new conditions. There were also substantial regional differences which should be borne in mind. Still, it is clear that once the right to hold serfs was abolished the nobility's days as the ruling class were numbered.

Despite enormous differences in wealth, the nobility were united by their sense of loss and endangerment. The Prussian envoy, Otto von Bismarck, reflected the fears of conservative interlocutors when he wrote in April 1861 that N. A. Milyutin, the prime instigator of reform, possessed the 'sharpest, most daring mind of all the progressives' while harbouring 'bitter hatred of the nobility'. Milyutin imagined 'the Russia of tomorrow as a peasant state featuring equality but no liberty with a great deal of intelligence, industry, bureaucracy and press, roughly along the lines of the Napoleonic model'.[16] Even proponents of reform concluded that the 'tyranny of freedom is no less dangerous than the tyranny of despotism'.[17]

The gentry's palpable loss of status in these years was reflected in the rising rebelliousness of the peasants, and life in the countryside grew uncomfortable and even dangerous at times for the upper classes. Nobles of modest means sought to move into the city; the wealthy and those who succeeded in selling their estates transferred capital outside Russia and took frequent foreign holidays. Between 1856 and 1860 alone, the number of travellers leaving Russia climbed from 17,000 to 275,000, and their lengthy sojourns outside the country put a heavy strain on the nation's reserves of foreign currency.[18]

Nobles living in the cities often found that the old sense of security had vanished from urban areas as well. The growth of a middle-class, capitalist economy stoked the feeling that the nobility was being sacrificed to an uncertain future. Revolutionary groups demonstrated, insurrectionary speeches could be heard at the universities and a series of mysterious cases of arson occurred; anarch-

---

see: V.M. Kabuzan, *Narodonaselenie v Rossii v XVIII – pervoii polovine XIX v.* (Moscow, 1963).

16. Bismarck to Schleinitz on 6 Apr. 1861, cited in B.A. Nolde, *Die Petersburger Mission Bismarcks 1859–1862* (Leipzig, 1936), p. 185; also E. Pyzuir, 'Bismarck's Appraisal of Russian Liberalism as Prussian Envoy in St Petersburg', *CSP* 10 (1968), pp. 298–311; cf. as well B. Jelavich (ed.), *Rußland 1852–1871. Aus den Berichten der Bayrischen Gesandtschaft in St Petersburg* (Wiesbaden, 1963).

17. 'Tyranny of Freedom': A.V. Nikitenko, *Moya povest' o samom sebe. Zapiski i dnevnik, 1804–1877 gg.* (St Petersburg, 1905²), vol. 2, p. 87 (11 June 1862).

18. A.N. Kulomsin in *Die finanzielle Sanierung Rußlands nach der Katastrophe des Krimkrieges 1862 bis 1878 unter dem Finanzminister Michael v. Reutern* (Berlin, 1914), p. 177.

istic values and revolt against traditional values were carried by young students into the very bosom of the family. Under these circumstances, many felt that the Apocalypse could not be far off.[19]

Thus alienation, isolation, loss of purpose and outright fear of anarchy and revolution profoundly disturbed an aristocracy which felt uprooted from the patriarchic security of Nicholaevan Russia. As the nobility's traditional dominant role melted away, fears arose that the country would be completely abandoned to the whims of an incompetent, corrupt and hated bureaucracy in whose upper reaches the same democratic levelling tendency was at work as in the 'nihilist lairs' of universities and gymnasiums.[20] The government did not seem able to stop the slide to perdition, and the 'Tsar-Liberator' reminded many of his contemporaries more of Louis XVI than a ruler who knew how to exorcise radical change. Revolution was becoming respectable, it was said, and was preparing to take its place at the Tsar's own table in the guise of certain senior bureaucrats.[21] Taken together, all these signs reveal a severe crisis of authority after 1860 which undermined the confidence of much of the upper class in the autocracy. The incessant flight of capital across the border clearly demonstrates what the social elite thought of its future under this government.

The sense of crisis was no less severe at the very pinnacle of society, at the imperial court and among ministerial bureaucrats. The diaries of the Minister of the Interior, P. A. Valuev, provide an inkling of the deep pessimism that held even the highest nobility and most illustrious servants of the crown in its grip, and moved the Grand Duchess, Mariya Nikolaevna, to comment in October 1861, 'On nous chassera tous d'ici à un an'. Lines such as this from the Tsar's own sister reflect the depressed state of mind that afflicted more than just a few sensitive souls.[22] In a memorandum to the Tsar, the Minister of the Interior wrote in 1862:

19. On the 'youth movement' of the reform period: A. Besançon, *Education et société en Russie dans le second tiers du XIX siècle* (Paris, 1974); T. Hegarty, 'Student Movement in Russian Universities, 1855–1861', PhD thesis, Harvard University, 1965.

20. F. Diestelmeier has written a thesis on the fear of revolution around 1860: 'Soziale Angst. Konservative Reaktionen auf liberale Reformpolitik in Rußland unter Alexander II (1855–1866)', Frankfurt, 1985. In the Soviet Union a group of researchers around M.V. Nechkina have studied the reforms from the point of view of a 'revolutionary situation'. See *Revolyutsionnaya situatsiya v Rossii, 1859–1861 gg.*, (6 vols., Moscow, 1960–74); for a critique of this concept see: C.C. Adler, 'The "Revolutionary Situation" 1859–1861', *CSS* 3 (1969), pp. 383–99.

21. Nikitenko, p. 103 (17 Oct. 1862).

22. *Dnevnik P.A. Valueva* 1 (1861–1864), (Moscow, 1961), p. 119 (12 Oct. 1861).

The isolation in which the government finds itself is a matter of serious concern to everyone truly faithful to Emperor and country. What is commonly called the nobility fails to understand its true interests, is dissatisfied, irritated, lacking in devotion, and split into a multitude of opposing views so that no part of it can be relied on at present for strong support. The merchant class is scarcely involved in politics, but in any case it is not trusted and exerts no helpful influence on the masses. Religious orders harbour some disorderly elements, and for the rest, do not support progress of any kind and have influence only when they oppose us or are somehow harmful. The peasantry forms a more or less independent and restless mass seduced by dangerous illusions and impossible dreams. Finally the army — the only magnet still holding the disparate elements of the state together in a kind of deceptive unity, a bastion of public order — even it is beginning to falter and cannot guarantee full security.[23]

Over and above this, solidarity was lacking even within the autocracy itself. Various ministries competed for access to the Tsar, and drew encouragement from his paralysing self-doubts and old-fashioned style of leadership. The tradition for individual ministers to present their reports directly in the Tsar's study split policy into a number of separate spheres. There were violent differences of opinion within the various branches of government which advised the Tsar and drew up proposals — the Council of State, the Committee of Ministers, and a number of ad hoc commissions. It was the Emperor's approval which brought laws and ukases into effect, but a host of shifting influences bore upon the decision-making process, turning the struggle for the Tsar's ear into a game of chance even for trusted advisors. Members of the royal family with vastly differing political views sought to sway their most illustrious relative; advisors from the school of Nicholas I warned the Tsar that the new regime would be the ruin of Russia; rational, progressive ministers of liberal inclination suffered under the weight of all the dealings and intrigue, the incompetence of their colleagues, and the wavering favour of their Emperor: 'Quels misérables hommes d'état nous sommes! Qu'avons-nous prévu, organisé, prévenu, accompli? Toujours aux expédients d'un jour à l'autre et jouant à sorte de loterie

23. P.A. Valuev, 'O vnutrennem sostoyanii Rossii (26 June 1862)', *IA* (1958/1), pp. 141–4. The minister was apparently not very worried about the proletariat in the factories; cf. in general: R.E. Zelnik, *Labor and Society in Tsarist Russia. The Factory Workers of St Petersburg 1855–1870* (Stanford, 1971) — this excellent study also demonstrates the increasing role of workers in internal security problems.

avec l'espoir de gagner un gros lot.'[24]

All this confusion and disagreement was intensified by what might be called the politicisation of society as reflected in the contemporary term *obshchestvennoe dvizhenie*. As large sections of the nobility demanded protection and the right to be heard, a rising tide of petitions and addresses flooded the government and quickly put the autocracy on notice that the changes planned or already in progress could not be handled in secret. Secrecy would also have worked against the government's strong desire to persuade the old elites, the very foundation of autocracy, at least to accept passively what was about to happen. To a certain extent, the process of reform had already become public when the decision was made to invite the provincial committees of the nobility and the deputies, who had been summoned to St Petersburg in 1859–60, to respond to a series of tabled questions.[25] The government quickly realised that the traditional voicelessness of Russian society, rigorously enforced by the police apparatus as recently as the time of Nicholas I, had become a relic of the past. 'Public opinion' (*obshchestvennoe mnenie*) was no longer a creature of the government. If reform was to succeed, critical thought could not be confined to émigré newspapers such as Alexander Herzen's *Kolokol* in London, but would have to find expression within Russia itself under relaxed, limited censorship.

As a result of the new attitudes forced on the government, the reform period witnessed the first flowering of political journalism in Russia.[26] It soon became clear that through the discussions and criticism in the press, which the politically aware classes read and absorbed, an independent locus of power had been created. Conservative, liberal, Slavophile and democratic voices all made themselves heard in the organs of public opinion; political groups coalesced and spoke out in the name of society, the state, the people and the best interests of the Russian Empire. A common thread to all the criticism was opposition to the bureaucratic machinery of the

24. 'What wretched statesmen we are! What have we foreseen, organised, prevented, accomplished? Always expedients from one day to the next and playing a sort of lottery with the hope of hitting the jackpot!', *Dnevnik Valueva* 1, p. 248 (20 Sept. 1863).
25. Emmons, *Landed Gentry*, pp. 209ff., 266ff.; Field, *The End*, pp. 265ff.
26. There are no adequate studies of the role of the press and the public in the reform period. New material can be found in: Yu. I. Gerasimova, *Iz istorii russkoi pechati v period revolyutsionnoi situatsii kontsa 1850-kh–nachala 1860-kh godov* (Moscow, 1974). For the state of censorship before 1861 see: Lemke, *Ocherki*; Field, *The End*, pp. 149ff.; I. Grüning, *Die russische öffentliche Meinung und ihre Stellung zu den Großmächten, 1878–1894* (Berlin, 1929), pp. 19ff.

state and demands for self-government and 'openness' (*glasnost'*).[27] No consensus existed, however, on the question of who should be responsible for self-government in the districts and provinces: aristocrats 'born' to mediate between the ruler and his people? owners of private property in their capacity as the most responsible group of citizens? the educated classes as the preceptors of the people and defenders of democratic rights? Such a welter of conflicting ideas and demands created a novel experience for the autocratic regime in Russia, and it had difficulty coming to terms with the new reality. Herbert von Bismarck's remark that the Russian press was the 'corollary' to missing parliamentary institutions was especially true during the reform period.[28]

The compensatory function of the press derived from the fact that the literate public, now interested in politics, was denied the right to participate in the decision-making process. Even convinced liberals seemed ready to eschew a representative body which would have competed with the autocracy and steered Russia towards constitutionalism. In view of the low general level of education among the Russian populace, many partisans of reform considered that, as far as constitutional matters were concerned, organic progress depended for the time being on the continuation of autocracy.[29]

The Tsar also did not want to hear of any pseudo-constitutional plans like those being considered in various ways and with varying degrees of seriousness by some members of the conservative nobility, slavophile writers, and even at times by the Minister of the Interior, Valuev. In the end, the Tsar did agree, as part of the reforms of 1864, to let people serve in self-governing institutions (*zemstvo*) for local administration and economic matters, though they were supervised by the bureaucracy. The local presence of the state was not to be replaced or even balanced by a zemstvo of all classes however. Elected bodies were meant merely to fulfil their imperial duties as a powerless extension of the administration. Since most of the nobility was slow to accept this dubious offer, and since liberal demands for self-government modelled after the English

27. Starr, pp. 201ff.
28. *GP* 5, p. 83; R. Wittram, 'Die russisch-nationalen Tendenzen der achtziger Jahre im Spiegel der österreichisch-ungarischen diplomatischen Berichte aus St Petersburg', in idem, *Das Nationale als europäisches Problem* (Göttingen, 1954), p. 201.
29. Cf. B. Chicherin, *O narodnom predstavitel'stve* (Moscow, 1866), pp. 412ff.; see also S. Benson, 'The Conservative Liberalism of Boris Chicherin', *FOG* 21 (1975), pp. 17–114.

system were not successful, the press remained for the time being the only institution in Russia capable of reflecting the public mood, whether critical or adulatory.[30]

There is no doubt that the Tsar and his ministers considered public opinion destructive. They deeply regretted the rising confidence of political journalism in Russia because it rarely reflected government views. The 'newspaper disease' (*gazetobolezn'*) took on unsettling proportions and even infiltrated the palace, the ministries and the offices of provincial officials.[31] The ponderous apparatus of state was not suited to developing a means of steering the press flexible enough as to meet the challenge from political journalism. The official publications of ministries and government provided no effective counterweight and an official gazette, *Severnaya Pochta* (Northern Post), founded by the Minister of the Interior in 1861, could not compete with the quality and resonance of the great St Petersburg and Moscow newspapers.

In discussing 'public opinion', one must remember that the views expressed in the press were those of a tiny minority of people living almost exclusively in the two capital cities. The literate audience that scrutinised these opinions formed a loosely associated 'public', but comprised only a small fraction of the Russian populace. However, in a country where 'politics' was necessarily a matter for small minorities, the effect of the press on relations between government and society was by no means negligible.

Autocracy's right to govern was not in question and the government was fully capable of suppressing any voices in the press that it found objectionable — even after preemptive censorship was abolished in the capital cities in 1865.[32] Nevertheless, the authorities continued to view the press as a kind of countervailing force. 'Not a single newspaper of any repute', claimed the Minister of the Interior in 1868, genuinely sympathises with the state; the government may find 'an occasional, fortuitous ally' in the press, but usually the government can 'only see it as an opponent.'[33] Valuev's successor,

30. Starr, pp. 241ff.; V. Garmiza, *Podgotovka zemskoi reformy 1864 g.* (Moscow, 1957).

31. *Dnevnik Valueva* 2 (1865–1876), (Moscow, 1961), p. 87 (12 Dec. 1865).

32. C.A. Rudd, 'The Russian Empire's New Censorship Law of 1865', *CSS* 3 (1969), pp. 235–45; D. Balmuth, 'Origins of the Russian Press Reform of 1865', *SEER* 47 (1969), pp. 369–88.

33. Valuev's report on the state of the press (8 Feb. 1868) in: *Dnevnik Valueva* 2, pp. 496ff. The Minister of the Interior's eloquent complaints about the press's hostile attitude to the government are also in the reports of 1862, 1864 and 1866 published by V. Garmiza in *IA* (1958/1), pp. 141ff.; cf. as well the unpublished thesis of G.D.

A.E. Timashev, also complained that parts of the press, especially the *Moskovskie vedomosti* (Moscow News), assumed 'the role of a supreme court' charged with judging 'the dignity and personal competence of the central organs of government'. This could not be tolerated, argued Timashev, by anyone concerned with upholding the authority of the administration.[34]

Other factors need also to be considered if the role and importance of public opinion in an autocratic system is to be understood. The craving for prestige among high-ranking government officials and their desire to govern in ideological harmony with their subjects increased rather than diminished during the reform period. The government's sensitivity was further heightened by uncertainty as to how far the process of reform should be taken, and by fear that developments could get out of hand. The highest authorities realised that as the old social order crumbled traditional society could no longer remain impervious: Neither the bureaucracy's traditional modes of expression, nor the orthodox pieties in which the Tsar customarily enveloped his speech when addressing the peasantry appealed to the new public. While the process of disintegration which ran right through traditional institutions could perhaps be slowed, it could clearly not be halted.

These nagging difficulties account for the ease with which some writers, wilful and critical despite their fundamental loyalty, could make themselves as indispensable to the government as they were irritating. The reputation and influence of these writers reflects the enormous difficulties the government was experiencing in formulating policies capable of producing a working consensus. No government scribe could compete with the Slavophile and Pan-Slav pathos of I. S. Aksakov, or with the emotional appeal of the Russian nationalist view of the state in the work of the Moscow press baron, M. N. Katkov.[35] The autocracy derived little comfort from the fact that the vehement nationalism of these and other opinion makers

---

Knutson, 'Peter Valuev: A Conservative's Approach and Reactions to the Reforms of Alexander II', University of Kansas, 1970, pp. 147ff.

34. A.E. Timashev, 'Report "On the Misuse of the Printed Word"' (20 Nov. 1869), *Dnevnik Valueva* 2, pp. 503f.

35. For a biographical orientation: M. Katz, *M.N. Katkov. A Political Biography 1818–1887* (Den Haag, 1966); S. Lukashevich, *Ivan Aksakov 1823–1886. A Study in Russian Thought and Politics* (Cambridge, Mass., 1965). For an example of a journalist's career in the reform period: E. Ambler, *Russian Journalism and Politics 1861–1881. The Career of Aleksei Suvorin* (Detroit, 1972).

proved in the end to have an integrating effect. Instead, it feared that the ideas generated in editorial offices could take on a life of their own and create pressures which would seriously inhibit the autocracy's freedom of action.

Finally, official policy makers were themselves divided by the same political disagreements that appeared in Russian newspapers and magazines. The 'government' was not a monolithic block of ideological allies; liberal, conservative and Slavophile proclivities or convictions gave rise to controversial opinions in these circles as well. Ministers were sometimes praised in the press, but it was not unusual to see them attacked.[36] In the struggle for influence that raged at the imperial Court and within the ministries, the weight of public opinion was of no small import since the press provided a barometer of popularity suggesting just who enjoyed public support. This was now becoming politically valuable in imperial Russia as well. As a result, some journalists became personal confidants of ministers and occasionally of the Court itself. One of the consequences of reform therefore was that journalism, even critical journalism, could no longer be eliminated from Russia.

There is no doubt that the crisis-ridden process of internal transformation during the sixties and seventies severely affected Russia's international standing. The very decision to reform had been provoked, as mentioned above, by international complications and setbacks; the results of reform now began in turn to affect international policy. Russian diplomacy in the wake of the Treaty of Paris cannot of course be interpreted solely as a reflection of internal problems. Certain policies and methods of operation were dictated by the constellation of great powers. Russia's international interests were determined by tradition and customary orientations. However, imperial Russia clearly needed an extended period of peace. Foreign policy had to serve the regeneration which it was hoped reform would bring; possible conflict had to be avoided. The new 'realism' of international abstinence practised by imperial diplomats under Prince A.M. Gorchakov thus seemed consistent with Russia's circumstances.

This defensive foreign policy was nevertheless always in danger of being overturned. St Petersburg had not retired from international power politics, and a revisionist tendency underlay both

---

36. For the conflict between Valuev and Katkov which made the Minister of the Interior think of resigning in 1865, see Knutson, pp. 188ff.

reform policies and imperial diplomacy. Reform had been embarked upon to help reverse the decline in international standing Russia had suffered in the Crimean War, to prevent the Russian Empire from going the way of the Ottoman Empire, and to make Russia in actual fact into the great power she claimed to be. This imperial strategy for security and internal development meant that reform policies were always exposed to pressure from what the leadership considered to be the external interests of the Empire. 'The primacy of domestic affairs' imposed policies that clashed with the regime's conception of Russia's 'dignity' and 'honour'.

Finally public opinion, that product of reform, was greatly concerned with Russia's imperial interests. It intruded into private areas of autocratic policy-making with demands the international ramifications of which would soon become apparent. It was tempting for the government to divert attention away from internal conflict and make dramatic foreign moves in an effort to brighten its tarnished authority. Russia's policy in the Balkans and her extensive expansion into Central Asia will be examined later in this context.

37. W.E. Mosse, *The Rise and Fall of the Crimean System 1855–1871. The Story of a Peace Settlement* (London, 1963); D. Beyrau, *Russische Orientpolitik und die Entstehung des Deutschen Kaiserreiches* (Wiesbaden, 1974), pp. 15ff.

2

Economic Conditions

More than any other critical area, the Russian economy provides a clear insight into the relationship between reform, structural backwardness and the imperial will to power. The nation's ability to develop its economy would determine whether imperial Russia could permanently keep pace in the competition with the great powers. Moreover, a study of Russia's economic potential shows how closely internal problems were bound up with international relations. An extended analysis of Russian economic history during the reform period is not necessary in order to see this connection.[1] Since broad sectors of the Russian economy were subject to state control, financial policy will suffice as a useful indicator. It reveals both the poverty of this underdeveloped country and the evolution of the economic crisis which figured among the internal factors conditioning foreign policy during the age of reform.[2] An overview of the evolution of the state budget gives a first impression (Table 1).

There would have been few grounds for optimism if the funds available for regenerating imperial Russia had been measured against all the demands and pressures placed on state finances after the Crimean War. The war had pushed Russia (which already suffered from chronic budget deficits) to the brink of bankruptcy and left massive deficits that exceeded the ordinary revenues of two budgetary years. The national debt owed to foreigners had risen to almost 500 million silver rubles. Equally disturbing was the fact that the supply of paper money had exploded because of letters of credit

---

1. For an introduction see: A. Gerschenkron, 'Agrarian Policies and Industrialization: Russia 1861–1917', *CEHE*, vol. 6, pp. 706–800; there is rich statistical information in: P.A. Khromov, *Ekonomicheskoe razvitie Rossii v. XIX–XX vv. (1800–1917)* (Moscow, 1950).

2. Besides the overview of A.P. Pogrebinskii, *Ocherki istorii finansov dorevolyutsionnoi Rossii* (Moscow, 1954) see, above all, the standard work by I.F. Gindin, *Gosudarstvennyi bank i ekonomicheskaya politika tsarskogo pravitel'stva (1861–1892 gg.)* (Moscow, 1960).

Table 1: Russian state finances indicators for 1861–80 (in mill. of rubles)

Year	Total state revenues	Revenue from alcohol excise tax	Revenue from tariffs	Revenue from loans	Total state expenditures	Expenses for debt repayment	Expenses of Ministry of War	Expenses of Ministry of Finance	Foreign trade balance	New railways (in km)
1861	417	126	33	—	414	51	116	94	+ 10	612
1862	337	130	33	15	393	53	114	55	+ 28	1278
1863	428	130	34	39	432	57	156	62	—	5
1864	391	114	27	44	437	74	155	59	+ 11	95
1865	401	124	26	28	428	72	140	68	+ 45	226
1866	442	122	32	78	438	75	130	80	+ 18	731
1867	483	134	37	68	460	82	127	80	− 20	465
1868	470	134	37	48	492	83	137	86	− 34	1748
1869	502	138	42	45	535	88	148	91	− 78	1380
1870	561	164	43	81	564	86	145	91	+ 24	2565
1871	588	175	49	80	557	85	159	91	+ 1	2910
1872	594	173	55	71	583	88	166	103	−108	719
1873	617	180	56	79	612	93	175	101	− 79	1846
1874	599	202	58	41	602	94	172	100	− 40	2014
1875	647	198	64	71	605	107	175	80	−149	809
1876	617	191	73	58	704	109	191	80	− 77	604
1877	879	191	52	330	1121	115	192	84	+207	1459
1878	971	215	81	345	1076	140	187	92	+ 23	1279
1879	965	229	93	303	812	172	187	94	+ 40	309
1880	741	223	96	90	793	173	209	113	−124	185

Source: P.A. Khromov, *Ekonomicheskoe razvitie Rossii v XIX–XX v.* (Moscow, 1950), pp. 462, 468, 494f., 514.

issued to finance the war. By 1858 only 16.2 per cent of Russian currency was still backed by the dwindling reserves of gold and silver stored in the casemates of the Peter and Paul Fortress and the ruble's rate of exchange fluctuated between 9 and 10 per cent below parity.[3]

Under these circumstances it was impossible to acquire new state loans to satisfy the finance department's hunger for cash. Russia's lack of real assets and unfavourable balance of trade led western banks to doubt her solvency. Prospects of raising substantial sums on internal financial markets were just as poor. By the end of the 1850s the Treasury owed the government-run credit agencies even more than the landowners who had been pawning off serfs to the agencies for years. Raising internal loans always meant further increases in the amount of unbacked paper money in circulation, and this was one of the great cancers on imperial finances.

All of this must be seen in conjunction with the heavy payments — no one knew exactly how large they would be — that fell on the Treasury in the period after the Treaty of Paris. Besides fixed expenses, the government had above all to tackle the pressing question of how to finance the extension of the railway system — an undertaking whose urgency was clear to all. When it also became apparent that compensation to the gentry for liberating the serfs would swallow up vast sums in advance payments, the financial system was shaken to the very core. Thorough reform of imperial finances would evidently be a prerequisite for other sorts of reform.

Within just a few years three apparent solutions had to be discarded:

1. The tax-exempt status of the nobility proved impossible to abolish and since substantially increased burdens on the rest of the population could threaten internal stability, only modest tax increases could be contemplated in the short term. This would do nothing, however, to solve the problems flowing from the nation's lack of capital. The fifteen kopek increase in the poll-tax imposed by the government in 1862 was also no solution.

2. The idea of enhancing state revenues by substantially increasing tariffs had also to be rejected. Russia's heavy industry had languished and the prodigious appetite of the expanding railway system could not be satisfied unless the borders were opened to

3. Information in Gindin, pp. 24ff., as well as Kulomsin in: *Finanzielle Sanierung*, pp. 174ff. For the Russian financial situation at the end of the Crimean War see the memorandum of A. Yu. Gagemeister (end of 1855) in *IA* (1956/2), pp. 103–25.

imports. The government drew the necessary conclusions and introduced the liberal tariff of 1857. The high protective barriers of the time of Nicholas I were thus eliminated, much to the disgust of manufacturers and textile producers in Moscow who thought cheap imports would sound the death-knell of industry in Mother Russia.[4]

3. Currency reform also had to be postponed. Calling in letters of credit, stabilising the silver ruble or even placing the ruble on the gold standard all proved impossible under the circumstances and the new Minister of Finance, Michael von Reutern, had to admit as much as early as the spring of 1862. There would have to be surpluses (and not deficits) in foreign trade if the ruble was to be backed. For the forseeable future there would be no balanced budget.

The reform movement and the railways had still to be financed, however, and the only possibilities left were to reorganise the Russian system of banking and credit, eliminate the state credit monopoly, quickly develop private banks, pass legislation governing stocks and credit, and encourage investment by means of state guarantees for foreign and domestic investors. Since the Treaty of Paris, a number of innovations had been moving fiscal policy in just this direction. Thanks to the dissolution of the traditional credit system in 1859, compensation to the nobility (425 million rubles) could be limited provisionally to debt conversion. The partial denationalisation of capital markets led to an upswing in railway business — handled by joint-stock companies and managed by foreign banks. To those awarded a concession, the Treasury guaranteed a minimal profit (usually 5 per cent of investment capital) and the right to import rails, locomotives, rolling stock and other material duty free. The entire world of Russian business, including the Court and senior bureaucrats, caught 'railway fever' after the 'Grande société des chemins de fer russes' was founded in January 1857 with the backing of 'Crédit mobilier' and banks in

---

4. For tariff policies after 1857 see: M.N. Sobolev, *Tamozhennaya politika Rossii vo vtoroi polovine XIX v.* (Tomsk, 1911), pp. 100ff., also: V.V. Potanin, 'Tarif 1857 g. i tamozhennaya politika Rossii 1856–1860 gg.', *VLU* 20/4 (1965), pp. 48–56; in addition, V. Wittschewsky, *Rußlands Handels-, Zoll- und Industriepolitik von Peter dem Großen bis auf die Gegenwart* (Berlin, 1905), pp. 116ff.; Blackwell, pp. 169ff.; for the interests of the bourgeoisie in Moscow see: V. Ya. Laverychev, *Krupnaya burzhuaziya v poreformennoi Rossii (1861–1900)* (Moscow, 1974), pp. 169ff.; for general information: M.L. Gavlin, 'Rol' tsentra i okrain Rossiiskoi imperii v formirovanii krupnoi moskovskoi burzhuazii v poreformennyi period', *IZ* 92 (1973), pp. 336–55.

Table 2: Railways in Russia

Kilometres of finished track

	Total	Amount of track in Asiatic Russia (including Manchuria)
1850	601	—
1860	1,589	—
1870	11,243	—
1880	23,982	125
1890	32,390	1,433
1900	56,976	8,869
1910	76,946	17,390

Russian railways in international comparison 1850–1900 (in km)

	1850	1860	1870	1880	1890	1900
Russia	601	1,589	11,243	23,982	32,390	56,976
Germany	6,044	11,633	19,575	33,838	42,869	51,391
Austria-Hungary	1,579	4,543	9,589	18,512	27,113	36,883
Great Britain	10,653	16,787	24,999	28,854	32,297	35,186
France	3,083	9,528	17,931	26,189	36,895	42,827
USA	14,515	49,292	85,139	150,717	268,409	311,094

Source: *Entsiklopedicheskii slovar' Russkogo Bibliograficheskogo Instituta Granat*, pt. 20 (Moscow, n.d.), Zheleznye dorogi, pp. 18f.

London and Amsterdam. When railway securities were issued under police protection in St Petersburg 'the crowd was so tumultuous that doors were broken in and people had to be held back with physical force.'[5]

All countries affected by modern capitalism in the nineteenth century underwent the 'transportation revolution' (Table 2).[6] But nowhere was railway construction so directly a creature of state initiative as in imperial Russia and nowhere did it have such a heavy

---

5. K. v. Schlözer, *Petersburger Briefe 1857–1862* (Stuttgart, 1921), pp. 37f. (19 April, 1 May 1857). On the Russian credit banks before 1861: S.A. Borovoi, *Kredit i banki Rossii (seredina XVII veka – 1861 g.)* (Moscow, 1958); A.J. Rieber, 'The Formation of La Grande Société des Chemins de Fer Russes', *JGO* 21 (1973), pp. 375–91; A.M. Solov'eva, *Zheleznodorozhnyi transport*, pp. 61ff.; also R.E. Cameron, *France and the Economic Development of Europe 1800–1914* (Princeton, 1961), pp. 275ff.
6. G.R. Taylor, *The Transportation Revolution 1815–1860* (New York, 1962).

impact on state fiscal policy. To the autocracy, a railway system was a basic necessity if its own position and the great power status of the country were to be preserved — 'The longer we delay, the further we shall fall behind Western Europe and the less we shall be able to develop our agriculture or even prevent its decline'.[7] Russia's ability to act on the international stage depended on the railway.

Even though the first phase of railway construction in Russia was, as elsewhere, the responsibility of private companies, and even though the finance department had decided to privatise the old state railways in the latter part of the 1860s, the government remained on the scene as the guiding hand to offer financial inducements. This can be seen in the import privileges granted to concessionaries and in the guaranteed minimal dividends. Under this arrangement the state was responsible for losses but could not make a profit. Such costly protection was needed because of Russia's economic backwardness and the bureaucratic control of its economy, for private capital could only be enticed into such an impoverished and unstable country by unusually strong guarantees and bright prospects of turning a profit.

All this state intervention underlines the strong link which existed between railways and Russia's political interests as a great power. The government secured overall control of railway construction through the concessions it distributed and economic profitability always had to be balanced against military considerations. Not only the Crimean War but also the Polish rebellion of 1863 demonstrated that the 'unity and integrity of the state', the mobility of the army and its ability to suppress 'particularist elements' on the periphery of the Empire all depended on improved transportation.[8] From an economic point of view the government considered railways to be a means of solving fiscal problems, not a way to encourage liberal capitalist development. Theories of free trade were looked upon with favour by Finance Minister von Reutern, but Russia's lack of capital and the autocracy's overriding desire to solidify its rule carried the day for government interventionism.

7. Minutes of a commission called by the Tsar to investigate the railway system (1865), cited in *Finanzielle Sanierung*, p. 188. For railway construction after 1860: N.A. Kislinskii, *Nasha zheleznodorozhnaya politika po dokumentam Arkhiva Komiteta ministrov*, vol. 1 (St Petersburg, 1901); A.P. Pogrebinskii, 'Stroitel'stvo zheleznykh dorog v poreformennoi Rossii i finansovaya politika tsarizma', *IZ* 47 (1954), pp. 149–80; Solovyeva, pp. 87ff.

8. On demands for strategic lines see: P.A. Zayonchkovskii, *Voennye reformy*, pp.119f.

The financing of Russian railways remained very much in the hands of foreigners and the future of the autocracy was therefore tied to a large extent to stock quotations. Russia was drawn by the 'cosmopolitan character' of its capital into world economic trends. The financial crisis of 1857 threw cold water on the first burst of enthusiasm for stocks and railways and cast doubt on contracts for concessions.[9] European banks, well-informed by telegraph of the Empire's problem with internal stability, had a large say in Russia's modernisation, and the ruble's rate of exchange was an excellent barometer of what they thought. Consequently, the reforms of the 'Tsar-Liberator' became vitally important for state credit. Loss of authority on the part of the autocracy, uncertainty about the consequences of agrarian reform, revolutionary agitation, discontent in the villages and among students, and especially the Polish rebellion meant that foreigners were not overly anxious to invest in the Empire and that Russian capital itself continued to flow out of the country.

One can gather from the sensitivity of European high finance to Russia's internal crises just how important the reports of the foreign press, diplomats and travellers were.[10] When pamphlets with gruesome pictures appeared promulgating the clichés of liberal Russophobia, it was not just the regime's 'honour' and 'dignity' that suffered but its credit-worthiness. The government's nervousness, its concern with international prestige, its tendency to indulge in displays of power, the efforts of its diplomats to improve Russia's image — all these characteristic behavioural traits of the Russian élite had an economic component.

Reutern analysed the financial crisis in Russia in a crisp and urgent report to the Tsar in September 1866, ten years after the Treaty of Paris. The situation was alarming, even if allowance is made for any self-serving dramatisation on the part of the Minister. The 'disorganised flow of money' remained the fatal flaw in the

---

9. On the 'cosmopolitan character' of capital see: Reutern, memorandum of 16 Sept. 1866 in *Finanzielle Sanierung*, pp. 16–96, here p. 39. On the crisis of 1857: S.G. Strumilin, 'Promyshlennye krizisy v Rossii 1847–1907 gg.', in idem, *Ocherki ekonomicheskoi istorii Rossii i SSSR* (Moscow, 1966), pp. 424ff.; A.F. Yakovlev, *Ekonomicheskie krizisy v Rossii* (Moscow, 1955), pp. 61ff.; L. Mendelson, *Ekonomicheskie krizisy i tsikly XIX veka* (Moscow, 1949), pp. 301–63; H. Rosenberg, *Die Weltwirtschaftskrise 1857–1859* (Stuttgart, 1934; rpt. Göttingen, 1974²).

10. Of the many contemporary descriptions see: A. Wagner, *Die russische Papierwährung* (Riga, 1868); C. v. Sarauw, *Das russische Reich in seiner finanziellen und ökonomischen Entwicklung seit dem Krimkriege* (Leipzig, 1873); F. Matthäi, *Die Industrie Rußlands* (2 vols., Leipzig, 1872, 1873).

system. Both the Treasury and private individuals, 'especially the landowners', could only obtain credit under the most difficult and ruinous of conditions. As the demand for capital expanded rapidly, private capital formation shrank 'far more drastically' than before the war. No longer was Russia believed 'safe from all revolutionary plots and financial crises'. The flow of foreign money into Russia therefore merely cleared the way for an ominous outflow of capital. Reutern feared for the nation's solvency, and foresaw a situation which would see Russian credit-worthiness on foreign markets destroyed and 'Russia reduced to a second-rate power'.[11]

No ministerial magic wand existed to dissipate the crisis. The national debt had risen again in the period between 1862 and 1865 by almost 360 million rubles, and only 8 per cent of the currency in circulation was backed. A difficult austerity programme was therefore inevitable. The budgets of the Ministries of War and the Navy could not be spared; Reutern also recommended the stabilisation of the rate of exchange at around sixty eight silver kopecks, the avoidance of new state loans and expensive reforms, the reduction of imports and expansion of exports, and a further 40 per cent increase in the poll tax 'even though this will weigh heavily on them [the people] and could provoke unrest'.[12] The sale of Alaska to the United States for 7.2 million dollars (about 11 million rubles) also was part of this programme.[13]

Despite the long-standing financial crisis, railways remained the apparent crux of government policy. According to Reutern, 'not just our currency and its rate of exchange, but also Russia's entire economy, financial system and even political importance' were bound up with railways. 'Our whole future depends on the railways.' It was of paramount importance, said von Reutern, that the confidence of foreign capitalists be regained, not least of all by reorganising the unprofitable, poorly managed and therefore much disparaged railway system. Decisive political action was necessary if the credit of the Russian state was to be restored. The regime would have to reinforce its inner stability and practice restraint in foreign policy by abstaining from 'interference in the political quarrels of other powers'.[14]

11. Reutern, 16 Sept. 1866 in *Finanzielle Sanierung*, pp. 21, 28f., 53.
12. Ibid., pp. 68f.
13. On the sale of Alaska see: S.B. Okun', *Rossiisko-amerikanskaya kompaniya* (Moscow, 1939), pp. 219–59.
14. Reutern, 16 Sept. 1866 in *Finanzielle Sanierung*, pp. 54, 95, 36; the following figures are also taken from this memorandum.

The heavy cost of reform was made apparent by the financial crisis — a matter of life and death for the state according to Reutern. The incessant flow of capital from the country showed clearly how suspicious the affluent classes – and wealthy country squires in particular – were of the Tsar's policies. In the year of the Polish revolt shipments of gold across European borders (in bars and notes) reached ten times the level of 1860. Between 1861 and 1866 the equivalent of more than 170 million rubles flowed out of Russia while capital imports reached only 37 million. The government was able to achieve a semblance of balance only with great effort and by means of aggravated debt incurred through a 15 million pound (96 million ruble) loan negotiated in 1862 and an Anglo-Dutch loan arranged in 1864 for 38 million rubles.

Besides a lack of confidence engendered by internal instability there were other reasons why Russia was starved of capital. The cotton branch of the textile industry in central Russia was hit hard when cotton grew scarce and rose in price as a result of the Civil War in the United States. Industry could not compensate for lost imports by increased shipments from the growing areas of Central Asia, especially since yields were reduced by poor harvests in 1864 and 1865. Last but not least, Russia's catastrophic financial position was further aggravated by the international crisis which saw several important European banks go bankrupt in 1866–7.[15]

Under the circumstances the government's ambitious plans of 1862–3 for the railways proceeded at a snail's pace. A number of private railway companies went bankrupt, leaving their debts to the Treasury. The southern railway was supposed to link Moscow with Sevastopol' by way of Kursk and Khar'kov, but by 1866 only the line to Orel had been completed, plus a stretch which would one day link Odessa with Kiev. At the same time, the extension to Vitebsk had been completed on the Riga-Dünaburg line, originally opened in 1862. The only railway to offer any hope of running at a profit, however, was the line between Ryazan' and Kozlov, built with German and English capital. It was, according to Reutern in 1869, 'the first of our railways to penetrate the rich grain-growing regions',[16] and since there was now a direct connection with

15. Strumilin, pp. 430ff.; Jakovlev, pp. 81ff., Mendelson, pp. 364–425.
16. Budget report of the finance minister for 1869 in *Finanzielle Sanierung*, p. 187; cf. V.M. Lyakhovskii, 'Zheleznodorozhnye perevozki i razvitie rynka. K istorii Ryazansko-Kozlovskoi dorogi 1860–70-e gody', *VMU-Ist* (1963/4), pp. 34–51, as well as the study of J. Metzer, 'Railroad Development and Market Integration: The Case of Tsarist Russia', *JEH* 34 (1974), pp. 529–49; Metzer, 'Some Aspects of

Moscow and with St Petersburg by means of the Nicholas Railway, a first step had indeed been taken in the urgent task of stimulating exports of grain. On the whole, however, the crisis-ridden year of 1866 (when the military value of railways was once more brought to the fore by the Austro-Prussian war) left little room for optimism.

By 1867, however, the railway business in Russia was beginning to shake off stagnation and enter a boom period. A number of factors played a part in this happy turn of events. As the economic crisis faded in the West, the government attempted to institute the stabilising policies which Reutern had recommended. New incentives to invest were introduced and the state's creditworthiness was improved because of restrictions on unproductive expenditures, increases in the poll tax and other levies, and cutbacks in internal reform as a result of an attempt on the Tsar's life in April 1866. Reutern even managed to find new sources of funding for the transportation system. The wherewithal to create a railway fund outside the regular budget and take out new state loans was provided by the sale of state-owned railways such as the Moscow–St Petersburg line, which alone went for over 105 million rubles.[17] With this fund the government helped to provoke a construction boom which lasted several years and which resulted in the German term *Gründerzeit* being taken over into Russian (*gryunderstvo*) to describe the years between 1868–9 and 1873–4.

The upswing was supported by a number of secondary measures as well. The new steep tariff of 1868[18] (25 to 30 per cent) provided protection for the textile industry in central Russia which had bitterly opposed the liberal tariff of 1857. On the other hand the new tariff favoured imports of pig-iron and steel for Russian ironworks and rolling mills, an underdeveloped industrial sector still recovering from the setback it had received when serfdom was abolished. For the sake of the railways, the Finance Minister now seemed to be moving towards differentiated policies designed to promote industry.[19] After 1866–7 Russian production of rails, carriages and locomotives was stimulated by state orders and sub-

Railroad Development in Tsarist Russia', PhD thesis, University of Chicago, 1972.

17. On the privatisation of the state railways see: Pogrebinskii, *Stroitel'stvo*, p. 162; P.A. Zayonchkovskii in *Dnevnik Valueva* 2, p. 484.

18. For the tariff of 1868 see: Sobolev, pp. 219f., 303ff.; Wittschewsky, pp. 129f. — For the demands of protectionist industrialists see: V. Ya. Laverychev, *Krupnaya burzhuaziya*, pp. 178ff.

19. For railway construction and the promotion of industry see: Gindin, pp. 191ff.; Soloveva, pp. 118ff., *passim*.

Table 3:   Growth of industrial production in Russia (not including Poland and Finland) 1860–1877 (1860 = 100)

	Coal production	Pig-iron	Steel & cast iron	Machine-building	Cotton & spinning products
	(1)	(2)	(3)	(4)	(5)
1860	100.0	100.0	100.0	100.0	100.0
1861	128.4	95.0	93.1	97.7	103.8
1862	115.4	74.8	83.0	99.2	93.5
1863	119.7	83.0	94.6	138.9	80.7
1864	133.4	89.3	87.6	159.5	109.0
1865	127.4	89.3	85.3	111.4	128.8
1866	152.0	91.0	90.0	110.7	167.3
1867	145.9	85.8	91.4	111.4	151.0
1868	150.3	96.8	110.0	135.9	147.5
1869	201.1	98.0	114.7	146.6	186.0
1870	231.2	107.0	121.8	217.6	201.0
1871	276.6	107.0	124.1	212.2	194.2
1872	362.3	119.0	131.0	251.1	214.4
1873	391.3	113.2	125.7	242.7	207.1
1874	430.7	113.2	145.7	314.5	213.0
1875	567.3	127.4	149.8	331.3	219.6
1876	608.3	131.8	146.9	345.0	214.0
1877	596.3	119.1	146.9	366.4	217.1

Source: A.F. Yakovlev, *Ekonomicheskie krizisy v Rossii* (Moscow, 1955), pp. 397, 400. Columns 1–3 and 5 were calculated on the basis of the amount of production (in poods) and column 4 on the value (in credit rubles).

sidies in order to lighten 'the heavy tribute of foreign payments'. The Ministries of War and Transportation as well as other government agencies were instructed to place their orders with domestic producers at all costs.[20] As in Germany in the late 1840s it turned out that railways could prove the locomotive of expansion for the whole of heavy industry. By the mid-1870s Russia built more carriages and locomotives than she imported. However the output of rolling mills lagged behind, hampered at first by the outmoded rails they produced.[21] Table 3 shows how rapidly industrial production

20. Reutern to the Tsar (1866), in *Finanzielle Sanierung*, pp. 192f.; Gindin, p. 35.
21. V.I. Bovykin, 'Probleme der industriellen Entwicklung Rußlands', in D. Geyer (ed.), *Wirtschaft u. Gesellschaft*, pp. 188–209, here p. 191. For the history of Russian industrial statistics and source studies of them see the critical work of Yu. Ya. Rybakov, *Promyshlennaya statistika Rossii XIX v. Istochnikovedcheskoe issledovanie* (Moscow, 1976), especially pp. 221–67.

Table 4: Russia's annual average foreign trade (in mill. of credit rubles)

	Total exports	Exports of grain	Total imports	Balance
1861–65	181.6	60.3	—	—
1866–70	263.7	104.8	290.6	− 26.9
1871–75	374.9	179.9	456.1	− 81.2
1876–79	543.6	305.9	520.2	+ 14.4
1880–85	565.2	296.6	528.5	+ 50.0
1886–90	665.7	342.6	415.0	+250.0
1891–95	628.0	306.3	451.6	+161.1
1896–99	694.5	326.9	—	—

Source: V.A. Zolotov, *Khlebnyi eksport Rossii cherez porty Chernogo i Azovskogo moryei v 60–90e gody XIX v.* (Rostov, 1966), pp. 97, 100, 103 (Tables 24, 27, 29).

soared above the base year of 1860.

Besides the growth of joint-stock companies, banks and rough and ready speculation, this *Gründerzeit* also spread transportation systems across the land. Baltic noblemen and zemstvo administrators joined the rush to the railways in increasing numbers. The total amount of track increased between 1868 and 1871 by more than 8,600 kilometres. By 1875 the southern lines were completed, the black earth zone was linked to ports on the Black Sea, the interior provinces were connected with Baltic harbours, the central Volga had been reached at Saratov and Tsaritsyn, and strategic railways penetrated the western provinces on the frontiers of Prussia and Austria. In the Caucasus trains ran as far as Vladikavkaz and from Tiflis to the port of Poti.[22]

Russian agriculture had been placing more and more goods on the market since the abolition of serfdom and exports grew accordingly. This was not all due to improved transportation or the increased productivity of modern agriculture however;[23] equally important was the fact that the burden of taxes and redemption payments forced most small peasant producers to sell their harvest rather than consume it. Rising exports during the upswing did not lead to a

22. For the opening of transportation routes in the Caucasus, see: A.T. Sagratyan, *Istoriya zheleznykh dorog Zakavkaz'ya 1856–1921 gg.* (Erevan, 1970).

23. For agricultural production and the agricultural market in Russia see the basic research of I.D. Kovalchenko and L.V. Milov, *Vserossiiskii agrarnyi rynok, XVII – nachalo XX veka. Opyt kolichestvennogo analiza* (Moscow, 1974), p. 243; also the production analyses for 1851–70 and 1878–82 by A.S. Nifontov, *Zernovoe proizvodstvo Rossii vo vtoroi polovine XIX v.* (Moscow, 1974).

spectacular surplus in foreign trade because these exports were surpassed in turn by rocketing imports (Table 4). State debts continued to grow (1 January 1871: c. 1,800 million rubles; 1 January 1875: 2,900 million rubles) and the financial situation remained the sore point of the Russian economy.

The level of economic activity Russia had experienced in the late 1860s began to tail off by the autumn of 1872 when shrinking sales and a falling stock-market announced the approach of a downturn. 'Bank mania' and 'showers of gold' had produced a dangerously overheated economy, and the situation was often compared to the situation in Germany as French reparations poured in. The crisis unfolded in 1873 — the same year that railway speculation in America collapsed and bank failures in Vienna, New York and Berlin shook the world of international finance.[24] However, this new crisis was conditioned by structural contradictions within Russian capitalism itself much more than the depressions of 1857 and 1866 had been. The economy hit rock bottom in 1875–6. The swollen network of Russian joint-stock, commercial and credit banks was especially hard hit, and the Strousberg scandal brought the Moscow Bank of Commerce and Loans crashing down, highlighting for the entire world the perilous state of Russian banking.[25]

Railway construction in 1875 and 1876 fell by 65 per cent in comparison with 1873–4 and the aftershocks of this set-back were not overcome until the early 1890s. The textile industry suffered more from reduced sales, diminished production and falling prices than machine-building which was supported by state contracts. The latter did nevertheless enter a period of sluggish growth in 1873. The depression was aggravated by poor harvests in 1875 and 1876; these had an immediate impact on Russia's foreign trade, which was further damaged by sinking prices on world grain markets. In previous years deficits in the balance of payments had been made up from budgetary surpluses, but in 1875 and 1876 a foreign trade deficit of 226 million rubles could not be covered and Russian reserves shrank accordingly. Reutern's old goal of making the paper ruble convertible at face value faded away, as did the creditworthiness of the state. The flight of capital only intensified.

Reutern concentrated primarily on the structural causes of the

24. Effects of the crisis in Russia: Strumilin, pp. 435ff.; Yakovlev, pp. 96ff.; Mendel'son, pp. 503ff.
25. For the Strousberg scandal see: J. Mai, *Das deutsche Kapital in Rußland, 1850–1894* (Berlin, GDR, 1970), pp. 56ff.

continuing economic decline and was less inclined to blame the foreign newspapers, with their exaggerated portrayals of Russia's economic plight. The Finance Minister believed with good reason that the most important source of Russia's woes was its surging dependence on foreign markets.[26] Imported capital occupied a proportionally larger place in the imperial economy during the sixties and seventies than it ever did again and consequently Russo-German relations in particular became extremely sensitive. The Germans were Russia's largest creditors, having invested a total of about 900 million marks (417 million rubles) in Russian railways between 1865 and 1876. As a result of the profound changes on world agricultural markets the German Empire had become Russia's best customer for its grain exports, while German industry began to conquer the expanding Russian market for manufactured goods.[27] The only long-term solution, so far as Reutern could see, was to reduce Russia's dependence by cutting back foreign loans, boosting exports and adopting tariff policies which would put 'narrower limits' on imports. A first step was taken with the imposition on 1 January 1877 of new import duties, payable in gold and amounting to a real increase of 40 to 50 per cent.[28] In making this move the Minister could count on the support of the engineering profession, which had been clamouring for tariff protection, and of the newly developed coal mining areas of southern Russia.

However, it turned out that new tariffs were not the opening shot in a sustained campaign to heal the economy, and in any case they had not been introduced solely in response to the depression. Since the autumn of 1876 Reutern could see that the Eastern crisis was likely to impose additional burdens on state finances. All hopes of quick economic recovery were dashed by Russian involvement in the Balkans, which led to partial mobilisation in November and war against the Porte in April 1877.[29] A massive issue of letters of credit would inevitably result in renewed expansion of the paper money supply and the Imperial Bank's first bond issue for 100 million rubles in November 1876 was only partially subscribed, despite public support for 'liberating the Balkan Christians'. Shaken capital

26. Reutern, memorandum of February 1877 in *Finanzielle Sanierung*, pp. 97–118.

27. Mai, *passim*; on the basis of contemporary sources: H. Müller-Link, *Industrialisierung und Außenpolitik. Preußen-Deutschland und das Zarenreich von 1860 bis 1890* (Göttingen, 1977).

28. For the introduction of the gold tariff in 1877, see: Sobolev, pp. 417ff.; for protectionist industrial interests after 1874 see: Laverychev, pp. 181ff.

29. Cf. chap. 4.1.

markets hindered the mobilisation of troops. Against this background of financial and economic crisis it is easy to understand why Reutern was probably the most determined opponent of policies which, as he wrote to the Tsar, 'would ruin Russia in the long run even if she should win the war'.[30] Ruination would be as inevitable as the consequences of 'two trains racing down the track toward each other'.[31] Foreign policy and economic crisis had never before been so closely interwoven in Russia as in those weeks when the Empire prepared to go to war — alone among the great European powers.

In response to the general question of how internal conditions affected Russia's foreign policy, a number of other points can be made in this short analysis focusing on the financial difficulties of the Empire. Firstly, Russia's chronic financial woes, weak industrial development and attempts to develop an infrastructure clearly militated against an aggresive foreign policy at this time. The Empire was dependent on foreign capital, and cautious policies designed to protect Russian prestige were therefore desirable. Russia's credit-worthiness had to be maintained, and Russian diplomacy under Gorchakov tried to promote this fundamental interest as best it could.

Secondly, military modernisation was progressing slowly because of the financial squeeze. Reforms proposed by the Minister of War, D.A. Milyutin, were delayed not just by conservative opposition but also by the understandable reluctance of the Finance Minister. Controversy still attended the introduction of general conscription in 1874 and new equipment for the army. Despite the obvious lessons of the Franco-Prussian War neither task had been completed by the time of the Balkan war.[32] Even in St Petersburg it was widely assumed that the Russian army was no match for a Western power, let alone for a coalition of powers. Russian inferiority had been alleviated by the great expansion of the railway system, but it had not been eradicated.

Thirdly, the inner stability of the regime and Russian credit-worthiness on foreign markets were closely connected. Crop failures, bank crises and reduced profits resulted in a declining stock

30. Reutern, memorandum for the Tsar (3 Oct. 1876) in *Finanzielle Sanierung*, pp. 121–30.

31. Reutern, notes from 12 Nov. 1876, ibid., pp. 131f.

32. Zayonchkovskii, *Voennye reformy*, pp. 136ff.; Miller, pp. 182ff.; W.C. Askew, 'Russian Military Strength of the Eve of the Franco-Prussian War', *SEER* 30 (1951/2), pp. 185–205.

market, the flight of capital and reduced foreign investment. All signs of political unrest, most evident after the Polish rebellion in the revolutionary movement, were also damaging to Russia's credit-worthiness. The Empire's dependence on foreign capital meant that economic and internal political events had serious consequences for its international position.

Fourthly, neither economic nor political stability could be achieved during the reign of Alexander. The cutbacks in politically significant reforms and their partial cancellation did nothing to reduce the mutual suspicion typical of the relations between rulers and ruled. As a result of domestic policies, the liberal minority was driven either to apathy or towards circles hostile to the regime, while most nobles remained unconvinced that the authorities had their interests at heart. The autocracy won some sympathisers thanks to state support for entrepreneurs, booming stock-market business and the speculative gains of some railway shareholders, but this was not enough to create a solid base of popular support. The option of buying social consensus by creating prosperous economic times had to be excluded because of Russia's chronic financial problems.

In conclusion, Russia's lack of capital, her financial dependence, her military and industrial underdevelopment, and her economic and political vulnerability were all reason for a defensive posture in foreign affairs. Yet the Empire expanded into Central Asia, persistently provoking England. Its interference in the Balkans finally led to war. This apparently contradictory behaviour on the part of the Russian autocracy deserves closer consideration.

3

The Role of Nationalism

As we have seen, Russia's freedom of action on the international stage was curtailed to a large extent by the crisis resulting from government efforts to transform the Empire through reform. Part of the reason was that the autocracy did not feel that it could count on the loyalty of politically important groups. The government's loss of authority, due as much to economic difficulties as to confused government policies, was reflected in the newspaper columns. Although in reality there was little chance of a succesful revolution in the 1860s and 1870s, the autocracy perceived this as a threat and behaved accordingly.

The sense of impending danger doubtless sprang less from foreign threats than from Russia's own domestic instability. Only the complexity of Russia's unsolved and perhaps insoluble internal problems can explain why the government felt so concerned about the Empire's international position. As with overcoming Russia's underdevelopment and financial weakness, establishing internal security was considered absolutely essential if power was to be maintained. The Tsar and the majority of his ministers realised that such security was not merely a matter for the police: a sufficient level of social consensus had also to be achieved. However, experience showed that neither political concessions nor economic largesse would suffice to establish this consensus because of the numerous rifts in society and the state's own lack of funds.

The question then arises as to whether and to what extent an atmosphere of confidence and consent could have been created by an ideology capable of spanning existing disagreements and contradictions. Was the regime able to inspire a sufficiently broad ideological movement by such means as convincing demonstrations of imperial power, revival of autocracy's charisma[1] or modern

---

1. M. Cherniavsky, *Tsar and People. Studies in Russian Myth* (New Haven, 1961);

strategies intended to arouse and integrate the population? It is doubtful whether the autocracy was flexible enough to bend the mobilising power of such ideologies to its purposes and apply it as a political instrument for preserving its authority.

As in other European countries which entered the phase of capitalist transformation in the early nineteenth century, the Russian period of reform witnessed the birth of a broadly-based nationalism.[2] When the traditional social order dissolved, the sense of loss engendered a search for a new national identity. Older forms of loyalty to the Russian Empire and the literary-philosophical Slavophile movement were assimilated.[3] This affinity for nationalist ideologies was not, of course, purely a product of Russian society and philosophy. Russia took leave of its traditions just at a time when nationalism was proving everywhere to be one of the most potent integrating forces in the process of social and economic modernisation. The Italian Risorgimento, the doctrine of nationalities proclaimed by Napoleon III and Bismarck's wars of unification expelling Austria from Germany and creating an empire with Prussia at its core all left their mark on the course of Russian nationalism. In the Polish rebellion, the nationalist movement in Finland and the tenacity of the Germans in preserving their heritage in the Baltic provinces, the longing for a national place in the sun could clearly be seen crossing the imperial borders and undermining Russia's empire of many peoples, or at least calling it into question. At the same time, ideas of national independence and national unity were changing the course of international politics. This was especially true of Eastern Europe, where the Ottoman Empire was disintegrating and the unity of the Austro-Hungarian Empire was permanently threatened. Russo-Austrian rivalries took on a new life because of the inroads made by nationalism among the Slavs of the Balkan provinces. Under these circumstances, Russian nationalism grew more and more potent.

The Polish question showed how imperial policies with a nationalist

---

D. Field, 'The Myth of the Tsar', in idem, *Rebels in the Name of the Tsar* (Boston, 1976), pp. 1–30.

2. For research on nationalism see: H. Mommsen and A. Martiny, 'Nationalismus, Nationalitätenfrage', *SDG* 4 (1971), pp. 623–95; H.A. Winkler (ed.), *Nationalismus* (Cologne, 1977); P.F. Sugar and I.J. Lederer (eds.), *Nationalism in Eastern Europe* (Seattle, 1969).

3. H. Rogger, *National Consciousness in 18th-Century Russia* (Cambridge, Mass., 1960); N.V. Riasanovsky, *Nicholas I and Official Nationality in Russia, 1825–1855* (Berkeley, 1967 [2]); E. Müller, *Russischer Geist in europäischer Krise* (Cologne, 1966); A. Gleason, *European and Muscovite. Ivan Kireevsky and the Origins of Slavophilism* (Cambridge, Mass., 1972).

tinge could have a unifying effect within Russia. The government had not satisfied public expectations during the troubled years leading up to the January rebellion of 1863, when Russian power in Congress Poland and the western provinces was imperilled.[4] The uncertain reaction of the bureaucracy to the troubles in Warsaw in the spring of 1861, awkward attempts at compromise with various groups of Polish nationalists, barely disguised concessions to demands for Polish autonomy, the remarkable protection afforded Alexander Wielopolski as a representative of the Polish nation in St Petersburg, all these signs of the government's willingness to appease provoked an increasingly angry public reaction in Russia. Suspicions were also raised by the Tsar's readiness to recall the Diet of the Grand Duchy of Finland at about the same time in April 1861, even though Finnish relations did not suffer from the same kind of historical experiences and bitterness as did those of Poland.[5]

Events in Italy and the images of Garibaldi adorning the walls of Warsaw, Helsingfors and other cities made many Russians fear for their multinational empire. The danger was charmingly symbolised by 'Garibaldi hats' which were then all the rage in women's fashion.[6] At a time when Italian unification and the policies of Napoleon III were disturbing the border provinces of the Empire, the autocracy's proposed concessions to non-Russian nationalists were taken as proof of weakness and a provocation of Russians themselves since they would not have benefitted from similar rights. The autocracy's policy towards the nationalities fuelled the crisis of authority originally ignited by the process of internal reform.

Valuev's plan, put to the Tsar in January 1863, to reform the Council of State along Austrian lines was an attempt at improving

4. The literature of the Polish rebellion is immense. For recent research, especially on Russian policies toward Poland, see: R.F. Leslie, *Reform and Insurrection in Russian Poland, 1856–1865* (London, 1963); I.M. Roseveare, 'From Reform to Rebellion: A. Wielopolski and the Polish Question 1861–1863', *CSS* 3 (1969), pp. 263–85; S.J. Zyzniewski, 'Milyutin and the Polish Question', *HSS* 4 (1957), pp. 237–48; Zyzniewski, 'The Futile Compromise Reconsidered: Wielopolski and Russian Policy in the Congress Kingdom 1861–1863', *AHR* 70 (1965), pp. 395–412; W.B. Lincoln, 'The Making of a New Polish Policy. N.A. Milyutin and the Polish Question 1861–1863', *PR* 15 (1970), pp. 54–66; F. Ramatowska, *Rzad carski wobec manifestacij patriotycznych w królestwie polskim w latach 1860–1862* (Warsaw, 1971); S. Kieniewicz, *Powstanie styczniowe* (Warsaw, 1972).
5. L. Krusius-Ahrenberg, *Der Durchbruch des Nationalismus und Liberalismus im politischen Leben Finnlands 1856 bis 1863* (Helsinki, 1934); K. Korhonen, *Autonomous Finland in the Political Thought of 19th-Century Russia* (Turku, 1967).
6. On the enthusiasm for Garibaldi: Schlözer, *Petersburger Briefe*, pp. 172, 259; *Dnevnik Valueva* 1, p. 190; F. Venturi, 'L'immagine di Garibaldi in Russia all'epoca della liberazione dei servi' in *Rassegna storica toscana* (1960), pp. 307ff.

51

relations between the autocracy and Russian society. 'Most gracious Sir,' he wrote to Alexander, 'grant Russia which loves You well and is truly devoted to Your service political pre-eminence [pervenstvo] over rebellious Poland. Let Russia herself take a step forward in the development of institutions of state.'[7] However, the emperor viewed any such step toward representative assemblies as inopportune and the Russian sense of national solidarity remained based on the patriotic feeling which swelled up during the Polish rebellion.

It is unlikely that massive public pressure caused the government to react so decisively to the collapse of its conciliatory policies in January 1863. The traditional interests of the Empire were at stake and the autocracy reacted spontaneously when it called in the army to suppress the insurrection and brutally pacify the Polish movement. The government did not fail to realise, however, that it now enjoyed the support of most Russians. Russophobic voices in the west served to strengthen the unity of purpose between government and people as did the challenge posed to Russian self-esteem when London and Paris tried to dictate conditions under which Polish autonomy could be restored. The fact that war in Europe no longer seemed such a remote possibility to many people furthered support for the government.[8]

Poland's political 'treachery' created a groundswell of nationalist feeling which carried away all the leading political journals and some influential voices within the central bureaucracy. The journalist Katkov in particular saw the Polish revolt as a 'European revolution' against Russia. Together with Slavophile writers, he gave vent to these feelings and tried to channel anti-Polish emotions into a movement for Russian national solidarity. Feared even by ministers, Katkov began to settle into his role as *praeceptor Russiae* and set out to fan the fires of patriotic enthusiasm. The enervating mood of depression lifted as bursting national pride ensured that Russia

7. Cited by P.A. Zayonchkovskii in *Dnevnik Valueva*, 1, p. 35. For Valuev's project for the Council of State see: Knutson, pp. 272ff.; for the text of the project: K.L. Bermanskii, 'Konstitutsionnye proekty tsarstvovaniya Aleksandra II', *Vestnik prava* (1905/09), pp. 223–91.
8. For the Polish rebellion as a problem in European politics see: V.G. Revunenko, *Pol'skoe vosstanie i evropeiskaya diplomatiya* (Moscow, 1957); W.E. Mosse, 'England and the Polish Insurrection of 1863', *EHR* 71 (1956), pp. 28–55; V.G. Chernukha, 'Vazhnoe svidetel'stvo o vneshnepoliticheskom aspekte pol'skogo vosstaniya 1863 g.' in *Issledovaniya po otechestvennomu istochnikovedeniyu* (Moscow, 1964), pp. 207ff.; E. Fleischhauer, *Bismarcks Rußlandpolitik im Jahrzehnt vor der Reichsgründung u. ihre Darstellung in der sowjetischen Historiographie* (Cologne, 1976), pp. 33–70; H.W. Rautenberg, *Der polnische Aufstand von 1863 und die europäische Politik* (Wiesbaden, 1979).

would be a country of the future. Pro-Polish manifestoes of solidarity in the democratic, *émigré* press and on the part of a few revolutionary demonstrators were swept aside by a tide of nationalist hostility. Exaggerated fears of Polish spies, arsonists and 'well-poisoners' incited Muscovites and others to consider forming a Home Guard. Contrary to the opinions of the Ministers of War and Finance, a flood of loyal addresses poured in to the Tsar suggesting that Russia would be able if necessary to 'do battle with Europe' if her honour was at stake.[9]

The unified national front that arose in Russia during the Polish rebellion had a palliative effect on Russia's own internal instability resulting from the great reforms. For a short time, social conflicts and economic deprivations were forgotten and the confidence gap between government and people narrowed. Slavophile liberals like N.A. Milyutin, Yu. F. Samarin and Prince V.A. Cherkasskii, who had been excluded from the reform process, played an important role in the administrative disciplining of Poland and thereby sought solace for their disappointments. However, national harmony was neither untroubled nor long-lasting. Conservatives grew refractory when it turned out that the Russian administration in the western provinces and Congress Poland was protecting the peasants while brutally punishing the Polish upper classes.[10] With their sense of international class solidarity, Russian aristocrats saw the same reforming forces at work that they had come to fear as the 'red democrats' of the St Petersburg bureaucracy. In the long run, however, Russian nationalism of all stripes served to bind together a traditional society in the process of decay. One can assume that Russians were particularly susceptible to nationalistic appeals precisely

9. Katkov to Valuev, 12 May 1863, in: *Russkii istoricheskii arkhiv (Prague)* 1 (1929), pp. 287f.; *Dnevnik Valueva*, 1, pp. 213f., 225, 232; *Nikitenko*, 2, p. 123. For Russian public opinion on the Polish rebellion see: H. Fleischhacker, *Russische Antworten auf die polnische Frage, 1795–1917* (Munich, 1941), pp. 93ff.; U. Picht, *Pogodin u. die Slavische Frage* (Stuttgart, 1969), pp. 237ff.; M. Katz, pp. 118ff.; Lukashevich, pp. 76ff.; M.B. Petrovich, *The Emergence of Russian Panslavism 1856–1870* (New York, 1956), pp. 172ff.; for a lonely spokesman for Poland from the liberal camp: I. Fleischhauer, 'Die Stellungnahme N.N. Strachovs zur Polenfrage', *JGO* 25 (1977), pp. 525–40. Soviet historiography has always emphasised the Russo-Polish solidarity of revolutionary groups; cf. the bibliography: *Vosstanie 1863 g. i russko-pol'skie revolyutsionnye svyazi 60-kh godov* (Moscow, 1960). There is no doubt, however, that the pro-Polish attitude of *Kolokol* curtailed Alexander Herzen's influence within Russia after 1863.

10. For Russian agricultural policies in Poland see: I.I. Kostyushko, *Krest'yanskaya reforma 1864 gv tsarstve Pol'skom* (Moscow, 1962); Leslie, pp. 136ff.; S. Kieniewicz, *Sprawa włościańska w powstaniu styczniowym* (Wrocław, 1953), p. 354ff.; Kieniewicz, *The Emancipation of the Polish Peasantry* (London, 1969), pp. 180ff.

because of all the social changes in their country. Perhaps that explains why Russian nationalism turned out to be so durable and did not require international crises to remain a vital force.

Beginning in the early 1860s, nationalist agitators found further grievances. Taking their cue from the barons' call for a united *Landtag* in the Baltic provinces, nationalists protested against the existence of a German territorial state within the Russian Empire.[11] The discussion may have produced less heat than the Polish question, but it was no less effective. With Katkov's publications leading the charge, most of the press in the capital cast doubt on the unquestioning loyalty which the Baltic German aristocracy had always accorded the Russian royal family. Criticism mounted as Bismarck's policies cast him more and more in the guise of a German Cavour who would unite his country into a powerful national state located at the heart of Europe.[12] Nationalists accused the Russian administration of acting more like representatives of the Baltic provinces in St Petersburg than the upholders of the imperial presence in the Baltic. Livonia, Kurland and Estonia should be fully assimilated into Russia, said the nationalists, all particular historical rights should be abolished, and the 'provincial separatism' imputed to German aristocrats by large sections of the Russian press should be dealt with decisively. Estonians and Latvians must not become 'sons of Germany', and the German nation should not be permitted a bulwark within the borders of the Russian Empire. In these matters it was political journalists and not the autocracy who came forward to speak and to demand action in the name of Russia.

In the rising clamour, Samarin's book on the borderlands of Russia (1868) probably succeeded in attracting most attention — thanks in part to the sharp reply it provoked from the Dorpat professor, Carl Schirren. Samarin took issue with the 'Germanising' of the 'Baltic Russian coast', and he encouraged the government to assume its responsibilities toward the Estonians and Latvians by

11. R. Wittram, *Baltische Geschichte* (Munich, 1954), pp. 181ff. For the socio-economic conditions behind the 'Baltic question', see the research, going back to the 1840s, of the Estonian agrarian historian J. Kakhk, in: *Die Krise der feudalen Landwirtschaft in Estland* (Tallinn, 1969), as well as G. v. Pistohlkors, 'Ritterschaft-liche Reformpolitik zwischen Russifizierung und Revolution' (Göttingen, 1978). Conservative reservations about incipient Russification can be seen in the notes of the Minister of the Interior (11 and 23 Sept. 1868), in *Dnevnik Valueva* 1, pp. 421–34; on that topic see: H. Stegmann, 'Graf P.A. Walujew. Zur baltischen Frage in der Zeit Alexanders II.', *BH* 13 (1967), pp. 59–83.

12. For the idea that Bismarck was 'Cavourising' Germany, see: Bennigsen (7 Feb. 1861), cited in Nolde, *Die Petersburger Mission*, p. 198.

rescuing them from the social and religious inferiority which the German barons would continue to impose. As in the crusade against the Polish aristocracy, political journalists clearly handled the question of nationality in terms much closer to the modern understanding of nationhood than did the Germans of the Baltic, who still thought primarily in the traditional terms of social hierarchy.[13]

Nationalism drew an extremely confused response from the government. Although it made an effort to suppress excessive outbursts, even the Court realised that anti-German feeling was not generated by just a few writers. Among senior bureaucrats, army generals and diplomats, it was common to take offence at government officials with German names. The nationalists had long enjoyed strong support at the Ministries of War and the Navy — if one wanted to become a patriot, one should be a Russian.[14] Now that a German Empire existed, the autocracy found it increasingly difficult to refrain from clamping down on the German-Protestant culture of the Baltic. However, when the government did begin cutting back German privileges, it was not out of sympathy with public nationalism but as a result of the general tendency toward administrative centralisation required by the reform process in Russia. Thus the autocracy's policy toward minority nationalities was much like that practised in Germany and Austria-Hungary.

Many studies have been made of Russian nationalism, its many moods and the people who inspired it. Slavophile philosophers wrote about them as early as the 1840s, though the discussion was confined to isolated groups and a few publications which the censor found acceptable. The 'Slavic idea' first aroused broad public interest in the patriotic atmosphere of the Crimean War as did the highly-strung Pan-Slavism promoted by such men as the Moscow history professor M.P. Pogodin. The latter movement reached out to embrace Russian Orthodox brethren outside the Empire and Slavs under Turkish or Austro-Hungarian suzerainty.[15] When the

13. Yu. Samarin, *Okrainy Rossii*, ser. 1: *Russkoe Baltiiskoe pomore*, vyp. 1 (Prague, 1868) (in *Sochineniya*, vol. 9, [1898]); R. Wittram, 'Carl Schirrens Livländische Antwort', in idem, *Das Nationale*, pp. 161–82; E.C. Thaden, 'Samarins's "Okrainy Rossii" and Official Policy in the Baltic Provinces', *RR* 33 (1974), pp. 405–15; G.I. Isakov, *Ostzeiskii vopros v russkoi pechati 1860-kh godov* (Moscow, 1961); L.K. Campion, 'Behind the Modern Drang nach Osten. Baltic Emigrés and Russophobia in 19th-Century Germany', PhD thesis, Bloomington, Ind., 1966; G. v. Pistohlkors, '"Russifizierung" u. die Grundlagen der baltischen Russophobie', *ZfO* (1976), pp. 618–31.
14. Cf. D. Beyrau, *Russische Orientpolitik*, pp. 15–22.
15. S.M. Levin, 'Krymskaya voina i russkoe obshchestvo' in Levin, *Ocherki po*

era of reform arrived, however, it became clear that the various ideological coteries behind the nationalism of the Russian public did not confine their interests to the Slavophiles. As long as concepts like 'people' (*narodnost'*) and 'orthodoxy' (*pravoslavie*) were linked to the institution of autocracy (*samoderzhavie*) they were accepted in conservative circles and attracted the support of the old Russian élites traditionally loyal to the Empire and proud of its might.[16] But the Slavophile understanding of 'society' and 'public opinion' extended beyond a narrow 'kvass patriotism' into liberal and even democratic spheres. Such notions were of course considered revolutionary by supporters of the old regime both inside Russia and without.[17]

The liberals' susceptibility to nationalism produced a problem similar in many respects to that of the National Liberals in Germany. Despite Russia's lack of national institutions and the final withering of the reform movement many liberals succumbed to the temptations of a kind of state nationalism, the future goals of which did not extend beyond enhancing Russia's role as a great power. Historians have assigned the welter of currents within Russian nationalism to the Procrustean beds of 'Pan-Slavism' or 'Pan-Russianism'.[18] Such a glaring simplification should not blind one to the fact that nationalism was a powerful force for unity precisely because it was seen as an ideological catch-all, with the various streams not too carefully defined in the public mind.

Russians were also drawn together by shared perceptions of external threats and enemies. Their Germanophobia soon proved far more effective a force for integration than anti-Polish feeling. With differing points of emphasis, both 'Russian' and 'Pan-Slavic' nationalism fastened onto resistance to German penetration and occasionally onto Germanophobia. These deep-rooted feelings provided a permanent base of support for Moscow industrialists in their economic demands for more tariff protection against the increasing competition from German goods. As early as 1864 Russian nationalists had revolted against the trade agreement with the

---

istorii russkoi obshchestvennoi mysli (Vtoraya polovina XIX–nachalo XX v.) (Leningrad, 1974), pp. 293–404; Picht, *Pogodin*; Petrovich, *Emergence*, pp. 26ff., 61ff.
    16. E.C. Thaden, *Conservative Nationalism in 19th-Century Russia* (Seattle, 1964).
    17. E. Müller, 'Zwischen Liberalismus und utopischem Sozialismus', *JGO* 13 (1965), pp. 511–30.
    18. T. Hunczak, 'Pan-Slavism or Pan-Russianism', in idem (ed.), *Russian Imperialism*, pp. 82–105.

German Zollverein, arguing that the motherland was in danger of declining into an agricultural adjunct to German industry. After Bismarck's conversion to agrarian protectionism in 1879, anti-German feelings were directed more and more at landowners reliant on the export trade.[19]

State nationalists derived inspiration for national policies and imperial displays of power from Bismarck's remarks about 'blood and iron' and from the mighty Prussian-German state arising in Central Europe. Russia, they said, was settling to the level of a second-rate power in the shadow of the German Chancellor. The government, paralysed by dynastic ties to the Kaiser, was allegedly unable to check the German elements in Russia, set foreign policy, and effectively defend Russian Poland and the western provinces in general against the German military machine. In the meantime, the nationalist party claimed, German capital and German concessionaries were taking over the Russian railway system. As a result, demands began to be heard for the assertion of Russian national interests, emancipation from Germany, Russification of the border areas, and a military strengthening of the western frontier.[20]

The Pan-Slavic branch of nationalism arrived at these same conclusions by way of Russia's problems with Austria-Hungary. In the emotional view of Pan-Slavs anxious to free their brothers in south-eastern Europe, the Habsburgs were not just rivals for the spoils of the collapsing Porte; Vienna was also frustrating the hopes of its Slavic subjects, and in Galicia it was harbouring the Polish nobility, banished sons of the Slavic family. In view of the 'special relationship' which Bismarck had built up with Vienna after the founding of the German Empire, Pan-Slavic publicists concluded that the tottering state of Austria-Hungary was incapable of any action in the Balkans that did not enjoy German backing. As time went by, this lent credence to the notion that there was a great historical dichotomy between Slavs and Teutons which one day

19. Laverychev, *Krupnaya burzhuaziya*, pp. 169ff.; Müller-Link, *Industrialisierung*, pp. 44ff., 51, 208f., is inclined to over-estimate the political role of the Moscow bourgeoisie; his interpretation of Russian nationalism — leaning on that of G. v. Schulze-Gävernitz — is coloured by the tariff wars of the 1890s and needs to be corrected. For the Russian bourgeoisie as an object of socio-historical research see: M. Hildermeier, 'Sozialer Wandel im städtischen Rußland in der zweiten Hälfte des 19. Jhs.', *JGO*, 25 (1977), pp. 525–66; A.J. Rieber, *Merchants and Entrepreneurs in Imperial Russia* (Chapel Hill, N.C., 1982).
20. On the effect of Bismarck's policies in Russia from 1866 to 1870 see: Beyrau, *Orientpolitik*, pp. 99ff., 140ff.; L.N. Narochnitskaya, *Rossiya i voiny Prussii v 60-kh godakh XIX v. za ob"edinenie Germanii 'sverkhu'* (Moscow, 1960); L.M. Shneerson, *Franko-prusskaya voina i Rossiya* (Minsk, 1976), pp. 141ff., 187ff., 240ff.

must be resolved in war. This stereotype seemed to be constantly reinforced on the German side by the attack Bismarck had inspired in the press against Pan-Slavism, the supposed incarnation of everything destructive and revolutionary.[21] After the German Reich was founded, even as sober a man as Minister of War Milyutin became obsessed with the idea that Russia must prepare 'to be attacked by Germany sooner or later'. Therefore the general staff concentrated on planning this conflict, despite the sinking feeling that Russia would not easily be able to make up the yawning gap in military potential.[22]

It is not easy to determine the exact impact of nationalism on Russian society as a whole or to show which social strata could be not only influenced but actually mobilised in a crisis. The problem is doubly difficult because nationalist attitudes cannot be separated from political views engendered primarily by the experience of radical change within Russia. It is no longer possible to make useful sociological analyses of who reads which leading newspapers and magazines. Opinions are correspondingly uncertain and contradictory, if one asks how much influence nationalists could bring to bear on governmental decisions (especially in foreign affairs and borderland policy) and how they did it. One can only have a rough idea of just how destabilising and dangerous were government decisions which offended the nationalistic expectations of the public. In general, the historical record contains only sweeping statements inclining towards hyperbole.

Given the present state of historical research, the best insight into the ability of nationalists to organise and fight for their ideals can probably be gained from a study of the 'Slavic movement', which brought Pan-Slavism to public attention after the Crimean War.[23] The Slavic Committee, founded in Moscow in January 1858 with the approval of the highest authorities, sprang from the initiative of a small circle of professors, journalists and well-known Slavophile writers in that city. For years their Pan-Slavic activities concentrated on cultural and charitable activities, and were of little concern to the bureaucracy in St Petersburg. Membership lists from 1862 to 1863 show that the committee had in the main attracted landowners,

---

21. R. Wittram, 'Bismarcks Rußlandpolitik nach der Reichsgründung', in *Rußland Europa u. der deutsche Osten* (Munich, 1960), pp. 161–84; E. Naujoks, *Bismarks auswärtige Pressepolitik und die Reichsgründung* (Wiesbaden, 1968).
22. Beyrau, *Orientpolitik*, pp. 264ff.; Müller-Link pp. 48ff. *passim*.
23. First and foremost: S.A. Nikitin, *Slavyanskie komitety v Rossii 1858–1876 gg.* (Moscow, 1960), pp. 9–155.

officers and academics, the educated and aristocratic elite of the old capital. Government and Court took little interest at first; nor did the rich Moscow merchants. The budget was very modest and sufficed, at most, for the donation of books and money or for a handful of student scholarships. In 1867, at the time of the so-called Slavic Congress in Moscow, receipts from membership fees and gifts barely reached 1,700 rubles.

This Congress, organised by the Moscow committee in May 1867 on the fringes of an 'Ethnographic Exhibition', attracted broad public attention and has often been the subject of scholarly research.[24] Slavic brotherhood, much talked about and celebrated at receptions and banquets, in theatres and concert halls, may have appealed emotionally to the participants, but did not help them formulate any clear political programme. In this, the year of the Austro-Hungarian Compromise and the rebellion on Crete, the regime in St Petersburg wished to keep its distance. The government was anxious to see to it that the presence of a substantial number of prominent Czech and Serbian representatives (from Hungary and the principality of Serbia) did not lead to political demonstrations. Calls for such demonstrations for a tripartite solution, for instance, could aggravate Russia's already sensitive relations with Vienna. The government particularly did not want to see the Serbs encouraged to undertake any military adventures. Therefore, the audience and private conversation granted by the Tsar to selected delegates was confined to harmless pleasantries. The participation of the Minister of Education, Count D.A. Tolstoi, was so arranged as to avoid the impression that the government was making any political commitments.

The conference organisers in Moscow, particularly Pogodin, Aksakov and Katkov, were primarily concerned with establishing personal contacts and with the publicity they would gain. The meeting confirmed the *raison d'être* of the Slavic Committee, but it must have been sobering to observe how much disagreement there was with the guests on fundamental issues. The Czech representatives, F. Palacky and F.L. Rieger, showed especially little sympathy for Russian condemnations of the Poles. In addition, most of the foreign guests did not accept a basic tenet obvious to the hosts — that, despite all the talk of brotherhood, the 'Slavic family' had a hierarchical structure in which the Russian element would dominate

---

24. Nikitin, pp. 156–259; Picht, pp. 186–202; Petrovich, *Emergence*, pp. 198–240; J.D. Morison, 'Katkov and Panslavism', *SEER* 46 (1968), pp. 422–41.

both politically and linguistically. The spectacular celebrations left memories of emotional processions, warm embraces and, probably, the sustaining impression that the common people of Moscow felt a strong sense of kinship with their Slavic brothers struggling for a place in the sun. Upon calm reflection, however, Slavic unity must have seemed a beautiful literary and academic mirage, full of internal contradictions and lacking political consequences.

The episodic nature of the Moscow meetings should not cloak the fact that the Slavic movement spread gradually in the following years. Soon it was not confined to the old capital: in 1868 a chapter of the Moscow Committee took root in St Petersburg with about 150 founding members. In the next two years, local committees were founded in Kiev and Odessa. A list of members and donors to the Moscow Committee in 1869–70 contains over 300 names. By 1874 there were 704 members, although only one-third paid fees. On the eve of the Balkan crisis, the sharply fluctuating membership of the Russian Slavic Committees had probably never exceeded 2,000 people, many of whom were not active. The nobility still dominated — landowners, government officials, army officers, intellectuals, professionals and a few churchmen. Only about 10 per cent of the members were businessmen, who since the municipal reforms of 1870 had begun to rival the nobility in local government. With the help of local manufacturers, Aksakov founded the newspaper *Moskva* in the old capital in 1867, and gradually managed to elicit more donations from the world of business because of his editorial policy in favour of protection for the textile industry. However, Aksakov's attempts to interest Moscow capitalists in economic opportunities in the Balkans and to win their support for Pan-Slavism did not meet with the desired success.[25]

There was, as we have seen, no dramatic strengthening of Pan-Slavism or Russian nationalism before the Balkan crisis. The militaristic chauvinism of General R.A. Fadeev, who joined forces with the opposition to resist the reforms of War Minister Milyutin, probably had greater impact outside Russia than within.[26] The Russian public also took no particular notice of Danilevsky's Darwinian style theory of cultural-historical types when it was published in 1869–71, though historians pronounce it 'the Bible of

25. Nikitin, pp. 46ff., 69ff.; Lukashevich, pp. 74f.; V. Ya. Laverychev, *Krupnaya burzhuaziya*, pp. 119ff.
26. Thaden, *Conservative Nationalism*, pp. 146ff.; Zayonchkovskii, *Voennye reformy*, pp. 289ff., Beyrau, *Orientpolitik*, pp. 286ff.

Pan-Slavism'.[27] Of greater importance was the development and spread of a system of national values that was derived from ideologies of national unification in the West and that helped bridge the gulfs within society.

Under the conditions prevailing in the Empire, no great political demonstrations were apparently necessary for the forms and attitudes of Russian nationalism to become firmly established. A deep craving for new ideals had been created by the hardships and the confusion of social roles which had accompanied the transformation of Russian society and which had been intensified by economic depression. Traditional patriotism, focusing on the person of the Tsar no longer sufficed for the rising bourgeoisie and those nobles who had lost their hereditary place in the social order. The new brand of nationalism, on the other hand, operated within a set of values capable of producing a modern sense of loyalty to one's country. The social pressure to conform to nationalistic movement often affected even educated liberals disinclined to crudely exaggerated behaviour.[28] The same is true of conservative aristocrats who, left to their own devices, were more inclined to be suspicious of the nationalism of the masses and to find it unpleasant.

One is therefore tempted to ask if more research could prove a correlation to exist between the worst periods of socio-economic crisis and peak susceptibility to nationalism. It is true that anti-Polish feeling reached its zenith at the very time it became clear just how destabilising the emancipation of the serfs and attendant social change would be. The economic crisis which peaked in 1865–6 also fits the pattern. In the mid-1870s, a wave of Pan-Slavic sentiment crested during the period of financial and economic crisis. The psychic effects of poor economic conditions were also aggravated by confused domestic policies and the activities of small revolutionary groups. In both decades, external events — the Polish rebellion and the Balkan crisis — probably do not suffice to account for the entire increase in Russian nationalism. It is most difficult of course to offer empirical evidence that could prove those assumptions beyond a doubt. However, given the lack of research into nationalism in Eastern Europe, it would clearly be wise to look into the

27. K. Pfalzgraf, 'Die Politisierung und Radikalisierung des Problems Rußland u. Europa bei N.J. Danilevsky', *FOG*, 1 (1953), pp. 55–204; R.E. MacMaster, *Danilevsky: A Russian Totalitarian Philosopher* (Cambridge, Mass., 1967).
28. R. Wortman, 'Koshelev, Samarin and Cherkasky and the Fate of Liberal Slavophilism', *SR* 21 (1962), pp. 261–79.

internal stimuli behind nationalism and the timing of its eruptions.[29]

If one accepts that Russian nationalism had a compensatory function, one is struck by the extremely reserved and even negative attitude the autocracy adopted toward it. Rather than trying to adapt to nationalism or even use it as a powerful tool for rallying the nation, the autocracy was more inclined to resist. There were good reasons for the aversion to nationalism that prevailed under Tsar Alexander II. Firstly, nationalism — like any mass movement — undermined the sole and complete authority of the autocracy. Nationalists claimed to speak in the name of the people; they presumed to formulate what Russian (or Slavic) interests were and to urge policy on the government. Secondly, nationalist agitators interfered directly in foreign relations, often offering blunt criticism of Russian diplomacy. Frantic activity and the rhetoric of diplomats could not really disguise the Empire's reduced ability to act on the international stage. The Pan-Slav wing of nationalism continually called both the Ottoman and Austro-Hungarian Empires into question. This was a constant challenge to the government and difficult for it to reconcile with the Emperors' League reconstituted by Bismarck. The effect which 'nationalistic harangues in the press' had on Russo-German relations is well known. On the whole then, nationalism seemed to challenge both the domestic and foreign strategies the autocracy had adopted to keep itself in power. This explains why the Tsar generally thought that stirring up nationalist emotions was more dangerous than dampening and disciplining them.

These observations have succeeded only in giving a rough outline of the situation. One should not be left with the impression that the relationship between the government and the nationalists was marked by unremitting hostility. Nationalism as an expression of the public mood and of the continuing, intractable process of social change could no more be repressed than public opinion and criticism in general. Moreover, the existence of a chauvinistic press was occasionally of use to the government when the demands and claims it wanted to put to foreign powers could not be handled through diplomatic channels or relations with friendly monarchs. When engaged in political negotiations or confidential discussions, even the Tsar was prone to the diplomatic practice of pointing out the constraints of hostile public opinion. Furthermore, the Russian

29. P.F. Sugar, 'External and Domestic Roots of East European Nationalism', in idem and I.J. Lederer, *Nationalism*, pp. 3–54.

press had assumed the task of engaging foreign newspapers in argument and counter-argument and tending to Russia's image beyond the frontiers. Katkov's publications in particular were invaluable in their role as adversary of the great German, English and French newspapers, especially as the autocracy's first attempts at steering public opinion were no match for the sophistication which western European governments had developed in handling the foreign press.

More important than these practical considerations was the fact that senior officials in Russia were by no means invulnerable to the blandishments of nationalism. Even though the autocracy energetically resisted any outside political influence nationalism penetrated vast sections of the bureaucracy, the officer corps and other government bodies. Even ministers, diplomats and the Palace itself were not immune, as it turned out, and were inclined, especially in a crisis, to bow before the nationalism of the Russian public. As the glory and prestige of the old regime and the autocracy faded, the temptation to embrace Russian nationalism grew. The government of Alexander II was forever caught on the horns of this dilemma, as can be seen in its policies towards the Balkans and the East.

4

Imperial Interests

The internal crisis in Russia during the 1860s and '70s did not necessarily ensure that the Empire's abstemious foreign policy — a rational, opportunist strategy of self-preservation — would be continued. Economic depression, the decay of the old order and the upper classes' lack of a well-defined social role aroused a psychological hunger that found satisfaction in nationalist ideologies. As these spread through society, there was increased pressure for the compensatory satisfaction of international displays of power. The uncertain relations between government and society thus became loaded with ideological dynamite. Russia's economic underdevelopment, precarious financial state and military inferiority were a powerful inducement to restraint in foreign affairs. However, these same factors could also tempt the autocracy to behave aggressively and to undertake offensive operations in order to reinforce the crumbling authority of the Tsar, relieve the pressure of internal problems, and satisfy the power elite's traditional sense of imperial prestige. In addition, there was the temptation to use a successful foreign policy to meet the challenge of the nationalists, establish internal stability and create a new consensus. In view of the antiquated and diffuse structure within which the political decision-making process in Russia operated, one can hardly impute to the autocracy a conscious strategy of diverting and channelling the crisis. However, Russia's lack of room for manoeuvre could very well have encouraged decisions which ran contrary to the requirements of a defensive foreign policy.

The domestic conditions and motivations behind foreign policy need to be examined in concrete historical situations in order to provide better evidence for the ideas and assumptions indicated above. This will now be attempted in the form of two 'case studies'. Russian policy in the Balkans and expansion into Central Asia seem appropriate choices for obvious reasons. That the constellation of international powers also influenced Russian behaviour and must also be considered, need not be emphasised. Interest in the internal motivations of foreign policy does not deny these external factors, despite the fears of many a respected historian concerned about the autonomy of *la grande politique*. This is especially true of the whole intricate Eastern Question and of the rivalry between Russia and England. Russia's precarious relations with Germany and France will be discussed later.

4.1 Policy and War in the Balkans

The public took a far greater interest in the Balkans and the 'Eastern Question' than in any other sphere of Russian foreign policy. This unusual sensitivity to the fate of ethnic and religious brothers under Turkish and Austro-Hungarian suzerainty is related to the import- ance of the 'Slavic idea' in the ideology of Russian nationalism. Older studies very often took the view that there was almost complete symbiosis between imperial Russia's traditional drive for hegemony and the popular crusade for the unity of Slavs and orthodox Christians. Both government policy and Russian Pan- Slavism were seen as being directed primarily at freeing Christian peoples from the Turkish yoke and attempting to seize Constanti- nople and the Straits, with the years of crisis and war between 1875 and 1878 providing a particularly telling example. The declaration of war against the Porte, military operations as far as the walls of the 'city of the Tsars', and the conditions for the peace of San Stefano all supposedly showed the autocracy succumbing to massive pressure from the Pan-Slavic movement in order to strengthen its control over Russian society.[1] Even though such undifferentiated judge- ments need some correction in the light of modern research, there is no doubt that a study of the Balkan crisis can help to elucidate the relationship between big power politics and nationalistic fervour.

1. H. Müller-Link recently analysed in detail the economic antagonism between Russia and Germany (*Industrialisierung u. Außenpolitik*, pp. 37, 56ff., 122f. *passim*). He interprets the decision to go to war as a 'flight forward', a reaction to the social and economic crisis of 1875–6. He thinks the bourgeoisie in Moscow was the driving force behind Russian nationalism's insistence on war. However, there is no evidence in the Russian sources that the highest levels of government came under massive pressure from economic interest groups. On the contrary, a feeling of economic crisis produced the strongest arguments *against* the war in decision-making circles. There was no calculated attempt to manage the crisis by engaging in a popular war and the discussions of whether to decide in favour of war or peace contain no mention of any hope that a war would revive the economy.

Far from slipping into oblivion after 1865, the Eastern Question remained a focal point of Russian interest. Revision of the Treaty of Paris was generally accepted as one of St Petersburg's central concerns. However, Russia's margin for manoeuvre was very limited because of the inner state of the Empire, especially its military weakness and the deplorable condition of national finances. Therefore, Gorchakov's diplomatic efforts had to be limited to deterring any changes in the Balkans that would have further diminished Russia's position. As things turned out, it was difficult enough satisfying just these minimal aims. Diplomatic co-operation with Paris brought no new guarantees, although St Petersburg did enjoy seeing its Austrian competitor humbled by Napoleon III in the late 1850s. It was obvious that the autocracy could not aspire to being a partner in Napoleon's 'Caesarism', even before Russia's vulnerability was clearly exposed by the Polish rebellion. St Petersburg had to accept the union of the Danubian Principalities under the Hospodar Alexander Cuza (1859) and even later, after the enthronement in Bucharest of Prince Karl von Hohenzollern-Sigmaringen (1866) was not able to decisively influence Romanian politics.[2]

Since 1864, N.P. Ignat'ev, the Tsar's Machiavellian envoy to the Porte, had been planning an active Russian role in the Balkans, in consultation with the Pan-Slavic movement and with the support of Prince A.I. Baryatinskii, Viceroy of the Caucasus. The chances for such a role seemed to improved after Austria's freedom of movement was reduced by her defeat at the hands of the Prussians. For a time even the more sober personalities in St Petersburg dreamed of seeing Russia rewarded by Prussia for her neutrality and compensated in the Balkans for the setback she had suffered because of the shifting balance of power in Germany. However, any hopes of arranging for a repeal of the Black Sea clauses in 1866 quickly proved illusory, as did as Gorchakov's belief that Russia had a role to play at a European conference in settling German affairs. In a year of financial crisis and economic depression, St Petersburg could not possibly go on the offensive. Although Katkov lamented any mention of limitations on the Empire as a 'continuation of

2. Mosse, *Rise and Fall*; B. Jelavich, *Russia and the Rumanian National Cause, 1858–1859* (Bloomington, Ind., 1959); V.N. Vinogradov, Rossiya i ob"edinenie rumynskikh knyazhestv (Moscow, 1961); E.E. Chertan, *Russko-rumynskie otnoshe-niya, 1859–1863 gg.* (Kishinev, 1968). Other literature is cited in Beyrau, *Orientpoli-tik*, pp. 36ff. *passim.*

nihilism',[3] all the signs indicated the wisdom of recognising the very real limits to Russian power.

A little later, the diplomatic exchange occasioned by the anti-Turkish insurrection on Crete in 1867–9 produced similarly disappointing results for Russia. While men like Ignat'ev thought that a general revolt in the Balkans against the Porte would, with Russian help, soon tear up the Treaty of Paris, the higher echelons in St Petersburg acted with the greatest circumspection and caution.[4] Although they recognised that Russia would only be able to restore the lost balance of power in Europe by extending her influence into the Balkans, Minister of War Milyutin warned against any military involvement and urged his colleagues to restrain the Serbs and Greeks from any military adventures.[5] The principle of non-interference enunciated by Gorchakov at the end of October 1867 was interpreted by many observers as lending encouragement to the rebels, but it too was consistent with a Russian policy in the Balkans that had been reduced to merely appearing to be involved while planning for the future. It was hard to see more than an empty dream in Aksakov's vision of Russia uniting the Slavs just as Prussia was uniting the Germans.[6] When it finally seemed that the Franco-Prussian War might give Russia its opportunity to fulfil these alluring dreams, the actual gains scored by Russian diplomacy were very modest. The Black Sea clauses were renounced with Bismarck's support, but this was considered a paltry reward for having helped neutralise the Austrian army.[7] There was no denying that Russia's position in Europe had again been substantially reduced by a revolutionary change in the constellation of powers, brought about by the defeat of France and the founding of the Reich.

These meagre results were very harmful to the already rather poor image accorded by the public to Russian diplomacy. The policy of *attentisme* forced on Russia by its own backwardness was

3. Cited in Beyrau, p. 57.
4. I.G. Senkevich, *Rossiya i kritskoye vosstanie, 1866–1869 gg.* (Moscow, 1970); for Ignat'ev's activity in Constantinople see: T.A. Meininger, *Ignatiev and the Establishment of the Bulgarian Exarchate, 1864–1872: A Study in Personal Diplomacy* (Madison, 1970).
5. Milyutin, 18 Dec. 1867, cited in Beyrau, pp. 96f.
6. I. Aksakov, 28 Feb. 1867 (*Polnoe sobranie sochinenii*, vol. 7, pp. 111ff.), cited in ibid., p. 102.
7. For the abrogation of the Straits conventions (31 Oct. 1870) and the ensuing Black Sea conference in London see: B. Jelavich, *The Ottoman Empire, the Great Powers, and the Straits, 1870–1887* (Bloomington, Ind., 1973), pp. 25ff., 47ff; Beyrau, *Orientpolitik*, pp. 225ff., 242ff.; as well as N.S. Kinyapina, 'Bor'ba Rossii za otmenu ogranichitel'nykh uslovii Parizhskogo dogovora 1856 g.', *VIst* (1972/8), pp. 35–51.

leading nowhere, and official policy makers in St Petersburg, not to mention the nationalist press, were becoming increasingly irritable. This was especially true in view of indications that the Eastern Question would soon arise again. When revolts in Bosnia and Hercegovina shook the status quo in the Balkans in the summer of 1875, the prestige of the autocracy was clearly in danger of once more being severely tested. There was no reason to believe that Russia's ability to act on the international stage was any greater during this particular crisis in the Balkans than it had been in previous years.[8]

Despite contemporary insinuations to the contrary, these insurrections were not a product of indirect Russian aggression aimed at freeing orthodox co-religionists from Ottoman rule. It was neither the machinations of tsarist agents nor the agitation of Russian Slavic committees that provoked revolt in the two Turkish provinces, but external conflicts in which St Petersburg played no part.[9] That does not exclude of course the exaggerated hopes which the rebels held of obtaining Russian assistance. From the beginning, Russian policy aimed at isolating and quelling the unrest by means of a diplomatic solution supported by the signatory powers of the Treaty of Paris and imposed on the Turks. Any unilateral action would deeply affect the European concert of powers and might inspire a return of the anti-Russian coalition formed at the time of the Crimean War. It was especially important to achieve consensus with Vienna and forestall an alliance between England and Austria.

St Petersburg's attempts to stop Serbia and Montenegro from intervening militarily on the side of the rebels was linked to the continuing dependence of Russia's Balkan policies on the approval of the great powers. A war between the two principalities and Turkey could easily force Russia's hand in a way that was inconsistent with its interest in preventing the conflict from spreading. Moreover, the Serbian regime of the liberal minister Ristić (which held Prince Milan to the constitution of 1869) was suspected of harbouring 'revolutionary' ambitions. In the view of officials in St

8. M. Ekmečić, *Der Aufstand in Bosnien. 1875–1878* (Graz, 1974), vols. 1, 2; Yu. A. Pisarev, 'Vosstanie v Bosnii i Gertsegovine i evropeiskie derzhavy (1875–1878)', *NNI* (1976/2), pp. 48–58.
9. For the diplomatic history of the crisis see the classic work by B.H. Sumner, *Russia and the Balkans, 1870–1880* (Oxford, 1937, 1962²) and G. Hüningen, *Nikolaj Pavlovic Ignat'ev und die russische Balkanpolitik, 1875 bis 1878* (Göttingen, 1968); for Russo-Serbian relations see the pioneering study of D. MacKenzie, *The Serbs and Russian Panslavism, 1875–1878* (Ithaca, 1967), as well as a study based on Greek archives: E. Kofos, *Greece and the Near Eastern Crisis, 1875–1878* (Saloniki, 1975).

Petersburg there were, therefore, also reasons of principle for not desiring closer co-operation. What little opportunity actually existed, in any case, to exert a calming influence on Belgrade and Cetinje soon became apparent. After Serbia and Montenegro declared war on the Turks in June 1876, the Russian government increasingly found itself in a position where its behaviour was determined by the course of the war. The revolt that broke out in Bulgaria in April 1876 sharply reduced the chances of containing the crisis and pushed the entire Eastern Question onto centre stage.[10] Now that the problem of the Straits was raised not only Austrian interests were directly affected but English interests as well. The principalities were waging war under the supreme command of a retired Russian general and military involvement of the Russian Empire could no longer be excluded as the *ultima ratio*. There was no doubt in the minds of contemporaries that the Tsar could not accept the crushing defeat of Serbia and Montenegro. The only question remaining was whether Russian diplomats would be able to prevent developments which would make imperial involvement in the war inevitable. In case of war, the guarantees provided by the Russo-Austrian agreements, concluded by Gorchakov and Andrassy in Reichstadt on 6 July 1876, were insufficient. If conflict with Austria arose, the Tsar could not be sure of Bismarck's active support. Finally, the English might come to the aid of the Turks if the Russian army marched into Bulgaria. Alexander was unwilling to run risks fraught with such danger solely 'pour les beaux yeux des Slaves'.[11]

There were internal reasons as well why Russia could not interfere with impunity in the spheres of interest of other powers in the Balkans. The Tsar and his advisors agreed that the Empire could not endure military conflict on a large scale. According to Milyutin (who was just completing the introduction of general conscription into the army at the time), the outcome of military operations could only be predicted with sufficient accuracy if those operations were safe from Austrian and English intervention. Minister of Transport

---

10. For the Bulgarian revolt see the documentation in: S.A. Nikitin et al. (eds.), *Osvobozhdenie Bolgarii ot turetskogo iga* (Moscow, 1961–7), vols. 1–3; A. Burmov (ed.), *Aprel'sko v-stanie 1876* (Sofia, 1954–6), vols. 1–3; S.I. Sidel'nikov, 'Sovetskaya i bolgarskaya istoriografiya Aprel'skogo vosstaniya 1876 g. v Bolgarii', *VIst* (1976/4), pp. 49–71; R.T. Shannon, *Gladstone and the Bulgarian Agitation 1876* (Hamden, Conn., 1975²).

11. Alexander II to Schweinitz (6 Aug. 1876) in: *Denkwürdigkeiten des Botschafters General v. Schweinitz* (Berlin, 1927), vol. 1, p. 337.

Poset and a commission of inquiry convened in July of 1876 painted
the deficiencies of the railway system in dark colours and doubted
that the railways could satisfy military requirements.[12] In view of
the alarming financial and economic crisis, Minister of Finance von
Reutern wanted to avoid even partial mobilisation. Despite all this
there were other factors pushing the government to consider seriously
the conditions under which Russian military intervention would
become inevitable. In order to discover what those factors were, one
needs to examine more closely the pressure exerted on the Russian
government in the autumn of 1876 when it became evident that
Serbia was going down to military defeat.

Only indirect references can be discovered in the statements of
Alexander II and his retinue. It seemed obvious that 'Russia's
honour and dignity' would require war with the Turks under
certain circumstances. For a long time though, even the Tsar and his
closest advisers did not know at exactly what point Russia's policy
of military restraint would reach its limits. What can be determined
with some certainty after the summer of 1876 are Russia's minimal
conditions for any diplomatic solution: the integrity of Serbia and
Montenegro would have to be preserved and administrative reform
carried out in the rebellious provinces. These basic conditions did
not conflict with the fundamental interests of the other big powers
concerned. All further kinds of territorial rearrangement and expansion of influence were extremely complex. They were negotiable
and were not to serve as a *casus belli*. It was clear that London and
Vienna would resist any unilateral strengthening of Russia's position, just as the Turks would clearly try to avoid any far-reaching
involvement on the part of the great powers. St Petersburg's extreme sensitivity to matters of prestige and the inconsistency typical
of Russian behaviour cannot be explained satisfactorily merely by
the very slow course of diplomatic negotiations. The dilemma in
which St Petersburg found itself can only be fully appreciated if the
effects of the Balkan crisis within Russia are also considered.

Since the beginning of Serbian and Montenegrin operations
against the Turkish army, a groundswell of sympathy among the
Russian people for their struggling co-religionists carried the Slavic
movement to new heights. All earlier expressions of sympathy were
easily outdone.[13] The brutal suppression of the rebellion in Bulgaria

12. Pogrebinsky, *Stroitel'stvo*, p. 167.
13. The stages and forms of mobilisation are described by Nikitin, *Slavyanskie
komitety*, pp. 260–342; see also: idem, 'Russkoe obshchestvo i natsional'no-

increased the groundswell and fuelled a strong desire for active involvement which spread from the Slavic committees and the nationalist press to the urban public, the clergy and substantial sections of the lower classes. There is much to indicate that 'Slavo-mania' spread among people who had never heard of Serbia, Bosnia and Bulgaria. The imaginations of the orthodox faithful, filled with the tales of martyrs and saints, were evidently highly susceptible to the sufferings of Christians in the Balkans.[14] Demonstrations, large contributions of money, and calls to arms of Russian volunteers plainly indicated that the Russian public was inclined to view unqualified support for Balkan Slavs as a 'holy duty'. Sceptical observers saw 'all Russia fallen victim to a sterile fever' and they spoke of 'Slavophile autoerotism'.[15] General M.G. Chernyaev, already known for the taking of Tashkent (1865) and editor of the reactionary Pan-Slav publication *Russkii mir* (Russian World), was celebrated as the hero of the hour. He had already gone to Belgrade in April 1876 and taken over supreme command of the Serbian army.[16] When it became evident that the fortunes of war were turning against Serbia, public concern rose to such a pitch that even liberal newspapers criticised the official policy of seeking a diplomatic solution to the conflict and considered massive military intervention justified. The 'Tsar-Liberator' was enjoined more and more vigorously to deliver the Slavic brothers from Turkish rule and lead them also to freedom.

This growing movement with in Russian society placed the regime in a difficult position. In lending support to the afflicted Serbs and Bulgarians, Russian society developed a sense of self-confidence which did not yet have an outlet in domestic politics

osvoboditel'naya bor'ba yuzhnykh slavyan v 1875–1876 gg.' in *Obshchestvenno-politicheskie i kulturnye svyazi narodov SSSR i Yugoslavii. Sbornik statei* (Moscow, 1957), pp. 3–77; T. Snytko, 'Iz istorii narodnogo dvizheniya v Rossii v podderzhku bor'by yuzhnykh slavyan za svoyu nezavisimost' v 1875–1876 gg.' ibid., pp. 78–106. There is rich material with analysis of Russian and Serbian sources, including the press in: MacKenzie, *The Serbs, passim*; see as well *Osvobozhdenie Bolgarii*, vol. 1, and I.V. Kozmenko, 'Iz istorii bolgarskogo opolcheniya', *Slavyanskii sbornik* (Moscow, 1948); Kozmenko, 'Russkoe obshchestvo i aprel'skoe bolgarskoe vosstanie', *VIst* (1945/5), pp. 95–108.

14. Schweinitz, *Denkwürdigkeiten* 1, pp. 386f. Almost all police reports confirm the spirit of self-sacrifice especially widespread among the lower classes, as well as a sharp increase in the influence of the press and the Slavic committees in the provinces; cf. the material in: *Osvobozhdenie Bolgarii* 1, pp. 333f., 343, 360ff., 364f., 380, 437, 463f., 467ff., 509.

15. *Dnevnik Valueva* 2, p. 381 (4 August 1876).

16. See D. MacKenzie, *The Lion of Tashkent* (Athens, 1974), especially pp. 117ff., on M.G. Chernyaev.

from which it was excluded. Although Pan-Slav activists avoided vehement accusations, their activity had to be seen as a conspicuous reproach of government inaction and evidence that the nation's honour was being defended not by the government but by society itself. There is no doubt that the Serbs in particular were comforted and encouraged in their exaggerated view of what they could achieve by public support in Russia and that they aimed to draw the Empire into the war.

The autocracy reacted to these challenges with ambivalence. Official St Petersburg was careful to preserve its aloof stance for reasons of foreign policy, offering neither credits nor delivery of weapons. However, it also offered no opposition (or only half-hearted opposition) to the mounting activities of the Slavic Committees, the Red Cross and other aid groups. The Tsar censured but finally accepted Chernyaev's strictly personal decision to go to Serbia and take command of a Serbian army in which, finally, over 600 Russian officers and several thousand soldiers served.[17] The recruitment of volunteers to help defend Serbia was left to private initiative, but the extreme tolerance shown this military aid lent it a quasi-official air. The Ministry of War even granted official leave of absence to officers. Thus the prestige of the autocracy was soon dangerously entangled in the events in Serbia, and a pall was cast over its policy of preventing war, even though there were many arguments in its favour.

There is little doubt that the Tsar fundamentally disapproved of the political influence which the public had acquired since the summer of 1876. The government could take no comfort from seeing an eccentric ideologue like Aksakov with his supporters at the Court, acting in the name of Russia and the Slavic cause as chairman of the Moscow Committee.[18] However, Alexander was neither able nor willing to resist the movement for solidarity with the Balkans — an indication of the autocracy's increasing desire not to resist society openly during this time of crisis and to give the impression that the authorities were, as always, close to the people. The process of adjustment to the public mood was a subtle one: the

17. At the end of September 1876 there were about 1,850 Russian volunteers (644 of whom were officers) in the Serbian army; by 1877 the Slavic committees had sent a total of about 5,000 volunteers to Serbia: cf. Nikitin, *Slavyanskie komitety*, pp. 319f.

18. For Aksakov's role during the Balkan crisis see: Katz, pp. 134ff., as well as the literature named in note 45. For the easy self-identification of the upper echelons of the Slavic committees with 'society' and the 'people', cf. Aksakov to N.K. Giers, 1 Sept. 1876 in *Osvobozhdenie Bolgarii* 1, pp. 374ff.

ruler and his ministers did not simply adopt wholeheartedly the overheated Pan-Slav feeling. Ignat'ev is often pictured in the literature as a rabid Pan-Slavist, but although he argued for a tougher stance than the ageing Gorchakov, his views were by no means foolhardy. Alexander's most influential advisor, Milyutin, was a sober, thoughtful man not inclined to become intoxicated by ideology. The temptation was great, though, to hear the voice of Russia herself in the demands of the Slavophile public and feel oneself bound to follow.[19] The attitude of the Tsar may have been affected by the fact that the Tsarina, the Crown Prince and some of the grand dukes succumbed to the patriotic mood and urged that more energetic steps be taken. In any case, such pleas must have made it easier for the Tsar to escape the constant vexation of such a complex issue by taking 'popular' decisions.

What seeped out from the ponderous decision-making process can only partly be explained by the mental state of the Tsar. Beyond mere personal predisposition, Alexander's hesitation was also a sign of the structural weaknesses of the political system. These weaknesses are perhaps best demonstrated by the poor coordination of Russian efforts on the diplomatic front.[20] Neither the Tsar, who spent weeks isolated in Livadiya in the Taurus Mountains, nor the Chancellor, as vain as he was immobile, could impose a unified policy on the unauthorised and competing activities of the ambassadors to Constantinople (N.P. Ignat'ev), London (P.A. Shuvalov) and Vienna (E.P. Novikov). The actions of the Russian consuls in the principalities completely evaded adequate control. The lack of leadership in Russian diplomacy irritated even well-disposed foreign negotiators. Attempts to pin Berlin down to binding agreements and to discover Vienna's true intentions ran aground on what was at times embarrassing dilettantism. Under the circumstances, the political powers which the Tsar had at his disposal to avoid the risk of war could not be used effectively. The frustration became unbearable when the agile Turks succeeded again and again, thanks to British backing, in dodging collective action by the European powers and even exploited their own internal confusion to neutralise Russian claims. 'Tout le monde contre nous'[21] — such impressions reinforced the spreading sense of resignation in St Petersburg and confirmed the

---

19. *Dnevnik Valueva* 2, pp. 373f. (2 July 1876).
20. *Briefwechsel des Botschafters General v. Schweinitz* (Berlin, 1928), p. 123 (4 Nov. 1876).
21. Schweinitz, *Denkwürdigkeiten*, 1, p. 428.

suspicion that Russia might be forced to act alone.

Government diplomacy was under pressure to produce results. That pressure originated in large part from the Pan-Slavic movement, but autocracy's international prestige was also on the line in the Balkans. The autocracy did not want to waste the confidence that the southern Slavs placed in Russia, and this special relationship was considered a political pledge that placed its policies in the Balkans on a higher plane than those of other interested governments. St Petersburg could only avoid serious loss of authority if it succeeded in persuading the other powers to impose political solutions on Constantinople which satisfied at least its minimal demands. Otherwise only decisive steps, backed by a willingness to intervene militarily, could succeed in channeling Pan-Slavic agitation (which always appeared rather unseemly to the regime and at times even revolutionary) along the desired path.

Under these circumstances the Tsar oscillated between impatience, fatalism and hope. Fateful decisions were finally taken in October 1876.[22] Despite the unrelenting opposition of the Finance Minister, the Tsar ordered that the army prepare for war while Ignat'ev's diplomatic efforts continued. By issuing an ultimatum to the Porte to conclude an immediate cease-fire on the Serbian front and begin peace negotiations within two months, the Russian government demonstrated its readiness to engage the Turks, alone if necessary. A spring offensive was planned on Romanian territory and would be legalised by means of a treaty with Bucharest.[23] Milyutin had auxiliary Bulgarian troops drawn up in Bessarabia, and Prince V.A. Cherkasskii, the prominent chairman of the Red Cross society, was designated leader of the Russian civilian government in Bulgaria.[24] Even before the mobilisation of six army corps was announced on 1 (13) November, the Tsar publicly paid tribute in Moscow to the 'Slavic cause' and evoked Russia's 'holy mission'.[25]

22. Hüningen, pp. 132ff.; Sumner, pp. 196ff. Important sources on the discussions in Livadiya are to be found in the notes and correspondence of the participants, especially Milyutin's diary: *Dnevnik Milyutina* 2, pp. 76ff.; A.G. Yomini's letters to N.K. Giers: C. and B. Jelavich (eds.) *Russia in the East 1876–1880* (Leiden, 1959), pp. 22ff.; N.P. Ignat'ev's memoranda in: *Istoricheskii vestnik* 136 (1914), pp. 77ff., as well as the memoranda and reports of Finance Minister Reutern, *Finanzielle Sanierung*, pp. 119ff.
23. M.M. Zalyshkin, *Vneshnyaya politika Rumynii i rumynsko-russkie otnosheniya 1875–1878* (Moscow, 1974).
24. For the actions of Prince Cherkasskii see his correspondence with I.S. Aksakov in: I.V. Kos'menko (ed.), *Slavyanskii sbornik* (Moscow, 1948), pp. 132ff.
25. Cf. S.S. Tatishchev, *Imperator Aleksandr II. Ego zhizn' i tsarstvovanie* (St Petersburg, 1903), vol. 2, p. 310.

It now seemed that the autocracy might be putting itself at the head of the Slavic movement. The new hard-line policy saved a defeated Serbia, and was received positively by the public. The Russian Slavic Committees were provided with official functions and the demoralised corps of Russian volunteers was disbanded.[26] However, the degree of relief which the politics of strength brought the Russian government should not be exaggerated. The nation's problems were shifted but not solved. The knowledge that a declaration of war would entail incalculable risks still motivated the Tsar and his advisors to continue their attempts to find a peaceful solution. However, as was seen again in the failure of the ambassadors' conference in Constantinople at the year's end, the disappointing experiences of the previous months were repeated again and again. Everything now depended on providing diplomatic backing for the planned offensive. When the time came to strengthen the Reichstadt agreements in new negotiations with Andrassy, it turned out that Austria's benevolent neutrality could be obtained only through further concessions. In the Budapest Convention of 15 January 1877, the Dual Monarchy was granted not only a renewal of its hold over Bosnia and Hercegovina but also a resolution of Serbian territorial questions at the expense of the regime in Belgrade. (These enhancements of its territory and power could, however, have all been achieved by Vienna without firing a shot.) The need to satisfy Austria's ambitions as much as possible was also gratified by the autocracy's acceptance of the Serbo-Turkish peace, signed in March 1877, and its refusal to urge Prince Milan once more to take up arms at Russia's side. The negotiations with England were even more difficult because London made it known that it would not tolerate the creation of a Greater Bulgaria under Russian domination or even a temporary occupation of the Straits.

If these sobering developments are considered together, it becomes clear that the tense situation in which the Russian leadership found itself had not dissipated by the spring of 1877. The Tsar was still struggling to escape from policies which had taken him prisoner and ministers were repeatedly confronted with a monarch who clung to the hope that war could still somehow be avoided. This hesitation can easily be explained as the result of a dilemma which men such as Miluytin and Reutern understood even better than the Tsar. The structural problems caused by internal reform were not

26. MacKenzie, *The Serbs*, pp. 154ff.

solely responsible for the catastrophic future perspectives evoked by the Minister of Finance. An economic depression descended over the country, aggravated by the poor harvest of 1875–6. 'Commerce has been flattened, almost no private credit is available, the population does not have a market for its agricultural products and therefore cannot purchase manufactured goods, the factories stand idle and offer no employment, private individuals go bankrupt every day and soon they will drag down the private banks with them.' Reutern's financial policies lay in ruins. The hopelessness of the situation was brought home to Reutern by the declining foreign demand for Russian grain as world prices fell, the almost insoluble problem of Russia's foreign debts, the depletion of the nation's gold reserves, and the prospect of having to cover all additional expenditures beyond those of the railway by openly or covertly issuing letters of credit. 'I am convinced that, quite apart from a war, merely a continuation of the uncertain political situation will lead Russia to wrack and ruin' — i.e., financial bankruptcy and economic confusion, the alienation of the conservative landowning class from the autocratic state, and a crisis which would create 'fertile ground for revolutionary and socialist propaganda'.[27]

The Minister of War had already warned against the consequences of a winter campaign. Strategic railways to the Danube did not exist. In February 1877 Milyutin was still arguing in much the same vein as his despairing colleague:

> The internal and economic transformation of Russia has reached a stage where every external disruption could lead to long-lasting disorder in the organism of state. . . . Not one of the reforms has been completed. . . . A war under these circumstances would be a very serious misfortune for us. The terrible loss of inner strength would be magnified by external exertions, every useful kind of work would be paralysed and the countless casualties of war could soon completely exhaust the country and even threaten Russia's greatness. . . .[28]

However, both the Tsar and the Minister of War were still enthralled by these very notions of the 'greatness' and 'honour' of

27. Reutern, 'Denkschrift für Alexander II' (11 Feb. 1877) in *Finanzielle Sanierung*, pp. 144ff. As a result of the economic emergency the population's ability to make 'voluntary sacrifices' in case of war was judged even by the secret police to be very limited: see N.V. Mezentsov's report to the Tsar (12 Nov. 1876) in *Osvobozhdenie Bolgarii* 1, pp. 506ff., as well as regional police reports in ibid., pp. 467ff., 532f., 594f.

28. *Dnevnik Milyutina* 1, p. 47.

the Empire. They were, after all, at the heart of the internal contradictions in Russian policy. While the diplomats failed to make progress in negotiations and at conferences, the mobilised army corps in their winter quarters developed a momentum of their own. In view of the millions of rubles already invested, only a miraculous diplomatic breakthrough in Russia's favour could justify demobilising them all. No such miracle occurred. The longer the uncertainty lasted, the more even Milyutin was inclined to contradict his own better judgement: 'in the absence of satisfactory guarantees,' he said, 'Russia's honour forbids us to stand about any longer with lowered guns just for the sake of peace.'[29]

There is no doubt that the precarious relations between the autocracy and the public continued to be largely responsible for this compulsive carelessness in the political decision-making process. Since the late autumn of 1876, the press had concentrated on the fate of Bulgaria, and by the winter of 1876/7 it was insisting that the time had come to end the nerve-racking suspense and fulfil Russia's 'holy duty' — whether by immediate, overwhelming collective action on the part of the powers or by force of Russian arms alone. The appeals and admonitions of the Finance Minister show that he considered it extremely unwise to divert attention away from internal tensions with a foreign war because such a war would aggravate the economic crisis, alienate social groups that supported the autocracy and encourage revolutionaries. Other influential voices in the Tsar's inner circle arrived at just the opposite conclusion: the government's vacillation and inability to act and its inclination to keep the peace at any price were driving a wedge between the Tsar and his people, were encouraging revolutionary agitation in Russia and the Slavic world and were partly responsible for the autocracy's loss of authority.

K.P. Pobedonostsev, the close companion of the crown prince, had seen such dangers approaching as early as June 1876:

The government must either take this popular movement in hand and lead it, or it will inundate the authorities and spread, wild and uncontrolled, animated by a sense of mistrust and hostility to the government. In that case, things will become very, very difficult. . . . Our people is capable of many marvellous virtues when it feels guided and led; if there is no guiding force, however, or if the task of leadership is shirked, then confusion, chaos and destruction will result. . . . If the present situation

29. *Dnevnik Milyutina* 2, pp. 135f. (19/1/1877), 137f. (8 Feb. 1877).

is not resolved or if it ends in a corrupt peace that disgraces us and delights our so-called allies, then the whole social agitation that now is directed outward will turn inward. The gulf between government and people could reach proportions never before seen in our history.[30]

What Pobedonostsev probably meant by this turning inward was the revival of those forces demanding internal reform. Now that even Turkey had a constitution, rebellious voices were pointing out 'that only two countries still lack constitutional government: the Russian Empire and the Celestial Kingdom of China'.[31] It is impossible to tell whether the first great nihilist trial, which aroused a great deal of public sympathy in the spring of 1877, strengthened the hand of those who favoured strong political action in the Eastern Question. What is certain is that the revolutionary movement cannot be excluded from the nexus of circumstances in which the government made its political decisions.[32] The inefficacy of diplomatic attempts to resolve the crisis, the mechanics of the military measures taken by the government and increasing unrest in politically concerned society were only the most important factors behind the final decision to declare war. The Turks' rejection of the London Protocol (31 March/12 April) determined the date of the Tsar's manifesto.

This is not the place to trace the events of the war in detail. One important domestic consequence of the commencement of military operations was that for the first time since the Polish rebellion the autocracy found itself fully in accord with public opinion.[33] Reac-

---

30. K.P. Pobedonostsev to the successor to the throne (25 June 1876), cited in F. Steinmann and E. Hurwicz, *Konstantin Petrowitsch Pobjedonoszew. Der Staatsmann der Reaktion unter Alexander III* (Königsberg, 1933), pp. 243; cf. Aksakov's speech on 6 March 1877 (*Sochineniya* 1, pp. 236ff.) whose sharp criticism of Russian policy earned him a rebuke from the Tsar: Mezentsov to Aksakov, 12 March 1877, in *Osvobozhdenie Bolgarii* 1, p. 619.

31. Police report to the Third Department (7 Feb. 1877), ibid., p. 595.

32. 'The Trial of the Fifty' (21 Feb.–14 March 1877). *Gosudarstvennye prestupleniya v Rossii v XIX v.* (Rostov, n.d.), vol. 2. Cf. as well Schweinitz's impressions, *Denkwürdigkeiten* 1, p. 411. For the activity of revolutionary organisations on the eve of the war see: P.S. Tkachenko, *Revolyutsionnaya narodnicheskaya organizatsiya 'Zemlya i Volya' v 1876–1879 gg.* (Moscow, 1961); B.S. Itenberg, *Dvizhenie revolyutsionnogo narodnichestva. Narodnicheskie kruzhki i 'khozhdenie v narod' v 70-kh godakh XIX v.* (Moscow, 1965); F. Venturi, *The Roots of Revolution* (London, 1960); idem, 'Problemi del populismo russo', *RSI* 83 (1971), pp. 314–84; J.E. Bachmann, 'Recent Soviet Historiography on Russian Revolutionary Populism', *SR* 29 (1970), pp. 591–612.

33. For Russian journalism after the outbreak of war see: MacKenzie, *The Serbs*, pp. 194ff.; Report of the Third Department (22 April 1877), in *Osvobozhdenie Bolgarii* 2, pp. 47f.; A.A. Ulunyan, *Bolgarskii narod i russko-turetskaya voina 1877–1878 gg.* (Moscow, 1971), pp. 130ff.

tionary spokesmen lauded the soothing effect of the war on the internal situation: the 'great mission' which Russia was preparing to undertake found 'its visible expression in the unity of the Russian people with the highest levels of governmental authority'; the resulting 'breath of fresh air' would supposedly engulf even those 'circles of raving doubters, calm their unnatural irritability, and distract them from their senseless and baneful schemes'.[34] Freed at last from all the vacillation and uncertainty, the Tsar must have relished riding a wave of affection and confidence. Evidently Alexander adapted quickly to his new role. Despite the efforts of official eulogists, doubt and disappointment had tarnished the myth of the Tsar-Liberator. Now it appeared once again in all its splendour, though in reference to the military might which Russia was deploying in foreign lands and no longer (as in 1861) to the domestic beneficence of the Tsar. To the public this was a war of liberation and it evoked the highest hopes. All that still remained to be achieved in the way of political liberation in Russia was quickly sublimated, as was shown just as the war reached its climax in a second gigantic trial of populist agitators whose courage put the St Petersburg public to shame.[35] The unsettled internal situation created such a psychological hunger for compensation that any possibility of a 'small peace' seemed excluded. The costs and casualties of the war could only be justified by the complete elimination of Turkish rule, the firm establishment of a Russian protectorate over liberated Greater Bulgaria, and possibly even the sight of the patriarchial cross shining over St Sophia. Attempts to satisfy such extravagant claims could not fail further to weigh down the government, quite apart from the many nuances that separated the Pan-Slav and Russian brands of nationalism.

The patriotic fervour did not allow the government to stop halfway — 'Russia would never have forgiven us for that,' said the Tsar in December 1877.[36] Military operations had been costly, Russia had suffered serious setbacks and the prestige of the military command under Grand Duke Nikolai Nikolaevich had not been enhanced.[37] The capitulation of the Turkish army did not seem

---

34. Katkov in: *Moskovskie vedomosti* 9 Oct. 1877, quoted in V.A. Tvardovskaya, 'Ideolog samoderzhaviya v period krizisa "verkhov" na rubezhe 70–80-kh godov XIX v.', *IZ*, 91 (1973), p. 218.

35. 'Trial of the 193' (October 1877 to January 1878): *Gosudarstvennye prestulpleniya v Rossii v XIX v. Sbornik pod red. B. Basilevskogo* (St Petersburg, 1906), vol. 3.

36. P.A. Valuev, *Dnevnik 1877–1884* (Petrograd, 1919), p. 22 (20 Dec. 1877).

37. For the course of the war, see the work by the Russian general staff: *Sbornik*

imminent until the end of 1877 when Plevna was finally captured after several unsuccessful attempts. Though the British threatened to land their fleet in the Straits even after a truce had been declared on 31 January 1878, the public and the high army command continued to insist that Constantinople should be occupied. This impossible demand forced the government to make dangerous political decisions and, without sufficient international backing, Ignat'ev was authorised to dictate conditions to the Turks at San Stefano which, as would soon be seen, dangerously overtaxed the military and political strength of the Empire.

The Peace preliminaries were signed (not without ulterior motive) on 19 February (3 March), the anniversary of the emancipation of the serfs and the coronation of Alexander II. This led the public to expect an extension of Russian power which would satisfy its highest hopes and justify the enormous human costs of the war. Thanks to Russia a Greater Bulgaria seemed about to take shape, including Macedonia and enjoying easy access to the Aegean Sea; Serbia, Montenegro and Romania would be freed from their tributary position and rounded off territorially; European Turkey would be reduced to small, unconnected territories — Constantinople with a very small strip of Rumelia, Thessaly, Epirus, Albania and Chalcidice with Salonika; Russia would be extended once again to the mouth of the Danube (at the expense of its Romanian ally) and would gain Batum, Kars and Ardahan; out of deference to Vienna, the fate of Bosnia and Hercegovina would not definitively be decided.[38]

Russia was clearly in for a rude awakening from such dreams of glory. St Petersburg had no real reason to believe it could long assert its claim against England and Austria to be the organising power that would re-shape the liberated Balkans. However, self-deception and a lack of clear direction prevented the government from defining a reasonable set of goals for the peace negotiations. Milyutin

---

materialov po russko-turetskoi voine 1877–1878 gg. na Balkanskom poluostrove (97 vols., St Petersburg, 1898–1911), as well as *Opisanie russko-turetskoi voiny 1877–1878 gg. na Balkanskom poluostrove* (9 vols., 6 supplemental vols., St Petersburg, 1901–1913). For Soviet presentations with a patriotic flavour, see: N.I. Belyaev, *Russko-turetskya voina 1877–1878 gg.* (Moscow, 1956); P.K. Fortunatov, *Der Krieg von 1877/78 und die Befreiung Bulgariens* (Berlin, GDR, 1953). For public unrest about the slow course of the war and the news blackout see: Giers to Ignat'ev (28 June 1877), in *Osvobozhdenie Bolgarii*, 2, pp. 144f., A.E. Timashev to Milyutin (2 Aug. 1877), ibid., pp. 222f.

38. Text in Sumner, *Russia*, pp. 627ff.; cf. S.L. Chernov, 'K voprosu o San-Stefanskom dogovore 1878 g.'. *ISSR* (1975/4), pp. 133–47.

made it clear that the Russian army could not hope to prevail in the looming conflict with the rival powers.[39] The war in the Balkans had demonstrated continuing deficiencies in assuring military supplies and provisions, the technical backwardness of Russian weaponry (especially that of the infantry), and the poor quality of leadership in the field.[40] For months top decision-makers in St Petersburg were paralysed by the fear that a great war could be ignited by the continuing confrontation between the British fleet and the Russian army before the walls of Constantinople. The Serbs were embittered by the creation of a Principality of Greater Bulgaria and felt constrained to align themselves with London and Vienna. Any visions of Slavic 'brotherhood' were thus reduced to shambles.[41] Uncertainty grew as to what would remain of St Petersburg's military conquests. In March 1878 Katkov wrote: 'Will Russia be a powerful, independent great power or will she not? Will she be the natural protector of those peoples of similar race who are bound by a foreign yoke? Will she so strengthen her position in the Black Sea that there need not be any concern about the economic future of the entire South?'[42] Russian diplomats had always assumed that the interests of England and Austria would have to be taken into account and substantial concessions made. Bismarck's reluctant offer to mediate as 'honest broker' vindicated the view that the results of the Russo-Turkish war would have to be submitted for consideration by the concert of European powers.

The bungling irrationality of Russian peace demands had landed the Tsar and his advisors in a ticklish situation and they contemplated the proceedings of the Congress of Berlin (13 June–13 July 1878) in a depressed frame of mind.[43] The terms of the Treaty of San Stefano could not be defended militarily, and it was impossible simply to stonewall Disraeli's ultimatums and Andrassy's ambitious pretensions. Nothing could compensate for the weakness of Rus-

39. *Dnevnik Milyutin* 3, p. 32 (22 March 1878), pp. 34f. (25 March 1878), *passim*.
40. L.G. Beskrovnyi, *Russkaya armiya i flot v XIX veke* (Moscow, 1973), pp. 408ff., 470ff.; Zayonchkovskii, *Voennye reformy*, pp. 338ff.
41. MacKenzie, *The Serbs*, pp. 248ff., 299ff.
42. Katkov in: *Moskovskie vedomosti*, 28 March 1878, cited in Tvardovskaya, p. 218.
43. On the Congress: Sumner, *Russia*, pp. 501 ff.; W.N. Medlicott, *The Congress of Berlin and After. A Diplomatic History of the New Eastern Peace Settlement 1878–1880* (London, 1963²); A. Novotny, *Quellen und Studien zur Geschichte des Berliner Kongresses 1878* (Vienna, 1957), vol. 1; R. Melville and H.-J. Schröder (eds.), *Der Berliner Kongreß von 1878* (Wiesbaden, 1982). For the Anglo-Russian confrontation in the Straits in the spring and summer of 1878 see the telegrams and notes of Count P.A. Shuvalov in: *KA* 4 (59) (1933), pp. 82–109.

sian diplomacy under the senile Gorchakov. When Shuvalov agreed with Salisbury to renounce the creation of a Greater Bulgaria and accept English control over Cyprus, the Russians felt deeply humiliated. Milyutin found the Tsar heavily influenced by the press, struck by the 'abuse in our newspapers, the fairy-tales and wild attacks propagated by real Russophiles' against concessions he himself had approved.[44] The depth of the disappointment, the sense of abasement and humiliation would probably not have been so great if Alexander had not been seduced by the success of Russian arms into letting the extravagant expectations of a public infected by nationalism form his conception of imperial honour.

The furious reaction of the public to the results of the Berlin Congress showed how quickly a loss of international prestige could engender substantial decline in the domestic authority of the regime. The social consensus of the 'wars of liberation' was lost, faith in the regime evaporated. The high-pitched emotions of the public produced a crisis of confidence that could not be dissipated by the denunciations of Russia's own diplomats or by press attacks on scheming Austrians, 'perfidious Albion', and Bismarck's self-interest. The widespread discontent was expressed most pointedly by Aksakov in his infamous remark that the Congress of Berlin was 'nothing other than an open conspiracy against the Russian people . . . with the connivance of Russia's own representatives'.[45] Even liberal newspapers like the *S. Petersburgskie vedomosti* or the *Russkie vedomosti* in Moscow spread the view that Russia should not lay down her arms until 'the house of cards of decisions' taken in Berlin had collapsed. Preparation for battle was seen as urgent, for 'a war is better than demoralisation'. According to the newspapers, Russia's internal problems also had be attacked in order to overcome as quickly as possible the flaws that were blocking the natural development of the life of the the nation and the satisfaction of the most important needs of society and the state.[46] Reform as preparation for war — such a concept underlines how directly Russia's internal problems were once again brought to the fore by the setback in foreign policy.

44. *Dnevnik Milyutina* 3, p. 78 (5 July 1878).

45. I.S. Aksakov, *Slavyanskii vopros 1860–1886* (Moscow, 1886), p. 303; also V.I. Ado, 'Berlinskii kongress 1878 g. i. pomeshchiché-burzhuaznoe obshchestvennoe mnenie Rossii', *IZ*, 69 (1961), pp. 101ff.; Ado, 'Vystuplenie I.S. Aksakova protiv Berlinskogo kongressa 1878 g. i. otkliki na nego v Rossii i Bolgarii', *ISSR* (1962/6), pp. 125ff.; Grüning, pp. 52ff.

46. For the quotes: *Petersburgskie vedomosti*, 13 June and 4 Aug. 1878, according to Ado, 'Berlinskii kongress', pp. 124f.

This relationship can only be adumbrated here. Soviet historians describe the period following the Russo-Turkish war as a time of 'crisis for the autocracy' or even as a 'revolutionary situation'.[47] They point in particular to revolutionary activities beginning in the spring of 1878 — a series of terrorist attacks that began with Vera Zasulich shooting General Trepov, the chief of police in St Petersburg (24 January 1878), and which eventually reached the Tsar himself, as well as such highly placed officials as the head of the Third Section. A jury acquitted Zasulich, to the accompaniment of applause from the public, indicating how far the autocracy's social base had crumbled. The liberal judicial system which the autocracy had created was being used to undermine the authority of the state and the government was forced to doubt the wisdom of its own actions. The struggle against the terrorist movement *Narodnaya Volya* (People's Will) raised questions that went beyond mere problems of policing. The amount of sympathy attracted by bomb-throwing 'nihilists' made it clear that broad sections of the public showed no sign of the loyalty which it was so often claimed they felt for the Tsar. At best he had their pity.[48]

Terrorism was seen as a sign of the death struggle of the regime. Consternation at the helplessness of the authorities turned in many cases into feelings of apathy and fatalism. Revulsion at political murder did not eliminate respect for the self-sacrifice of the young assassins. 'As the state decays more and more,' said the German ambassador, General von Schweinitz, 'nihilist sects grow bolder, and discontent among all the educated classes becomes more pronounced.' The autocracy no longer really existed, according to Schweinitz, for it had been 'reduced to self-preservation'. The ambassador was shaken by the 'frivolity of the upper classes' and the 'indifference of the middle classes' when a group of young soldiers were killed in a dynamite attack on the Winter Palace in February 1880.[49]

47. For the following, on the basis of broad documentary material: P.A. Zayonchkovskii, *Krizis samoderzhaviya na rubezhe 1870–1880 godov* (Moscow, 1964); also M.I. Kheifets, *Vtoraya revolyutsionnaya situatsiya v Rossii (konets 70-kh – nachalo 80-kh godov XIX v). Krizis pravitel'stvennoi politiki* (Moscow, 1963).

48. For the 'Narodnaya Volya' (People's Will) see: S.S. Volk, *Narodnaya volya, 1879–1882 gg.* (Moscow, 1966); *Revolyutsionnoe narodnichestvo 70-kh godov XIX v.* (Moscow, 1965), vol. 2.

49. Schweinitz, *Denkwürdigkeiten*, 2, p. 48 (March 1879), p. 102 (20 Feb. 1880); cf. as well: *Briefe über die gegenwärtige Lage Rußlands*, 11(23) April 1879–6(18) April 1880. Translated from the Russian (Leipzig, 1881). For the reaction in the press to terrorism see: Tvardovskaya, pp. 219ff.

This loss of authority, brought to the fore by the disappointing outcome of the war, was largely responsible for the fact that a handful of determined revolutionaries could threaten to topple the regime. Even the Tsar now demanded a change in direction. The outcome was an attempt to combine energetic steps against the small revolutionary groups with policies designed to reinspire confidence between autocracy and public. This formed the basis for the benevolent 'dictatorship' of Count M.T. Loris-Melikov.[50] The supposed revival of governmental liberalism never broke free of its inner contradictions. The emergency regime failed both to overcome the defects in the decision-making process and to create a firm consensus among influential groups by introducing overdue plans for reform. After the period of economic prosperity created by the war had petered out, the economic and financial collapse forecast by Finance Minister Reutern before his resignation began in earnest. Deliberation over changes in the educational system and the press alternated between liberalism and repression; plans to do something about the pitiable state of the Russian peasantry ran aground on fiscal limitations. Finally, the much discussed revival of semi-constitutional projects died with the Tsar-Liberator when his life was extinguished by *Narodnaya Volya* in March 1881.

This outline of the autocracy's response to the crisis shows how inseparable was the connection between the inner problems of the Empire and war and politics in the Balkans. Aroused by nationalism, the public put heavy pressure on the government to prove itself. This so increased the uncertainty, confusion and lack of direction in government policy that even the highest officials could no longer foresee the consequences of their decisions. The claim that St Petersburg gave in to Pan-Slavic demands in its handling of the Eastern Question does not really get to the heart of the matter. Russia would have intervened diplomatically as the ultimate authority in the Balkans with or without the Slavic Committees. The political élite conceived of Russia as an imperial power whose traditional interests and prestige were at stake, and non-interference would have been out of the question. However, the slide into policies that constantly put the government in a position where it could be pressured, and the decision finally to break with the mutually helpful concert of powers cannot be satisfactorily explained on their own intrinsic merits. Russia's structural weaknesses

---

50. Zayonchkovskii, *Krizis*, pp. 148ff., 230ff.; cf. as well chap. 5.

and the fragility of the regime must be examined as well. Only then does it become apparent why the government was unable to cope with all the pressures arising from the Eastern Question, the economic crisis and increased nationalist fervour, and why the government resorted to a solution which would have seemed foolhardy if looked at coolly and rationally.

There is very little to indicate that the decision to wage war resulted from a sober consideration of the alternatives. The Tsar was more resigned than confident of victory when he decided that Russia should march on its own. Evidently the danger which the diplomatic strategy of *attentisme* posed for the internal stability and external prestige of the autocracy seemed greater than the dangers of war — the probable ruin of state finances, the termination of development policies for the economy, and the international danger that St Petersburg ran. The regime definitely did not decide to go to war because it had succumbed to the allures of its imperial war aims: no one could seriously have thought that these exaggerated war aims, which conflicted with strong Austrian and English interests, would prove acceptable. Nor were imperial policies in the Balkans activated by a desire to conquer new markets for the Russian economy and penetrate the Balkans economically. Commercial pressure groups did not influence the decisions taken by the Tsar. In the early 1880s, when Russian railway interests in Sofia collided with Austrian interests, leading functionaries in the Foreign Ministry opined that Russia had 'nothing either to buy or sell in Bulgaria'.[51]

All that remained was the hope that the decision to go to war would rally public support within Russia. However, the expectation that the popularity of the war would rub off on the authority of the autocracy quickly proved illusory. Rather than increasing the Tsar's margin for manoeuvre, the war seriously reduced it. Autocracy's prestige came to depend on the acclamation of social forces whose loyalty could only be permanently sustained by glorious victories and gains in Russia's international influence and power which were simply not possible in 1877–8. The sobering experience of the Berlin Congress revealed an Emperor without clothes, and the 'crisis of autocracy' continued.

---

51. Yomini to Giers, 4 Nov. 1880, cited in: C. Jelavich, *Tsarist Russia and Balkan Nationalism. Russian Influence in the Internal Affairs of Bulgaria and Serbia, 1879–1886* (Berkeley, 1958), p. 69. Müller-Link's view (*Industrialisierung*, p. 209) that the Russian bourgeoisie wanted to maintain its market in the Balkans 'even at the cost of a war' is not tenable. Russian trade with the Balkans was minimal.

4.2   Expansion into Central Asia

As we have seen, the war in the Balkans did not reinforce the shaken authority of the government and only aggravated the permanent structural crisis in Russia. The question therefore arises of how imperial successes in Asia (which created quite a stir at the time) fit into the nexus of causes and effects outlined above. Not only was Russia's position in the Far East substantially improved under Alexander II but, more importantly, Russia acquired vast territories in Central Asia. The roots of this traditional expansion reach all the way back to the pre-Petrine era, but the rapidity of military and colonial conquests after the Crimean War and especially after the mid-1860s vastly surpassed anything seen before. A new phase of imperial expansion had evidently begun in response to changed circumstances.[52] This policy of conquest stands in marked contrast to St Petersburg's indecisive, hesitant reactions to the Eastern Question. In Central Asia a sense of strength and superiority seemed to take hold and the government felt few compunctions about embroiling Russia in a permanent confrontation with the British Empire. Russian operations in Asia seem also to have been unaffected by the fits of depression which arose from contemplating all the problems within Russia itself.

The educated classes in Russia had long cherished the belief that the Empire had a 'civilising mission' to fulfil by way of geographical expansion into Asia — much the same as the English and French in their colonies. This belief was given new life by the Crimean War. Slavophile writers (who had been particularly humiliated by the Russian defeat) and many others thought that Russia should now push more vigorously the historic advantage she enjoyed in the East.[53] The psychological hunger for compensation that this reflects was reinforced by a desire better to protect the Empire's holdings in Asia against attack by the same powers that had already once allied themselves against Russia.

After the Peace of Paris interest in defending Russian dominions focused primarily on the Caucasus. The imperial government had been expressing a desire to secure these domains permanently ever

52. For Alexander II's entire Asian policy see: O. Hoetzsch, *Rußland in Asien. Geschichte einer Expansion* (Stuttgart, 1966).

53. Evidence in: N.V. Riasanovsky, 'Asia through Russian Eyes', in W.S. Vucinich (ed.), *Russia and Asia. Essays of the Influence of Russia on the Asian Peoples* (Stanford, 1972), pp. 3–29, 369ff.

since the time of Nicholas I. After 1856 the time had come for action, and within just a few years the rebellious mountain peoples had been subdued and the Caucasus secured.[54] St Petersburg also undertook new initiatives along the military border in Central Asia between the Aral Sea and the 'New Siberian Line' and in the extreme Far Eastern regions as far as the Pacific coast.

After Japanese ports were opened up, an agreement was reached with the Tokugawa shogunate in 1855 dividing the Kurile Islands between Russia and Japan. In 1858 a commercial accord was added.[55] Of particular importance was the acquisition of the Amur area and the Far Eastern coastal province, acquisitions which were confirmed in writing during the Second Opium War under the shadow of Anglo-French military operations against China. The Sino-Russian treaties of Aigun (16/28 May 1858) and Peking (2/14 November 1860) brought the regime, hungry for prestige, territories intended to reinforce Russian interests in the Pacific against the increasing influence of England and France.[56] The founding of Vladivostok, 'Ruler of the East', and the figure cut by the celebrated Governor-General of eastern Siberia, Count N.N. Murav'ev-'Amurskii', provided symbols which attested to the undiminished power and grandeur of the Russian Empire.

Russia's incipient special relationship with China and her

54. J. Hoffmann, 'Das Problem einer Seeblockade Kaukasiens nach dem Pariser Frieden von 1856', *FOG* 11 (1966), pp. 130–175; Hoffmann, 'Die Politik der Mächte in der Endphase der Kaukasuskriege', *JGO* 17 (1969), pp. 215–258; on the prehistory: L.H. Rhinlander, 'Russia's Imperial Policy: The Administration of the Caucasus in the First Half of the 19th Century', *CSP*, 17 (1975), pp. 218–35; A.V. Fadeev, *Rossiya i Kavkaz pervoi treti XIX v* (Moscow, 1960); also W.E.D. Allen and P. Muratoff, *Caucasian Battlefields. A History of the Wars on the Turko-Caucasian Border 1828–1921* (Cambridge, 1953).

55. G.A. Lensen, *The Russian Push toward Japan: Russo-Japanese Relations 1697–1875* (Princeton, 1959); Lensen, *Russia's Japan Expedition of 1852 to 1855* (Gainesville, Fl., 1955); E. Ya. Fainberg, *Russko-yaponskie otnosheniya 1697–1875 gg.* (Moscow, 1960; J.J. Stephan, *The Kuril Islands, Russo-Japanese Frontiers in the Pacific* (London, 1975), chap. 3.

56. The Russo-Chinese treaties of 1858 and 1860 in: *Russko-kitaiskie otnosheniya 1689–1916 gg.* (Moscow, 1958), pp. 29ff. Soviet historians now interprete these treaties as acts of Russian charity for a China under threat from Great Britain and France, cf. M.I. Sladkovskii, 'Otnosheniya mezhdu Rossiei i Kitaem v seredine XIX v.', *NNI* (1975/3), pp. 55–64; Sladkovskii, *Istoriya torgovo-ekonomicheskikh otnoshenii narodov Rossii s Kitaem (do 1917 g.)* (Moscow, 1974), pp. 233ff.; A.N. Khokhlov, 'Vopros o voennoi pomoshchi Rossii Kitayu v kontse 50-kh — nachale 60-kh godov XIX v' in *Strany Dal'nego Vostoka i Yugo-Vostochnoi Azii* (Moscow, 1967); L.G. Beskrovnyi and A.L. Narochnitskii, 'K istorii vneshnei politiki Rossii na Dal'nem Vostoke v XIX v.', *VIst* (1974/6), pp. 14–36; in addition, A.L. Narochnitskii, *Kolonial'naya politika kapitalisticheskikh derzhav na Dal'nem Vostoke 1860–1895 gg.* (Moscow, 1956); R.K.I. Quested, *The Expansion of Russia in East Asia 1857–1860* (Kuala Lumpur, 1968).

strengthened position on the Pacific did not lead, however, to any immediate plans for further expansion. Another generation was required for China to be included in long-term imperialist strategies. The sale of Alaska to the United States, arranged by the Ministry of Finance, and the liquidation of what remained of the bankruptcy of the 'Russian-American Company' (1867) were further indications that the Far East still played only a marginal role in Russian policy and the public mind.[57] Nevertheless, a treaty was signed with Japan in 1875 giving Russia control over Sakhalin Island in return for abandoning the Kuriles. Japan had speedily begun to modernise after the restoration of the Meiji in 1868 but did not become a serious rival of Russia until the mid-1890s when the imperialism of both powers was unleashed under new conditions, resulting in attacks on Korea and Manchuria.[58]

Although the government of Alexander II did not undertake anything in the Far East to detract from the primacy of internal reform, as much cannot be said of expansion into Central Asia during the 1860s and 70s. We shall therefore discuss in more detail the advances of 1864 to 1884 which brought under Russian suzerainty the khanates and emirates of Turkistan and the Transcaspian desert areas as far as the frontiers of Afghanistan and China. The fact that these conquests made animosity between England and Russia a constant factor in world politics[59] forces one to relate the motives and expectations behind colonial policies to the huge internal problems Russia was facing.

While the Tsar's policies in the Balkans were bound up with the European political system, Russian conquests in Central Asia were similar in many ways to the colonial expansion of western powers at the same time. Military expeditions were undertaken into expanses of territory under no strong control, conquistadors sought fame, exotic populations untouched by 'modern culture' were subdued and the ideological justification was offered that 'semi-barbaric

57. S.B. Okun, pp. 219–259; in general: W.A. Williams, *American-Russian Relations, 1781–1947* (New York, 1952); H. Chevigny, *Russian America. The Great Alaskan Venture 1741–1867* (London, 1967).

58. The text of the treaty of 7 May 1875 is in Lensen, *The Russian Push*, pp. 501ff. On the modernisation of Japan see: W.G. Beasley, *The Meiji Restoration* (Stanford, 1972). For a comparative approach see: C.E. Black et al., *The Modernization of Japan and Russia* (New York, 1975); Black, 'Russian History in Japanese Perspective. An Experiment in Comparison', *JGO* 23 (1975), pp. 481ff. Cf. as well chap. 9.

59. For Central Asian expansion with emphasis on the Anglo-Russian confrontation in Persia, see the general work of F. Kazemzadeh, *Russia and Britain in Persia, 1864–1914. A Study in Imperialism* (New Haven, 1968), esp. pp. 3–99 with mention of the older English literature.

tribes' were being civilised. It was hoped in addition that the new colonies would provide new markets and sources of raw materials for commerce and industry. A comparison with the opening up of the American West might be suggested by the frontier theory of Frederik Turner, but in reality there are few significant parallels.[60] In Central Asia there was no question of free farmers seizing land and opening new areas to agrarian capitalism. A movement to settle these lands would have helped alleviate the overpopulation of rural areas in Russia, but even later such a movement never became very important.

In his famous dispatch to the capitals of Europe in 1864, Gorchakov sought to justify the advance of the young General M.G. Chernyaev to the very gates of Tashkent and assuage the feelings of the other powers by comparing Russia's behaviour in Central Asia with that of 'all other civilised states' which found themselves in contact with wild, nomadic populations. The security of Russia's frontiers and commerce required that expensive expeditions be mounted time and again and that unruly tribes be pacified more or less directly. 'Like the United States in America, France in Africa, Holland in her colonies, and England in East India' Russia was now being swept 'less out of ambition than absolute necessity' down a path 'where it is extremely difficult simply to stand pat'.[61] Here Gorchakov evokes the suggestive picture of involuntary expansion and conquest as the destiny of civilised powers; at the same time it is intimated that no one can say where the expansion will stop. Gorchakov's contemporaries were well acquainted with the tendency to view colonialism as an inevitable fact of life. The same is true of the feeling that the drive to cross frontiers escaped rational explanation: 'General Chernyaev has taken Tashkent,' noted Minister of the Interior Valuev in July 1865, 'and nobody knows why . . . . There is something erotic (*nechto eroticheskoe*) in everything that happens on the distant frontiers of the Empire.'[62] A

---

60. On the limits and possibilities of a comparison: D.W. Treadgold, 'Russian Expansion in the Light of Turner's Study of the American Frontier', *Agricultural History* 26 (1952); D. Gerhard, 'Neusiedlung u. institutionelles Erbe. Zum Problem von Turners "Frontier"', in Gerhard, *Alte u. neue Welt in vergleichender Geschichtsbetrachtung* (Göttingen, 1962), pp. 108–40; J.L. Wieczynski, 'Toward a Frontier Theory of Early Russian History', *RR* 33 (1974), pp. 284–95.

61. Gorchakov's circular (22 Jan., 3 Dec. 1864): C. de Cardonne, *L'Empereur Alexandre II* (Paris, 1883), p. 587; extracts in Hoetzsch, *Rußland in Asien*, pp. 27, 78; for recent work on the campaigns of 1864–5 see: K. MacKenzie, *The Lion of Tashkent. The Career of General M.G. Cherniaev* (Athens, 1974), pp. 34ff., 51ff.

62. *Dnevnik Valueva*, 2, p. 60f. (20 July 1865).

similar interpretation can be found in the theories of Joseph A. Schumpeter, who thought imperialism arose from an atavistic, warlike drive for conquest 'without recognisable limits'.[63]

The historical literature is often content to ascribe imperial policies in Central Asia to the laws of geography, nature or Russian history. For the rest, judgements about the course of imperialism and the reasons for it are coloured primarily by the military and colonial character of Russian expansionism. Strategic factors are always emphasised as the prime elements in planning operations and in the daily administration of the newly conquered territories. The ambitions of military men hungry for medals and promotions played a large role in the conquests. They undertook operations without official authority and continually confronted St Petersburg with new *faits accomplis*. Military logic was such that new actions were continually deemed necessary. The antagonism between England and Russia is considered to be another important factor and it explains Gorchakov's attempt to slow things down or at least smooth them over. Connections with Russian policies in the Balkans and the Caucasus and rivalries between the Foreign Ministry and the Ministry of War are also considered important. Economic motives too are not ignored — especially the desire for cheap raw cotton to supply the Russian textile industry and for widened trade relations with markets in Asia. However, only Soviet historians (and not all of them) think that the 'economic interests of the Russian bourgeoisie' were a central reason for colonial policies in Central Asia. They claim that the development of capitalism in the Russian heartland was hindered by strong feudal remnants and that it therefore sought an outlet in the economically underdeveloped areas of Central Asia. By conquering new markets on the periphery of the Empire, capitalism began to develop 'in the broad expanses' with results that were 'progressive from an objective point of view' for the peoples of the conquered territories. However, Russia herself supposedly suffered a negative effect. While capitalism sought expansion in the peripheral regions, the disintegration of the ruling landowning class in Russia was at least delayed (though not halted) as was the transformation of the autocracy into a 'bourgeois monarchy'.[64]

---

63. J.A. Schumpeter, 'Soziologie der Imperialismen', *ASS*, 46 (1919), pp. 1–39, 275–310.

64. The prime importance of economic interests in developing Russian capitalism was underlined by the studies of N.A. Khalfin: *Politika Rossii v Srednei Azii*

This line of thought paves the way for the thesis that colonial policies in Central Asia tended to stabilise the system. The concept of 'feudalistic military imperialism' borrowed from the older school of Soviet research into imperialism is based on a similar interpretation. These economic explanations tend to be extremely abstract, and this limits their usefulness in concrete historical analysis. It cannot be denied that there always was an economic component in diplomacy and considerations of military strategy. However, it is equally clear that the capture of Turkistan did not stem from any expansionist strategy on the part of the capitalist captains of commerce and industry.[65]

After the end of the Crimean War academics, ministerial civil servants, representatives of the armed forces, enterprising merchants and others with a variety of grand designs urged the government to turn its attention to opening up Central Asia to communications and economic penetration. The memoranda, petitions and newspaper articles which flooded in well before any large military operations began argued that cotton could be planted as a source of raw materials for the cotton processing industry in Central Russia, at that time almost completely dependent on American exports; they drew the government's attention to the possibilities inherent in increased trade with Tashkent, Bukhara, Samarkand and other places; they pointed to the desirable effects of encouraging greater navigation on the Caspian and Aral Seas and the Amu-Darya and demonstrated the usefulness of railway lines reaching deep into the heart of Asia. Reports that mercantile agents were arriving from England by way of Afghanistan acted as a perpetual stimulus. By the end of the 1850s military topographical expeditions and diplomatic emissaries were being dispatched to the emirates and khanates of Turkistan, into Persian Khorasan and Chinese Kashgar. The young Ignat'ev had gone to Bukhara and Khiva in 1858 before taking over the Asiatic Department of the Foreign Ministry (he was

1857–1868 gg. (Moscow, 1960); *Prisoedinenie Srednei Azii k Rossii (60–90e gody XIX v).* (Moscow, 1965); 'O dvizhushchikh motivakh politiki Rossii v Srednei Azii (60–70e gody XIX v.)', *ISSSR* (1972/4), pp. 128–35; *Rossiya i khanstva Srednei Azii (pervaya polovina XIX v.)* (Moscow, 1974). For another view emphasising the Anglo-Russian confrontation as a motive for expansion see: M.K. Rozhkova, *Eko-nomicheskie svyazi Rossii so Srednei Aziei 40–60-kh godov XIX v.* (Moscow, 1963), p. 224 *passim*; N.S. Kinyapina, 'Srednyaya Aziya vo vneshnepoliticheskikh planakh tsarizma (50–80e gody XIX v.)', *VIst* (1974/2), pp. 36–51; K.M. Anwar, *England, Russia and Central Asia. A Study in Diplomacy 1857–1879* (Peshawar, 1969).

65. For the limited initiative and willingness to run a risk of industrial and commercial circles in Moscow, see: V. Ya Laverychev, *Krupnaya burzhuaziya v poreformennoi Rossii 1861–1900* (Moscow, 1974), pp. 195ff.

nominated ambassador to Constantinople in 1864). In his reports, Ignat'ev recommended that henceforth military operations should be undertaken to protect Russia's commercial interests.[66] When American cotton exports dried up during the Civil War and prices on world markets rose, arguments favouring Russian expansion into Central Asia grew louder and awakened the interest of the Moscow bourgeoisie.

There is nothing to indicate, however, that Russian merchants or industrialists had gained a decisive influence over the deliberations of the autocracy. The state was deeply committed to supporting commerce and manufacturing, but this support was intended primarily to serve fiscal goals and was orientated toward balancing the budget, maintaining the balance of payments and, especially, financing the costly railway system. Capital markets were small, and the national budget was in a state of crisis, highly indebted and almost always run at a deficit. Under the circumstances no great investments could be made in Asia.[67] The Minister of Finance remained determined to keep the budget of the War Ministry under control, and insisted from the beginning that the costs of military operations should be covered by the regular budget. During the period when Turkistan was being subdued the military budget was not enlarged. This too is an indication that the advance into Asia was not viewed as a precautionary measure in defence of economic imperialism. The siren songs of those championing expansion into Central Asia were more than offset by the critical voices who warned of the costs and dangers of taking on new financial burdens.

The army had therefore continually to justify its actions to the Finance Minister and to broad sections of the public. This was the reason for the unconvincing assurances that while the costs were few the future advantages accruing to Russia from its Asian storehouse would be many. The generals themselves strove to awaken commercial interest. When the governor-generalship of Turkistan was established under K.P. Kaufman in 1867, Chernyaev saw to it personally that a collection of agricultural and commercial products from the newly conquered areas could be viewed at the Ethnographic Exhibition in Moscow.[68] General Kaufman introduced

66. J.W. Strong, 'The Ignat'ev Mission to Khiva and Bukhara in 1858', *CSP* 17 (1975), pp. 236–59; G.B. Ritschie, 'The Asiatic Department During the Reign of Alexander II, 1855–1881', PhD thesis, Columbia University, 1970.
67. A.L. Popov, 'Iz Istorii zavoevaniya Srednei Azii', *IZ* 9 (1940), pp. 198–242.
68. Khalfin, *Politika Rossii*, p. 227.

measures to improve agricultural methods in the area under his command, not least because the military government had to maintain itself to a large extent on what the conquered territories themselves produced.[69] The treaties with Bukhara (1868) and Khiva (1873), containing preferential tariffs for Russian caravans, were also meant primarily to strengthen Russia's military position. St Petersburg decided to leave both these khanates as autonomous protectorates and not to formally annex them (as happened to Kokand in 1875), in conformity with the governor-general's wish to keep the conquered tribes pacified through graduated forms of direct and indirect rule. The construction of the Transcaspian Railway (begun in 1880–1) was also primarily a military undertaking and economic considerations were not taken into account when the decision was made where to lay the track. This colonial railway was not extended beyond Samarkand until 1899 and not joined with Russia's European railway system until 1905, by way of Tashkent and Orenburg. Not until the time of the first industrial boom under Finance Minister Witte were conditions ripe for gradually integrating the colonies into the main Russian economy.[70] Despite rising imports of raw cotton from Turkistan, the importance of Russian Central Asia in the internal economy remained extremely small until the 1890s. Only 5 per cent of all Russian imports came over Asian borders in 1880, and Asia only took 3 per cent of Russian exports.[71]

During this time of expansion, Russia was never in the throes of the kind of 'colonial fever' that gripped Germany. The Russian public did not take a great deal of interest in the conquests. When victory reports (for instance of the slaughter in Geok Tepe) elevated the public mood, it was only because they helped to dispel disappointments on the European front and depressing news concerning

69. D. MacKenzie, 'Kaufman of Turkestan: An Assessment of his Administration, 1867–1881', in *SR* 26 (1967), pp. 265–85; E.M. Crean, 'The Governor-Generalship of Turkestan Under K.P. v. Kaufmann 1867–1882', PhD thesis, Yale, 1970.

70. J. Stadelbauer, *Bahnbau u. kulturgeographischer Wandel in Turkmenien. Einflüsse der Eisenbahn auf Raumstruktur, Wirtschaftsentwicklung u. Verkehrsintegration in einem Grenzgebiet des russischen Machtbereichs* (Berlin, 1973), pp. 83ff.

71. O. Hoetzsch, 'Russisch-Turkestan u. die Tendenzen der russischen Kolonialpolitik', *Schmollers Jb.*, 37 (1913), pp. 903–41, 1427–73. More recent studies: R. Pierce, *Russian Central Asia. 1867–1917. A Study in Colonial Rule* (Berkeley, 1960); E. Allworth (ed.), *Central Asia. A Century of Russian Rule* (New York, 1967); S. Becker, *Russia's Protectorates in Central Asia, Bukhara and Khiva 1865–1924* (Cambridge, Mass., 1968); D. MacKenzie, 'Turkestan's Significance to Russia 1850–1917', *RR*, 33 (1974), pp. 167–188; M. Sarkisyanz, 'Russian Conquest in Central Asia. Transformation and Acculturation', in W.S. Vucinich, *Russia and Asia*, pp. 248–88.

the inner state of the Empire. This attitude even informs Dostoevskii's passionate commentary celebrating Skobelev's victory in January 1881.[72] The dominant view was the one Katkov expressed in 1865, a few weeks before the capture of Tashkent: 'Whatever makes Russia greater there [in Asia], weakens her in Europe. Russia's role as a great power is not based there but on her rule over the western marchlands and in her position on the Black Sea. Our history is played out in Europe and not in Asia.'[73] Such views went largely unchallenged, and not only in the mid-1860s. Personalities anxious to arouse public emotion did not believe for a moment that their goal could be achieved by means of ideologies promoting Russia's mission in Asia. It is not an accident that men like Ignat'ev and Chernyaev, who played a highly visible role in Russian expansion into Central Asia, also figured prominently in the 1870s in the Pan-Slav movement. General Skobelev, a kind of Russian Boulanger, thought Russia should seek its historic destiny in the inevitable struggle with the Teutons, in the defeat of the German *Drang nach Osten*.[74]

These observations underline two facts. Firstly, Russian colonial expansion was not undertaken for its own sake. It was supported by Pan-Slavic and imperial Russian ideologies that focused on Russia's position in Europe. Secondly, the invasion of Central Asia was closely connected (both politically and militarily) to the confrontation with the European powers, especially the antagonism between England and Russia. The roots of this conflict were not to be found in the border lands between Turkmenistan and Afghanistan but in the Near East, where the question arose of what would happen to the Straits when the 'sick man' of the Bosporus finally died. The rivalry with Austria over the Balkan peoples broadened this field of interest and extended it to include the new German Empire, whose Chancellor maintained a special relationship with Vienna. The Russians noted with some suspicion that the German Chancellor never ceased encouraging St Petersburg to continue its drive deep into Asia. Central Asia therefore played a subsidiary role in Russia policy-making: its importance was derived not from the intrinsic value of the conquered territories but from the role it played in European affairs.

---

72. Dostoevskii, *Geok Tepe. Chto takoye dlya nas Aziya?* (*January 1881*).
73. *Moskovskie vedomosti*, 2 March 1865, cited in Hoetzsch, *Rußland in Asien*, p. 78.
74. N. Knorring, *General Michail Dm. Skobelev* (2 vols., Paris, 1939–40).

Russia's confrontation with England, which almost erupted into open warfare after the capture of Merv in 1884, has been thoroughly researched. There is no doubt that most stages of Russian expansion were prompted and governed by a desire to resist the English. This can be seen as early as the first stirrings of Russian designs on Central Asia after the Treaty of Paris. The reaction in England to the Polish rebellion also influenced St Petersburg's deliberations about connecting the military lines to Orenburg and Siberia (1863). Since then the view had become widespread that, in case of war, British power could only be effectively countered in Asia. In rivalling the international position of the mighty British Empire, Russia hoped to satisfy her own thirst for prestige and to prove, despite any lingering self-doubts, that the Tsar was still at the helm of a true world power. This craving for equal status could best be satisfied in Central Asia which England could penetrate only with difficulty and where Russia was invulnerable. In January 1865, Milyutin wrote to the Asiatic Department: 'It is unnecessary for us to beg the forgiveness of ministers of the English crown for each advance that we make. They do not hasten to confer with us when they conquer whole kingdoms and occupy foreign cities and islands, nor do we ask them to justify what they do.'[75]

Such self-assurance was probably most pronounced in the Minister of War (the driving political force behind expansionism) and in his generals and officers — the 'Turkistanians'. When in 1869 the question of the Amu-Darya arose once again and operations were initiated to conquer the Bay of Krasnovodsk, the War Ministry's official journal termed Russian plans 'a worthy response to the opening of the Suez Canal'.[76] Easy victories over the militarily inferior tribes of Central Asia made it easier for Russians to ignore the unpleasant fact that their army was incompetent to fight a major European war.[77] The Russian armed forces enjoyed the international attention which these campaigns attracted. Their *faits accomplis* (which placed Russian diplomats and occasionally the Tsar himself in an embarassing position) and even the repeated instructions from St Petersburg to go no further, strengthened their sense of power over the central authorities.

75. *Dnevnik Milyutina*, 1, p. 35.
76. Popov, *Iz istorii*, pp. 225f.
77. In this respect, cf. the comments of the Minister of War: *Dnevnik Milyutina* 1, p. 218 (26 Aug. 1875). On Milyutin's decisive role and contradicting the widespread view that the generals in Turkestan acted on their own: P. Morris, 'The Russians in Central Asia, 1870–1887', *SEER* 53 (1975), pp. 521–38.

It is easy to see why the Foreign Minister worried constantly that unlimited expansionism could lead to a dangerous confrontation with the British, whose politicians and journalists reacted with nervous hostility to the spread of Russian power in Asia. However, despite their efforts to calm troubled waters, negotiate spheres of influence and force the army to heed the requirements of foreign policy, Russian diplomats also grew accustomed to the new role which the Empire's military and colonial expansion had bestowed on them. Russian diplomats in London did not hesitate to announce in 1875, before the final liquidation of the Khanate of Kokand, that Russia reserved to herself 'full freedom of action'.[78] During the crisis in the Balkans, thoughts of sending a military expedition to India by way of Herat were not confined to the 'over-heated imaginations of army cadets' (O. Hoetzsch). St Petersburg itself toyed with the idea in view of British resistance to Russia's demands on the Porte, the rampant ideology of Empire under Disraeli, and the creation of a realm in India linked to the British crown. General Stoletov's adventurous mission to Kabul, initiated by Kaufman during the Congress of Berlin, was consistent with Russia's efforts to compensate for her weakness in Europe. The limitations of Russian power were demonstrated in 1879 when force of arms turned Afghanistan into a protectorate of the Indian Viceroy. However, this also prompted St Petersburg to begin its long-planned invasion of the deserts of Turkmenistan.

The latter operation in particular was plainly undertaken to relieve Russian gloom over internal conditions. The angry threats hurled at Albion by Katkov were quite properly labelled 'theatrical nonsense' by Otto Hoetzsch, but they serve to show once again that no one in Russia thought the Empire's existence was at stake over events in Asia. 'The English tremble over India,' wrote Katkov, 'but need we tremble over Tashkent? Russia would remain Russia even without Central Asia, but what would England be without India?'[79] It was Russia's place in Europe which kept nationalism alive. War and the colonisation of Central Asia were merely a way of compensating for the fears and unrequited hopes that resulted from the internal crisis and from Russia's limited ability to act in Europe.

---

78. Proof from British documents in: F. Kazemzadeh, 'Russia and the Middle East' in I.J. Lederer (ed.), *Russian Foreign Policy. Essays in Historical Perspective* (New Haven, 1966'), pp. 500f.
79. *Moskovskie vedomosti*, 16 August 1879, cited in: Hoetzsch, *Rußland in Asien*, p. 116.

Nevertheless, in the early 1880s Russia's enormous colonial acquisitions began to develop a life of their own which soon carried them beyond their original purpose.

It is well known that tension between London and St Petersburg rose when Russia conquered the oasis of Akhal in 1881 and that it reached dangerous levels when Merv was annexed in 1884.[80] The Anglo-Russian confrontation in Central Asia was on the verge of escaping the Tsar's control and endangering Russia's European interests rather than fortifying them. Action was therefore taken to control the danger of war in September 1885, when a first agreement was reached concerning the course of the Russo-Afghan border. In judging this *modus vivendi* another factor must be considered: as a result of Russia's expansion into Transcaspia and especially its conquest of Turkoman oases on the approaches to Herat, Persia was now drawn into the theatre of conflict much more than before. Researchers have developed an impressive array of material showing how directly the lengthy struggle between the British and Russian ambassadors in Tehran was linked to Russian military operations and the counter-measures taken by the Indian Viceroy and the cabinet in London.[81] If Russia's desert colony was to be secured, St Petersburg had to gain lasting influence in Persian affairs.

In summary, Russian expansion into Central Asia had the following causes and effects during the 1860s and 1870s:

1. The precarious relations between the autocracy and the Russian public remained basically unaffected by the successful military campaigns in Turkistan and Turkmenistan. There was nothing to compare with the lively interest taken by broad sections of the Russian public in the Balkans. Unlike the Eastern crisis, affairs in Central Asia never exposed the government to the pressure of aroused public opinion. Events along the Amu-Darya or the Afghan frontier did not awaken the nationalism of the Russian people, and these colonial military adventures made a correspondingly low contribution to government stability. On the other hand, the government apparently had no reason to fear a dangerous sapping of its internal authority if Russian advances were rebuffed on any of these fronts.

2. Expansion doubtless aroused economic expectations, although the latter had little impact on political and military decisions. There is

---

80. M.N. Tikhomirov, *Prisoedinenie Merva k Rossii* (Moscow, 1960).
81. Kazemzadeh, *Russia and Britain*, pp. 57ff. *passim*.

nothing to indicate that economic depressions (like those occurring in 1865–6 and 1873–6) prompted or accelerated military and colonial expansion. Attempts were made to justify the conquests with economic arguments. It was said, for instance, that the cotton industry in Central Russia required a reliable supply of raw materials. However, although the government did consider the interests of textile producers and the caravan trade, Central Asia was of limited importance in determining Russian financial and economic policies. For the time being, expansion along the peripheries of the Empire was not important to the agricultural base of the Russian economy.

3. Colonial policies which brought Russia into conflict with outposts of the British Empire in Afghanistan and Persia must be ascribed above all to the political élite's desire for prestige. The regime, feeling threatened by its limited capacity for action in Europe and by all the internal crises afflicting Russia itself, was anxious to show off its imperial power and experience military success. The regime could find compensation on the Central Asian periphery of the world political scene where, unlike the Balkans or the Straits, there was no need to fear the collective action of other powers. Feelings of backwardness and weakness could be exorcised in Asia where Russia claimed to have a civilizing mission. Here it was possible to meet one of Russia's foremost rivals and compete for glory and prestige at a relatively low cost and a known level of risk. The army could experience a sense of success, due not only to victories over hopelessly inferior opponents but also to the inspiring feeling that in Central Asia at least imperial Russia was frustrating the ambitions and interests of the mighty British Empire.

4. Even if Russia's policy of conquest is understood as compensatory, one should not forget that it still drew the Empire fully into the competitive system of modern imperialism. English capital markets were closed to Russia after the 1870s, and the government calmly accepted the dangerously mounting dependence of Russian finances on money and security markets in Berlin. In the long run, this imposed new burdens on the autocracy and made the cost of Russian backwardness doubly heavy. In 1881 the alarming financial situation did result in an order to retreat out of the Kuldja area of Chinese Turkistan which had been occupied ten years earlier — an indication that the government did not feel up to more military entanglements.[82] The enormous discrepancy between Russia's

82. I.C. Hsü, *The Ili Crisis. A Study in Sino-Russian Diplomacy, 1871–1881*

backwardness and its claims to be a great imperial power could not long be papered over by colonialism in Central Asia. One result was that Witte developed an industrialisation strategy which, combined with theories of economic imperialism, burst into China in the 1890s.

As previously pointed out, the connections between Russian expansion into Central Asia and Anglo-Russian rivalry in Persia should not be overlooked. The conquest of Turkmenistan broadened the basis of Russian policy toward Persia, a policy which in the aftermath of the Treaty of Turkmenchay (1828) had been largely determined by imperial interests in the Caucasus. Besides Persian Azerbaijan and the coastal regions of the Caspian Sea, Russian power now spread into the north-eastern provinces of Persia. As early as the 1870s, St Petersburg was becoming very sensitive to British initiatives in Tehran.[83] Abrupt Russian intervention in 1873 forced the Shah to cancel a large contract granting a railway monopoly and exclusive rights of exploitation to the firm of Reuter & Co. From 1879 until the First World War, the Shah was protected by a brigade of Cossacks commanded by Russian officers — a permanent reminder of the Tsar's presence. Russia also tried to give her role as protector an economic dimension by stimulating trade. This had been stagnant since 1830 and Russia always ran a deficit. It was therefore to be hoped that the Persian market could be closed as much as possible to foreigners, because Russian goods could not compete internationally. The inclusion of routes through the Caucasus within the Russian tariff system in 1883 was a first step in this direction. Soon afterwards, state export subsidies were introduced, benefitting primarily cotton manufacturers in Moscow and south-Russian sugar producers.[84]

Trade with Persia now became an additional responsibility of the Ministry of Finance, although such trade certainly could not help soften depressions in Russia or even amount to much in the economy as a whole. Despite continual increases in trade, shipments to Persia had rarely exceeded 3 per cent of total Russian exports by 1913. Russian wares succeeded in dominating the Persian market only because St Petersburg, anxious to profit from Russia's geo-

---

(Oxford, 1965); text of the Treaty of St Petersburg (12 Feb. 1881) in *Russko-kitaiskie otnosheniya 1689–1916*, pp. 54ff.

83. Kazemzadeh, *Russia and Britain*, pp. 100ff.

84. On the following: M.L. Entner, *Russo-Persian Commercial Relations, 1828–1914* (Gainesville, Flo., 1965), has a great deal of statistical data.

graphical position, stubbornly opposed further improvements in Persia's system of transportation. Successive projects to build railways linking Tabriz with railways in the Caucasus, or Tehran with ports on the Caspian Sea came to nothing — not to mention the ambitious dreams of constructing a main Trans-Persian route to challenge the British on the Persian Gulf.[85] Not just the Treasury's chronic lack of capital but also the never-ending concern that England might be incited to massive counter-measures undermined such dreams and persuaded the government to satisfy itself with improvements to postal and caravan routes.

While Manchuria received the industrial overflow created by Witte's expansionary policies in the 1890s, no effort was made to use Russia's penetration of Persia to further the internal economic needs of the Empire. Compared with Russia's huge investments in the Far East, 'ruble imperialism' in Persia was rather modest. The Persian Discount and Loan Bank (*Uchetnossudni bank Persii*) was operated by the imperial Treasury after 1894, and financial operations — including two loans of 22.5 million rubles in 1900 and 10 million in 1902 — were calculated primarily to keep the highly indebted Shah in line and to outdo the British Imperial Bank of Persia.[86] Russia was only able to maintain its influence because of Persia's continued backwardness and the suppression of all attempts at modernisation. Furthermore, the delicate balance between Russian and British interests might have been upset if Persia had not been maintained in a state of underdevelopment.

85. F. Kazemzadeh, 'Russian Imperialism and Persian Railways', *HSS* 4 (1957), pp. 355–73; cf. B.C. Bush, *Britain and the Persian Gulf 1894–1914* (Berkeley, 1967); J.B. Plass, *England zwischen Rußland und Deutschland. Der Persische Golf in der britischen Vorkriegspolitik, 1899–1907*(Hamburg, 1966); G.L. Bondarevskii, *Angliiskaya politika i mezhdunarodnye otnosheniya v basseine Persidskogo zaliva* (Moscow, 1968).

86. B.V. Anan'ich, *Rossiiskoe samoderzhavie i vyvoz kapitalov 1895–1914 gg. (po materialam Uchetno-ssudnogo banka Persii)* (Leningrad, 1975); P. Luft, 'Strategische Interessen u. Anleihepolitik Rußlands in Iran', *GuG* 1 (1975), pp. 506–38. Cf. chap. 13.

5

The Limits of Imperial Policy

Internal conditions continued to restrict the Russian Empire's freedom of movement in the 1880s. As was mentioned earlier, Alexander II relied on the emergency programme of Count Loris-Melikov during the final, crisis-ridden phase of his reign. Melikov's stabilisation policies were designed to stop the dizzying slide in the Tsar's prestige, halt the erosion of government authority and power, and create a new basis for confidence in the regime. To this end, Melikov planned to wipe out terrorism, suppress revolutionaries and subdue the students. More important, he also tried to persuade the public that the Tsar was inclined to permit public participation in finding a solution to the grave problems facing the nation. New life was to be breathed into the institutions of self-government in rural and urban areas and selected representatives were to be allowed a hand in drafting laws in the Council of State. The Tsar, despite many reservations, signed a plan to this effect on the eve of his assassination. This programme did not result from any constitutional conspiracy to replace autocratic rule with representative government. The autocracy simply felt it would be unable to resolve the intractable structural crisis afflicting Russia without the moral support of society. Since this government programme was aimed in no small measure at lessening distress in the countryside and securing the obedience of peasants exhausted by taxation, autocracy was especially anxious to gain the loyalty of the landed gentry. Hence the call to grant the zemstvos more responsibilities and reform the Council of State.[1]

This 'dictatorship of the heart' did not have much chance of success. Time was running short for the Minister of the Interior and his supporters in the bureaucracy, and their options were extremely

1. For a fundamental study of the experiment in internal stabilisation see: Zayonchkovskii, *Krizis samoderzhaviya.*

limited. The government was unable to solve the enigma of the peasantry, and economic concessions could not be used to purchase the trust of the landowners — state finances were too shaky, with no improvement in sight. Moreover, industry and commerce were stagnant. After a period of expansion generated by the war effort, the economy collapsed and a prolonged slump seemed unavoidable. In the wake of setbacks suffered during the war in the Balkans, the government could not gamble again on the dubious effects of whipping up nationalism or using foreign adventures to distract attention from the internal crisis. Russia had no capacity for striking political moves.

The international weakness and isolation of the Empire after the Congress of Berlin did indeed leave little reason to hope that the internal emergency could be alleviated by foreign successes. However, the disappointing result of the war in no way diminished the autocracy's traditional claim that the system of great powers should include an imperial role for Russia. The government therefore had to continue bearing the burdens imposed by this claim: rivalry with Austria-Hungary (given new impetus by the Congress of Berlin) and confrontation with England (now made unrelenting by colonial expansion into Central Asia). No guarantee existed for the time being that these two foreign powers would not join in a coalition against Russia. No one even knew exactly how to secure the influence Russia still exercised in Bulgarian affairs.[2] It was doubtful whether the Treaty of Berlin would prove lasting, and long shadows were cast over relations with Germany. There was an acute danger that London would incite the Porte to reoccupy Eastern Rumelia and would post its fleet in the Sea of Marmara to block Russian counter-measures. After San Stefano the traumatic realisation spread that Russia would not be able to prevent or repel a landing by the British. If the 'sick man of the Bosporus' ever decided to collaborate, the consequences for Constantinople and the Straits would be equally depressing. No European power was likely to grant the Tsar possession of 'the key to his own house', even though the health of Russian finances now depended on agricultural exports. Most of Russia's grain exports flowed through ports on the Black Sea; the Black Sea clauses were no longer just a matter of prestige or military advantage.[3]

2. The standard study of Russian policies toward Bulgaria and Serbia is: C. Jelavich, *Tsarist Russia and Balkan Nationalism* (Berkeley, 1958).
3. V.A. Zolotov, *Khlebnyi eksport Rossii cherez porty Chernogo i Azovskogo*

Under the circumstances, it is easy to understand why Russian diplomats would attempt to extract basic guarantees from Berlin. The feelers put out to Bismarck in 1879 by P.A. Saburov (Russian ambassador to Athens) during a period of steadily worsening Russo-German relations should be understood in this context. In the end, Saburov's initiative resulted in the formation of the 'Three Emperors' League' in June 1881. St Petersburg's motives in the days leading up to the signing of this *entente à trois* have been well established by S.D. Skazkin in a classic study based on unpublished Russian documents.[4] Bismarck's policies have all been well documented and need not be reiterated here.[5] If one bears Russia's internal crisis in mind when one examines these complex negotiations, a few important facts become apparent.

1. The characteristic low morale of Russian diplomats, the weakness of their organisation and the lack of rational planning influenced the course of the conversations in Berlin. While old Gorchakov plotted away in Baden-Baden against a Russo-German *entente*, N.K. Giers, who was actually in charge of the Foreign Ministry, was experiencing great difficulty in pinning down the Chancellor, disciplining the ambitious Saburov and gaining the latter's support for a clear set of goals for the talks. The expectations which the Tsar's negotiator took with him to Berlin were skewed by his overestimation of the power and political weight Russia had at its disposal when trying to engineer a compromise with Austria guaranteed by Germany. The ambassador tried repeatedly to get Bismarck to agree that Constantinople would devolve to Russia if Turkey collapsed. Thanks above all to Milyutin, the Tsar was not given to such illusory demands. During the deliberations in St Petersburg, Milyutin supported Giers in his attempts to preserve

---

morei v 60–90e gody XIX v. (Rostov, 1966), pp. 97–103; B. Jelavich, *The Ottoman Empire, the Great Powers and the Strait Question, 1870–1877* (Bloomington, Ind., 1973).

4. S.D. Skazkin, *Konets avstro-russko-germanskogo soyuza. Issledovanie po istorii russko-germanskikh i russko-avstriiskikh otnoshenii v svyazi s vostochnym voprosom v 80-e gody XIX st.* (Moscow, 1928, 1974²): in the 2nd edition, published by the Institut istorii SSSR AN SSSR, the important chapter on Bulgaria in the 1928 edition (pp. 195–337) was reduced to just four pages (pp. 235–9). For the creation of the Three Emperors' League see: M. Hammer, *L'entente des trois empereurs: Recherches sur les méthodes et l'orientation de la politique extérieure russe entre 1879 et 1881* (Berne, 1973); also: W.H. Brennan, 'The Russian Foreign Ministry and the Alliance with Germany', *Russ. History* 1 (1974), pp. 18–30.

5. B. Waller, *Bismarck at the Crossroads. The Reorientation of German Foreign Policy after the Congress of Berlin 1878–1880* (London, 1974); Müller-Link, *Industrialisierung und Außenpolitik*.

the capacity of the European concert to function. Gier's plan to leave Constantinople in Turkish hands and aim at a federation of small autonomous states in the Balkans under European guarantee sprang from his desire to secure a long-lasting peace.[6]

2. At this time the Minister of War was, in fact, the chief architect of Russian foreign policy. Milyutin helped produce a realistic analysis of Russia's limited margin for manoeuvre. The truth about the Minister of War contrasts sharply with the distorted picture which Bismarck (for reasons of domestic policy) had willing journalists draw of a man filled with revolutionary Pan-Slav ambitions plotting a war with Germany. Troop movements into Poland repeatedly annoyed the German Chancellor, but they were the make-shift defensive posture of a ponderous army and not a reflection of Russia's readiness for war. The danger of 'Pan-Slavism', often evoked in Berlin and Vienna, was described privately by Milyutin as a chimera. He vigorously denied insinuations that the Tsar's government intended to bring the Slavic peoples under Russian rule, though Russia would be called upon 'in the natural course of events' to act as their advocate and protector. Since this obligation was inviolate, conflict was possible, according to Milyutin, with those powers which sought to suppress their Slavic populations, especially Germany and Austria. Russia should therefore be prepared. 'In the face of the boundless ambitions of the German Chancellor, the fantastic plans of Lord Beaconsfield, the isolated and humiliated position of France and the inevitable fall of the Ottoman Empire, events can soon unfold which would not permit Russia to sit by idly.'[7] Milyutin considered it to be in Russia's interest that the danger of a European war be reduced, for no one knew better than he how unprepared the Empire was for military conflict. A treaty guaranteeing the status quo and precluding war with Germany and Austria would relieve the pressure and provide the government with an opportunity to master the dangerous internal crisis, such as would not be gained from an accord with France.

6. Skazkin (1974), pp. 123ff.; cf. J.Y. Simpson, *The Saburov Memoirs or Bismarck and Russia* (Cambridge, 1929), pp. 50ff. Giers did not find out about the Three Emperors' Treaty of 1873 until early October 1879; until then only Gorchakov, Milyutin and the crown prince had been informed, cf. *Dnevnik Milyutina*, 3, p. 169.
7. Milyutin, note of November 1879, cited in Skazkin (1974), pp. 167f. Important information about the difficulty of coming to a decision can be found in the War Minister's diary: *Dnevnik Milyutina* 3, pp. 154ff. *passim*. In his private notes Milyutin repeatedly denied the accusation he hated Germany and sought a war — see the diary entries of 23 Aug. 1879, 15 March 1880, 27 May 1880 (ibid., pp. 157f., 233, 254).

3. The problem with such a treaty was the well-known aversion of the Russian press to any indication that St Petersburg might once more be allowing the German Chancellor to arbitrate on fundamental Russian interests. Public sensitivity reached a fever pitch during the Russo-German 'newspaper war' of 1879 which erupted in the wake of an 'epidemic embargo' (*Pestsperre*) levied by Bismarck on Russian exports on meat.[8] Every move which could be taken as seeking accomodation with Vienna was immediately suspected of 'treason'. Even Alexander II was consumed with suspicion as a result of Russia's military inferiority, its financial dependence on capital markets in Berlin and the Russophobic arguments being heard in Germany in support of Bismarck's new protective tariff. Hence Alexander's excitable reaction to Berlin's policy of 'pin pricks'. St Petersburg's extreme sensitivity becomes understandable if one considers that government prestige at the time was in disastrous decline. There was no doubt that negotiations in Berlin had to be kept secret, but this also meant that the government could not reap any public benefit from its limited successes. The regime could not therefore help stabilise itself by pursuing rational policies on the international stage.

4. After the sudden demise of his father, Alexander III continued the negotiations with Bismarck and finally ratiried the 'Three Emperors' League'. This seems to indicate that no realistic alternative existed at the time. While the new Tsar guided internal policy in a different direction, international diplomacy stayed on course. The final arrangement was, to be sure, not without advantages as far as St Petersburg was concerned. The treaty of 6 (18) June 1881 imposed limits on the special relationship between Berlin and Vienna arising from the Austro-German alliance. It guaranteed the benevolent neutrality of Russia's partners in case of war with England (and Russian neutrality in the event of a Franco-German war). It reinforced the principle, undermined by the British, that the Porte was to keep the Straits closed to warships in accordance with international law. Any change in the *status quo* in the eastern Balkans required the consent of the three emperors and the Turkish occupation of Eastern Rumelia was to be considered a cause for war. The 'reunification' of this province with the Principality of Bulgaria was left to 'circumstances' (*la force des choses*).[9]

---

8. Grüning, *Die russische öffentliche Meinung*, pp. 63ff. Cf. also, H. Heilbronner, 'The Russian Plague of 1878–1879', *SR* 21 (1962), pp. 89–112.
9. Art. 4 of the treaty protocol of 6(18) June 1881.

5. These terms met only the minimum demands of the Tsar's diplomatic staff. Within the exclusive circle of those Russians permitted any information, it had to be admitted that guarantees of neutrality did not provide Russia with much security in its confrontation with the British Empire. Neither Bismarck nor the Austrian Foreign Minister, Baron Haymerle, were prepared to guarantee the future of the Straits on terms which Russia would have liked. St Petersburg succeeded (with German help) in extracting a promise from Austria to renounce the Sanjak of Novibazar but had to recognise Vienna's right to annex Bosnia and Hercegovina if it so desired. Of greater import was the fact that the treaty failed to define the spheres of interest of the two rival powers. Russian documents reveal differences of opinion in St Petersburg as to whether such a demarcation was desirable.[10] On the one hand the backwardness of the Empire seemed to militate in favour of safeguarding the eastern Balkans by treaty against the economic expansion of Austria and Germany. In the end, though, the opinion prevailed that fixing spheres of interest would inhibit Russia's ability to respond to the peoples of the Balkans. The emperors contented themselves with a mere promise to prevent their agents and representatives from mutual interference, thus making future conflict virtually inevitable.

In order to determine which factors influenced Russian foreign policy after Alexander II was assassinated, internal conditions must once more be reviewed. Judging by the new Tsar, one would expect an era of determined reaction and conservative stabilisation. By the end of April 1881, Loris-Melikov's projects had been abandoned. Soon thereafter, ministers suspected of being liberal or revolutionary were dismissed, Milyutin included, and the chief procurator of the Holy Synod, K.P. Pobedonostsev, was busily defending the autocratic rule of his old protégé against all constitutional temptation. This attitude was in line with the Russocentric precepts which Katkov espoused in his Moscow publications; the *Moskovskie vedomosti* had long been calling for a strong state and for the spiritual unity of Tsar and people.[11]

The appointment of Ignat'ev as Minister of the Interior reflects

10. Skazkin (1974), pp. 171ff.
11. For the new regime of Alexander III it is best to see: Zayonchkovskii, *Krizis*, pp. 300ff.; for the character of the chief procurator, see the excellent bibliography by R.F. Byrnes, *Pobedonoscev. His Life and Thought* (Bloomington, Ind., 1968); for Katkov: Tvardovskaya, *Ideolog samoderzhaviya*, pp. 254ff.

Pobedonostsev's conviction that the crisis made it necessary for the Tsar to attract prominent figures from the Pan-Slavic movement. It was well known that the Tsar had been close to these circles during the war in the Balkans, and was apparently still well disposed towards them. According to Schweinitz, the new regime seemed to rest 'on Pobedonostsev who controls heaven, Katkov who controls the people, and Ignat'ev who moves the nether world'.[12]

The military chauvinism of General Skobelev was also given rein. His much discussed appearances seemed able 'to paralyse or even smother nihilism by awakening a martial patriotism'.[13] Pobedonostsev himself implored the Tsar to receive this hero 'heartily'. He was 'personally perhaps an immoral man' but possessed 'great moral influence on the masses. The people believe him and follow him'. The Tsar must not miss the opportunity to win over to the autocracy the integrating influence of such a voice.[14] The curious combination of state nationalism, exultant Slavophilia, and the militant emotionalism of the 'Turkistanians' indicate the weakness of the new regime. Among the zealous adherents of this 'saviour of the motherland' the Tsar was useful only as a figurehead. It was therefore impossible for the autocracy to create a 'strong national authority' securely in its hands by aimlessly whipping up nationalism. Schweinitz argued that in the general process of decomposition the 'central ruler' had no other choice but 'war or destruction', an expression which was still current among German diplomats at a much later date.[15] However, employing a bellicose foreign policy to relieve the internal crisis was not really a practicable alternative.

In April 1882 Ignat'ev recommended to the Tsar that he summon a national assembly of three thousand representatives in order to demonstrate concretely, in the historic setting of Old Moscow, the 'unity of Tsar and people'. However, Pobedonostsev and Alexander recognised the dangers which might arise from a union with Pan-Slav schemers and dreamers, and the Minister of the Interior was relieved of his duties.[16] The Tsar remained the personal symbol of

12. Schweinitz, *Denkwürdigkeiten* 2, p. 194 (5 April 1882).

13. Valuev, *Dnevnik 1877–1884* (Petrograd, 1919), p. 187 (17 March 1882). On Skobelev's anti-German appearances, cf. *KA* 2 (27), pp. 215–25.

14. Pobedonostsev to the Tsar, May 1881, in: *K.P. Pobedonostsev i ego korrespondenty. Pis'ma i zapiski* (Moscow, 1923), vol. I/l, pp. 233f.

15. Schweinitz, *Denkwürdigkeiten* 2, p. 196 (5 May 1882); on the continued influence of this interpretation, cf. Bülow to H. v. Bismarck (5 May 1887) in: W. Bußmann (ed.), *Staatssekretär Graf Herbert v. Bismarck. Aus seiner politischen Privatkorrespondenz* (Göttingen, 1964), p. 441.

16. For Ignat'ev's ministry: Zayonchkovskii, *Krizis*, pp. 379ff.; for his successor,

autocratic Russia. The possibilities inherent in this arrangement were celebrated with Byzantine splendour during the coronation in May 1883. However, the gigantic celebration of Tsar and traditional rule had lost its magnetic effect 'in an age of railways and nihilists'.[17] The nostalgic spectacle did not cloak the fact that Alexander's government could not afford simply to stand pat within the dazzling halls of the Kremlin.

The determination of Alexander III and his advisers to press ahead with reaction was not without its effect in the long run, however. Firm intervention by the police succeeded in putting a stop to revolutionary terrorism.[18] After years of terror disseminated by *Narodnaya Volya* the attractiveness of a return to law and order in a climate of reaction should not be underestimated. The anxieties of living in a permanent state of emergency began to wane. The proscription of the reform impulse satisfied the virulent need for security and, in particular, the expectations of the old ruling classes. As Prince V.P. Meshcherskii, one of the Tsar's most influential intimates had predicted, a substantial portion of the public grew as accustomed to 'the sounds of conservative speech' as it had previously been to flights of liberal oratory in the age of reform.[19]

Above all, though, the regime catered to the wishes of the landowning aristocracy. The new Minister of the Interior, Count D.A. Tolstoi, had given the government a stronger profile after 1882 with the intention of rallying to the throne the privileged classes which had often been the object of the reformers' disdain. On the hundredth anniversary of the charter issued by Catherine II, the rights of the noble corporations were solemnly confirmed and Russian aristocrats informed that theirs was the task of reinforcing the stability of the state in town and the countryside. The path was cleared for the 'counter reforms' of 1889–92, which badly damaged any claim the zemstvos had of representing all estates.[20] A Nobles'

D.A. Tolstoi, including his time as Minister of Education (1866–80) see: A. Sinel, *The Classroom and the Chancellery: State Educational Reform in Russia Under Count Dmitry Tolstoy* (Cambridge, Mass., 1973).

17. Schweinitz, *Denkwürdigkeiten* 2, pp. 230f. (16 May 1883); also Valuev's diary notes, *Dnevnik 1877–1884*, pp. 228ff. (16 May 1883).

18. S.S. Volk, *Narodnaya volya, 1879–1882* (Moscow, 1966), pp. 133ff.

19. Meshcherskii's report to the Tsar (21 Oct. 1882), cited in a valuable study by Yu. B. Solov'ev which opens up many unpublished diaries and memoirs: *Samoderzhavie i dvoryanstvo v kontse XIX v.* (Leningrad, 1973), p. 90; cf. the published memoirs of V.P. Meshcherskii, *Moi vospominaniya* (2 vols., St Petersburg, 1898).

20. For reactionary politics under Alexander III: P.A. Zayonchkovskii, *Rossiiskoe samoderzhavie v kontse XIX st. Politicheskaya reaktsiya 80-kh godov* (Moscow,

Land Bank was founded in 1885 to solve the economic woes of the landowners, but such attempts to improve the situation were very limited because of the economic depression and lack of capital in the national treasury.

No less important for reactionary stabilisation was the discovery that if autocratic rule was dressed in the garb of Russian nationalism it could engender a conservative national ideology. The bureaucratic police state took its lead from Katkov's newspapers, which gave the civil service a fairly clear idea of what was expected of it. Variations on the 'national policy' could be found everywhere and the style of the Russian reaction spread to the non-governmental sphere. Monuments to it were raised on all sides, the most impressive examples visible to this day in the decorative architecture of Old Moscow. The enormous public buildings of the Moscow City Duma (today the Lenin Museum), the Historical Museum and the rows of shops on Red Square (today GUM) still leave their stamp on the centre of the Soviet capital almost a century later.

Bureaucratic nationalism found an easy outlet in the provinces which were not ethnically Russian. Policies of Russification, already tested in the 1860s, were strengthened affecting primarily German institutions in the Baltic provinces. As before, the authorities counted on the sympathy of the Estonian and Latvian populations. Even more than the German upper classes, however, these populations were expected to 'become Russians'.[21]

German municipalities and educational systems, the Lutheran Church and the associations of German knights saw their remaining privileges reduced and the strength sapped from many of their institutions. Russian was pushed through as the language of education and of the civil service, the Russian system of courts and police was introduced, and Russian functionaries streamed in. The German element was stirred into 'that Sarmatian stew' in which — in the derogatory words of the Riga city council — 'the great "Russian concept" is concocted out of Orthodoxy, nihilism, bureaucracy, paper rubles, brandy and dynamite'.[22] That the Russifi-

1970); L.G. Zakharova, *Zemskaya kontrreforma 1890 g.* (Moscow, 1968); for policies toward the nobility: Solov'ev, *Samoderzhavie*, pp. 165ff.; for nobles' organisations: A.P. Korelin, 'Rossiiskoe dvoryanstvo i ego soslovnaya organizatsiya 1861–1905', *ISSSR* (1971/5), pp. 56–81.

21. General M.A. Zinov'ev in an administrative report from 1886, cited in R. Wittram, *Baltische Geschichte*, p. 227.

22. M. v. Oettingen, *Stadtrat in Riga* (1887), cited ibid., p. 224. On the effect of Russification policies cf. M. Haltzel, *Der Abbau der deutschen ständischen Selbstver-*

cation of the Baltic provinces brought no foreign complications was due, in no small measure, to the fact that Bismarck thought he should not endanger his 'line to St Petersburg'.

The new regime's policy towards the Jews followed in the wake of official nationalism. The liberal concept of assimilation, pursued by the government of Alexander II, was finally abandoned in order to intensify the special laws for subjects of the Hebrew faith. Increasing susceptibility to anti-Semitism went hand in hand with a hatred of capitalism, especially among the administrators of the Ministry of Interior. The continuing boycott of Russia organised by the big Jewish banks (such as the Rothschild group, Bleichröder) was a direct result of the anti-Jewish outrages that began in 1881. The Tsar and more particularly the Finance Minister opposed these pogroms, but the local police forces exhibited a distinct tendency to manage the unhappiness and despair of the lower classes by permitting or encouraging anti-Semitic riots and by claiming that the Tsar was of a mind to punish the 'enemies of the cross'.[23] Thereafter, anti-Semitism remained part and parcel of reactionary ideologies which opposed social and economic change and saw in Jewish capitalists a symbol of the calamities afflicting Mother Russia. The impression of national consensus built on ideology should not obscure the fact that such policies could not make good the structural damage inherited from the age of reform. Stabilisation remained superficial.

It is not easy to resist the temptation to draw a more detailed picture of the heart of the regime and of the personalities to be found there. Alexander III was not the sort of man to infuse his personal rule with a sense of dynamism and coherence. He ruled instead with the fear and insecurity in which he held his ministers. There was no unified government policy and the various ministries remained as isolated from each other as before. The Tsar was rarely

---

waltung in den Ostseeprovinzen Rußlands 1855–1905 (Marburg, 1977); A. Hendriksson, *The Tsar's Loyal Germans: The Riga German Community. Social Change and the Nationality Question, 1855–1905* (New York, 1983); Pistohlkors, *Reformpolitik*.

23. On Russian anti-Semitism and Jewish policies after the 1880s see: H. Rogger, 'The Jewish Policy of Late Tsarism. A Reappraisal', *The Wiener Library Bulletin*, 25 (1971), pp. 42–51; Rogger, 'Russian Ministers and the Jewish Question, 1881–1917', *CSS*, 8 (1975), pp. 15–76; Rogger, 'Government, Jews, Peasants and Land in Post-Emancipation Russia', *CMRS* 17 (1976), pp. 5–25, 171–211; I.M. Aronson, 'Russian Bureaucratic Attitudes toward Jews 1881–1894', PhD thesis, Northwestern Univ., 1973; Aronson, 'The Attitudes of Russian Officials in the 1880s toward Jewish Assimilation', *SR* 34 (1975), pp. 1–18. On the anti-capitalist vein of Russian anti-Semitism see: H.D. Löwe, *Antisemitismus u. reaktionäre Utopie, 1890 bis 1917* (Hamburg, 1978) chaps. I–III.

intelligent enough to grasp complex issues, and ruled his land like a deaf, highly suspicious rural patriarch with the uncouth manners of the gambling hall. Nevertheless, even his limited mind grasped the power of the press and its ability to confirm his own position and make the public aware of the benefits of a strong, invincible state.[24]

As a result of this insight, Katkov gained virtually unlimited freedom. This press baron had his own standards for measuring the failings of ministers and government agencies, and the biting criticism he directed at them (far beyond what was allowed liberal publications) provided a reliable means of discipline. It made the Tsar's advisors more dependent on their lord and master, but undermined the already shaky reputation of the bureaucracy. 'Katkoff règne, mais ne gouverne pas.'[25] The dreaded man did not suffer from a sense of false modesty. He took his leave of the Tsar with the words, 'ministers consulted me, governors-general in important positions confided their intentions in me, and foreign politicians had to reckon with me. My name was synonymous with a political programme'.[26] Katkov's power, which was not reduced until shortly before his death in 1887, shows how weak the institution of autocracy had become and how the need had developed for a voice to speak in place of the voiceless Tsar. The influence of Meshcherskii, which reached even into the palace household, demonstrates equally well the unpredictable nature of the Tsar's decisions. This dubious boyhood companion emerged from the past to influence life at the Palace, his diary tailored to suit the Tsar's frame of mind. As the ruler's paid herald, he made known in his newspaper *Grazhdanin* what might pass for official views.[27]

There is much evidence that such a state of affairs inspired confidence in neither the Tsar nor his most illustrious servants. The multitude of extant diaries and letters reflect an atmosphere of unmitigated fear of the future, continual erosion of authority, and the stagnation of the *ancien régime*. Some of its representatives even recognised that their day had passed. 'Everybody whom truth does not leave indifferent feels melancholy and depressed. When we

---

24. For the Tsar's personality and style of government see: Zayonchkovskii, *Rossiiskoe samoderzhavie*, pp. 35ff.; Skazkin (1974), pp. 197ff; Solov'ev, *Samoderzhavie*, pp. 44ff. *passim*.
25. Valuev, *Dnevnik 1877–1884*, pp. 223f. (15 Feb. 1883). For press policies and censorship: Zayonchkovskii, *Rossiiskoe samoderzhavie*, pp. 262ff.; E.M. Feoktistov, *Vospominaniya. Za kulisami politiki i literatury, 1848–1896* (Leningrad, 1929, repr. Cambridge, 1975), pp. 239ff.
26. Katkov to the Tsar (February 1884), cited in Solov'ev, *Samoderzhavie*, p. 92.
27. On Meschcherskii: ibid., pp. 85ff.

compare the present with the past, with the distant past, we realise that we are living in a strange, unknown world in which everything is leading inexorably back to primaeval chaos (*k pervobytnomu khaosu*), and we feel helpless in the midst of all this fermentation.'[28] The *Weltschmerz* which moved the chief procurator to pen these words when expressing his condolences to the Tsar on the occasion of the sixth anniversary of the murder of Alexander II was a common phenomenon among the Russian elite of this time, though not everyone could formulate the sense of loss quite so philosophically as Pobedonostsev. This basic mood reveals the fearful realisation, in stark contrast with all the talk of a 'national policy', that social transformation, socio-cultural change, and the capitalist reorganisation of the economy were eating away at the heart of the autocratic system.

The government lacked the will to make any powerful foreign moves likely to offset the widespread sense of pessimism. Leading military officers were very worried about Russia's strength in view of the increasing superiority of potential foes. The catastrophic financial state of the Empire induced the Tsar to keep a tight rein on army expenditure (a measure which might have seemed reasonable if the generals had been informed of the Three Emperors' League). In 1882 the new Minister of War, P.S. Vannovskii, had to accept an austerity budget which cut the military budget (fixed each time for five years) by almost 25 per cent. Funding did not reach the 1881 level again until 1891. The effect on the armed forces can be seen in a drastic reduction of troop strength by about 10 per cent. It was impossible to mobilise as planned: about 14,000 reserve officers would have been needed to prepare the army for war. Progress was also very slow in procuring new equipment for the army and in constructing strategic railways, forts and barracks. The short-term programme, viewed by chief of staff N.N. Obruchev as indispensable in order to keep pace at least with the military strength of Austria-Hungary, had to be stretched over fifteen to twenty years because of objections from Finance Minister Bunge.[29] Construction of naval vessels also stagnated. The plan put forward by Navy Minister I.A. Shestakov in May 1882 remained a *pia desiderata* because of lack of funds. By the end of the 1880s the Black Sea fleet

28. Pobedonostsev to the Tsar (4 March 1887) in: *Pis'ma Pobedonostseva k Aleksandru III* (Moscow, 1925), vol. 2, pp. 138f.
29. These particulars in Zayonchkovskii, *Samoderzhavie i russkaya armiya na rubezhe XIX–XX stoletii* (Moscow, 1973), pp. 80f., 123f., 215ff.

had not even reached the strength of the Turkish fleet, while the Baltic fleet would have had great difficulty in repelling an English landing on the Baltic coast.[30] There is nothing to indicate that responsible military figures advocated an aggressive policy. Increased military spending was not one of the Tsar's priorities, and one has to accept at face value his often repeated wish for years of 'complete calm'.[31] In December 1882, shortly before taking up his ambassadorship to Turkey, A.I. Nelidov recommended to the Tsar that he prepare militarily and diplomatically to seize the Straits, but this alluring plan was entrusted to the future as a 'distant ideal'.[32]

Even a cursory glance at international engagements in the 1880s will show that the Russian Empire did not enjoy the peace it desired. The extended conflict with England on the Afghan border, the Bulgarian crisis, the continuing rivalry with Austria-Hungary, and tense relations with the German Empire — all compelled Russia to continue to play its traditional role as a great power and to concern herself with asserting Russian interests. In addition, the standards of the 'national policy' subscribed to by the autocracy under Alexander III did not permit any relaxation of imperial interests. The ideal of a powerful state (encouraged by the Tsar through the mouthpiece of eloquent journalists like Katkov in an attempt to shore up his own authority) now came back to haunt imperial foreign policy by making demands on it. The economic crisis eliminated any real possibility of an aggressive foreign strategy, so that the regime's only recourse was to feign power and hold tight to the unpopular alliance offered by Bismarck in 1881.

During the 1880s Russia's imperial interests could be pursued with least concern in Central Asia, though there was some risk even there.[33] Russia and England went to the brink of war in the spring of 1885, after the Russians had run the risk of heightened tension and captured Merv in 1884. Despite his desire to avoid military conflict, Alexander III was not able to halt expansion into Central Asia. The Indian Viceroy's protectorate over Afghanistan (consolidated after 1879–80) set in motion once more the struggle for position between England and Russia, and Geok Tepe and Merv can be seen as the Russian response. In accordance with its diplomatic

30. L.G. Beskrovnyi, *Russkaya armiya i flot v XIX veke. Voennoekonomicheskii potential Rossii* (Moscow, 1973), pp. 517f.; cf. Solov'ev, *Samoderzhavie*, pp. 79f.
31. Schweinitz, *Denkwürdigkeiten* 2, p. 237 (23 June 1883).
32. Marginal note of Alexander III on a memorandum from A.I. Nelidov (6(18) Dec. 1882), in: *KA* 46, pp. 182–7.
33. Cf. chap. 4.2.

tradition St Petersburg included the Turkoman oasis in its Transcaspian holdings as a 'natural' and necessary rounding off of the Russian sphere — 'commandé . . . par la necessité de nous assurer une position défensive contre l'hostilité . . . anglaise'.[34] There was, however, no revival of Skobelev's plans for Herat and beyond. In the view of the Tsar, the conquest and pacification of Turkmenistan was in no way comparable to the expansionist policies of the European powers in Asia and Africa: 'We have no use for colonialism . . .'[35] To the Russians, the Transcaspian desert was already an integral part of the Empire.

From the beginning Giers had counted on a diplomatic solution to the new problem of demarcating the Afghan border, but when a detachment of Afghan warriors (with their British officers) was annihilated in the disputed Penjdeh area in March 1885, the conflict seemed to slip out of control. Fortunately, Gladstone had reason to let war fever fade as quickly as possible, and the British cabinet was no more interested in war than the Tsar. Troubled relations with the Porte, tensions with France on account of Egypt and signs of a Franco-German *rapprochement* persuaded the Foreign Office to accept a compromise favourable to Russia.[36] The Three Emperors' League, which had been renewed in 1884, was probably also responsible in part for Russia's ability to continue its customary imperial postures during the Afghan crisis.[37] However, in 1885 the League was put to a test that Russian policy was unable to bear.

Unlike events in Central Asia, the Bulgarian crisis (unleashed by Alexander Battenberg's proclamation of the union of the two Bulgarias in Septemter 1885) made the imperial government painfully aware of its limited power. German historians in particular have seen in Russia's reaction the unbounded aggressiveness of Russian Pan-Slavism once more at work — that same collection of subvers-

34. Giers to Baron Staal, Russian ambassador to London, 17 July 1884, in *Correspondance diplomatique de M. de Staal 1884–1900* (Paris, 1929), vol.1, p. 48; cf. A. v. Erdmann, 'Nikolaj Karlovič Giers, russ. Außenminister 1882–1895', *ZOG* 9 (1935), pp. 495ff., 505.
35. Diary entry of state secretary Polovtsov, 25 Oct. 1885 in: *Dnevnik gosudarstvennogo sekretarya A.A. Polovtsova, 1883–1886* (Moscow, 1966), vol. 1, p. 344.
36. For the military aspects of British diplomacy: R.L. Graves, *Russia and Persia and the Defence of India, 1884–1892* (London, 1959), pp. 70ff.; P.C.M.S. Braun, *Die Verteidigung Indiens. Das Problem der Vorwärtsstrategie* (Cologne, 1968), pp. 137ff.; Kazemzadeh, *Russia and Britain*, pp. 94ff.; also in general: B. Jelavich, 'British Means of Offence against Russia in the 19th Century', *Russian History* 1 (1974), pp. 119–35.
37. On the renewal of the Three Emperors' League in 1884 see: Skazkin (1974), pp. 240ff.

ive forces which (supposedly) finally destroyed the peace agreement fathered by Bismarck.[38] On closer inspection, however, these conclusions (drawn from German and Austrian documents) seem unreliable. It is true that the Russian press, including even liberal newspapers, vehemently insisted that Russia intervene in the Balkans, while bitterly condemning Austrian ambitions and barely concealing its distrust of Germany. However, the simplistic interpretation according to which a weakened Giers was sympathetic to Germany but came under pressure from a militant, Germanophobe public, does not get to the heart of the matter. It merely touches on the superficial aspects of a deeper problem, typified by a depressing diminution of Russia's international standing. St Petersburg found itself in an extremely embarrassing position when Eastern Rumelia was reunited with the Principality of Bulgaria (as provided for in the Three Emperors' League) and the Greater Bulgaria of San Stefano seemed, for an instant, to appear on the horizon as a consequence of the Serbo-Bulgarian War. The paradox, that the union of Philippopolis seemed an insult to Russian interests and not the fulfilment of long cherished hopes, shows the débâcle of Russian policy in the Balkans.[39] The Bulgarian crisis once more underlined Russia's inability to play an active role in European affairs.

The fact that a land freed by Russian arms and soaked in Russian blood could elude the imperial grasp within just a few years was closely related to Russia's economic backwardness and to flaws in the autocratic system. Even under Alexander II it was apparent that the political apparatus set up in Bulgaria by St Petersburg could not provide a progressively stronger hold over the country. The limited intelligence of a petty German prince had sufficed to undermine the system of balances in the constitution of Trnovo, proclaimed in 1879. St Petersburg had thought of this constitution as a kind of balm on the humiliated Bulgarian sense of national pride and as a model for the future of those provinces still under Turkish rule. In addition, it had been a response to Austrian policy which was growing increasingly attached to conservative clients in the Balkans and especially in Serbia.[40]

38. The vilification of Russian policy promoted by Bismarck is shown very well in: H. Hink, *Bismarcks Pressepolitik in der bulgarischen Krise und der Zusammenbruch seiner Regierungspresse 1885–1890* (Frankfurt, 1977); also, Müller-Link, *Industrialisierung u. Außenpolitik*, pp. 293ff., 309ff.

39. Extensive comment on this: C. Jelavich, *Tsarist Russia and Balkan Nationalism, passim*. On Russia's policies toward Bulgaria 1881–1884 see: Skazkin, *Konets* (1928), pp. 212–333.

40. On the Bulgarian constitution: C.E. Black, *The Establishment of Constitu-*

Unlike his father, Alexander III had not initially been adverse to his ambitious young relative's destruction of constitutionalism in Bulgaria. However, it became apparent as early as 1882–3 that Russian representatives in Bulgaria were not able to subordinate the prince. The Ministry of War and the Foreign Ministry both proved incapable of elaborating a coherent policy, nor did they succeed in managing their own agents. The generals and officials sent to Sofia were generally of a low calibre and unable to rise above the oriental bribery and intrigues of the local milieu to develop a co-operative plan likely to win over the political forces within the principality. The defects in Russian organisation and personnel in Bulgaria were a provincial reflection of the situation in St Petersburg itself, and they made it possible for Battenberg to escape his would-be protectors.

No less important was the fact that Russia was not able to employ economic means in order to reinforce its influence in Bulgaria. Finance Minister Bunge reacted coolly when proposals were made to lend support to Russian companies competing with the Austrians, and in the spring of 1883 Russia had to admit defeat in the long struggle over railway concessions. Russia's backwardness was highlighted by St Petersburg's inability to penetrate Bulgaria economically and seal it off from the capital and expanding commercial relations of more advanced countries. The autocracy could not employ modern methods to advance its imperialist interests,[41] and since the army was too weak to rely on for the defence of Russian spheres of interest in the Balkans, St Petersburg could not bring sufficient pressure to bear on Bulgaria. All that remained was diplomacy, which proved as inadequate as ever in this zone where the interests of the great powers overlapped. At the ambassadors' conference in Constantinople the union of Eastern Rumelia with the Principality of Bulgaria could no longer be undone. Giers had to be satisfied with an outcome that placed legal limits on Battenberg's plans but left the actual union intact.[42]

---

tional Government in Bulgaria (Princeton, 1943, repr. 1970).
    41. C. Jelavich, *Balkan Nationalism*, pp. 65ff.; G.W.G. Hallgarten, *Imperialismus vor 1914* (Munich, 1963), vol. 1, pp. 227ff.; Skazkin (1928), pp. 256ff.; cf. V. Paskoleva, 'Über den wirtschaftlichen Einfluß Österreich-Ungarns auf Bulgarien 1878–1918' in F. Klein (ed.), *Österreich-Ungarn in der Weltpolitik 1900–1918* (Berlin, 1965); in general: A. Gerschenkron, 'Some Aspects of Industrialization in Bulgaria' in idem, *Economic Backwardness in Historical Perspektive. A Book of Essays* (Cambridge, Mass., 1962), pp. 198–234; W. Zorn, 'Umrisse der frühen Industrialisierung Südosteuropas im 19. Jh', *VSWG* 57 (1970), pp. 500–33.
    42. C. Jelavich, *Balkan Nationalism*, pp. 216ff.

One must appreciate this painful experience in order to understand the outrage of the Russian press and senior levels of government. The bitterness was directed at England and Austria-Hungary as much as at the arbitrary actions of the Prince. The cabinet in London was accused, not without justification, of having connived with Vienna in encouraging Battenberg in his struggle against Russia.

The Tsar's latitude to respond was extremely limited. There is no indication that Alexander III seriously considered armed intervention to drive his 'ungrateful' cousin from Sofia. He repeatedly rejected as 'nonsense' the arguments of Russian agents in favour of military occupation saying that 'it would be inexcusable and even criminal to expect Russia to fight a war with Turkey and possibly Europe' on account of Bulgaria.[43] The Tsar believed that Russia could not risk a war, a conviction shared not just by the Foreign and Finance Ministers but by the chief of staff as well. The Empire's catastrophic financial and economic state (approaching bankruptcy during the Bulgarian crisis) made armed intervention impossible. No military operations were considered, even at the height of the tension in the late summer months of 1886. Alexander's argument that 'our sole main objective' was the capture of Constantinople and the Straits functioned, under circumstances, as a psychological excuse with no practical consequences.

In the event, Russia resorted to an officers' conspiracy arranged by the military attaché in Sofia with the knowledge of the Tsar. But even this tack, which compelled Battenberg to abdicate (after his forced abduction and unexpected return on 26 August/7 September), turned out to be a hollow victory. The Russian success was undermined by the mission of General N.V. Kaulbars, which was overseen personally by the Tsar. Within two months this emissary, behaving like a governor and interfering clumsily in Bulgaria's internal affairs, had created an impossible situation. In November 1886 he returned to Russia with his retinue of advisors and agents under a storm of belligerent protest.[44] With the exception of a few unsuccessful conspiracies against Stambolov's government, imperial Russia's days in Bulgaria were over. The Bulgarian National As-

---

43. Ibid., p. 256; also Alexander III to General Obruchev, 12(24) Sept. 1885, in *KA* 46, p. 180.
44. On Russia's role in Battenberg's fall and on Kaulbars' mission: *Avantyury russkogo tsarizma v Bolgarii. Sb. dokumentov* (Moscow, 1935), pp. 3ff., 23ff.

sembly resisted Russia's candidate for the throne, Prince Min-
grelskii, and elected instead Ferdinand von Coburg (June 1887). St
Petersburg refused to recognise Ferdinand for an entire decade, so
complete was its humiliation.[45]

The Tsar and his Foreign Minister did not need the howls of the
press to realise that a renewal of the Three Emperors' League was
out of the question. The loss of Bulgaria had demonstrated that this
treaty did not guarantee Russian interests. Austria's position in the
Balkans seemed so strong that even Bismarck failed in his campaign
for an exact definition of respective spheres of influence. Under the
circumstances, the secret Reinsurance Treaty with Germany proved
to be the only way to avoid complete isolation.[46] Even at the
moment of signing, Germany's promises were of no particular
practical value in respect to Russian interests in Bulgaria and the
Straits. Unfortunately, the Tsar had no other choice: in 1887, at the
time of the crisis in relations with Germany, important prerequisites
were still lacking for an alliance with France. Alexander III's deep
aversion to republican France continued to weigh heavily, even
though Moscow journalists openly sympathised with the French.
Bismarck's psychological warfare against Boulanger also kept Russian diplomats fully aware of the dangers inherent in a tilt toward
France.[47]

The shrill tone of Russian journalists did more at this time to
influence the image which Russian policies projected than did the
behaviour of the Tsar and his minister, Giers. The contradiction
between official policy and 'public opinion' was clearly visible,[48]

---

45. J. v. Königslöw, *Ferdinand v. Bulgarien. Vom Beginn der Thronkandidatur
bis zur Anerkennung durch die Großmächte, 1886–1896* (Munich, 1970); B. Jelavich,
'Russo-Bulgarian Relations, 1892–1896', *JMH* 24 (1952), pp. 341–51; A.K. Martynenko, *Russko-bolgarskie otnosheniya 1894–1902 gg.* (Kiev, 1967).

46. On sources and history of the research: H. Hallmann (ed.), *Geschichte u.
Problematik des deutsch-russischen Rückversicherungsvertrags von 1887* (Darmstadt,
1968). P.A. Shuvalov's reports of his conversations with Bismarck: *KA* 1, pp. 92–127.
The diary entries of a ministerial aide in the Foreign Ministry are informative:
Dnevnik V.N. Lamzdorfa 1886–1890 (Moscow, 1926) — for excerpts in German
translation see: *BM* 9 (1931), pp. 158–77; see also, V. Frank and E. Schüle, 'Graf
Pavel A. Suvalov, russischer Botschafter in Berlin, 1885–1894', *ZOG*, 7 (1933), pp.
535ff.

47. A. Dorpalen, 'Tsar Alexander III and Boulanger Crisis in France', *JMH* 23
(1951), pp. 122–36; G.P. Morozov, 'Russko-frantsuzskie otnosheniya vo vremya
voennoi trevogi 1887 g.', *FE* (1959), pp. 248–81; reports of Mohrenheim, the Russian
ambassador in Paris, to Giers in: *KA* 5 (72), pp. 51–109; also Hink, *Bismarcks
Pressepolitik*, pp. 112ff.; H. Krausnick, 'Holsteins großes Spiel im Frühjahr 1887',
Geschichte u. Gegenwartsbewußtsein. Fs. f. H. Rothfels (Göttingen, 1963), pp.
357–427.

48. Grüning, *Die russische öffentliche Meinung*, pp. 86–139.

and since the press was presumably subject to censorship, this contradiction gave rise to two main interpretations in other countries. The apparently uncontrolled criticism of Russian diplomacy, especially in Moscow newspapers, was interpreted by some as a sign of the autocracy's weakness and of the gathering strength of an influential brand of Pan-Slav chauvinism which intended to force the Tsar to turn his back on Germany and practise a 'free-hand' policy. Others assumed that the government's real intentions were being revealed in the press and that the discrepancy between official moderation and public intransigence was a calculated means of preparing the way for a new course, which would steer Russia into an alliance with France. This assumption was a matter of grave concern (especially in Germany) and it moved Bismarck to complain about the 'duplicity' of Russian policy. The plans of the German general staff for a preventive war belong in this context.

Sober analysis reveals that the much discussed 'press campaign' in Russia during 1886–7 did not produce anything close to the degree of public arousal generated by the Slavic Committees ten years earlier. There was no expanding or even organised social movement. The nationalist press did, however, have much closer ties to what might be called government circles than it did in 1876–7, and the discrepancy between official policy and the views of the press show how far the imperial pretensions of the regime outran its capabilities. The interests and claims espoused in Katkov's articles did not conflict in theory with those of the Tsar and the Russian élite, but they could not be satisfied in reality. What the *Moskovskie vedomosti* demanded was viewed as desirable but not yet practicable. The government could not afford to give in to demands for a policy of non-aligned 'free rapprochement' with a France under threat from Bismarck. However, the fact that the Tsar allowed Katkov to continue to agitate indicates the lack of firm direction in government policy-making.[49]

The criticism of foreign policy shows the weakness of the Russian system of leadership. While journalistic demonstrations of national and imperial pride may have had a beneficial domestic effect by compensating for the humiliating series of set-backs suffered by Russian foreign policy, the government was clearly placed in an

49. For Katkov's agitation beginning in 1886 for a tilt toward France cf. his letters to the Tsar (26 Dec. 1886, 8 Jan. 1887, 31 March 1887) in: *KA* 3 (58), pp 60–85; also I.S. Rybachenok, 'Raznoglasiya v pravyashchikh krugakh o napravlenii vneshnei politiki, v 1886–87 gg.' *VMU*-Ist (1973/5), pp. 78–87; A.Z. Manfred, *Obrazovanie russko-frantsuzskogo soyuza* (Moscow, 1975), pp. 228ff.

extremely awkward position that cannot have benefitted its authority. The public could not be allowed to know that some degree of security for the Empire could be achieved only through co-operation with Germany. Nevertheless, St Petersburg's orientation towards Berlin, the result of economic dependence and military weakness, did become increasingly apparent. The press helped to cover up the lack of any political alternative by creating the impression that St Petersburg wanted to distance itself from Berlin. By the same token, though, the autocracy had to accept that the 'public' could not simply be ignored when it was harming the Tsar's prestige. Katkov was indispensable when it came to defending Russia against the campaign which Bismarck unleashed in the newspapers under his control, and when it came to warning the Tsar about semi-revolutionary' subversive tendencies in the Russian press.[50] However, when Alexander III was personally offended in March 1887 by Katkov's revelation of secret provisions 'very harmful to Russia' in the Three Emperors' League, he could only vent his anger in private: 'Katkov wishes to play the role of a dictator...this foolishness must be controlled.'[51] But the Tsar dared not make his reproach public. As Pobedonostsev knew, the *Moskovskie vedomosti* had become a moral institution in which the autocracy participated. To disavow Katkov would have been to encourage the 'enemies of [autocratic] order'.[52]

The deplorable state of the Russian autocracy, both internal and external, had never been so abundantly clear as in the second half of the 1880s. The regime was dependent for support on forces which contradicted its foreign policy and undermined its prestige, and the Tsar was incapable of breaking the string of defeats which Russia had suffered in foreign relations. By 1887 Bismarck believed he was strong enough to use economic pressure to compel Russia to remain true to its alliance with Germany. More than even before, he disciplined Russia by raising German agricultural tariffs and thus damaging Russia's foreign creditworthiness.[53] This came at a time when the new Minister of Finance, A.I. Vyshnegradskii, was renewing attempts to master the economic crisis and reduce the foreign consequences of backwardness by expanding exports and increasing protectionism. It was clear that Russia would only regain

50. For a detailed analysis: Hink, pp. 127ff.
51. Grüning, p. 111.
52. Pobedonostsev to the Tsar, 11 March 1887.
53. Cf. chap. 7.

her ability to act on the international stage and stabilise her political system when she had fought her way out of poverty and economic stagnation and developed her financial and economic resources to the level needed to carry out the imperial policies of a great power.[54] The survival of autocracy depended therefore on how and at what cost an economic recovery was possible that could raise the Empire to the level of its competitors, namely the highly industrialised nations of the West.

54. For economic conditions cf. chap. 6.

PART II

Borrowed Imperialism 1885–1905

6

Backwardness and Industrialisation

Russia's limited ability to act on the international stage and the prevailing sense of confusion, fuelled by bitter disappointments and fear for the future, can only be understood in the context of the social and economic problems besetting the Empire. As was indicated earlier, the economic depression of the 1880s placed severe restrictions on Russia's foreign policy. There were structural reasons for the nation's lack of capital reserves and the situation had been aggravated by debts contracted to finance the war in the Balkans. As long as the depression lasted, there could be no improvement in the situation. The Empire had, therefore, to continue to rely on a defensive strategy for security, as seen in the limits placed on military spending and in the stagnant state of railway construction.[1] Russian behaviour during the Bulgarian crisis seemed to reveal increasing self-restraint. Despite all the clumsy obtrusiveness, risk of serious conflict was avoided. The same self-restraint can be seen in the government decision to preserve the traditional German alliance despite opposition from the public. St Petersburg accepted the fact that Russia was not prepared for new directions or for a great power policy of unlimited options.

Russia's financial and economic difficulties were closely related to various aspects of the social crisis. This crisis resulted primarily from the poverty of the rural population. Its increasing size meant that average landholdings continued to shrink — from 4.8 *desyatina*

---

1. For the depression of the 1880s: A.F. Yakovlev, *Ekonomicheskie krizisy v Rossii* (Moscow, 1955), pp. 127ff.; L. Mendel'son, *Ekonomicheskie krizisy i tsikly XIX v.* (Moscow, 1949), pp. 590ff.; production statistics in P.A. Khromov, *Ekonomicheskoe razvitie Rossii v XIX–XX vekakh (1800–1917)*, (Moscow, 1950), pp. 452ff.; for public finances and state incentives for the economy (until 1892): I.F. Gindin, *Gosudarstvennyi bank*.

per male inhabitant in 1860 to 2.6 *desyatina* at the turn of the century. The reduced circumstances of many landowning nobles was no less important for the stability of the regime. The amount of land in the hands of the nobility declined between 1863 and 1887 by 0.7 per cent per annum and even by 1.6 per cent per annum between 1887 and 1905.[2] While the social costs of emancipation threatened the financial viability of the lower classes in the countryside, the sensitive relations between the autocracy and 'society' were permanently damaged by the deteriorating position of the landed gentry. The poverty of the peasants and the economic decline of the gentry both pointed to the regime's inability to offer the rural classes any prospect of future development. The amount of capital the government had at its disposal was limited, and its attempts to preserve the position of the nobility, proceed with overdue reform of the tax system and speed up redemption payments were very weak. These social and economic dilemmas must be taken into account if one is to explain the political elite's depressed, and at times even fatalistic, attitudes which influenced foreign policy again and again.

Closer examination of the development of the Russian economy and the social consequences of that development will show that the structural problem lasted well beyond the end of the nneteenth century. Despite all the other transformations over the years, this problem remained one of the constants of imperial foreign policy as well. Every attempt to overcome economic underdevelopment and improve the nation's shaky financial condition only aggravated the poverty of the peasants and hastened the disintegration of the gentry's estates. A striking example of this is the industrialisation strategy of Finance Minister Witte who tried in the 1890s to reinforce Russia's claim to be a great power.[3] When the autocracy attempted to increase the Empire's international competitiveness by energetically attacking economic underdevelopment, it furthered the erosion of its own social base. The vicious circle could not be broken. The suspicion that the autocracy would be doomed if the nobility did not survive strengthened the conservative rebellion

2. I.D. Koval'chenko, 'Sootnoshenie krest'yanskogo i pomeshchichego kho-zyaistva v zemledel'cheskom proizvodstve kapitalistecheskoi Rossii' in *Problemy sotsial'no-ekonomicheskoi istorii Rossii* (Moscow, 1971), pp. 171–94; on the situation of the landed gentry see: A.P. Korelin, 'Dvoryanstvo v poreformennoi Rossii, 1861–1904 gg.', *IZ* 87 (1971), pp. 91–173.

3. J. Nötzold, *Wirtschaftspolitische Alternativen der Entwicklung Rußlands in der Ära Witte und Stolypin* (Munich, 1966); T. v. Laue, *Sergei Witte and the Industrialization of Russia* (New York, 1963).

against the times but did not give it any chance of final success. State sponsored industrial expansion was undertaken at the expense of the peasantry and of agrarian interests, and it resulted in continually worsening social tensions. The danger to the government inherent in these policies became fully visible in 1905, when war and revolution erupted at the same time and the new forces which had been gathering strength in the factories of industrial Russia began to flex their muscles. Under the pressures of the Russo-Japanese War the autocracy lost control of both domestic and foreign policy.[4]

One should not be misled into thinking that government economic and financial policies were dominated by the social and economic interests of the rural gentry. Already at the time of the emancipation of the serfs the government had felt obliged to reduce substantially the privileges of the nobility and interfere 'from above' in the economic circumstances of the old ruling class. It will be remembered that the majority of nobles opposed this policy. The reactionary regime of Alexander III would certainly have preferred to abandon the complete transformation of rural conditions, but it was forced to see through the agrarian reforms of his predecessor. In the very year in which the throne changed hands, the purchase of allotment land was made obligatory, and those strata of the rural gentry that had resisted so far were finally forced to give up their rights of ownership over peasant land. The compensation wrung out of the Finance Minister (80 to 88 per cent of the redemption payments) satisfied no one.

There were excellent reasons for interventionist agricultural policies, even though they caused conservative pressure groups to protest against the increasing 'impoverishment' (*oskudenie*) of the upper classes. Although the autocracy had espoused policies intended to protect the nobility in the 1880s, nothing could be done from an economic point of view, and the policy remained based more on ideological and psychological compensation. Despite all attempts to lend support (such as that offered by the Nobles' Land Bank founded in 1885), the amount of land controlled by the Russian aristocracy continued to decline. In 1892–3 a survey of the situation was undertaken by a 'Commission for the Support of Noble Estates', but attempts to stop the rapid decline failed. Even the much discussed idea of saving country estates by introducing primogeniture came to nought.[5]

4. Cf. chap. 10.
5. On policies toward the nobility: Solov'ev, *Samoderzhavie*, esp. pp. 167ff.;

Notwithstanding substantial imperfections, the statistics demonstrate well what 'impoverishment' meant for the aristocratic economy.[6] Between 1862 and 1882, 18 per cent of estate lands were transferred to proprietors who were not noblemen (not including lands assigned to the peasant communes). In the next twenty years (until 1902) a further 21 per cent were transferred. By 1905 the amount of gentry land had shrunk to 59 per cent of the amount in 1862. If one examines the regional effects of this process it becomes apparent that areas in the Great Russian heartland of the Empire were much more strongly affected than the western provinces. The Polish aristocracy which predominated in the west had managed to retain 80 per cent of its land in 1902. However in the Moscow region, the cradle of the Russian nobility, where only a minority had participated in agriculture before 1861, only 45 per cent of what had originally been gentry land was still in their hands forty years after the emancipation. In these results can be seen the inability of the upper classes to adapt to the changed conditions of estate farming. The incentive to sell unprofitable farms was increased by the effects of the worldwide agricultural crisis and by rapidly rising prices for land which quadrupled and quintupled within a generation. As estates became a commodity, they began to change hands very frequently. Between 1863 and 1904 about 90 per cent of all gentry land changed ownership.

The remarkable retreat of the aristocracy from the land clearly demonstrates the increasing dissolution of the traditional bond between autocracy and landowners as the interests of the nobility no longer coincided with agrarian interests. In 1877 56 per cent of all nobles (the personal nobility included) owned land; by 1895 this proportion had sunk to 40 per cent and by 1905 had shrunk a further 10 per cent. One must also remember that more than half of all gentry landowners held meagre amounts of land: 50.2 per cent in 1877 and 58.9 per cent in 1905 owned fewer than 100 *desyatina*, and of these four-fifths held fewer than 50 *desyatina*. These disparities in holdings reveal the traditional fragmentation of the nobility. A common class interest was merely an ideological pretense.

The political importance of these findings cannot be measured

---

201ff.; cf. Solov'ev, 'Samoderzhavie i dvoryanskii vopros v kontse XIX veka', *IZ* 88 (1971), pp. 150–209; Solov'ev, 'Pravitel'stvo i politika ukrepleniya klassovykh pozitsii dvoryanstva v kontse XIX veka' in *Vnutrennyaya politika tsarizma* (Leningrad, 1967), pp. 239–80.
6. The following data according to Korelin in: *IZ* 87, pp. 143ff.

precisely. It is clear, though, that the Russian elite within the army and the bureaucracy was detaching itself more and more from its original links with the interests of aristocratic landowners.[7] In 1897, 71.5 per cent of those in the top four ranks of the civil service were still of noble lineage, but the number of landowners in these upper echelons had declined steadily since the emancipation of the serfs. In 1854 only 11.4 per cent of the in service privy councillors (second rank, including ministers and senators) had no country estates, and only 31.7 per cent of the privy councillors (third rank); by 1888 these proportions had risen to 45 per cent and 55.7 per cent respectively. Only 31.3 per cent and 29.6 per cent respectively possessed an inherited estate, and of these only one-third possessed estates of over 1,000 *desyatina*. By 1901 only 29.9 per cent of civil servants in ranks I to IV inclusive owned an estate.

The percentage of 'landless' officers was even higher. Most were not very well off, and by 1897 about half were of non-noble birth. The army rolls of 1903 have only been analysed so far as generals are concerned. It turns out that 58.7 per cent of generals and 80.8 per cent of lieutenant-generals did not own a country estate. The corresponding figures for major-generals and leading figures on the general staff were 89.8 per cent and 94.8 per cent respectively. The Soviet thesis that the expansionary policies of the Empire were precipitated by 'feudal militarism' rests therefore on rather thin evidence.

The 'class character' of the Russian state under Alexander III simply cannot be adequately understood if it is thought to be based on the interests of the agrarian-feudal strata. Russian economic and financial policy demonstrates this clearly enough. Policies of the Russian Finance Minister which hurt the landed gentry will be described in detail later, in relation to extreme protectionism and the Russo-German tariff wars.[8]

'High society' in St Petersburg had little understanding of economic and fiscal affairs, not to mention the structural causes of Russia's backwardness. This may explain the peculiar position in which the Finance Minister found himself in the autocratic

---

7. The information here and hereafter in: Korelin, pp. 156ff.; Zayonchkovskii, *Rossiiskoe samoderzhavie*, pp. 112 ff.; idem, *Samoderzhavie i russkaya armiya*, pp. 207ff. For a (poorly-proven) contrary position, see: A. M. Davidovich, *Samoderzhavie v epokhu imperializma. Klassovaya sushchnost' i evolyutsiya absolyutizma v Rossii* (Moscow, 1975) and a review of this work by M. Hagen in: *JGO* 25 (1977), pp. 444–7; the social history of the officer corps, see: H.P. Stein, 'Der Offizier der russischen Heeres zwischen Reform u. Revolution', *FOG* 13 (1957), pp. 396–507.

8. Cf. chap. 7.

decision-making process. That position was as difficult as it was influential, and at times he was known as the 'President of the Imperial Bankruptcy Board'.[9] Usually, ministers reacted very coolly to demands from agrarian interests for government aid and only reluctantly granted special concessions. Their policies were dictated by fiscal concerns and they increasingly saw the promotion of industry as their most important task. There was, however, no possibility of pursuing an expansive industrial policy with the help of large foreign loans during the depression of 1882 to 1886. Above all, state finances had to be set on a solid footing.

The Kiev professor N. Kh. Bunge became the country's chief financial officer in 1881. He was concerned mainly with limiting the supply of paper money (which had swollen dangerously during the war in the Balkans), with discharging the enormous national debt and, if possible, withholding the declining value of the ruble at a reasonable level. In this he was continuing the efforts of Reutern who was probably the first Russian Minister of Finance to realise the connection between the socio-economic structural crisis, the internal danger faced by the regime, and the government's limited margin for manoeuvre in foreign policy. In order to achieve Bunge's economic goals, military and railway expenses had to be cut. However, reduced demand on the part of the state only made the economic depression worse. Little headway was made with the old plan to get rid of the poll tax.[10]

Alexander III loyally supported Bunge's restrictive financial policies which were designed to restore the state's credit-worthiness. The regime thus demonstrated some capacity to learn, and the Tsar understood that the state's lack of capital rendered any burdensome foreign expenses unacceptable. At the same time, however, Bismarck thought that lack of capital would not make the Russians the least bit more peaceful. They would 'spend the necessary money for railways and wars whether they have it nor not'.[11] The Tsar's behaviour disproved such hypotheses.

Under conditions of economic depression, Bunge's financial successes could only be few and far between. The Minister did achieve

9. *Dnevnik Lamzdorfa* 1, p. 30 (5 Jan 1887).
10. For Bunge's financial policies: *Gosudarstvennyi bank*, pp. 53ff. *passim*; J.L. Pesda, 'N.Kh. Bunge and the Russian Economic Development, 1881–1886', PhD thesis, Kent State Univ., 1971; for an intensive study of contemporary German material see: Müller-Link, *Industrialisierung u. Außenpolitik*, pp. 21ff. For the abolition of the head tax: N.I. Anan'ich, 'K istorii otmeny podushnoi podati v Rossii', *IZ* 94 (1974), pp. 183–212.
11. H. v. Bismarck to Rantzau, 14 Mar. 1884, in: Bußmann (ed.), p. 220.

a small but continual decline in the supply of credit notes and in the size of the national debt, a 20 per cent increase in key tariffs (1885), providing modest compensation for the sinking profits from grain exports, and a positive balance in foreign trade by restricting imports. (This positive balance was not, however, sufficient to cover current foreign obligations or to stabilise the value of the ruble.) In order to balance the state budget new credits had to be arranged on capital markets, but within Europe Russian bonds and railway debentures were accepted only in Berlin. Even there the terms were poor (as the 6 per cent gold dividend of 1884 demonstrates), and Bismarck's political pressuring had to be taken into account. The large Jewish banks, especially the Rothschilds in London and Paris, maintained their boycott in protest against Russia's anti-Semitic policies. In the budgetary proposals of 1885 the estimated payments on interest and principal surpassed the 236 million rubles in the war budget by almost another 25 million rubles. The Russian balance of payments for the years 1882 to 1886 showed a deficit of 765 million rubles, while the trade surplus during the same period only reached an annual average of 65.9 million rubles. By 1887 the exchange rate of the credit ruble had sunk to 55.7 per cent below parity as a result of economic stagnation and the German *Lombardverbot*.[12] The Finance Minister was decried as a 'doctrinaire free trader' and there are many indications that his dismissal at the end of 1886 was arranged by Pobedonostsev and Katkov. These preceptors of the Tsar had made themselves spokesmen for the widespread sense of unease within the business community, and they doubted Bunge's ability to master the declining currency, slackness in the economy and foreign competition. Unlike his predecessor, the new Minister, I.A. Vyshnegradskii, was experienced in financial dealings and a firm proponent of high protective tariffs. Foreign observers gained the impression that when Vyshnegradskii took office 'industrial interests were themselves sitting in the Minister's chair'.[13] Vyshnegradskii did indeed embark on an era of extreme protectionism, and by means of rigorous budget management, succeeded in creating the fiscal foundation for notable industrial growth. His tariff policies

12. V. Wittschewsky, *Rußlands Handels-, Zoll- u. Industrie-Politik von Peter dem Großen bis auf die Gegenwart* (Berlin, 1905), pp. 135ff., 175; M.N. Sobelev, *Tamozhennaya politika Rossii vo vtoroi polovine XIX veka* (Tomsk, 1911), pp. 427ff., 692.; Müller-Link, pp. 214ff.
13. G. v. Schulze-Gaevernitz, 'Der Nationalismus in Rußland u. seine wirtschaftlichen Träger', *PJ* 75 (1894), p. 350. For the accusations that Vyshnegradskii enriched himself personally: 'Dnevnik Polovtsova', *KA* 46, pp. 110f. (29 March 1895).

(the relationship with Bismarck's aggressively anti-Russian tariffs will be discussed later) were praised as 'a masterpiece of state welfare' for entrepreneurs.

It is easy to see why Vyshnegradskii did not win any friends in agricultural circles. He was blamed not only for repeated increases in Russian tariffs on agricultural machinery but also for high German tariff barriers on Russian grain. Plans to appease large agricultural producers by reducing railway rates did not succeed. Protectionism served to aggravate, not reduce, the conflict between Russian industrialists and agricultural interests — an important legacy for the future. The kind of solidarity between 'smoke-stack, and straw' (*Schlot und Halm*) which Bismarck had achieved with tariffs in Germany could not be expected in Russia.[14] Reactionary, rebellious noblemen had their customary view confirmed that men of gentle birth were being hurt and humiliated by the government's financial policies. In 1890 the nobility was given more control over rural self-government when laws governing the zemstvos were revised. This can be interpreted as an attempt by the government to provide the old ruling class with political compensation for its economic decline, which was being hastened by protective tariffs. The flood of official decorations and other signs of royal appreciation can probably be seen in the same light, as can the introduction of 'land captains' (*zemskie nachalniki*) intended to supervise the peasant districts.[15]

After several substantial tariff increases in 1887 and 1890, Vyshnegradskii's protectionist industrial policies were crowned by the carefully prepared tariff of 11 June 1891.[16] Imports were taxed an average of one-third of their value, and taxes on some goods reached prohibitive levels. The new tariff on pig-iron was higher than both the English market price and the prime costs of new iron foundries in Russia. So the tariff barriers behind which Russian heavy industry was to grow were almost insurmountable. Professor D.I. Mendeleev, who inspired these policies, made it clear that protection

14. Cf. H.-H. Wehler, *Bismarck u. der Imperialismus* (Cologne, 1969), pp. 95ff.; H. Böhme, *Deutschlands Weg zur Großmacht. Studien zum Verhältnis von Wirtschaft u. Staat während der Reichsgründungszeit* (Cologne, 1966), pp. 561ff., 603f.
15. For the revision of the zemstvo laws and the new controlling organs of the peasant administration see: Zayonchkovskii, *Rossiskoe samoderzhavie*, pp. 366ff., 401ff.; L.G. Zakharova *Zemskaya kontrreforma* (Moscow, 1968).
16. Tariff law of 1891: Sobolev, pp. 699–796; Wittschewsky, pp. 151ff.; for Mendeleev's role: S.A. Pokrovskii, *Vneshnyaya torgovlya i vneshnyaya torgovaya politika Rossii* (Moscow, 1947), pp. 284–93; I.F. Gindin, 'D.I. Mendeleev o razvitii promyshlennosti v Rossii', *VIst* (1976/9), pp. 210ff.; for the German view of Vyshnegradskii's tariff policies: Müller-Link, pp. 314ff.

against foreign competition should focus primarily on raw materials, iron and machine building. The Moscow Chamber of Trade and Manufacturing wanted equal protection for all branches of commerce and complained about the tariffs on cotton, but its advice was ignored. Only a single representative of the landed nobility was asked to sit on the tariff commission on which, excepting government bureaucrats and financial experts, representatives from the stock exchange and industry were in the majority.[17] The funds raised by the tariff (82.2 million rubles in 1892) seem rather modest when compared with the incentives which the tariff law offered for developing heavy industry. The tax on tea remained by far the greatest source of revenue (24.5 million rubles in 1892), followed by import duties on cotton (11.5 million rubles) and spirits (3.4 million rubles).[18] As these figures show, the main reason for high industrial tariffs was protectionism and not the fiscal benefits which could be derived from them.

There is no doubt that the world economic recovery of 1887–8 greatly aided the Finance Minister's plans for development. The positive effects can be seen in rates of industrial production.[19] Heavy industry in particular benefited from the upswing, while the textile industry remained below the level of 1881. The production of pig-iron (and soon of steel) broke out of the recession of the previous five years and entered a phase of continual growth. Coal production had hardly been affected by the depression, but after 1888 it too leapt ahead. An important factor in these achievements was increased liquidity on European capital markets. This produced better terms for borrowers and created interest in direct investment in Russia.[20] Even the supply of credit increased on Russian money markets.

It is important to remember that Vyshnegradskii's protectionism was closely related to further attempts to raise capital on foreign markets. Imports of capital had stimulated railway construction in Russia during the 1860s and 70s and remained essential for industrial development. It turned out that Vyshnegradskii was rapidly able to counteract the damage which Bismarck had done to Russian creditworthiness in 1887. Through huge loan conversions in

---

17. Sobolev, pp. 699–704.
18. Ibid., pp. 792f.
19. Statistical proof in Khromov, pp. 452ff.; Jakovlev, pp. 397ff.
20. Direct investment: J.P. MacKay, *Pioneers for Profit. Foreign Entrepreneurship and Russian Industrialization, 1885–1913* (Chicago, 1970); B. Ischchanian, *Die ausländischen Elemente in der russischen Volkswirtschaft* (Berlin, 1913).

1888–9, he succeeded in transferring to France those Russian securities that were squeezed off the German market, thus lending an economic underpinning to St Petersburg's new political orientation. (These financial operations had a big influence on foreign policy and will be discussed later.)[21] In the midst of all these events the Tsar and his Minister never doubted that Russia had to preserve the peace.[22] With Alexander's help, Vyshnegradskii managed, in the autumn of 1889, to dodge Chief of the General Staff N.N. Obruchev's plan to finance a costly armaments programme stretching over six years. However, it was becoming increasingly doubtful whether the military budget could continually be held at the reduced figure of 1884 in view of German military equipment levels.[23] In both the Foreign Ministry and the Ministry of Finance pessimistic complaints made the rounds about the disastrous international armaments race.

The 'Vyshnegradskii system' of protective tariffs and substantial loans cannot be fully understood without considering its fiscal objectives. These were to produce equilibrium in the balance of payments, stabilise the credit ruble and, if possible, provide gold backing for the Russian currency. In order to achieve all this, more had to be done than simply limiting unproductive state expenditures. Exports had continually to be increased by a substantial margin if Russia was to attain not mere equilibrium in the balance of payments but a surplus large enough to cover her high foreign debts. Simple appeals to Russian agriculture to increase the supplies it brought to market would not be very effective. The relatively abundant harvests of 1887 and 1889 abetted the Finance Minister, but no one doubted that the customary cycle leading to poor and even catastrophic years would continue — the success of the export drive literally depended on the weather. Russian grain exports also faced a particularly difficult time because of continually sinking prices on world markets and Bismarck's tariff wars.[24]

If healthy exports of agricultural products were to be assured under the circumstances, means of fiscal coercion had to be imposed

21. Cf. chaps. 7, 8.
22. *Dnevnik Lamdzdorfa*, 1, p. 50 (12 Jan. 1887).
23. Ibid., pp. 217f. (9 Nov. 1889), pp. 351ff. (26 Nov. 1890).
24. Vyshnegradskii's 'export offensive': Wittschewsky, pp. 140ff., 148, 175; B. Bonwetsch, 'Handelspolitik u. Industrialisierung. Zur außenwirtschaftlichen Abhängigkeit Rußlands' in Geyer (ed.), *Wirtschaft u. Gesellschaft*, pp. 277ff.; S.A. Podrovskii, *Vneshnyaya torgovlya*, pp. 298ff. Harvest statistics: A.S. Nifontov, 'Statistika urozhaev v Rossii v XIX v', *IZ* 81 (1968), pp. 216–58. The average price for grain in Russia sank between 1881 and 1894 by about half — from 119.4 to 59.3 kopecks per pood, Wittschewsky, p. 143.

on the majority of the population. By sharp rises in indirect taxation, Vyshnegradskii forced the small peasant producer to forego consuming the meagre harvest from his small plot (intended to cover personal need) in order to sell it at extremely low prices. The proportion of market grain which the peasants gave over to commerce was probably around 65 per cent in 1890. This had tended to increase ever since the emancipation of the serfs, and it rose even more under mounting tax pressure.[25] By forcing the starving peasants to consume less, the government did achieve its goal of large increases in Russian exports. In the years between 1887 and 1891, average yearly trade figures showed a favourable balance of 300 million rubles. During the same period 25 per cent of marketed grain was exported, accounting for 47 per cent of west European imports of agricultural produce.

The dangers inherent in these policies soon became clear. The terrible harvest of 1891–2, mass hunger and the attendant cholera epidemic cut into grain exports and lowered the value of Russian securities on foreign markets.[26] The long-planned attempt to float a loan of 300 million francs at 3 per cent interest failed — not least because of opposition from the Rothschilds and other consortia of Jewish banks.[27] In addition, little headway was being made in the negotiations with Berlin over a commercial treaty which would have allowed Russia to participate in Caprivi's tariff convention.[28] In order to avoid aggravating the famine further, Vyshnegradskii was compelled to halt all grain exports. This painful setback coincided with the final blow: a cyclical downturn in industrial production which affected the textile industry in particular because of the rapidly declining internal demand for goods. Vyshnegradskii's policies, pushed through at the expense of the peasantry, had obviously gone wrong, and in March 1892 he proposed a progressive income tax to ward off looming national bankruptcy. In the Tsar's inner circle such a plan was simply taken as a sign that the faltering minister was suffering from 'paralysis of the brain'.[29]

26. G.B. Robbins Jr., *The Famine in Russia 1891–1892: The Imperial Government Responds to a Crisis* (New York, 1975); S. Bensidoun, *L'agitation paysanne en Russie de 1881 à 1902* (Paris, 1975), pp. 302ff.

27. B.V. Anan'ich, *Rossiya i mezhdunarodnyi kapital, 1897–1914. Ocherki istorii finansovykh otnoshenii* (Leningrad, 1970), p. 13; R. Girault, *Emprunts russes et investissements français en Russie 1887–1914* (Paris, 1969), pp. 188ff. For obstruction by the Rothschild bank: *Dnevnik Lamzdorfa* 2, p. 107 (26 Apr. 1891), p. 198 (15 Nov. 1891).

28. Cf. chap. 7.

29. *Dnevnik Polovtsova* 2, p. 442 (5 Apr. 1892); see also the explanations of P.A.

However, if Russia's backwardness was to be overcome and her status as a great power confirmed, no real alternative existed to Vyshnegradskii's financial and economic policies. No one made this clearer than Vyshnegradskii's famous successor, Sergei Yul'evich Witte, architect of the industrial take-off in Russia during the second half of the 1890s. Witte considered it his task to 'overcome as quickly as possible the lag resulting from 200 years of economic sleep in Imperial Russia'.[30] As the director of the largest private railway company in the Empire, Witte had entered the Ministry of Transport before making his way to the pinnacle of the Ministry of Finance in August 1892. He was without a doubt the most important political figure in the service of the last two Tsars, a man who had risen from titular councillor to the seat of power in St Petersburg in just a few years. However he did very little to change Vyshnegradskii's system. Instead, he increased the financial leverage which his predecessor had developed and applied it in grand style.[31] Continuity in policy can be seen everywhere: the extreme tariff of 1891 was strictly adhered to, many more foreign loans were contracted, and fiscal methods were used more often to put state finances on an even keel. There was in the autocracy probably no more eloquent a proponent of industrial protectionism, imported foreign capital and direct foreign investment, and no more dynamic an advocate of rapid industrial growth. The virtuosity of Witte's performance continued to intoxicate many a later biographer.[32] The new Finance Minister did not doubt for an instant that the state had to play the dominant role in 'the development of capitalization in Russia' and that government initiative would be largely responsible for the growth of Russian industry.[33]

The dangers and dilemmas which had bedevilled Vyshnegradskii's financial policies continued to haunt his successor and were not diminished by Witte's successes. Indeed, the risks mounted to breath-taking proportions. However, Witte's achievements were also impressive. Helped by the end of the great world depression, the minister cleared the way after the mid-1890s for a kind of

Zayonchkovskii, ibid., p. 516. Cf. also *Dnevnik Lamzdorfa* 2, pp. 310f. (8 Mar. 1892).

30. S.J. Witte, *Vorlesungen über Volks- und Staatswirtschaft* [1901–02] (Stuttgart, 1913), vol. 1, p. 60.

31. Laue, *Sergei Witte*, passim.

32. S. Yu. Witte, *Vospominaniya* (Moscow, 1960), vols. 1–3; the first Russsian edition was published in Berlin in 1922.

33. Witte, *Vorlesungen*, 1, pp. 131f.

Table 5: Russian import tariffs 1881–1900 (as a % of product value)

	Agricultural products	Raw materials & semi-finished goods	Finished goods	Imported goods as a whole
1881	30.3	11.8	21.2	16.5
1885	41.1	13.8	24.9	23.7
1887	59.2	16.7	32.1	29.2
1888	70.4	18.1	28.6	31.9
1890	59.6	18.3	26.0	28.7
1895	63.9	24.5	24.1	31.9
1897	67.8	29.5	26.5	35.2
1898	69.4	31.8	25.8	36.2
1900	71.7	23.7	24.6	32.5

Source: Khromov, *Ekonomicheskoe razvitie Rossii*, p. 485.

industrial boom never before seen in Russia, a boom with all the signs of an 'industrial revolution'. As always, the leading sector in the economic recovery was railway construction. Rates of growth before the crisis of 1900 surpassed even American levels. Between 1896 and 1901 almost 20,000 kilometres of track were laid. The policy begun in the 1880s of nationalising large private railway companies was continued — their losses had to be borne in any case by the national treasury because of terms in the original concessions. Low freight rates, the 'heart of the railway system' according to Witte, were supposed to make the new routes attractive and profitable.[34]

Increased government demand and high tariff barriers had a particularly beneficial effect on heavy industry. Pig-iron production doubled between 1887 and 1892 and had doubled again by 1899. With an output of 165.4 million poods, production reached a peak at the turn of the century that would not be reached again until 1906, after a period of crisis, war and revolution. Steel production had already entered on a phase of continual growth in 1889, and by 1901 output had risen by 200 per cent. Rates of growth in the coal industry were almost identical. The boom also gave a powerful boost to urbanisation. The building industry profited both from the construction of new industrial plant and the extension and moderni-

34. Statistical evidence of industrial expansion in Khromov, pp. 452ff.; cf. also Mendel'son, pp. 687ff.; on railway construction: A.M. Solov'eva, *Zheleznodorozhnyi transport*, especially pp. 251ff.; J. Metzer, 'Railroads in Tsarist Russia: Direct Gains and Implications', *Explorations in Economic History*, 13 (1976), pp. 85–111.

Table 6: State revenues 1881–1899 (in mill. of rubles)

Budgetary year	1881	1886	1891	1892	1893	1894	1895	1896	1897	1898	1899
Ordinary receipts	652	781	892	970	1046	1154	1256	1369	1416	1585	1673
Excise & profit taxes	117	97	53	56	60	60	63	54	55	56	60
Alcohol tax	225	237	247	269	261	297	298	322	333	392	421
Other taxes	16	35	64	75	85	100	110	106	121	126	139
Tariffs	86	112	128	131	166	184	179	182	196	219	219
Railways	19	52	99	111	120	155	218	312	293	363	358
Redemption payments	—	49	69	77	99	93	101	97	89	86	95
Extraordinary receipts	155	178	37	199	174	79	162	44	43	88	184
Amount of this in loans	91	150	2	166	164	53	157	33	40	83	182

Source: Khromov, *Ekonomicheskoe razvitie Rossii*, pp. 498–503

Table 7: State expenditure 1881–1899 (in mill. of rubles)

Budgetary year	1881	1886	1891	1892	1893	1894	1895	1896	1897	1898	1899
Ordinary expenses	732	836	875	911	947	991	1138	1129	1300	1358	1464
National Debt	196	264	248	251	267	271	285	268	259	274	276
Min. of War	226	212	226	236	237	239	285	294	294	303	336
Min. of the Navy	30	45	45	48	51	51	57	60	85	67	84
Min. of Finance	108	116	113	120	124	132	141	189	204	214	237
Min. of the Interior	67	73	80	82	83	84	86	90	80	80	82
Min. of Education	17	21	23	22	22	22	24	25	26	27	29
Min. of Transportation	12	26	56	67	76	98	163	196	227	265	288
Extraordinary expenses	108	113	240	215	114	164	383	255	195	414	322
Railways	28	63	44	101	63	78	102	132	131	139	166
Loan repayment & conversion	50	50	94	—	13	1	124	5	33	64	100
Foreign currency supply, debt repayment	—	—	—	—	—	—	158	118	31	75	50
Arms and the military	30	—	27	26	37	43	—	—	—	90	—

Source: Khromov, *Ekonomicheskoe razvitie Rossii*, pp. 518–23

Table 8: Economic growth indicators for 1880–1913

Year	Population[1] (in millions)	Coal production (in mill. of poods)	Pig-iron production (in mill. of poods)	Steel & cast iron (in mill. of poods)	Gold production (in tonnes)	Oil production (in mill. of poods)	Railways (in 1000s of km)
1880	97.7	200.8	27.4	36.6	43.3	—	22.9
1885	108.8	260.6	32.2	33.9	33.0	115.0	26.0
1890	117.8	367.2	56.6	49.5	39.4	226.0	30.6
1895	123.9	555.5	88.7	81.6	41.1	377.0	37.0
1900	132.9	986.3	179.1	165.2	38.8	631.1	53.2
1905	143.9	1139.7	166.8	162.1	33.5	455.9	61.1
1910	160.7	1526.3	185.8	205.7	53.9	588.4	66.6
1913	170.9	2200.1	283.0	—	49.2	561.3	70.2

Year	Spun and woven goods (in mill. of rubles)	Cotton consumption[2] (mill. of poods)	Cloths & worsted cloth (mill. of rubles)	Grain production (mill. of poods)	Sugar production (mill. of poods)	Imports (mill. of rubles)	Exports (mill. of rubles)
1880	154.4	5.7	84.2	—	12.5	622.8	498.7
1885	165.7	7.6	64.2	—	20.9	495.4	537.9
1890	208.6	8.3	54.6	—	24.6	406.7	692.2
1895	350.7	12.3	—	2681	32.3	526.1	689.1
1900	493.5	16.0	92.3	2950	48.5	626.4	716.2
1905	560.8	16.7	113.3	2984	52.1	635.1	1077.3
1910	959.5	22.1	123.7	3693	63.0	1084.4	1449.1
1913	—	25.9	—	4240	75.4	1374.0	1520.1

1. Excluding Finland, Bukhara and Khiva
2. Statistics based on cotton imports from America and Central Asia

Sources: A.F. Yakovlev, *Ekonomicheskie krizisy i Rossii*, pp. 397–401; Khromov, *Ekonomicheskoe razvitie Rossii*, pp. 452–5, 459

sation of the cities.[35] Tariff and commercial policies, foreign loans, encouragement for investors and new transportation routes were all interconnected in this period of economic prosperity. Rapid growth in the size of the national budget also bears all the hallmarks of an economic take off. The powerful upsurge seemed to indicate that Russia's underdevelopment would be overcome within a reasonable space of time and its ability to compete internationally restored.

Witte clearly understood the connection between backwardness and Russia's diminished international position, and he touted his development strategy as being absolutely necessary if the autocracy was to retain power. No sacrifice was too great to attain the goal of stabilising the system internally and externally. However, despite all his successes, Witte was unable to improve Russia's financial position. The state's hunger for capital reached undreamed-of proportions during his tenure as Finance Minister. The spending increases resulted from the enormous development projects which the Minister drove forward as quickly as possible — especially the Trans-Siberian Railway, begun under Vyshnegradskii and eventually thrust beyond the frontiers of the Empire itself. However, the new Russian domains in Manchuria proved to be an extremely costly undertaking for the Ministry of Finance.[36]

Increases in military expenditures too could not be resisted. The budget of the Ministry of War (224.7 million rubles) had been frozen at the 1884 level and had received very few supplements from outside; however, in reaction to the increasing power of the German army a large increase was ordered in 1894. Despite substantial increases in military spending, from 280.3 million rubles in 1894 to 333.5 million in 1899, Russia was unable to keep pace in the arms race of the great powers.[37] Minister of War A.N. Kuropatkin considered trying to agree with Vienna on a freeze with regard to the new automatic weapons and this led to the Tsar's remarkable disarmament proposals of 1898-9 and an unprecedented conference in the Hague. But 'Russia's strange sentimental talk' provoked only

---

35. On urbanisation: L.M. Ivanov, 'O soslovno-klassovoi strukture gorodov kapitalisticheskoi Rossii', *Problemy sotsialnoekonomicheskoi istorii Rossii* (Moscow, 1971), pp. 312–40; R.H. Rowland, 'Urban In-Migration in Late-19th-Century Russia', PhD thesis, Columbia University, 1971; J.H. Bater, *St. Petersburg: Industrialization and Change* (London, 1975).
36. Cf. chap. 9.1.
37. L.G. Beskrovnyi, *Russkaya armiya*, pp. 485, 600f. The data refer to the actual military expenditures, not the sums that appear in the state budget, cf. table 6.

concern and surprise in European capitals, especially Paris.[38] It should also be pointed out that Russian expansion in the Far East had increased the need to build up the fleet, and this also swallowed substantial sums after 1897. (A few years later the Japanese fleet revealed the ineffectiveness of Russian efforts.) No Russian minister could seriously expect that a principled condemnation of the arms race would soon produce reductions in the military expenditures of the Empire. 'Militarism,' said Witte, 'forces states continually to prepare for war and create and enlarge a class of people that is interested in war.' However, militarism was accepted as a fact of life in St Petersburg (as in other European capitals) and there was a widespread feeling 'that the coming war [would] include all European countries'. Witte had therefore to accept the priority of armaments over 'increases in the cultural and productive strength of the people'.[39]

It was clear from the beginning that the means to develop industry and the military might of the nation could not be squeezed from a population that was already extremely hard pressed. An alcohol monopoly was introduced in 1894 to replace the old excise tax on spirits but, like other fiscal innovations, it did not produce substantial gains in revenue until later. No great increases in revenue could be expected from import duties either. The gruelling tariff war with Germany (finally halted by the commercial treaty of 1894) had shown the Minister that an autonomous Russian tariff was no longer possible.[40] More dubious means of raising capital such as issuing unbacked paper money were rejected. Witte only once recommended such tactics when construction on the great Siberian line had to be pushed through quickly;[41] thereafter he always resisted such temptations. The reason was that increasing the number of outstanding letters of credit would have blocked the only plausible way to finance the grandiose plans of state and encourage private entrepreneurship — continued access to international money markets.

In order to attract more and more foreign capital into Russia, Witte would have to do something which his predecessors had

---

38. 'Dnevnik Polovtsova', *KA* 46, p. 121 (11 June 1899); Russian documents on the Hague Conference in *KA* 50/51, pp. 64–96; ibid., 54/55, pp. 49–79; the French documents in: *DDF* 1, pp. 14, 475ff.; cf. also D.L. Morill, 'Nicholas II and the Call for the First Hague Conference', *JMH* 46 (1974), pp. 296–313.
39. Witte, *Vorlesungen*, 1, pp. 80ff.
40. Bonwetsch, 'Handelspolitik', pp. 280ff.
41. *Dnevnik Polovtsova* 2, pp. 460, 517.

never attempted: steer a financial course that would make the ruble a hard currency. Witte planned on obtaining huge loans, and it was essential that the ruble, which was being maintained at 66.67 per cent below parity, be placed on the gold standard by 1897.[42] This would ensure the long-term integration of the Russian economy within the international system, as Witte's foreign financial policies over the following years demonstrated. Further increases in Russia's foreign debt were therefore a hallmark of the Witte era. Tied to fluctuations in the world economy and dependent on the liquidity of capital markets in Europe and their readiness to invest, the Minister's strategy for economic expansion was extremely prone to sudden crisis. Russia's friends and foes alike were forever tempted to buy politically acceptable behaviour from St Petersburg by granting or refusing financial help.[43] The fragility of these policies for extensive development became apparent when recession struck around the turn of the century and conflict broke out in Manchuria — a conflict that was closely related to 'the Finance Minister's foreign policy'.[44]

No less troublesome than the international complications were the conflicts which Witte's policies provoked in Russia itself. Much more than Vyshnegradskii, Witte became enmeshed in battles with the landed gentry and its conservative ideologues, who had succeeded in strengthening their influence at the Court after the throne changed hands in 1894. Nicholas II was highly susceptible to advice from members of his large family, and Witte had continually to seek assurances that he had the loyalty of the young ruler.[45] Witte's critics complained about his criminal neglect of agrarian interests and evoked, as they had for many years, the looming ruination of

42. A.I. Bukovetskii (ed.), *Materialy po denezhnoi reforme 1895–1897 gg.* (Petrograd, 1922), vol. 1; O. Crisp, 'Russian Financial Policy and the Gold Standard at the End of the 19th Century', *EcHR* 6 (1953), pp. 156–72; now also in: Crisp, *Studies in Russian Economy before 1914* (London, 1976); I.M. Drummond, 'The Russian Gold Standard 1897–1914', *JEH* 36 (1976), pp. 663–88, gives an opposing view to the sceptical judgements passed on the economic justification of the gold standard in H. Barkai, 'The Macro-Economics of Tsarist Russia in the Industrialization Era', *JEH* 33 (1973), pp. 339–72; cf. A. Kahan, 'Government Policies and the Industrialization of Russia', *JEH* 27 (1967), pp. 460–77; also P. Gregory and J.W. Sailors, 'Russian Monetary Policy and Industrialization 1861–1913', *JEH* 36 (1976), pp. 836–51.
43. Cf. chap. 8.3.
44. Th. v. Laue, 'Problems of Modernization', in I.J. Lederer (ed.), *Russian Foreign Policy*, p. 79.
45. For a drastic characterisation of the inexperienced Tsar and the political and moral quality of his entourage: 'Dnevnik Lamzdorfa', *KA* 46, p. 27 (17 June 1899). This assessment is corroborated by Witte's bitter judgment; cf. Vitte, *Vospominaniya*, vols. 2 and 3 *passim*.

the country estates. Twenty-six marshals of the gentry, enjoying the protection of Minister of the Interior Goremykin, addressed a lengthy list of complaints to the Tsar in which they demanded fundamental change in financial policy, i.e. new state subsidies. In particular they wanted preferential credit conditions, lower freight rates and lower tariffs on imported agricultural machinery.[46] Witte responded to such pressures in a lengthy treatise in which he defended his view that the nobility had no right to claim preferential treatment and should adapt to the realities of the market.[47] However, his opponents enjoyed the strong support of I.N. Durnovo, chairman of the Council of Ministers, and V.K. Pleve, later Minister of the Interior, and they constituted a formidable group. This was demonstrated beyond a doubt in 1897–8 during discussions about reforming the Nobles' Bank and calling a 'Special Conference on Questions Pertaining to the Nobility'.[48] In both cases Witte was overruled, and in March 1897 he was forced to dip into the national treasury and lower interest rates for noble debtors from 4.0 to 3.5 per cent.

In general, though, providing support to landowners in straitened circumstances was not a priority of the Minister of Finance. What he was anxious to see was a substantial improvement in the living conditions and economic circumstances of the peasantry. His reasons were mainly financial: the peasants' inability to pay much in taxes, he explained to the Tsar, was the reason why the Russian national budget was only one-third that of the French budget (proportional to the population) and less than half even of the Austrian budget.[49] Witte's arguments in favour of better protection for the peasantry ran aground not only on the resistance of his opponents but also on his own economic policies.[50] Witte wanted to solve the permanent agricultural crisis by abolishing communal land tenure but this was out of the question so long as there were no returns from expanding industry to permit the channelling of profits back into agriculture. Witte knew that economic progress in Russia was not yet self-sustaining despite high rates of industrial growth.

Witte's opponents castigated him for selling out the country to

46. Solov'ev, *Samoderzhavie*, pp. 234ff.
47. Cf. Witte's lengthy comment on a petition of the marshals of the nobility (1897) in: *IA* (1957/4), pp. 125–55.
48. Solov'ev, *Samoderzhavie*, pp. 220ff.
49. Witte to the Tsar, October 1898, in: Witte, *Vospominaiya* 2, pp. 522–8.
50. 'Dnevnik Polovtsova', *KA* 46, pp. 118f. (4 Jan 1899).

foreign capitalists. In his defence against their attacks and insinuations Witte tried to demonstrate that for the time being Russia
could not afford to renounce either high protective tariffs or foreign
capital.

> Capital, like knowledge, has no homeland. . . . It is said that the flow of
> foreign capital threatens the country's character, and that our own capital
> resources would suffice if we did not rush things. But a big country
> cannot wait. . . . Access to foreign capital is the best means of meeting
> our mounting needs and of increasing the productivity of our excess
> supply of labour that is not put to any use in order to speed up the
> accumulation of wealth and increase the prosperity of our people. That
> this does not pose a danger to the independence of a country is proven
> . . . by the examples of England, Germany, France and the United
> States. They did not lose their independence because they created indus-
> try with the help of foreign capital. [Witte thought it obvious that
> sacrifice would be necessary]. . . . Nothing in the world is free.[51]

He was fully aware that Russia would have to accept dependence
on foreign countries for a transitional period until she could stand
on her own two feet.

In reaction to the 'kvass-patriotism' of his adversaries who complained about the 'economic occupation' of the Empire by foreigners, Witte pointed out very bluntly that Russia's political independence was not assured so long as the country was economically
dependent:

> Russia's economic relations with western Europe are still very similar to
> the relations between colonies and their mother countries. The latter
> regard their colonies as a rich market where they can sell without
> interference the products of their labour and industry and which they can
> force to hand over the raw materials they need. The economic power of
> the states of western Europe is based on this, and the essence of that
> power is the defense of old colonies and the conquering of new ones. To
> a certain extent, Russia is still one of these hospitable colonies for all the
> industrially developed states. She generously supplies them with cheap
> products from her land and pays dearly for goods manufactured by the
> labour of industrialised countries. However, there is one essential differ-
> ence in comparison with the situation of colonies: Russia is a powerful,
> politically independent state. It has the right and the might not to remain
> eternally in debt to the economically more advance states. . . . Russia

51. Witte, *Vorlesungen*, 1, pp. 140f.

herself wants to be a mother country [*metropoliya*], and an indigenous national industry has begun to grow on the basis of peasant labour freed from the chains of serfdom. If promises to become an auspicious counterweight to foreign domination [*vladychestvo*].[52]

The Finance Minister had seen again and again, especially during negotiations with bank consortia in Paris and Berlin, how 'harmful and ignoble' it was for Russia to have her 'foreign policy exposed to the dangers of pressure from foreign exchanges'. This dependence became expecially troublesome during the recession of the winter of 1899–1900 when Russia's access to capital markets in Europe was almost cut off, and her French ally would agree to grant more funds only if St Petersburg built expensive strategic railways in Central Asia and Poland.[53] Witte expected that the state's credit needs would be covered in the medium term on Russian money markets, but this had to remain a theoretical hope. A more realistic approach was to reduce the costs of industrialisation by encouraging foreign capitalists to increase direct investment in Russian joint-stock companies or to open up businesses in Russia.[54] Witte thought this form of direct participation was less susceptible to various crises than paper securities because the interest which foreign investors would take in the prosperity of the companies and enterprises they were helping to finance, would be relatively independent of disagreements in foreign policy. Around the turn of the century about one-half the money invested in Russian trade and industry (c. 11,000 million rubles) belonged to foreigners. In order to increase these sums the substantial limitations placed on foreign, and especially

52. Witte to the Tsar, 22 Mar. 1899, in: *Materialy po istorii SSSR* (Moscow, 1959), vol. 6, pp. 159–222, here pp. 176f. This memorandum was first published in an English translation by T. v. Laue in: *JMH* 26 (1954), pp. 64–74. For the arguments of the opponents of the Finance Minister around Grand Duke Alexander Mikhailovich: 'Dnevnik Polovtsova', *KA* 46, pp. 119f. (13 Feb. 1899); cf. as well Yu. B. Solov'ev, 'Protivorechiya v pravyashchem lagere po voprosu ob inostrannykh kapitalakh v gody pervogo promyshlennogo pod″ema', *Iz istorii imperializma v Rossii* (Moscow, 1959).
53. Witte, 'Most humble report' (February 1900), *IM* (1935/2–3), pp. 131–9, here: p. 136; cf. Anan'ich, *Rossiya*, pp. 33ff., 61f.; Girault, *Emprunts*, pp. 329ff.
54. A summary of the state of research may be found in: B. Bonwetsch, 'Das ausländische Kapital in Rußland', *JGO* 22 (1974), pp. 412–25. For the history of joint-stock companies and laws governing the operation of joint-stock companies in Russia see: L.E. Shepelev, *Aktsionernye kompanii v Rossii* (Leningrad, 1973), here especially pp. 168ff., 179ff., 201ff.; cf. as well the literature mentioned in note 20. For the development of banking: I.F. Gindin, *Russkie kommercheskie banki. Iz istorii finansovogo kapitala v Rossii* (Moscow, 1948), pp. 37ff., 73ff. *passim*; I.V. Bovykin, *Zarozhdenie finansovogo kapitala v Rossii* (Moscow, 1967), pp. 201ff.; also the survey by O. Crisp, 'Russia', in R.E. Cameron (ed.), *Banking in the Early Stages of Industrialization* (New York, 1967), pp. 183–238.

Jewish, capitalists would have to be eliminated. In view of strong xenophobic and anti-Semitic feelings in Russia it would not be easy to persuade the prevaricating Tsar that a thorough revision was necessary of laws governing commerce and industry (including the stock market). Powerful arguments would be needed. The Empire, said the Minister, was such a 'strong political organism' with 'such enormous political strength and power' that Russia would doubtless succeed, as had other comparable powers, in assimilating foreign capitalists and enterprises and in keeping Russian industry 'completely national'.[55]

In 1899 Witte expressed the hope that by about 1903 Russia would have traversed the critical period during which it was dependent on the West. As things turned out, however, this was the very moment when the extremely serious consequences of his bold attempts to overcome Russia's backwardness finally caught up with the Minister himself. The turning point in Witte's development strategy came with the cyclical downturn which began around the turn of the century in the wake of falling values on the stock exchanges. The failure of this strategy can be ascribed in no small part to his policies in the Far East. Since 1895–6 the Minister had been implicating Russia's internal economic development in an area where modern imperialisms were in conflict.[56] His Asian strategy was based on the belief that the dynamism of young Russian industries could only be assured if Russia penetrated Siberia in order to conquer territories and markets in Asia which had not yet been opened up by economically more advanced powers. It was in Manchuria that Witte tried to realise his goal of seeing the Russian Empire recognised not as a colony of the West but as a 'mother country' equal in status with the other great powers. This was a substantial change in Russian foreign policy, and more traditional policy-makers in St Petersburg realised as much around the turn of the century. The Minister of War, A.N. Kuropatkin, felt compelled to warn the Tsar in March 1900 that Russia could be dragged into the 'terrible struggle for markets' if the feverish growth of industry resulted in overproduction in Russia as well. Russian military power would then enter into an 'entirely new period, alien to its historical experience'. It would no longer be fighting for 'our faith, the Tsar and the motherland . . . but to a large extent for the

---

55. Witte, 'Februar 1900', *IM* (1935/2–3), p. 136.
56. For Far Eastern policies, cf. chap. 9, sections 9.1 and 9.2.

interests of the captains of industry'.[57]

Witte called this outburst 'an astonishing paradox'. Vastly over-estimating Russian possibilities, Witte did not want to accept any territorial limitations and hoped to imitate American policies of the 'open door' and 'peaceful penetration'. Railways were the key to his concept of economic imperialism. At times Witte even went so far as to maintain that driving eastwards and expanding markets there would solve the dilemma posed by Russia's lack of independence: payments due to western creditors could then be covered by profits from flourishing trade with the East.[58] The preparations for this experiment and its results will be described in more detail below.

The plans of the powerful Minister of Finance soon aroused traditional foreign interests concerned about military spheres of influence and naval bases. That they would thwart his programme of penetration became clear as early as 1897–8 when Russia seized Port Arthur. Witte's policies were suddenly caught up in the competition of the imperialist powers, in the 'scramble for China'. It was an international web of conflict which exceeded the resources of the Empire. When Russian troops occupied Peking and halted in Manchuria in August 1900, Witte feared that a war would lead to domestic disturbances.[59] Japan had begun a process of partial mod-ernisation at about the same time as Russia, and its armed aggression a few years later would make the limitations of Russian power painfully apparent. Under the double pressure of internal crisis and military defeat the political system threatened to collapse. The costs and disproportionate consequences of industrial growth had be-come self-evident.

Witte's modernisation programme increased Russia's dependence on foreign countries and the problems that resulted will be looked at in greater detail in the ensuing chapters. Firstly, the tensions arising from the conflict between protective tariffs and agricultural exports will be examined. Secondly, the impact of Russia's lack of capital on her foreign policy will be investigated. Russia was doubly dependent for her economic development — on Germany as the biggest purchaser of agricultural goods and on France as the main creditor of the Russian government. It therefore seems advisable to look at the effects of Russia's lack of capital in two specific areas: in

57. Kuropatkin to the Tsar, 14 March 1900, with marginal notes in Witte's hand ('astonishing paradox'), quoted in Anan'ich, *Rossiya*, pp. 25f.
58. Witte, 22 Mar. 1899, in *Materialy po istorii SSSR* 6, pp. 188f.
59. 'Dnevnik Polovtsova', *KA* 46, pp. 131f. (13 Aug. 1900).

the context of relations between St Petersburg and Berlin and in the context of the Franco-Russian Alliance. Finally, the qualitative changes which appeared in Russia's foreign policy during the period of industrial expansion, will be examined focusing on the relation between internal economic expansion and imperialist expansion. This connection can clearly be seen in Russian policy in East Asia.

7

Trade and Tariff Policies:
St Petersburg's German Partner

Until the 1880s the political relationship between Berlin and St Petersburg was kept on an even keel, despite mutual irritation, by strong commercial and financial relations between the two countries. German portfolios contained about 2,000 million marks in Russian securities in 1885, including most of the credits for the war of 1877–8. German capital financed the construction of railways in Russia, German heavy industry was the largest supplier of industrial raw materials, equipment and technical know-how, and Germany offered the largest market for Russian exports of grain. Both German industry and Russian agriculture felt an increasing pressure to export, and a relationship of mutual dependence developed. This dependence lent economic and social support to the political alliance between monarchs and governments, just as the friendship between monarchs and governments benefitted the economic and financial relationship.[1]

1. Russo-German economic relations between 1879 and 1904 have been well researched, so the supporting evidence for this chapter can be kept brief. The following discussion is based for the most part on recent studies which have substantially expanded our knowledge: S. Kumpf-Korfes, *Bismarcks 'Draht nach Rußland'. Zum Problem der sozialökonomischen Hintergründe der russisch-deutschen Entfremdung im Zeitraum von 1878 bis 1894* (Berlin, GDR, 1968); J. Mai *Das deutsche Kapital in Rußland, 1850–1894* (Berlin, GDR, 1970); H. Müller-Link, *Industrialisierung u. Außenpolitik. Preußen-Deutschland u. das Zarenreich von 1860 bis 1890* (Göttingen, 1977); B. Vogel, *Deutsche Rußlandpolitik. Das Scheitern der deutschen Weltpolitik unter Bülow, 1900–1906* (Düsseldorf, 1973). The best account of the importance of trade policies for the industrialisation process within Russia can be found in: B. Bonwetsch in Geyer (ed.), *Wirtschaft u. Gesellschaft*, pp. 277–99.
The work of Kumpf-Korfes and Mai is especially valuable because of its detailed assessment of both German and Russian sources and literature. The connection between foreign policy and economics in the history of Russo-German relations is not made into its own special problem the way it usually is in a Marxist-Leninist approach. This is done, however, in Müller-Link's impressive and informative thesis completed at the university of Bielefeld. The relationship between economic interests and *grande politique* is understood as a function of differing conditions during

As a source of capital and an importer of grain, Germany was of fundamental importance to the financial, industrial and communications policies of the Russian Empire. St Petersburg's diplomacy was fully consistent with its strategy for development, aimed at overcoming industrial underdevelopment, chronic financial difficulties and military inferiority. The preference for Bismarck's Germany gave Russia an ability, however limited, to manoeuvre internationally in her rivalry with Austria and England. Thanks to the German connection, Russia was able to compensate somewhat for the diminished position in which her structural problems had placed her and to continue to play her traditional role as a great power. This role was necessary if the autocratic system was to survive.[2]

The partnership created by the many political and economic links between Russia and Germany was very unequal, as evidenced in the fundamentally Germanophobic tone of Russian nationalism. This inequality did not result merely from the differing degrees of development within industrialised Germany and agrarian Russia. St Petersburg had no other choice than the German market and no foreign policy alternative — at least until the end of the 1880s. The Russian Empire was an important part of Bismarck's alliance policies but a break between the two countries would not have put Germany in such a precarious position as Russia. Though fears of a Franco-Russian alliance had been fomenting in Germany, there was no real possibility of such a combination for the time being. England was a possible future partner in the Triple Alliance, renewed in 1887 (as demonstrated by the Mediterranean Agreements signed at the end of the year), but she would not ally herself with Russia.[3]

---

industrialisation and expressed in very pointed fashion, despite limited acquaintance with the state of Russian and Soviet research; cf. the seminal study of H. -U. Wehler, 'Bismarcks späte Rußlandpolitik 1879–1890' in Wehler, *Krisenherde des Kaiserreiches 1871–1918* (Göttingen, 1970), pp. 163–80. In going back to the Caprivi era, B. Vogel's thesis (University of Hamburg) offers a precise history of the development of the Russo-German trade treaties of 1894 and 1904. This is also touched upon in the thesis of H. Altrichter, which concentrates on the problem of parties in the Reichstag participating in devising trade treaty policies: H. Altrichter, *Konstitutionalismus und Imperialismus. Der Reichstag und die deutsch–russischen Beziehungen, 1890–1914* (Frankfurt, 1977). Recent Soviet research has involved relatively little work on the connection between foreign policy and the economy in the context of the Russo-German relationship. An exception is the study by V.S. Dyakin, *Germanskie kapitaly v Rossii. Elektroindustriya i elektricheskii transport* (Leningrad, 1971); also: G.S. Holzer, 'German Electrical Industry in Russia: From Economic Entrepreneurship to Political Activism, 1890–1918', PhD thesis, Univ. of Nebraska, 1970.
2. Cf. chap. 5.
3. P. Rassow, 'Die Stellung Deutschlands im Kreise der Großen Mächte

The Russian Empire was also more vulnerable from an economic point of view, and the German Chancellor was not immune to temptations to exploit this weakness politically, especially after 1879. German industry and the Berlin banks had of course grown accustomed to commerce with Russia; however, they had sufficient flexibility and adaptability to absorb or circumvent tighter restrictions, as they did after 1885 when the Russian tariff soared. On the other hand rising German tariffs on agricultural products threatened to topple St Petersburg's system of capital imports, agricultural exports and fiscal protection for expanding industry.

Protectionism was clearly the Achilles' heel of the Russo-German *entente*. Where an alliance supposedly existed, barricades were being erected on both sides. St Petersburg and Berlin completed the transition to protective tariffs between 1877 and 1879, and thereafter the political and economic links between the two countries became increasingly strained. There was an air of inevitability in the mounting economic antagonism because neither Germany nor Russia could renounce protectionism. In Russia the protective tariff was a prerequisite for any real attempt to overcome economic backwardness and serious financial difficulties; in Germany tariffs were closely related to complex problems arising from financial reform, military policies and the agrarian-industrial accord. The ulcer on Russo-German relations began to be felt in the second half of the 1880s during a time of deep economic depression. The political alliance could scarcely be held together while Russia smarted from the loss of Bulgaria. The 'stop-gap moratorium' of the Reinsurance Treaty[4] did not suffice to curb the onset of the tariff war and the chauvinistic fervour which accompanied it.

Two interrelated sets of decisions caused the tariff conflict to escalate: increases in the Russian tariff in April 1885 and again in May 1887 (on pig-iron, coal, iron-ore, non-ferrous metals, machinery, agricultural equipment etc.) and the German tariff ordinances of May 1885 and December 1887. The situation was further aggravated by the so-called *Lombardverbot* placed by Bismarck on Russian securities in November 1877. These measures compelled the autocracy to take decisions with international consequences

---

1887–1890'. *Mainzer Akd. d. Wiss. u. d. Lit. Abh. d. geistes- u. sozialwiss Kl.* (1959), pp. 179–231.
    4. Wehler, 'Bismarcks späte Rußlandpolitik', p. 179; cf. Müller-Link, *Industrialisierung*, pp. 319ff.

which would soon become apparent.[5]

Given the state of research on the subject, detailed analysis of the reasons why Bismarck set a collision course may be omitted. The tariff war and the proscription of Russian securities were the result of elaborate calculations on the part of the German Chancellor who was not least concerned with managing internal political tensions. Though under attack, protectionism was still the strongest bond holding together the cartel of large landowners and heavy industrialists which Bismarck wanted to preserve.[6] The authoritarian rule of Prussia's traditional ruling classes depended on it for stability. Agricultural tariffs and a refusal to take Russian securities as collateral for loans therefore fulfilled three functions:

1. They indicated to the large landowners east of the Elbe, whose loyalty could not be won without economic compensation, that Bismarck would protect major agrarian interests even during recession.

2. They demonstrated to entrepreneurs orientated towards exports, especially in the industrial part of Upper Silesia, that the government was ready to respond to the prohibitive tariffs of the Russians with strong measures against Russian grain exports. Limitations imposed on German exports to Russia would be met with counter-pressure.

3. They were intended to pacify the circles around Moltke and Waldersee which were planning a preventive war and help in frustrating the political ambitions of the general staff.[7] In proclaiming the *Lombardverbot* Bismarck showed that he was even willing to see most of the profitable business which Berlin banks did in Russian securities evaporate because of tumbling prices and capital withdrawals.

Like the German government, the Russian administration also found its policies caught up in the escalating tariff conflict during the precarious year of 1887. Each side viewed its own behaviour as a necessary response to the provocation of the other side; each considered its own position inalienable and expected the other to make concessions. Like the German Chancellor, the Russian Fi-

5. Kumpf-Korfes, *Bismarcks Draht*, pp. 50ff., 121ff., 154ff.; Müller-Link, pp. 264ff., 291ff., 321ff.

6. Cf. the interpretation of H. Rosenberg, *Große Depression u. Bismarckzeit. Wirtschaftsablauf, Gesellschaft u. Politik in Mitteleuropa* (Berlin, 1967), esp. pp. 169ff., 258ff.

7. Wehler, 'Bismarcks späte Rußlandpolitik', pp. 174f., 380; Müller-Link, pp. 303ff., 341f.

nance Minister had to deal with pressure groups over the tariff issue. Protectionist industrial circles in Central Russia and the Urals had an influential spokesman in Katkov who saw no reason to separate loan policies, protective tariffs and diplomacy and who vigorously attacked St Petersburg's orientation toward Germany. Bunge's authority melted under the heated attacks and intrigues of the Moscow patriots eager for tariffs. When Bunge's successor, Vyshnegradskii, took office in January 1882, he was met with a wave of proposals and petitions expressing the demands and complaints of commerce and industry. With Russia in the grip of a depression and the government unable to hand out any subsidies or large contracts, the call for help against foreign, especially German, competition could not be ignored. It was a plausible reaction on the part of those who saw their profit margins rapidly disappearing.[8]

Agricultural interests were orientated towards external markets and exports and they were therefore the most determined opponents of St Petersburg's tariff policies. They had strong support among the political élite within Russia. The Council of State was the most important advisory body in the legislative process, and most of its members were favourably disposed to the large landowners suffering under German grain tariffs and the collapse in prices on the world market. To agrarian interests, Russian tariff barriers were hardly less offensive than German barriers: these interests purchased artificial fertilisers and agricultural machinery from foreign countries and tariffs were driving up the price. Large landowners blamed the Ministers of Finance for the fact that the government could not do anything about German protectionism and did not consider offering tariff concessions in return for a reduction in Bismarck's tariff on agricultural products. The Ministers of Finance had every reason not to underestimate the power of this lobby. It always became dangerous when the costs of industrialisation began driving small farmers to starvation, putting the fearful chorus of agrarian interests in a position where it could convince the Tsar to dismiss the Minister of Finance. This is how Vyshnegradskii finally met his demise.[9]

In looking at the structural peculiarities of Russian protectionism,

8. Gindin, *Gosudarstvennyi bank*, pp. 56ff.; Laverychev, *Krupnaya burzhuaziya*, pp. 183ff.; Kumpf-Korfes, pp. 60f.; also pointed interpretations from a contemporary German point of view in: G. v. Schulze-Gaevernitz, 'Der russische Nationalismus u. seine wirtschaftlichen Träger', *PJ* 75 (1894), pp. 337–64; Schulze-Gaevernitz, *Volkswirtschaftliche Studien aus Rußland* (Leipzig, 1899).
9. Cf. chap. 6.

one should remember that, unlike Germany, tariff policies only benefitted industry. Protective tariffs did not alleviate the existing antagonism between Russian agriculture and industry but made it a permanent feature of national life. The only factor uniting trade, industry and agriculture was economically-motivated Germanophobia and its corollary — Francophilia. Public opinion was saturated with such sentiments in the spring of 1887 when the war psychosis which Bismarck had provoked loomed large.[10] The dilemma of government industrialisation policies was that protectionism hurt those very social classes that had always been the foundation of the autocracy. Tariffs were meant to assure the future of autocracy, but they also undermined what remained of its social base after the period of reform.

Those who wanted to modernise backward Russia by means of railways and industry had to accept both protective tariffs and the bitter opposition of agrarian, conservative interests. A high tariff barrier was one of the firmest foundations on which industrialisation in Russia could be based. It was essential for promoting unimpeded economic growth, for cutting back imports to improve the balance of trade and help balance the budget, and for attracting direct foreign investments which, unlike state loans, did not particularly affect the balance of payments.

However, Russian ministers of finance could not afford to be indifferent to German tariffs on grain. Russia's international solvency depended on the surplus brought in by agricultural exports. That surplus was derived, however, from an extremely weak agricultural sector; it was squeezed out of the mass of small peasant producers by taxes which forced them to sell their generally meagre harvest at low prices, This Russian *Hungerexport* was possible only because fiscal measures compelled the impoverished population to forego consumption. When wheat and rye came across the German border they were hit with a tax of one mark per 100 kg until May 1885, then three marks per 100 kg until December 1887. Subsequently the Prussian tariff rose by another two marks.[11] Under such conditions proceeds sank, despite increases in the volume of exports. So Bismarck's grain tariffs were paid in part by Russian

10. H. Hink, 'Bismarcks Pressepolitik'; Grüning, *Die russische öffentliche Meinung*, pp. 106ff.; G.P. Morozov, 'Russko-frantsuzskie otnosheniya vo vremya voennoi trevogi 1887 g.', *FE* (1959), pp. 248–81; A.Z. Manfred, *Obrazovanie russko-frantsuzskogo soyuza* (Moscow, 1975), pp. 191–234.
11. Kumpf-Korfes, pp. 50, 123.

peasants. Prices also rose on the German domestic market and the lower classes in Germany were increasingly offered up to 'bread profiteers'. Bismarck's tariffs cut into the Russian balance of trade and threatened conversion of the foreign debt, efforts to strengthen the currency and industrial progress in general.

In summary then, the Russo-German tariff war was virtually inescapable. Protectionism was equally essential on both sides though for different reasons. For Bismarck tariffs were an element in his strategy for ruling and preserving the existing system; for the Russian Finance Minister they were an essential part of the plan for economic development. The functional equivalence in both countries made for unyieldingly opposed positions. Giers and Ambassador Shuvalov in Berlin, supported by Schweinitz in St Petersburg, strove in vain to halt the escalating conflict: a tariff war would excite the 'passions of the population', aggravate 'the unfortunate and idiosyncratic aversion that is deeply imbedded in both peoples' and possibly drive 'the most influential sections of Russian landowners' into war with Germany.[12] However, neither Bismarck nor Vyshnegradskii were prepared to make a deal — the former because he believed he could apply most pressure and bring the Russians to heel by economic means, the latter because he considered tariff increases inevitable for the sake of national finances.

Despite dark threats from Berlin and a campaign in the German press Vyshnegradskii did not shrink from imposing a substantial increase in Russian import duties in May 1887. This had less to do with aggression than with the difficult position in which he found himself. After the defeat of his predecessor Vyshnegradskii's tenure in the Finance Ministry stood or fell on whether the chronic deficit in the balance of payments could be eliminated. Opponents of protective tariffs in Russia did not get far against Vyshnegradskii's argumentation. There is no doubt that German business in Russia suffered no small damage as a result. By 1886 exports to Russia had already shrunk by about one-third in value as compared with 1880 and the German share of total Russian imports had dropped from 45 to 31 per cent. The new tariff was particularly hard on exports of pig-iron which in 1888 attained only one-seventh of the level reached in 1886 (10,115 metric tons as opposed to 70,521 metric tons).[13] If one considers the fact that the Russian tariff ordinance came at the same time as a *ukaz* forbidding foreign nationals to

12. Ibid., p. 59.
13. Ibid., pp. 52, 120.

acquire property in the Vistula provinces and reducing their rights of inheritance (14/26 March) then the widespread desire for counter-measures becomes understandable. Leaders of the agricultural and heavy industry cartel (iron and steel interests in Upper Silesia and Silesian magnates with large estates in Russian Poland) demanded that the government punish the Russians with a tariff war and credit restrictions. Bismarck accordingly encouraged an anti-Russian campaign in the press, but he did not block Russian securities and increase agricultural tariffs until the late autumn of 1887, wanting first to see the Reinsurance Treaty concluded.

Recent researchers are agreed that Bismarck's calculations misfired.[14] German retaliation did not destroy Vyshnegradskii's protectionist measures, and Alexander III was neither forced to come and do penance in Berlin nor rigorously to control attacks on Germany in the press. The unusually good harvests of 1887 to 1889 came to the aid of the Russian Minister of Finance. Increased market supplies made it possible to limit the damage done to grain exports and prevent an alarming decline in the foreign trade surplus. The government was not forced to abandon the long-term plans which Vyshnegradskii had introduced to reorganise the Russian system of tariffs, and the ultra-protectionist tariffs of June 1891 eventually came into effect.

Of equal importance was the fact that the blow aimed at Russian securities was absorbed without catastrophic effects. The *Lombard-verbot*, accompanied by a press campaign against Russian securities, led to the desired collapse in prices, but the bonds and shares available on the Berlin exchange at discount rates soon found new purchasers elsewhere. At first the Russian national Treasury accepted a large number of the available securities (not without help from large German banks that had financial dealings in St Petersburg and were adversely affected as well). Not even the low prices worked to Vyshnegradskii's disadvantage for they helped him to speed up the planned conversion of foreign loans, an operation which capital markets in Paris were well placed to support. Most Russian securities did make their way to France after 1888 — not under the best of conditions but the Finance Minister managed to derive some benefits from this as well.[15] Moreover high finance in

14. Evidence in Müller-Link, pp. 339ff.
15. A.L. Sidorov, 'Konversii vneshnikh zaimov Rossii v 1888–1890 gg.', *IA* (1959/3), pp. 99–125; R. Girault (Zhiro), 'Finansy i politika vo franko-russkikh otnosheniyakh 1887–1889 gg.', *FE* (1967), pp. 136–58; Girault, *Emprunts russes*, pp. 156ff.; Wittschewsky, pp. 164ff.; Müller-Link, pp. 332ff.

Paris could be expected, with the tolerance or even help of the government to remain open to further requests for loans. French banks thus provided St Petersburg with what it had previously sought from Germany.

Bismarck's action meant that the Russo-German relationship lost one of its underpinnings. The secret Reinsurance Treaty, that stop-gap measure of cabinet politics, did not inspire a great deal of confidence either in the palaces or in the diplomatic chancellories. When Wilhelm II ascended the throne and took over the reins of power in Berlin in June 1888, dynastic sympathies cooled as well. Neither German industry nor Russian grain interests could do without the other's market, making high tariffs all the more poisonous to the general atmosphere. With trade relations deeply disturbed, involvement in the other's economies through capital investments reduced, and an alliance which provided questionable guarantees — suspicions, phobias and a sense of threat could not fail to emerge. Political consequences soon followed. Offers from France had been flowing in since the spring of 1887, and even provincial publications in Russia had aired the idea of reinforcing the transfer of loans to France with further agreements. However, the Tsar and the Foreign Minister found this rather unseemly and dangerous for the time being. Even Vyshnegradskii was anxious not to turn his back completely on Berlin, for in the long run his tariff system could only be shielded against external pressures if a commercial agreement could be concluded, bringing the tariff war to an end.

The 'new course' set by Caprivi in the spring of 1890 did not give any immediate ground for optimism. The trade policies of the new Chancellor seemed to be steering toward an Austro-German economic block protected by conventional tariffs. This was no less depressing for St Petersburg than the refusal to replace, with comparable guarantees, the expired Reinsurance Treaty.[16] In contrast, the Triple Alliance, established by Bismarck and formally ratified in May 1891, seemed very stable, as far as St Petersburg could see, and increasingly open to England.[17] No new facts emerged to undermine the inner logic of a Franco-Russian *rapprochement*. Particularly helpful in dispelling conservative aversions to the French

16. For Caprivi's policy on trade agreements see: Vogel, *Deutsche Rußlandpolitik*, pp. 17ff.; Altrichter, *passim*; Kumpf-Korfes, p. 130ff.
17. P. Jakobs, *Das Werden des französisch-russischen Zweibunds 1890–1894* (Wiesbaden, 1968), pp. 73ff.; Manfred, *Obrazovanie*, p. 321.

republic were the arguments brought to the Tsar's cabinet by the Russian general staff, concerning the increasing strength of the German army. The Foreign Minister could not approach an under-standing with France without major pangs of conscience, but even he finally accepted *la force des choses*. When the French fleet visited Kronstadt in July 1891 and the Tsar saluted the *tricolore*, even diplomats sentimental about regal friendships could no longer think of any convincing arguments against a Franco-Russian *entente* (15/27 August).[18] In the following two years the protectionists in St Petersburg and Berlin engaged in a vicious exchange of blows while the general staffs of France and Russia negotiated. In the autumn of 1893, while Giers grew resigned to this military alliance,[19] the Russo-German tariff war reached full pitch.

An explanation is needed as to why this war did not end with Russia's capitulation and why it brought Vyshnegradskii's succes-sor, Witte, even a measure of success and a favourable press. The course of the conflict is well known: apparently undaunted by German threats, the government in St Petersburg ordered a further 20 per cent leap in the tariff in July 1890. In June of the following year a new, carefully elaborated set of tariffs came into effect at the same rate. Imported goods were on average taxed at one-third of their value. The tariffs had an almost prohibitive effect on heavy industrial goods, to which German interests were especially sensitive.[20] After the increases, the Russian 'Mendeleev tariff' surpassed any in the world, including those of the United States which had just erected new barriers against 'free' world trade in the form of the McKinley tariff of 1890.

If one considers the extent to which Russia depended on exports this rigorous insistence on the right to set tariffs at any level might seem a very dangerous game. In 1891–2 Caprivi was busy arrang-ing treaties to discriminate again, and apparently permanently, against Russia's foreign trade. Mutually complimentary commercial agreements had been concluded with Austria-Hungary, Italy, Ro-mania, Serbia, Bulgaria, Belgium and Switzerland, and these set conventional tariffs for rye and wheat at 1.50 marks per 100 kg below the rate imposed on Russia by the German tariffs of 1887.[21]

18. Jakobs, pp. 84ff.; Manfred, pp. 322ff.
19. Cf. chap. 8.
20. Sobolev, *Tamozhennaya politika*, pp. 699ff.; S.A. Pokrovskii, Vneshnyaya torgovlya, pp. 273ff.; Kumpf-Korfes, pp. 118ff., 132ff.; Bonwetsch, pp. 280ff.
21. For the following see: Wittschewsky, pp. 154ff.; E. Zweig, *Die russische Handelspolitik seit 1877* (Leipzig, 1905), pp. 37ff.; Pokrovskii, pp. 397ff.; M.N.

Enquiries in Berlin revealed that Russia could only benefit from similar favourable treatment if she granted substantial concessions to German exports. Nevertheless Witte apparently felt strong enough by June 1893 to push through a double tariff with further increases of 20 to 30 per cent. He intended to force Berlin either to grant most favoured nation status or to agree to a long-term commercial treaty with conventional tariffs without any substantial damage to the Russian tariff system. Two months later German imports were hit with another increase of 50 per cent, in full recognition of the fact that the German government would respond in kind.[22] The Russian Finance Minister thus succeeded, in remarkable harmony with Caprivi, in provoking a crisis which very soon forced the parties to seek an agreement. By October 1893 a Russo-German tariff conference was underway and attempts were being made to put an end to the battles of the previous few years. In the commercial treaty of 10 February (29 January) 1894 Caprivi granted the Russians what he had originally wished to confine to his partners in the Austro-German customs union.[23] Berlin, not St Petersburg, had made the decisive concession and Caprivi's political downfall was not unrelated to this fact.

Why was Witte able to act with such remarkable firmness? St Petersburg's new French partner could not be called on for emergency help in this struggle. Paris could take over from the German market so far as securities were concerned but not in respect to grain. The Méline tariff of 1892 had closed off France just

---

Sobolev, *Istoriya russko-germanskogo torgovogo dogovora* (Petrograd, 1915), pp. 54ff.

22. The following statistics show the decline in German exports to Russia as a result of the tariff war (monthly average in hundreds of kg.):

	1892 Aug./Dec.	1893 Jan./Feb.	1893 Aug./Dec.	1894 Jan./Feb.
Pig-iron	26,782	7,668	25,101	100
Iron bars & hoop-iron	109,633	46,327	43,539	2,438
Hardware	31,700	14,318	21,347	4,395
Machines	40,832	14,936	27,817	6,226
Copper	11,350	8,080	1,913	—
Phosphates	26,782	923	22,693	200
Cotton	13,765	7,188	3,916	522

Source: Per Pokrovskii, *Vneshnyaya torgovlya*, p. 310.

23. *RGbl* (1894), no. 8; M.H. Kloessel, *Der deutsch-russische Handelsvertrag* (Bielefeld, 1895).

as effectively as Germany to agricultural imports. The commercial treaty concluded between St Petersburg and Paris in June 1893 promised Russia hardly any advantages worth mentioning besides most favoured nation status. Above all, it did not modify the marginal role played by France in Russia's foreign trade. Besides Germany, Great Britain was Russia's most important trading partner, but exports in that direction had not risen noticeably during the Russo-German tariff war.[24]

Procedures intended partly to subvert or evade German tariffs brought some relief. These measures included reducing railway freight rates to the German and Austrian borders, or using Holland, Romania or Austria as intermediaries to pass on Russian grain to Germany at conventional tariff rates. In addition, the poor harvests of 1891 and 1892 brought a marked reduction in the amount of Russian grain on the market and what remained could be profitably sold within Russia itself. Due to the catastrophic famine, the fall in prices which the German tariff war threatened to inflict on Russian agriculture never occurred. This exceptionally unfortunate chain of events makes it clear that Witte could not hold out forever. He needed the help of other unique factors to withstand the trial of strength with Germany.

In the end, the Finance Minister did not have to rely on the resilience of the Russian people alone. Despite his weakness he could imitate the politics of strength because his German competitor was hardly in a better position. Caprivi had been forced to seek new directions for German trade, not least because in 1889 the French government had moved to exclude Germany from its system of commercial treaties and conventional tariffs. By the Frankfurt Treaty (1871) Germany had gained most favoured nation status and the right to participate in all the advantages granted to French trading partners, but now this right was cancelled.[25] Thus the need arose to create Germany's own trading and tariff union. Caprivi was forced to deal with additional economic and internal political problems. His defensive strategy was hampered both by increases in agricultural prices in 1890 and cyclical depression in industry in whose interests the 'new course' had been established. The

24. Cf. table 9. For the trade agreement between Russia and France see: Girault, *Emprunts*, pp. 239ff.
25. R. Poidevin, *Les relations économiques et financières entre la France et l'Allemagne de 1898 à 1914* (Paris, 1969), pp. 93ff. For the Treaty of Frankfurt and trade policy: Böhme, *Deutschlands Weg*, pp. 308ff.

Chancellor's plans for a customs union aimed therefore at enhancing the ability of German industry to export goods while agreeing in return to accept a reduction in agricultural tariffs. While Germany's new commercial treaties with her partners in the Triple Alliance and Romania were a step in this direction, they also led to the dissolution of the internal cartel which Bismarck had created. Caprivi's position was weakened by the risk this entailed.

St Petersburg trade policies aimed for obvious reasons at including the Russian Empire among the exporters of agricultural goods favoured by Germany. It is equally obvious that this aim would be resisted by Caprivi who knew that the inclusion of Russia would strengthen the position of his agrarian opponents and negate the value of the Central European union as a political alliance. In the end, Witte was able to exploit high tariffs to extract a trading agreement largely because of Caprivi's internal political problems. The Russian Minister of Finance received involuntary support from German industry, which was most anxious to gain access to the Russian market, and Caprivi was heavily dependent on the support of industry, not least to help ward off the storm of protest directed at the Chancellor by the Farmers' League founded in 1893.[26]

As the 1894 agreement between Berlin and St Petersburg demonstrates, Witte's strategy was successful. The ending of Russian autonomy in tariff matters and the relief Witte was obliged to grant German exports were more than offset by the advantages accruing to Russia from Germany's conventional tariff. The conclusion of the tariff war indicates that the pressure to export was no weaker in Germany's highly developed industrial economy than in backward agrarian Russia. The notorious term, Russian *Hungerexport*, found a notable parallel in Caprivi's dictum: 'We must export: either . . . goods or . . . people.'[27] Since the 1870s the mutual dependence of the two unequal partners had been partly based on this truth, which is why St Petersburg and Berlin continued to need each other even after the traditional political alliance had crumbled and financial connections had loosened.

The treaty, signed in March 1894 for a period of ten years, clearly enhanced Russo-German trade relations and marked the beginning

26. H.J. Puhle, *Agrarische Interessenpolitik u. preußischer Konservatismus im Wilhelminischen Reich* (Hanover, 1966); S.R. Tirell, *German Agrarian Politics After Bismarck's Fall. The Formation of the Farmers' League* (New York, 1951); v. Laue, *Witte*, pp. 109ff.; Bonwetsch, pp. 281f.
27. Vogel, *Deutsche Rußlandpolitik*, p. 29.

of an era of relatively untroubled expansion (Table 9). In 1902, Germany took 41 per cent of Russian exports (compared with 24 per cent in 1892), and shipped back 35 per cent of Russian imports (in comparison with 25 per cent). Thus the relations which had existed back in the 1870s were virtually restored. During the period of economic growth of the second half of the 1890s there was a strong increase in the volume of trade. Germany succeeded in strengthening its dominant position *vis-à-vis* the Russian market, but Russia also succeeded in making optimal use of its export opportunities. After a decline in exports to Germany caused by poor harvests and the tariff war, Russian shipments increased sharply, to more than double their previous value by 1894 and again by about 28 per cent over the next five years. Thereafter the expansionist tendency evened out considerably and exports remained at their 1898 level (as a result of stagnant foreign demand) during the period of economic crisis at the beginning of the century. While Russian exports to Great Britain reached 40 to 50 per cent of the German level between 1898 and 1902, exports to France reached only 15 to 20 per cent of the German level.[28]

Despite their shortcomings, Russian import statistics also reveal that the treaty of 1894 stabilised Germany's position as Russia's premier trading partner. Russian imports from the German Empire rose by 30 per cent between 1892 and 1894 and by the same amount before 1898; they remained at around this level during the ensuing years of economic crisis. By way of contrast, British exports to Russia reached only about half the level of German exports, French exports barely attained more than 11 to 13 per cent of the German share of the market and American exports stood at about 20 per cent of the German share. Economic expansion under Witte produced an enormous demand for machinery and industrial equipment in Russia, but her foreign trade balance remained strongly positive after 1894, both in respect to Germany and overall. Total annual surpluses hovered around 100 million rubles until the turn of the century and then increased rapidly during the depression (1902: 271 million rubles).

The irritations which cropped up in Russo-German trade relations after 1894 remained bearable so far as St Petersburg was concerned. Individual complaints were ironed out at a joint trade conference in 1897, and when the time came, around the turn of the

28. Girault, *Emprunts*, pp. 311ff.

Table 9: Russian foreign trade 1890–1913 (in mill. of rubles)

	1890	1892	1894	1896	1898	1900	1902	1904	1905	1906	1907	1908	1909	1910	1911	1912	1913
Imports from																	
Germany	114.6	101.7	143.0	190.2	202.2	216.9	208.5	228.5	240.4	298.4	337.4	348.4	363.3	449.8	487.8	532.3	652.2
Great Britain	93.0	101.2	132.8	111.3	115.3	127.1	99.2	103.4	97.4	105.7	114.9	120.3	127.9	153.8	155.1	142.4	173.0
USA	54.8	38.0	45.7	65.7	50.1	44.2	39.9	62.9	40.8	47.5	55.6	79.2	57.2	74.4	102.5	87.4	79.1
France	17.3	18.5	28.2	23.4	27.1	31.4	26.9	26.5	26.1	28.7	29.4	36.3	49.5	61.0	56.8	56.3	57.0
Total imports	416.1	403.9	559.5	589.8	617.5	626.4	599.2	651.4	635.1	800.7	847.3	912.6	906.3	1084.4	1161.7	1171.8	1374.0
Exports to																	
Germany	166.3	116.3	247.2	292.5	335.1	331.7	352.0	379.0	505.0	576.3	524.8	448.1	637.0	650.6	774.7	721.5	672.0
(Russ. statistics)	177.9	138.2	147.9	184.0	179.4	187.6	203.2	234.8	255.3	284.7	291.0	279.0	387.1	390.6	490.5	453.8	453.6
Great Britain	203.7	118.5	175.3	160.9	139.9	145.6	189.1	230.4	249.2	225.4	228.5	220.5	288.9	315.5	337.0	327.8	267.8
France	49.4	35.1	56.2	58.2	68.6	57.4	55.1	61.8	64.5	76.5	73.4	64.6	89.1	93.6	90.8	98.2	100.9
Holland	43.5	19.5	53.0	70.9	72.3	69.3	103.1	99.3	126.8	108.0	114.4	93.8	189.2	196.0	188.8	154.0	177.4
Total exports	703.9	475.6	668.6	688.5	732.8	716.4	860.3	1006.4	1077.3	1094.9	1053.0	998.3	1427.7	1449.1	1591.4	1518.8	1520.1
Grain exports	344.9	164.1	381.4	322.5	370.9	304.7	432.2	495.3	568.3	472.0	430.6	379.6	749.4	745.9	739.5	551.3	594.5
Grain exports as a % of all exports	49.0	34.5	57.0	46.8	50.6	42.8	50.3	49.3	52.8	43.1	40.9	38.0	52.2	51.5	46.5	36.3	39.1

Sources: Bonwetsch, 'Handelspolitik und Industrialisierung', pp. 282, 289; cited in Khromov, *Ekonomicheskoe razvitie Rossii*, pp. 474, 486–93; S. Zuckermann, *Der Warenaustausch zwischen Deutschland und Rußland* (Berlin, 1915). Tables I, II. German trade statistics were used for Russian exports to Germany. The variation in comparison with the Russian statistics results in part from the fact that the latter ascribed to Holland shipments that were discharged in Rotterdam but sent on to Germany.

century, for the Ministry of Finance to consider renewing the treaty, there appeared no reason not to continue with the system of conventional tariffs already in effect. This does not exclude a strong desire on the Russian side to adjust the tariffs on individual imported goods — to modify the tariff rates accepted in 1894 in order to take into account the expanded capacity of Russian industry. By the late summer of 1900 it was evident that revisions in the treaty could not be handled as a routine matter for experts.[29] The impetus once more to inject political ill-will and public feeling into Russo-German trade relations came from Berlin where the conservative Farmers' League was engaged in a continual campaign of massive opposition to a policy of conventional tariffs and most favoured nation status. Reducing this pressure was a key element in Chancellor von Bülow's attempts to create a broad national consensus. For reasons of domestic harmony, the German system of tariffs had therefore to be thoroughly revised and levels raised substantially, especially on agricultural goods.[30]

The preparation of a German 'compromise tariff' was clearly a matter of grave concern in Russia and most unwelcome to the Minister of Finance. After the draft tariff bill was published in July 1901, Witte had little reason to hope that Russo-German trade could be continued on the basis of the 1894 agreement. The proposed minimum tariff of 5.50 marks per 100 kg of wheat and rye was a clear increase over the old tariff, and the Russian press took strong exception to the German plans, for obvious reasons. Witte too let it be known that if more constraints were placed on Russian agricultural exports, he would reject the treaty and would not hesitate to impose countervailing measures. However, Witte's ability to affect internal German decisions was very limited. The warning that England would be the major victor in a Russo-German tariff war had little effect after the Anglo-Japanese Alliance was signed in February 1902.[31] Witte also failed to succeed in his attempts to engage the Austrian government in a common front against German tariff policies. However, Bülow's position in domestic German politics did offer the Russian Minister of Finance an opportunity that could be exploited.

Bülow was faced with the problem of how his desire for a

29. For the history leading up to the trade treaty of 1904 see: Sobolev, *Istoriya*, pp. 127ff.; Wittschewsky, pp. 364ff.; Bonwetsch, pp. 283ff.; Vogel, pp. 56ff.
30. For the struggle over the German tariff see: Vogel, pp. 30ff.
31. Ibid., p. 33.

political *rapprochement* with Russia could be reconciled with the necessary increases in Germany's tariffs on agricultural goods. The Chancellor wished to gain Russian support for Germany's essentially anti-British international policy (*Weltpolitik*) and this moved the Russian government to emphasise the incompatibility of political friendship with commercial confrontation. Authoritative publications such as the official *Novoe vremya* warned against the illusion 'that a close alliance could exist between peoples with tense economic relations'.[32] However, declarations such as these were not particularly effective. A more important point of attack was the fact that the trade agreement with Russia would be a test of whether the new German tariff could be applied to other countries. During the Caprivi era St Petersburg had had to fight to gain a place within a system of conventional tariffs already in place, but now Germany's other trading partners recognised that the new Russo-German treaty would serve as their model.

Witte could therefore rest assured that a large part of Bülow's political authority depended on reaching an agreement with Russia. Firstly, the Russian Finance Minister tried to disrupt the lengthy process of drawing up the new German tariff by making proposals of his own. He suggested either that the treaty of 1894 should be extended without alteration or that negotiations for a new treaty should begin immediately. At the same time he expedited work on revised Russian tariffs which would substantially increase the 1891 rates and restore the tariff differential (harmful to German exports) between goods coming by sea and land. When Berlin categorically refused to extend the old treaty and the Reichstag passed the tariff law of 13 December 1902 Witte matched the German conditions with new Russian tariffs (13/26 January 1903). The positions of both sides had been set.[33]

As with Bülow's compromise rates, Witte's tariff had not been elaborated solely from the point of view of Russo-German trade. The thorny problems of balancing the budget and dealing with deficits in the balance of payments could no more be overlooked than conditions affecting the development of specific branches of industry. In the midst of an economic crisis the Minister of Finance knew that he could not permit any reduction in the protection of

32. *Novoe vremya*, 19 July (1 Aug.) 1901, cited in Vogel, p. 39.
33. Sobolev, *Istoriya*, pp. 170ff.; cf. V.S. Dyakin, 'K otsenke russko-germanskogo torgovogo dogovora 1904 g.', *Problemy istorii mezhdunarodnykh otnoshenii* (Leningrad, 1972), pp. 156–73.

industry. Since this was difficult to arrange without further discriminating against agricultural interests, everything depended on out-manoeuvering his critics. The tariff of 1903 which promised to ease imports of fertiliser and agricultural equipment did not satisfy the agrarian camp. It was therefore all the more important that Witte make as favourable an impression as possible when presenting the concerns of Russian agriculture to the Germans. This explains his negotiating tactics which were forceful, frequently abrupt and calculated to produce delay. Witte probably realised that the minimum German tariffs would inevitably have to be recognised in the long run and that a tariff war was out of the question. He therefore aimed at more modest results: the Germans, he hoped, would agree to accept an increase in Russian tariffs and a few compromises in their agrarian tariffs on fodder barley and livestock. Actually, Witte and his expert advisors did not really expect that Russian agricultural exports would suffer very much because the rising German demand for imports made it likely that Bülow's tariff would harm German consumers more than Russian agriculture.[34]

St Petersburg's position was assisted primarily by the German Chancellor's ambition to forge new political alliances, by the trade agreement's role as a model for the entire German tariff system, and by Witte's counter-strategy of increased Russian tariffs. Threatening signs of an economic and social crisis were undermining the 'Witte system' at the time, and the Minister had every reason to avoid compromises damaging to his prestige. This explains why, first of all, he rejected Bülow's attempts to gain tariff concessions in return for satisfying the Russian desire for capital loans on the German market. That Witte succeeded in breaking up such a compromising combination while reaching a satisfactory loan agreement cannot be ascribed solely to his close connections with the Mendelssohn banking house in Berlin, the most important pillar in Germany's 'Russian consortium'. No less helpful were the fears of the Foreign Ministry that a blunt refusal of St Petersburg's requests for capital would drive Russia 'completely into the embrace of France'.[35] Witte balanced himself very cleverly between Paris and Berlin. In April 1901 successful loan negotiations were concluded with France, making it possible for the irrepressible

---

34. Cf. Bonwetsch, 'Handelspolitik'; Bonwetsch, *Kriegsallianz u. Wirtschafsinteressen*, pp. 12ff. For a detailed analysis of the development and completion of negotiations for a trade treaty see: Vogel, pp. 124ff., 174ff.
35. Vogel, pp. 74ff., 82ff. For Franco-German rivalry over capital markets in Russia, cf. R. Poidevin, pp. 45ff., 286ff.

Witte to unsettle the German diplomats with a display of unshakeable self-confidence and to portray the arrival of Russian railway securities on the Berlin market as an example of Russian generosity. Witte did not even have to make any trade concessions in obtaining the state loan for 200 million rubles at 4 per cent interest, which was offered in Berlin in April 1902 and quickly subscribed many times over. Bülow arranged the approval of the *Reichsbank* in order to dampen the Franco-Russian connection, promote the Russo-German *rapprochement* and help reconcile St Petersburg with Germany's minimum tariffs.[36]

In the end, Russia's bargaining position could not be tampered with the promise of loans. Although Witte had been dismissed as Minister of Finance in August 1903, he remained in charge of the commercial treaty and did not feel inclined to retreat from his hard-headed obstinacy. Even after the outbreak of Russo-Japanese hostilities, he let it be known that Russia did not require German capital for the time being because her French ally had come to her aid with a loan (May 1904).[37] The war had an effect, of course, on the treaty negotiations but not in a way particularly damaging to Witte. It helped him to gain the Tsar's assent to the basic trade and tariff provisions which had been worked out as early as the spring of 1903. In May 1904 a ministerial conference approved his plan only to accept the German minimum tariffs if Berlin acknowledged the Russian tariff and granted a measure of additional relief.[38] Bülow and Witte then met on the island of Norderney to establish the treaty which was signed in Berlin on 28 July 1904. While the Germans gained nothing that Russia was fundamentally opposed to conceding,[39] it was possible to counter the vehement protests of the agricultural lobby with the argument that the government had been obliged to bow before German demands because of the pressures of war. German capital markets which Bülow had sealed off from the Russian Government during the decisive phase of the negotiations were now reopened. This was all the more important to St Petersburg in that the Russian war effort in the Far East was dependent on the continual influx of foreign capital.[40]

36. Cf. also Anan'ich, *Rossiya*, pp. 49ff., 70ff.; Girault, *Emprunts*, pp. 340ff.
37. Anan'ich, pp. 105ff.; Girault, pp. 402ff.
38. Bonwetsch, *Kriegsallianz*, pp. 14ff.
39. The text of the treaty is in: *RGBI* (1905), no. 7.
40. For Russian financing of the war of 1904–05 see chap. 10.

8

Capital Imports and the Alliance: Franco-Russian Relations

The astonishing industrial boom of the 1890s would doubtless never have occurred without the combination of capital imports and high protective tariffs which Witte fought so hard to achieve. At the time protective tariffs were being raised everywhere to promote economic development, and they were not a specifically Russian phenomenon. However, the extent of Russian dependence on foreign capital for internal development was an unusual consequence of late industrialisation in an agrarian country whose political elite was determined she would remain a great power. The question posed here is to what extent this dependence influenced the foreign policy of the Russian Empire. The answers offered by historians have aroused controversy.

The Franco-Russian Alliance, resting on the *entente* of 1891 and the military convention which followed, has long prompted historians to try to elucidate the connection between political, military and economic interests. The Alliance offers a prime example of the political effects of Russia's dependence on foreign capital. The very chronology of its development demonstrates an apparently logical chain of financial and political arrangements: The *Lombardverbot*, ordered by Bismarck in 1887, drove Russian securities from the German market; since the Parisian banks had an unquenchable thirst for fixed-interest government securities and railway bonds, France willingly accepted those Russian securities; direct investments, especially in mining and metal-working, also contributed to making French high finance the main creditor and partner in the expansion of Russian industry and the transportation system; an alliance of governments and general staffs soon followed.

The controversies to which these observations give rise easily degenerate into a kind of shadow-boxing, with historians insistent on quarelling over the 'primacy of the economy' versus the 'primacy of politics'. Such squabbles have always been tempting and not only because of the fundamental disagreements between Marxist and non-Marxist historians. No less important is the fact that the traditional separation of diplomatic and economic history has reduced the possibility of synthesised analysis. Historians who confine their studies to diplomatic documents conclude that economic or financial motives played an insignificant role in negotiations over the *entente* and military convention — especially in Russia's case.[1] Studies of the movement of capital on the other hand leave such an impression of Russian dependence that political and military agreements seem to have been a direct result of the financial relationship.[2] In view of all the excellent research which has been done on the creation of the Dual Alliance and on French and Russian policies regarding capital and loans, conditions seem ripe for breaking down the historiographical barriers.

Detailed studies of the Franco-Russian *rapprochement* show no sign of a causal connection between Vyshnegradskii's financial operations and politico-military decisions. In assessing capital

1. The painstaking thesis of P. Jakobs, *Das Werden des französisch-russischen Zweibundes* (Wiesbaden, 1968) is confined to a study of the political and military negotiations and so remains fully in the tradition of older standard histories of diplomacy. Cf. W.L. Langer, *The Franco-Russian Alliance 1890–1894* (Cambridge, Mass., 1929); B. Nolde, *L'alliance franco-russe. Les origines du système diplomatique d'avant la guerre* (Paris, 1936). For the prehistory of the Alliance, see the recent contribution by G.F. Kennan, *The Decline of Bismarck's European Order: Franco-Russian Relations 1875–90* (Princeton, N.J., 1979).
2. Russia's reliance on capital loans and the French 'diplomatie du franc' originated the politico-military alliance and held it together, according to R. Girault, who conducted the leading research into French loans to Russia and direct investments there (*Emprunts russes*, 1973). The late A.Z. Manfred has warned against 'overestimating the direct influence of economic factors' on politics in a study of the early history of the Alliance reaching back to the brink-of-war crisis of 1875 (*Obrazovanie russko-frantsuzskogo soyuza* [1975]). He also objects to Girault's interpretation, claiming that the financial operations of 1888–89 had 'almost no influence on decisions about political fates (na reshenie politicheskikh sudeb)' (p. 288f.); cf. also Manfred's older study, *Vneshnyaya politika Frantsii 1871–1891* (Moscow, 1952), pp. 377ff., 446ff., 471ff., and Manfred, 'Oformlenie russko-frantsuzskogo soyuza', *NNI* (1975/6), pp. 114–32. Closer to Girault's views is the presentation of Russia's financial relations in: B.V. Anan'ich, *Rossiya i mezhdunarodnyi kapital* (1970), as well as the study of Yu. B. Solov'ev, 'Franko-russkii soyuz v ego finansovom aspekte (1895–1900 gg.)', *FE* 1961, pp. 162–206. Both Leningrad historians come from the school of B.A. Romanov, who bequeathed influential pioneer work in his study of the connection between diplomatic and financial history. Cf. primarily: *Rossiya v Mandzhurii 1892–1906. Ocherki po istorii vneshnei politiki samoderzhaviya v epokhu imperializma* (Leningrad, 1929), English translation: *Russia in Manchuria* (Ann Arbor, 1952); Romanov, *Ocherki diplomaticheskoi istorii russko-yaponskoi voiny 1895–1907 gg.* (Moscow/Leningrad, 1947, 1955²); and the source volume: Romanov (ed.), *Russkie finansy i evropeiskaya birzha 1904–1906 gg.* (Moscow/ Leningrad, 1926).

flows, one must bear in mind that the efforts of the Finance Minister to find purchasers for the securities flowing out of Germany and back to St Petersburg in many cases succeeded only in Paris.[3] Panamanian stocks had created a flurry of excitement on the Parisian market and created favourable conditions for loans to the Russian state and railway network. Parisian bank syndicates scented a high rate of profit and their representatives haunted the antechambers of the Ministry of Finance in St Petersburg. The French government was anxious to end the international isolation of France and saw in Russia a natural partner against Germany. It therefore found no reason to veto the sale of Russian securities. Public opinion was well disposed. The broad social spectrum of French pensioners and investors showed sufficient confidence to purchase the high interest-bearing bonds and mortgages backed by the Russian national Treasury. Contributions from St Petersburg to a newspaper campaign helped keep excitement high.[4]

Vyshnegradskii's position meanwhile was not especially favourable. The appalling budgetary situation left him little room or time to work towards an improvement of conditions. Moreover, he shared the view of the Tsar and the Foreign Minister that all political entanglements should be avoided in financial transfers. Alexander III's deep aversion to republicanism and Giers's fear of imperilling the Berlin connection meant that as late as 1890 a political *entente* seemed unthinkable, not to mention a military alliance. However, the suggestive power of loan conversions was at work in Russia as well. Broad sections of the public inclined to support the insistent campaign in Moscow newspapers for closer ties with France and consequently saw political overtones in St Petersburg's financial manipulations. Vyshnegradskii tried to internationalise the 1888–9 agreement with Parisian banks by persuading financiers in London and Berlin to participate. However, his attempts to avoid a new dependence did not diminish the public's

3. The following presentation adheres for the most part to the basic view of Girault, Anan'ich and Solov'ev. For the loan conversions of 1888–9 cf. chap. 7, note 15. For the prerequisites of French capital exports see: R.E. Cameron, *France and the Economic Development of Europe 1860–1914. Conquests of Peace and Seeds of War* (Chicago, 1961, 1965²); Cameron, *French Foreign Investment 1850–1880* (Chicago, 1955); G. Ziebura, 'Interne Faktoren des französischen Hochimperialismus 1871–1914', in W.J. Mommsen (ed.), *Moderner Imperialismus* (Stuttgart, 1971), pp. 85–139; Poidevin, *passim*.

4. As part of its loan policies, St Petersburg continually had the Ministry of Finance make gifts to the French press in order to influence it. Cf. the papers of the long-time Russian financial agent in Paris, A. Raffalovitch [Rafalovich], *L'abominable vénalité de la presse. . . . D'après des archives russes, 1897–1917* (Paris, 1931).

impression that Russia's ties were with France alone. Almost all the converted loans went to France, and other contributions to the understanding were not long in coming. In 1889 Russian business-men visited the World Exhibition in Paris with the approval of the Tsar, and the War Ministry ordered 500,000 new Lebel guns from France.[5]

The importance of these links for the political discussions which began the following year should not be exaggerated. While the diplomats and generals engaged in desultory conversation, Vyshne-gradskii vigorously argued against a Franco-Russian alliance. There is nothing to indicate that he could have been constrained to change his mind by loan blockades such as the one decreed to the Roth-schild banks against St Petersburg. When Ribot enquired of the Russian ambassador in May 1891 whether the Finance Minister might be interested in concluding a trade agreement with France instead of with Caprivi, his offer met with a very chilly reception in St Petersburg. Vyshnegradskii never doubted that Russia could replace her German trading partner. German trading policies — the continuing tariff war and discrimination against Russian grain ex-ports — made him very anxious to clear up relations with Berlin and prepare the way for a favourable trade agreement, even if Russia had to make concessions. Giers, who was strongly opposed to any identification of Russia with French desires for revenge against Germany, found Vyshnegradskii a reliable ally in this matter. The Finance Minister was of the opinion that France, under pressure from the Triple Alliance, was heading for 'another Sedan' and that Russia could not therefore even be sure of an economic partnership.[6]

It appears then that there was no intentional plan to pave the way for an alliance lurking behind St Petersburg's loan policies. Russian securities were sold in Paris solely for financial reasons to do with pressures on European capital markets, and Russian officials re-sisted all political interpretations. However, one should not over-look the fact that intensive economic relations soon developed a momentum of their own. St Petersburg's economic policies and the extensive programme of economic development which Witte pursued in the 1890s were highly dependent on foreign help, and

5. Girault, pp. 156ff., Manfred, *Obrazovanie*, p. 281. On Vyshnedgradskii's maxim, supported by Giers, that the competition between Parisian and Berlin banks should be exploited see: *Dnevnik Lamzdorfa* 1, pp. 137 (15 Feb. 1889), 238f. (7 Dec. 1889).

6. Jakobs, pp. 77f., 109; on the break with Rothschild: Girault, pp. 188ff.; *Dnevnik Lamzdorfa*, 2, p. 214 (8 Dec. 1891).

the close financial relations between France and Russia did not fail to engender political consequences. Early in 1895 more than half of all Russian securities handled on financial markets were in French hands (5,153 million francs); French capital also participated in the economic boom in Russia in the 1890s by way of rapidly rising amounts of direct investment (1895: 433.6 million francs, 1902: 1108.6 million francs).[7] Russia was quickly coming to depend on French money markets, much as she had long depended on German tariff provisions. Russia's partners were of course economically dependent on her as well. However, the difference between the backward Russian Empire and France of Germany was that Russia was incomparably more vulnerable than her competitors to external pressures, especially during times of crisis.

The question of a Franco-Russian *entente* arose for the first time in the spring of 1887 when Bismarck began stirring up war hysteria against France in order to push through his plans for the Septennate. In its alarm, Paris sought to discover what St Petersburg would do in case of a German attack on France, thinking that a Russian promise of neutrality would help check German aggressiveness and save the peace. The Russian press was very interested in a partnership with France. Although the idea that Germany could defeat France and reduce it to the level of a second-rate power was alarming to offical St Petersburg as well, Giers and the Tsar refused any binding commitments. The reason could be found not just in conservative aversions to a republic which seemed, under Boulangism, to be returning to its Bonapartist past. More important was St Petersburg's feeling that the traditional German connection was indispensable and that Russia could not risk being drawn into military conflict.[8]

After it became apparent that the Three Emperors' League would not be renewed, Bismarck and Shuvalov began, in January 1887, to discuss a bilateral understanding similar to the one which eventually saw the light of day as the Reinsurance Treaty. German guarantees provided the only support Russia could find in her continual confrontation with England and Austria, two rival powers who,

<hr>

7. Girault, pp. 106f.; cf. O. Crisp, 'French Investment in Russian Joint-Stock Companies 1894–1914', in *Business History* 2 (1960), pp. 75–90.

8. Morozov, *Russko-frantsuzskie otnosheniya*, pp. 248–81; Manfred, *Obrazovanie*, pp. 191ff.; also, with letters and reports to Giers from Mohrenheim: 'Bulanzhizm i tsrarskaya diplomatiya', *KA* 72, pp. 51–109; on the effect within France: P.H. Hutton, 'Popular Boulangism and the Advent of Mass Politics in France 1886–1890', *JCH* 11(1976), pp. 85–106.

together with Italy, were once more at this critical juncture maintaining the status quo in the Mediterranean and in south-eastern Europe. As England drew closer to the Triple Alliance of Germany, Austria and Italy, the anti-French and anti-Russian slant in this ingenious combination became apparent. Statements to the effect that Russia was uncommitted papered over the policy of *attentisme* by which official St Petersburg hoped to survive the crisis. Despite Bismarck's lack of enthusiasm Russia felt neither willing nor able to choose between Paris and Berlin.[9]

The Franco-Russian contacts in the spring of 1887 form part of the preliminaries leading up to the *entente* because the idea of a *rapprochement* between Russia and France was first broached at this time. However, by 1891–3 the Foreign Minister still feared as much as ever that an alliance with France would result in the burning of all bridges to Berlin. What had changed was that Giers had been unable to get Caprivi's signature on anything to compensate for the loss of the Reinsurance Treaty. St Petersburg found itself faced with a German-Austrian understanding as well as a renewed Triple Alliance with which England was in contact. Direct links, as seen in the Heligoland-Zanzibar treaty of 1890, seemed likely.[10] Never before had Russia's isolation been so complete and the Berlin connection so uncertain. The Russo-German tariff war made the situation even worse.

The military balance had also shifted. Russia's chronic financial woes forestalled large-scale rearmament, but this was not the case in Germany where the military had not ceased to grow since 1887/8.[11] The Russian general staff had upset Berlin by stationing troops close to the border in order to compensate for the Germans' ability to mobilise much more quickly, but such a strategy had become very implausible by the end of the 1880s. Chief of the general staff N.N. Obruchev reluctantly had to concede that while Russia may have been Austria's equal she was no match for German military power. The friendship between Berlin and Vienna left little hope that Germany would stand idly by during a conflict between Russia and Austria. St Petersburg also felt that the reactions of the young

9. H. Krausnick, 'Rückversicherungsvertrag u. Optionsproblem 1887–1890', *Geschichtliche Kräfte u. Entscheidungen. Festschrift f. O. Becker* (Wiesbaden, 1954), pp. 210–32; Müller-Link, *Industrialisierung* (pp. 306ff., 347ff.) underestimates the reservations Russian policy-makers had about ties with France.
10. Jakobs, pp. 73ff.; T.A. Bayer, *England u. der Neue Kurs* (Tübingen, 1955).
11. Cf. L. Rüdt v. Collenberg, *Die deutsche Armee von 1871–1914* (Berlin, 1924), pp. 27ff.

German Kaiser could not reliably be predicted. The rising tide of suspicion sharpened the fear that 'personal rule' in Berlin could lead to a collision course with Russia and possibly an offensive war.[12]

The military was in fact the driving force behind the Franco-Russian Alliance. Obruchev thought that a future was would involve all the European powers and he adopted a two-pronged approach. Firstly, he wanted to see the mobilisation of the French and Russian armies synchronised in case of conflict and, secondly, he hoped that in the event of war between France and Germany the Alliance would allow Russia an opportunity to settle old scores with Austria. The military power of Russia's potential partner had increased under Boulanger and Freycinet, giving such plans an air of plausibility.[13] The French general staff, on the other hand, wished to secure Russian support against Germany without having to declare war at an awkward time if hostilities erupted between Russia and Austria. These differences in military interests complicated the negotiations between generals Boisdeffre and Obruchev and compromise became necessary.

Giers had much stronger misgivings about an alliance. Even the sensational visit of the French fleet to Kronstadt, where the Tsar had managed to tolerate the Marseillaise, could not reduce the Foreign Minister's opposition to a military convention. Giers therefore strove to keep the political agreements free from all 'compromising' commitments. The *entente* which finally received Alexander's assent in August 1891 was so fashioned that Russia was not automatically liable to treaty obligations which pre-empted all room for manoeuvre. Giers sought a cordial relationship with Paris, 'a certain counterweight' and 'a beneficial balance of forces', not a military alliance which would necessarily offend Germany. Giers found enough security in a promise to consult in case of crisis or aggression, which remained vague regarding the mutual steps to be undertaken immediately.[14] Vyshnegradskii also believed that a military alliance was not in Russia's interest. In view of the alarming state of imperial finances he considered it essential that every

12. For Obruchev's assessment of Russia's military position see Jakobs, pp. 34ff. *passim.* Fears that Wilhelm II would pursue a policy of aggression are expressed in *Dnevnik Lamzdorfa* 1, p. 105 (24 Apr. 1891).
13. D.B. Ralston, *The Army in the Republic: The Place of the Military in the Political Evolution of France 1871–1914* (Cambridge, Mass., 1967).
14. For the Tsar's and Foreign Minister's reservations about a military alliance see Jakobs, pp. 84ff., 133ff. For Vyshnegradskii's position: *Dnevnik Lamzdorfa* 2, pp. 189f. (23 Feb. 1892), 310f. (8 March 1892).

international risk be avoided which might threaten 'peace and quiet'. As before, Vyshnegradskii apparently preferred settling with Germany to seeking a *rapprochement* with France. The economic and financial emergency in Russia was therefore a reason to reject the Alliance and not to join it.

More than two years passed before Minister of War Vannovskii could persuade the irresolute Tsar to confirm the military convention (in the version of 17 August 1892). The Panama scandal which had tainted the Russian ambassador in Paris, Mohrenheim, provided Giers with an opportunity continually to stoke the Tsar's anti-republican sentiments and at the same time dampen his anger with his German nephew.[15] In October 1893 the stopover of the Russian fleet in Toulon was coordinated with the visit of two French cruisers to Copenhagen where Alexander was sojourning. It seems to have been this visit and not the German military law of 1892 which finally nudged the Tsar at the year's end into ordering a resigned Giers to ratify the convention.[16]

The Franco-Russian Alliance was a defensive agreement directed against the powers of the Triple Alliance. In the case of a German offensive against France or an Italian offensive supported by Berlin, Russia was to attack Germany with between 700,000 and 800,000 men. France promised to reciprocate with 1.3 million men should Russia be attacked by Germany or by Austria with support from Berlin. The commitments were strengthened by a clause requiring immediate full mobilisation if a single member of the Triple Alliance mobilised. Procedures governing joint action at the level of operations were to be worked out in the near future by the general staffs.

Thus late in 1893 the traditional pattern of Russian diplomacy was broken and a new alliance steered through. This occurred not because of the Finance Minister's desire for loans but because of the military planners' strategy for security. However, it was inevitable that financial relations and the politico-military alliance would continually become entangled.[17] The mutual dependence created resembled the relationship between creditor and debtor, but the specific weight of the two allies cannot be adequately assessed simply by totalling up Russia's growing mountain of debt. Her

15. Jakobs, pp. 144ff.; Girault, pp. 215ff.
16. Text of the convention: *DDF* 2X, No. 488; *Sbornik dogovorov*, pp. 281ff.; for a precise analysis of the course of the negotiations and the drafts of the military convention see: Jakobs, pp. 106ff., Manfred, *Obrazovanie*, pp. 342ff.
17. On the direct effect see Girault, pp. 242ff.

political and military importance to France compensated to a large extent for her financial weakness. Despite her dependence and internal crises, Russia never before the First World War sank to the level of the Ottoman or Chinese Empires and certainly never to the status of a colony. Russia remained a partner of some stature and not simply a pawn of French policy.

This partnership, based on financial dependence, was evidently prone to work more to the disadvantage of the Russians than the French. However, the government in Paris did not enjoy unlimited opportunities to impose its will on St Petersburg by squeezing supplies of credit. Although the government and financial oligarchy in France usually operated in close co-operation, the Foreign and Finance Ministers had always to consider, when influencing the stock-market, the stabilising effect of capital exports within France. The state was compelled to pull gently on the levers of financial power, and it usually relied only on recommendations (which the banks rarely refused).[18] One must also bear in mind that the French Republic was not exactly a rock of stability during the 1890s. It was shaken by crises and scandals and strained by the colonial confrontation with England. Unsteady, industrially stagnant France was in no position to turn the Russian Empire into an inferior satellite.

Nevertheless St Petersburg did not find it easy to preserve a balance in the alliance. The difficulty can clearly be seen in the interconnected political and financial relationship. After concluding the military convention Witte soon discovered that the Alliance did not necessarily provide a reliable means of quenching his virtually unlimited thirst for capital. The French ministries and senior financial circles offered stiff resistance in 1894–5 to Witte's financial representatives, especially his Parisian agent A. Rafalovich and the prominent St Petersburg banker A. Rothstein who was entrusted with special missions.[19] They were accused of flooding Parisian markets with Russian securities, and it was claimed that new offerings would merely lower the value of the securities already listed. At the same time, however, the press and the Bourse reacted with utmost sensitivity to any Russian attempt to find new creditors in Berlin, London or New York. While the kingpins of French finance laid exclusive claim to St Petersburg's foreign credit (either implicitly or often explicitly), they did not offer Witte preferential treatment.

18. Ziebura, 'Interne Faktoren', pp. 111ff.
19. Solov'ev, 'Franko-russkii soyuz', pp. 164f.

The Finance Minister therefore had good reason to do all he could to preserve Russian access to the German market and to make enquiries in England and the United States as to the possible interest of financial circles. The outlook in London and New York was not good however. Banks in Berlin and London helped place a loan for 400 million francs in 1894, but thereafter Russian agents had little success either in England or the United States.[20] Repeated contacts with Nathan Rothschild made it clear to Witte's emissaries that British bankers would only listen to Russian requests if a political settlement could be arranged between St Petersburg and London. Even the signing of an Anglo-Russian accord governing mutual railway interests in China (16/28 April 1899) brought no noticeable change. In the summer of 1899 a London bank accepted 2.975 million pounds worth of state guaranteed railway bonds at four per cent interest, but this did little to change the atmosphere, especially since only about a quarter of the securities stayed in England despite their relatively low value. Rothstein conducted lengthy negotiations in 1898–9 with the American financial magnate, J.P. Morgan, but this too came to nothing. Witte's strategy of zig-zagging back and forth between bourses in America and the European capitals was therefore not a complete success. Only the big German banks, with Mendelssohn and Bleichröder leading the way, were interested in Russian railway securities.[21] The leverage this gave Witte in Paris was, however, limited. During his term in office (1892–1903) the Finance Minister managed to find purchasers for about 2,200 million rubles worth of securities, and of these about half went to France and a quarter to Germany. This relationship shows that Russian capital imports were politically highly sensitive to the force fields of international governments and high finance.

The French government left no stone unturned in its attempts to turn the Russian connection to the advantage of its imperialist interests in East Asia and the Middle East.[22] It tried again and again to grant or withhold loans as a means of ensuring loyalty. When Paris supplied credits to its Russian ally, they were usually accompanied by desires for military, diplomatic or economic favours. Since this angling for a double return was usually frustrated by Witte's opposition and succeeded only rarely, strong feelings of

20. The following according to Anan'ich, pp. 29ff.
21. Vogel, *Deutsche Rußlandpolitik*, pp. 78f.
22. W. Zürrer, *Die Nahostpolitik Frankreichs u. Rußlands 1891–1898* (Wiesbaden, 1970). For Far Eastern policies see chap. 9.

friendship seldom arose between the partners in the alliance.

Russian and French financial interests could occasionally coincide, of course, as can be seen in East Asian policy at the time of the Sino-Japanese War. In the summer of 1895 Mohrenheim, Rothstein and French Foreign Minister Hanotaux prepared the way for a loan that was to advance both Witte's desire for 'peaceful penetration' of Manchuria and France's wish to stem the activities of German and English companies in China. A consortium of French banks (Crédit Lyonnais, Hottinguer, Banque de Paris et des Pays-Bas) saw to it that Li Hung-chang was able to pay the indemnity owed Japan with the help of a Russian loan. This opened the door to Russian desires to build a Chinese Eastern Railway, and the newly founded Russo-Chinese Bank began making arrangements the following year.[23]

Franco-Russian relations within the Alliance also affected the 400 million franc loan of July 1896 which Witte wanted in order to shore up his monetary reform. This time the explosive situation in south-eastern Europe was involved. St Petersburg dodged French requests for Russian involvement in the debt administration of the Ottoman Empire while annoying Paris by pressing ahead with ambitions in the Bosporus. Witte probably felt strong enough in this situation to resist excessive French demands because he could point out to the French the more than obvious willingness of German banks to supply Russia with credit.[24]

In the ensuing years Russian negotiators in Paris met with increasing attempts at coercion. The demands increased in 1897 when Witte negotiated the acceptance of mortgages from the Nobles' Land Bank and the time arrived for a new loan to China. The Parisian Rothschilds again insisted that St Petersburg allow them a monopoly on loans and accused Witte of having discriminated against France by placing railway bonds in Berlin. Pessimistic judgements about Russia's chances for success with her development programme appeared in the press. The discord increased when the ruble was put on the gold standard and bimetallists in France suffered losses. Finance Minister Cochery intervened against the Russian method of side-stepping French financial authorities when selling securities, and Hanotaux complained about the Alliance's lack of effectiveness.[25]

23. On the loan to China and the Russo-Chinese Bank see Romanov, *Russia in Manchuria*, pp. 65ff.
24. Solov'ev, pp. 169ff.; Zürrer, pp. 149ff., 183ff.
25. Solov'ev, pp. 173ff.; Anan'ich, pp. 18f.

St Petersburg sensed that the Quai d'Orsay and the Ministry of Finance were subtly joining forces and working with the banks in order to frustrate Russian wishes. Demands began to be heard that Russia should adopt a more lenient tariff on French goods — industrial orders from Russia would be a useful means of boosting stagnant French exports. Unedifying squabbles ensued. Hanotaux complained to Witte that St Petersburg's trade policies were helping Germany establish economic hegemony over the Russian market, while Witte countered by pointing to the high prices of French industrial goods and the unjustified increases in French tariffs on Russian exports of grain. The discord intensified in the summer of 1897 when St Petersburg prepared once more to come to the assistance of Peking with a loan obtained from a number of international lenders. The French Foreign Minister demanded greater influence in the administration of the Russo-Chinese Bank and threatened to close French money markets to this financial arm of Russian policy toward China. Witte, who did not intend to yield in matters related to China, tried in vain to reduce tensions by ordering locomotives from France.[26]

The irritations within the Franco-Russian Alliance grew even worse in 1898–9, for several reasons. Following the monetary reform the hunger of the Russian national Treasury for capital grew particularly acute while the French had all but lost their appetite for new Russian securities. As was mentioned earlier, St Petersburg could not win over any English or American banks at this time. In the late summer of 1898 only mortgages from the Nobles' Bank were being accepted in Paris, and railway loans, which were subject to a high capital levy in France, were again acceptable only in Berlin. This left the financial requirements of the Russian Empire far from covered. Rising expenditure on defence and a negative balance of payments meant that Witte was confronted with a virtual state of emergency. Since the spring of 1898 he had been under pressure from the new Minister of War, Kuropatkin, who demanded additional funds to re-equip the Russian artillery in response to the German introduction of the 77 mm automatic cannon, which further added to their superiority. Russian policy in the Far East had become more militant since the seizure of Port Arthur, and it too continually required new expenditures, not to mention the cost of the Trans-Siberian Railway, the Manchurian line and the new naval

26. Solov'ev, pp. 182ff.

programme.[27]

The critical state of national finances also provoked the note circulated by Foreign Minister Count Murav'ev on 24 August 1898. This led in turn to the convening of an international peace conference in the Hague the following year. Witte was not opposed to this initiative, though he could hardly expect that Russian proposals 'to put an end to the progressive development of new armaments' would meet with the approval of the great powers. Still, two possible benefits did arise: the proposal gave the Minister an opportunity to escape, at least for a short time, the insistent budgetary demands of the military not by virtue of spending more money but by means of a spectacular diplomatic display. Furthermore, assurances that Russia was prepared, under the right circumstances, to freeze arms expenditures and the peace-time strength of her army and navy sent a discomfiting message to allied France. The French military attaché in St Petersburg understood full well that Witte was in a tight corner and needed money more than anything.

This strategy was not successful, however. France, already worried about the Fashoda Incident, was startled and did move to consider Russia's needs. However St Petersburg's interests were not served by the impression that Murav'ev's note was possibly 'the start of the disintegration' of the Franco-Russian Alliance. In October 1898 Kuropatkin and then the Foreign Minister travelled to Paris to confirm Russia's commitment to the alliance. Shortly thereafter Witte arrived to enquire into French willingness to supply credits.[28]

The Finance Minister found that neither the French Government nor the banks were prepared to make any special offers, and financial markets in Paris remained difficult. Despite ongoing negotiations through financial intermediaries and diplomats only internal Russian loans (mortgages from the Nobles' Bank) could be placed in 1899 and these in inadequate amounts. Larger grants of credit ran up against the financial recession (aggravated by the Boer War) which was spreading throughout Europe. Russian securities were not the last to suffer. French financial aid evidently could not be expected during a period of world economic crisis unless political concessions were forthcoming. Not just tariff concessions and contracts for French industry were demanded but also strategic

27. Cf. chap. 9.
28. Solov'ev, pp. 189ff.; cf. chap. 6, note 38.

military projects which the French general staff wanted in order to strengthen the Alliance's position against Britain. The outlines of the Alliance were re-confirmed by both partners in the summer of 1899 by express guarantees that the agreements of 1891–3 remained in force. However, Foreign Minister Delcassé was only willing to put up a new 200 million ruble loan if Russia began construction on the railway between Orenburg and Tashkent, a line that would link the Transcaspian railway with the network in Central Russia. Witte finally promised to do so very reluctantly; for him construction and completion of railways in the Far East were more important than unprofitable lines which could only please the general staffs.[29]

As the international economic and financial crisis deepened, Russian finances suffered accordingly. In addition, a lasting strain was imposed on the national Treasury by the costs of the military expedition to Manchuria which was the Russian response to the Boxer Rebellion. In the summer of 1900 Witte hoped in vain that a contract concluded with J. P. Morgan after difficult negotiations would have a 'moral effect' on capital markets. However, the New York banker was only prepared to grant 50 million dollars, and when the time came to complete the contract he wished to attach new conditions. The angry Minister of Finance simply cancelled the arrangement.[30] Another attempt consisted of trying to float on foreign markets securities for internal state loans at 4 per cent interest, but this was only moderately successful. Demand had fallen sharply. Only after the 5 per cent capital levy had been dropped for foreign purchasers did St Petersburg succeed in the spring of 1901 in inducing the Parisian Rothschilds to accept the securities. However, Witte had to agree not to offer any other state or state-backed securities on foreign markets for the period of one year (until March 1902). At the same time French Foreign Minister Caillaux compelled St Petersburg to support Russian industries which had benefitted from French direct investment and were now threatened by the economic crisis.[31]

Delcassé's visit to St Petersburg in April 1901 did nothing to solve

29. Anan'ich, pp. 39f.; Girault, pp. 335ff.; on the renewal of the alliance through an exchange of letters through the foreign ministers (27 July [8 Aug.] 1899) see: A. Zayonchkovskii, *Podgotovka Rossii k mirovoi voiny v mezhdunarodnom otnoshenii* (Moscow, 1926), pp. 88f.; Text: *Sbornik dogovorov*, pp. 319ff.
30. Anan'ich, pp. 44ff.
31. Ibid., pp. 49ff. For an extensive look at French direct investment and industrial participation see Girault, pp. 107ff., 261ff., 354ff.

Witte's problems. Further financial burdens could be expected when the revised military convention was ratified, requiring Russia to send 300,000 men to her Central Asian borders with India and Afghanistan in the event of a British attack on France. The French Foreign Minister wanted Russia to participate in the Baghdad railway project and insisted once again on the building of strategic railways. It was no longer only a question of the line between Orenburg and Tashkent but of an additional project which had already been negotiated between the general staffs: a 1,100 km long, double-track railway that would lead from the junction at Bologoe (on the line between St Petersburg and Moscow) by way of Velikie Luki and Polotsk to Siedlce in Congress Poland and shorten by four days the time taken to concentrate mobilised field units against Germany. Faced with the double pressure of Kuropatkin and Delcassé, Witte did not make much headway with the Tsar. Without having achieved any financial guarantees, the Finance Minister had to accept Nicholas II's instruction of May 1901 to begin construction on this economically unprofitable railway. Witte's stubborn attempt to cover the costs with a new French loan of 200 million rubles led to a debilitating controversy with Caillaux. In the Foreign Ministry too there were grave misgivings that projects to build strategic railways would harm relations with London and Berlin. Not until August could France be induced to approve the requested loan after Witte had promised not to approach the Parisian market again until 1904.[32]

The poor climate for Russian imports of capital in France is indicated by an intensive newspaper campaign sparked off by the crash of Russian industrial stocks. Russia's criticial economic situation was conveyed to the general public in sombre terms, and the St Petersburg authorities were accused of systematically discriminating against French investors. The French press was not even mollified by Delcassé's invitation to Nicholas II to visit Dunkirk in September 1901 in order to offset the Tsar's presence at manoeuvres of the German fleet. Furthermore, Witte had to yield to the views of his Parisian agent that henceforth a 'tribute' of about 150,000 rubles a year would be necessary to improve Russia's image among French

32. Anan'ich, pp. 62ff.; C. Andrew, *Théophile Delcassé and the Making of the Entente Cordiale, 1898–1905* (London, 1968), pp. 125f.; revision of the military convention: *DDF* 1/XVI, no. 208; for the negotiations on Russian participation in the Baghdad Railway see: G.L. Bondarevskii, *Bagdadskaya doroga i proniknovenie germanskogo imperializma na Blizhnii Vostok (1888–1903)* (Tashkent, 1955), pp. 232–43.

stock-brokers.[33] In fact no further Russians loans could be arranged in France before the Russo-Japanese War.

Berlin alone offered an outlet. In view of French rebuffs Witte pressed ahead with discussions begun with the Germans in 1901. In March 1902 a substantial loan of almost 200 million rubles was arranged by a consortium put together by Mendelssohn — a not unfortuitous result from the Russian point of view. The rapid consummation of the deal thwarted the plans of those German diplomats who had intended to make the loan contingent on Russian promises to make tariff concessions in the forthcoming negotiations for a commercial treaty.[34] Since the loan included Russia's share of a contribution to help subdue the Boxer Rebellion in China, it also served to frustrate France's desire to steer Russian policy in the Far East by applying financial pressure. Witte took advantage of the opportunity to demonstrate publicly that Russia was by no means dependent on financial aid from France. In an article in the St Petersburg *Vestnik finansov, promyshlennosti i torgovli* (April 1902) he interpreted the German loan in the following way: It disproved intimations in the French press that Russia was misusing the Alliance as a tool of financial coercion and that she was a financial drain on small French capitalists; the Franco-Russian Alliance had nothing to do with foreign financial policies, and economic matters were dominated 'in our materialistic age' by commercial interests; the German example proved that Russia did not need the Alliance to do business on capital markets in Europe.[35]

The robust self-confidence with which Witte played off French and German interests against one another underlines the fact that Russia's financial dependence did not automatically translate into political subservience. Franco-German antagonism opened up a freedom of movement for Russian policy and made it possible for the autocracy either to resist untoward French demands or to satisfy them with minor concessions (as happened when direct investments from France were given fiscal support). The cabinet in Paris felt obliged to deal tactfully with its eastern ally, not least because of Bülow's attempts to wean her away. France had a national interest in Russian stability, partly because of Russia's importance as an ally but also because of the effects of the financial relationship on French society. Bankruptcy in St Petersburg would have been a disaster for

33. Anan'ich, pp. 75ff.
34. Vogel, *Deutsche Rußlandpolitik*, pp. 75ff.; Anan'ich, p. 86.
35. Ibid., p. 93.

the broad classes of French investors (including even parts of the petty bourgeoisie) and would have had a substantial impact on the French government's own internal position. Around the turn of the century about a quarter of all French foreign investments, c. 7,000 million francs, were in Russian industries securities.[36] Russia's solvency and her continued participation in the Alliance were both fundamental to French policy. This continued to be true when Russia's borrowed imperialism entangled her in a war with Japan and the ensuing revolutionary convulsions cast serious doubt on the regime's ability to survive. In the summer of 1905 Paris managed to use a temporary financial blockade in order to convince a harassed St Petersburg to discontinue the war with its associated heavy losses; however, the creditor's perfect sense of her own self-interest led her in the end to take steps to ensure that the debtor did not sink beneath the waves of revolution. Republican France made no mean contribution to the survival of tsarist Russia.[37]

36. Cf. the table in Ziebura, 'Interne Faktoren', p. 113.
37. Cf. chap. 10.

9

Expansion in Eastern Asia

Industrialisation in Russia was accompanied by other international consequences besides the commercial and financial dependence outlined above. State-directed economic expansion soon penetrated the most distant realms of the Empire, making Russian policy (especially in the Far East) more and more the domain of the Minister of Finance. Thus the characteristics of modern imperialism began to mark the traditional strategy of military-colonial penetration (which had still been dominant at the time that Transcaspia was conquered and which had been exercised in Persia together with the means for securing economic influence).

Witte's East Asian policy was a prime example of the dynamic welding of traditional power politics, forced industrialisation and imperialist expansion: its chosen vehicle was the railway; its instrument was bank capital and loans closely connected to the national treasury; its stated goal was the long-term opening up of markets, the 'peaceful penetration' of economically underdeveloped territories where a power-vacuum existed and the strengthening of the imperial position of the Russian Empire. Witte's international competition stemmed from the modern imperialisms of the industrially developed nations which at the time were also opening up new outlets in China as well as in Africa.

After the Treaty of San Stefano Russia had avoided in Europe the extraordinary kinds of risk which she now ran in East Asia. While the tension in Central Asia and Persia was largely confined to competition with England, the vital interests of all the great powers were involved in China. Not just the European 'concert' composed of the usual constellation of powers was involved in East Asia: the rise to power of a rapidly modernising Japan and the awakening of American interest in China had created an imbalanced system prone to conflict where costs could not be accurately predicted. St Petersburg's ability to calculate and steer its policies rationally would show whether Russia could now measure up to the demands imposed on a modern 'world power'.

The limitations on the Russian advance came from more than just the competing powers. Within a few years it became clear that they resulted no less from the internal structural weaknesses of the Empire: the autocracy provided weak leadership and was unable to weld together the conflicting ambitions of the various elites; rural Russia was devastated and impoverished, and this aggravated the nation's chronic social and political instability; finally, industrialisation had bred Witte's borrowed imperialism.

9.1 *The Concept and Reality of 'Peaceful Penetration'*

As the pioneering research of B.A. Romanov has demonstrated, Russian expansionism in the Far East was closely related to Witte's financial and economic strategy.[1] Thanks to protectionism and capital imports the grand experiment of industrialisation was now to benefit from the new resources and markets of Asia. Russian industry would have its own huge territory to exploit with all the advantages of proximity. Witte's strategy was not unrelated to his view that only by becoming a metropolis herself could Russia overcome her historic 'backwardness' and her subservient role as a colonial source of exploitable resources for the more developed powers, with the threat to national independence which that entailed.

Like no other government official before him Witte understood the economy as a category of power. For him, Russia's imperial interests were subsumed in economic modernisation, the trans-

1. Besides the works of B.A. Romanov mentioned in chap. 8, note 2, cf. the extensive survey of the history of Russian expansion in the Far East in: A. Malozemoff, *Russian Far Eastern Policy 1881–1904* (Berkeley, 1958); D.J. Dallin, *The Rise of Russia in Asia* (New Haven, 1949); see also: B.H. Sumner, 'Tsardom and Imperialism in the Far East and Middle East 1880–1914', *Proceedings of the British Academy 1941* (London, 1942). The definitive Soviet work on big power policies in the Far East before the Sino-Japanese War: A.L. Narochnitskii, *Kolonial'naya politika kapitalisticheskikh derzhav na Dal'nem Vostoke (1860–1895)* (Moscow, 1956); also the overviews in *Istoriya diplomatii* (Moscow, 1963[2]), vol. 2., pp. 209ff., 297ff., 353ff., 541ff. A careful study of Chinese reactions to Russian policy on the basis of Chinese and Russian sources can be found in the still unpublished thesis of P. M. Kuhfuß, 'O-kuo u. Li Hung-chang. Rußland in den Horizonten der chinesischen Selbststärkungs- u. Fernost-Politik der späten Ch'ing-Zeit', Tübingen, 1977; also I. C.Y. Hsü, *The Rise of Modern China*, (Oxford, 1975), pp. 406ff.; for the institutional basis of China's foreign policy see S.M. Meng, *The Tsungli Yamen. Its Organization and Functions* (Cambridge, Mass., 1962).

portation revolution and the enduring acquisition of a dominant role between Europe and Asia. A fundamental prerequisite in the Finance Minister's eyes was the construction of an immense Trans-Siberian Railway, to surpass all known projects in sheer size. This main thoroughfare would open up the untold treasures of Siberia to the Russian economy and ignite an economic boom. It would act as the conduit for dynamic policies aimed at establishing the Russian Empire as an economic power in neighbouring East Asia. Russia would become a 'large producer and consumer' in her own right, as Witte made clear, and not just a country through which international trade flowed.

Such plans to reach out toward China, Korea and Japan had a visionary aspect foreign to Witte's predecessors. Very concerned about his budget of restraint, Vyshnegradskii had agreed only very reluctantly in 1891 that work should be started on a trans-Siberian line to be commenced simultaneously in Vladivostok and western Siberia. Both the financing and the economic benefits seemed dubious to him. Witte paid little attention to such narrow-minded concerns typical of the traditional fiscal thinking of the Ministry of Finance. His modern, imperialistic style was plainly visible in his very first statement of accounts, issued in November 1892, in which rational economic thinking and extravagant irrationalism lay side by side: the railway project was an 'event of earth-shattering importance' that would introduce a new era in the history of humanity and revolutionise economic relations between states.[2]

This forecast coincided with the spirited appeal that had already been made at the Nizhnii-Novgorod Fair in 1889 when the Siberian line was being planned. At that time spokesmen for Russian business had evoked the inestimable advantages of this railway which would link 400 million Chinese and 35 million Japanese to Europe and put Russian commerce in a position to survive the 'economic war' that had broken out in the Pacific between the great powers. World trade would stream through the railway because the journey from Europe to Vladivostok and on to Shanghai would take only eighteen to twenty days, twenty-five days fewer than via the Suez Canal and fifteen days fewer than by way of the Canadian Pacific

2. Romanov, *Ocherki*, pp. 23f. For construction of the Trans-Siberian Railway see H. Tupper, *To the Great Ocean. Siberia and the Trans-Siberian Railway* (London, 1965); V.F. Borzunov, 'Istoriya sozdaniya Transsibirskoi zheleznodorozhnoi magistrali XIX–nachala XX veka', PhD thesis, MGU, Moscow, 1972; also: R.B. Valliant, 'Japan and the Trans-Siberian Railroad 1885–1905', PhD thesis, University of Hawaii, 1974.

Railway opened in 1886.[3]

These commercial considerations were very close to Witte's own calculations, but he knew that arguments stemming from the business lobby were unlikely to advance his design politically. Such individual voices carried little weight. Since the Minister was seeking a consensus within high society in St Petersburg, it is not surprising that he soon fell back on the old notion of Russia's 'historic mission' in Asia. His commentary on the petition of a Lamaist zealot, the Buryat Mongol P.A. Badmaev, is a telling example of how the Minister had to justify himself. This scheming adventurer offered, in February 1893, to incite Tibetans, Mongolians and Chinese to rebel against the Manchu dynasty and submit to the 'White Tsar'. The territory acquired would then be secured by means of a railway running deep into the Chinese interior and linked with the Trans-Siberian line. If this project went forward, Witte promised the Tsar, Russia would control the entire area between the Pacific coast and the peaks of the Himalayas, and would be master not only of Asian affairs but of European affairs as well. Choosing his words to suit Alexander III, Witte evoked the ideological ingredients of a peculiarly Russian imperialism, of Russia's 'cultural mission' guided by her own principles of Orthodoxy, Autocracy and the spirit of the Russian people, and not by western kinds of 'Europeanization'.[4]

It is hard to say whether this ideological justification expressed a firm conviction or was subtly adapted to the Tsar's powers of comprehension. The public had not been electified by expansion into Central Asia, and the idea of a Russian mission in Asia met with little support.[5] However, even altered political conditions did not deter Witte from giving his policies an ideological cast in order to fire the Tsar's imagination. The Minister may have been encouraged to engage in such excesses by the fact that Prince E. Ukhtomskii was both a personal confidant of Nicholas II and a prominent proponent of Russia's mission in Asia. The rather sober lectures given by Witte to Grand Duke Michael Aleksandrovich in 1901–2 were still not free from these views: 'Russia does not need colonialism. Her foreign policies are not only peaceful, they are cultural in the true

---

3. G. Krahmer, *Sibirien u. die Große Sibirische Eisenbahn* (Leipzig, 1897), p. 97.
4. Romanov, *Russia*, pp. 46f.; Malozemoff, pp. 48ff.
5. For the idea that Russia had a mission to fulfil in East Asia cf. also H. Gollwitzer, *Die gelbe Gefahr. Geschichte eines Schlagworts. Studien zum imperialistischen Denken* (Göttingen, 1962); N. Riasanovsky, 'Asia Through Russian Eyes', in W.S. Vucinich (ed.), *Russia and Asia* (Stanford, 1972), pp. 3–29.

sense of the word. Unlike the efforts of western European powers to subjugate the peoples of the East economically and often politically, Russia's mission must be protective and elevating.'[6] At the time of course the dangerous consequences of Russia's Far Eastern policies were already being laid bare by the crisis in Manchuria, and Witte's concept of 'pénétration pacifique' was in shambles. The Minister was constrained to moderate the megalomaniac estimates of Russian capacities which he himself had promoted and which as late as February 1903 had encouraged the otherwise rather inhibited and anxious Nicholas II to dream of the day when he would rule not just over Manchuria but over Korea, Tibet and Persia as well.[7]

The various methods which Witte used to promote his expansionist ideals serve as a reminder that from the very beginning he had to struggle to ensure that his policies triumphed over other, often hostile interests. His plans for economic imperialism competed with military, naval and certainly diplomatic ambitions and axioms. Witte had to face the fact that the Foreign Ministry and the Ministers of War and the Navy would be troubled by his projects. In addition, plans for railways and the ensuing development of territories in Russian Asia necessarily constituted massive interference in the administrative authorities of eastern Siberia. Witte therefore had obstacles to overcome on many sides, either by artful persuasion or by exploiting his increasingly powerful position.

The demands of the Far Eastern province probably created least problems for Witte. Like the Finance Minister, the Governor-General of Amur province expected that the railway would bring settlers and economic penetration of the lands he controlled as well as a counterweight to feared strong foreign influence from the Chinese and other 'foreign races' in Transbaikal and the trading centres of the Amur. The catastrophic famine of 1891–2 lent urgency to acquiring more land and settling the virgin territories of the East. A standing committee was established in late 1892 to steer construction of the railway. As the line progressed the committee planned to implant peasant villages inhabited by people from the overpopulated interior provinces every 100 versts along both sides of the track. They would be provided with land and fiscal incentives by the domanial ministry and sent into the remote areas opened up to inner colonisation by railway engineers and their labourers.[8]

6. Witte, *Vorlesungen*, 1, p. 204.
7. 'Dnevnik Kuropatkina', *KA*, 2, p. 31 (16 Feb. 1903).

Witte in the meantime had his mind on more than just peasant settlers. The Siberian railway (he thought) needed a chain of industrial workshops and public utilities in order to open up Siberia's mighty rivers and sources of raw materials and to give the line a material basis for its existence. The stimulating cumulative effect of railway construction, implantation of industry and colonisation would then seem to justify the exorbitant costs which the rapidly progressing work placed on the national treasury and the Tsar's taxable subjects after 1894.

Witte did not have any serious problems with the Governor-General of the Amur province until May 1896 when he received a concession from Li Hung-chang, confidant of the Chinese empress dowager, to build the railway to Vladivostok directly across Manchuria. The Finance Minister's critics thought this decision a 'huge historical miscalculation' and argued that the Amur and Ussuri lines should receive priority. Witte's Chinese Eastern Railway would be militarily indefensible, they said, especially since rapid 'Russification of Manchuria' was highly unlikely. Moreover, the railway could become immensely dangerous to the Russian colonisation of Transbaikal, particularly on account of the Japanese.[9]

By the mid-1890s railway and economic planning in the Far East were indeed no longer reducible to problems that could be handled in an informal conference of the Finance Ministry with the Siberian authorities. The grand project of a Trans-Siberian railway had in the meantime become a prime concern of foreign policy and it had very direct military consequences. Intervention by the 'East Asian Triple Alliance' (Russia, France and Germany) in the Sino-Japanese Treaty of Shimonoseki (1895), the ensuing defensive alliance between Russia and China in 1896 and finally the seizure of Port Arthur and Kwantung in 1897–8 confirmed how quickly Witte's railway programme could become a tool of international politics, with unforeseen complications for Russia.

In assessing the risks inherent in such international policies one must remember that Russia was involved in the Eastern Question at

---

8. D.W. Treadgold, *The Great Siberian Migration* (Princeton, 1957), pp. 108ff.; also generally: F.X. Coquin, *La Sibérie. Peuplement et immigration paysanne au dix-neuvième siècle* (Paris, 1969); B.V. Tikhonov, 'Pereselencheskaya politika tsarskogo pravitel'stva v 1892–1897 godakh', *ISSSR* (1977/1), pp. 109–20.

9. Cf. the opinion of Governor-General Dukhovskii (11 [23] Jan. 1896) in *KA* 52, pp. 83ff with Witte's reply (31 Mar. [12 Apr.] 1896, ibid., pp. 91ff.; also: S.J. Witte, *Erzwungene Aufklärungen aus Anlaß des Berichtes des Generaladjutanten Kuropatkin über den Krieg mit Japan* (Vienna, 1911), pp. 56ff.

least as intensively as in East Asia. This is not the place to delve further into the events in the Near East between 1895 and 1897 (in which the Anglo-French confrontation in the Eastern Mediterranean and North Africa played a large part).[10] Toward the end of 1896 St Petersburg found itself tempted to land in the Bosporus and prepare the way for the realisation of a traditional Russian goal in the Near East — mastery of the Straits. A plan recommended by A.I. Nelidov, Russian ambassador in Constantinople, seemed to offer Russia an opportunity to erect her very own 'Gibraltar' at the entrance to the Black Sea in the wake of intervention by the great powers in internal Turkish affairs.[11] Russia thus drew so close for a time to Salisbury's policies that her French ally became upset. France was similarly worried by Russia's tendency to accede to British desires in Egypt and by her refusal to join the Ottoman debt administration dominated by French capital.

Important in this context is the fact that both the Russian military and the Tsar were favourably disposed to a quick attack on the Bosporus and were even prepared to abandon the system of great powers if necessary. Witte alone warned of the 'harmful consequences' of such an action. When the idea was eventually abandoned it was less because of Witte's complaints than to strong opposition from Paris. In view of the Finance Minister's projects in the Far East at the time this episode would seem to indicate that his chances of permanently isolating the peaceful penetration of China from the effects of opposed military and diplomatic ambitions were slim. One year after Nelidov's plan was scuttled, the Tsar ordered that Port Arthur be taken. Besides all the immediate reasons for this step, it can also be seen as compensation for the Bosporus expedition that never happened.

One is forced to admit that such military aspects of expansionism were included from the beginning in Witte's development strategy in East Asia. Even the decision to begin construction on the Trans-Siberian Railway in March 1891 was prompted primarily by strategic and diplomatic considerations and not by commercial or demographic concerns. Since the great powers were becoming more active in the Far East, the Pacific outposts of the Empire (which had been peacefully acquired in the 1850s) had to be made defensible

10. Zürrer, *Nahostpolitik*, pp. 106–204.
11. Sources on deliberations about the Nelidov plan: *KA* 47/48, pp. 55–70; also V. Khvostov, 'Problemy zakhvata Bosfora v 90-kh godakh XIX v.', *IM* 20 (1930), pp. 100–29.

and an ice-free port annexed on the Korean coast if possible. News that the English were helping to build railways in northern China strengthened the impression that Russian holdings in the Far East were in jeopardy so long as Vladivostok was not linked to Russia's internal railway network.[12]

It is easy to see why the Sino-Japanese War for pre-eminence in Korea cast an unexpected spotlight on strategic considerations and prompted momentous decisions.[13] However, it was neither the military nor even Russian diplomats who set long-term Russian policy in the Far East: Foreign Minister Prince Lobanov, Chief of the General Staff Obruchev and Grand Admiral Aleksei Aleksandrovich were primarily concerned with the traditional confrontation with England. They advised seeking a compromise with Japan and negotiating advantageous concessions: an island off the eastern coast of Korea or an ice-free port linked to the coastal province and, if possible, a strip of land along the Manchurian border to make it easier to lay out the Siberian railway. Witte, however, turned these arguments around and won the day with a policy directed against Japan. The Japanese attack had really been directed against Russia, he said, not China. The Treaty of Shimonoseki was actually a preventive strike against the Siberian line which would henceforth require an expensive contingent of hundreds of thousands of troops to defend it. If southern Manchuria remained in Japanese hands, all Korea would soon be lost and the Mikado would make his entry into Peking. Russia should therefore do all she could to drive Japan once more from the Chinese mainland, even at the risk of an outbreak of hostilities.[14]

The danger of war implied in Witte's ultimatums turned out to be less than immediate. It was not the bombardment of Japanese ports, as the Minister had proposed, but diplomatic intervention coordinated with Paris and Berlin which forced Japan by May 1895 to vacate the Liaotung Peninsula (including Port Arthur) and content herself with Formosa and an indemnity from China. In the Moscow Protocol of 28 May (9 June) 1896, Tokyo had to agree that 'the

12. Romanov, *Ocherki*, pp. 20ff.; also the literature cited in notes 1 and 22, as well as the excellent survey of Japanese foreign policy in general in: J.W. Morley (ed.), *Japan's Foreign Policy 1868–1941. A Research Guide* (New York, 1974); for a competent survey see I. Nish, *Japanese Foreign Policy 1869–1941* (London, 1977), pp. 34ff.
13. For Russian policies on the Sino-Japanese War see the documents in: *KA* 50/51, pp. 3–53, *KA* 52, pp. 62–83.
14. Minutes of the special meeting on 30 Mar. (11 Apr.) 1895: *KA* 52, pp. 78–91; cf. Romanov, *Russia*, pp. 50ff.

fundamental integrity and independence of Korea' was inviolate and that nothing could be done in this regard which St Petersburg opposed.[15] With this return to the status quo, Japanese ambitions in Manchuria and Korea were dealt a serious blow while Russia became Peking's partner and saw no reason to reduce her sphere of activity in East Asia. However, in the long run the humiliation of Japan turned out to be a pyrrhic victory. A vehement desire for revenge prompted the Japanese to undertake a rearmament campaign which finally led to Russia's own Waterloo.[16]

Witte had insisted on buying Peking's 'friendship' at Japan's expense. Russia's self-appointed role as 'China's saviour' promised to give her an uncomfortable but useful place of privilege at the Chinese court and a foundation on which St Petersburg's programme for East Asia could develop. Witte tried to imitate the economic imperialism of the 'open door' (though he considered Russian dominance in Manchuria non-negotiable). The events of the next few years are familiar: In June 1895 the Russian national Treasury negotiated and guaranteed a loan for China supplied by Parisian banks (400 million francs at 4 per cent); with the help of this loan Peking's war indemnity to Japan was paid and the international debt administration which banks in Berlin and London were anxious to see was avoided. The financial relationship between Russia and France — their common interest within the Dual Alliance — was extended to East Asia where it met up with English and German consortiums who fairly frequently joined forces. In September 1895 the Russo-Chinese Bank was founded using French capital in the usual way. The Minister of Finance, who once more had recourse to the services of Rothstein and Prince Ukhtomskii, thus gained a flexible instrument for the long-range financing of his borrowed imperialism.[17]

Witte's efforts bore their first fruits a year later. Thanks to the funds borrowed in Paris, Witte won for the Russo-Chinese Bank a concession to build the Chinese Eastern Railway and the Russian

15. Romanov, *Russia*, pp. 102ff.; Malozemoff, pp. 87ff.; K. Krupinski, *Rußland u. Japan. Ihre Beziehungen bis zum Frieden von Portsmouth* (Königsberg, 1940), pp. 59ff.; text of the protocol: G. Krahmer, *Rußland in Ost-Asien* (Leipzig, 1899), pp. 180ff.; for a research paper: Hosoya Chihrio, 'Japan and Russia', in Morley (ed.), pp. 340ff.

16. On the Japanese armaments programme see Romanov, *Ocherki*, pp. 30ff.

17. Romanov, *Russia*, pp. 63ff.; Malozemoff, pp. 69ff.; Girault, *Emprunts russes*, pp. 305ff.; O. Crisp, 'The Russo-Chinese Bank', *SEER* 127 (1974), pp. 197–212. For the text of the loan contract of 24 June (6 July) 1895: *Russko-kitaiskie otnosheniya 1689–1916*, pp. 67ff.; Sladkovskii, *Istoriya*, pp. 422f.

railway programme set off in a momentous new direction. The lengthy negotiations were prepared by Peking's ambassador, Count Cassini, and helped along by a Russo-Chinese mutual assistance pact. Now, the infrastructure of the 'informal Empire' which the Finance Minister intended to erect in Manchuria seemed secure. A complicated financial deal, including special funds to be credited to Li Hung-chang's own privy purse, made it possible for the Russian state to acquire the majority of shares in the Chinese Eastern Railway Company created to build and maintain the line.[18]

In order to win the political approval of the Chinese government the Finance Minister pointed to Russia's altruistic friendship and her desire to protect China. Opposition within Russia was overcome with the help of a number of political, military and economic arguments: in view of the increasing international competition Russia had no other choice than to follow 'the example of her economic rivals'. The railway project would strengthen the Empire's influence and prestige, keep foreign concessionaries out of northern China, shorten the route to Vladivostok by more than 1000 versts and make it possible, in case of crisis, for Russian troops to quickly reach Manchuria, the Yellow Sea and the Peking area. Witte believed he could guarantee protection for track laid through the extra-territorial strip of land by quietly dispersing soldiers among the workforce and subsequently by making use of railway police. He roundly dismissed fears that the Chinese Eastern Railway was an 'enormous political risk', would make military occupation of Manchuria inevitable, and would provoke the division of China by the great powers.[19]

With the Russo-Chinese defensive alliance of 22 May (3 June), the railway concessions treaty of 27 August (8 September) and the company charter of 4 (16) December 1896, Witte thought he had secured Russian dominance in northern China — not by annexation and military bases but by economic penetration and courteous treatment of the Palace in Peking.[20] To him, it would be just a matter of time before Russia's railway empire in Manchuria gained a spur to a port on the Yellow Sea. In his reaction to new Chinese requests for credit in December 1897, the Minister of Finance once

18. Sino-Russian defensive alliance of 22 May (3 June) 1896: *Russko-kitaiskie otnosheniya*, pp. 73f.; concession treaty for the Chinese Eastern Railway of 27 Aug. 1896: ibid., pp. 74ff.; Sladkovskii, pp. 426ff.
19. Cf. Witte's memorandum of 31 Mar. (12 Apr.) 1896, in *KA* 52, pp. 91ff.
20. Terms of the articles of association of the Chinese Eastern Railway Company in: Krahmer, *Rußland*, pp. 207–18.

more clarified his final goals: exclusive rights throughout Manchuria and Mongolia for the construction of railways, the exploitation of natural resources and the creation of industry, as well as a railway in southern Manchuria and port facilities for Russia's warships and merchant fleet.[21]

Witte also wanted to establish an economic base to help solidify the political gains which the Russians hoped to secure in Korea at the expense of the Japanese. Since the minimal amount of trade passing over the Korean border offered few opportunities, the Minister created the necessary financial basis for further initiatives in September 1897 when a Russo-Korean Bank was established (modelled on the Russo-Chinese Bank) and a financial agent was sent to Seoul. Witte's immediate goals were to bring the administration of Korean tariffs under Russian tutelage, acquire concessions to open up gold and copper mines on the Yalu river, and generally keep the entire country open to Russian influence.[22]

There was no genuine basis for the belief that such an extensive economic empire could be accumulated without political and even military complications. Those who portray Witte as a pacifist who thought only in economic terms, fall victim to the brilliant gloss which the fallen Minister cast over the successes and failures of his days in office in the course of his skilful memoirs.[23] Only a dreamer (which Witte certainly was not) could have indulged in the vain hope that financially weak, backward Russia could have successfully modelled her East Asian policies along the lines of the 'informal' approach adopted in China primarily by the United States. It was much more likely that Witte's 'peaceful penetration' would soon become caught up in the traditional methods of establishing influence. In reality, expansion would no longer be linked to economics but to military conquest, territorial annexation and Russification — as in the case of Transcaspia. The plausibility of this assumption is indicated by actual events, from the seizure of Port Arthur in December 1897 to the Russian occupation of Manchuria in the wake of the Boxer Rebellion.

There have been many descriptions of the events which led to Russia gaining first a lease on Port Arthur and Dairen (Dalny) on 15

21. Malozemoff, p. 102.

22. Romanov, *Russia*, pp. 109ff.; Malozemoff, pp. 90ff.; cf. H. Conroy, *The Japanese Seizure of Korea, 1869–1910* (Philadelphia, 1960); for the preliminary history see: F.F. Chien, *The Opening of Korea, 1876–1885* (n.p., The Shoe String Press, 1967).

23. v. Laue, *Witte*, pp. 146ff.; Vitte, *Vospominaniya* 2, pp. 42ff., 132ff., 159ff.

(27) March 1898 and a little later, on 6 July, the sought-after concession to build the southern Manchurian line.[24] Here we shall simply look at St Petersburg's *modus operandi* and at some events which had further consequences. One of the salient features of the autocratic decision-making process was that the acquisition of these two ports and the surrounding area of Kwantung was not based on any rational plan, still less a sober calculation of the costs which would result. It was instead a reaction intended to compensate Russia for the German landing in Kiaochow. This lightning stroke in Wilhelm II's struggle for a 'place in the sun' had left Russian diplomats feeling badly outmanoeuvred,[25] and the Foreign Minister Murav'ev (not the navy), insisted on this reaction. The Russians had long hoped to gain an ice-free port which would relieve their Pacific fleet of the embarrassment of having to winter in Nagasaki, and this desire had taken on a special urgency after Shimonoseki. However, at the meeting of ministers which preceded the arrival of Russian warships in Port Arthur (14 December 1897), Vice-Admiral Tyrtov had evidently had his eyes on a base on the east coast of Korea, rather than one in an area which could be reached from Vladivostok only via the easily blockaded Straits of Tsushima. Only General Vannovskii had agreed in principle with Murav'ev's proposal to seize this territory, recently returned to China with Russian help. Vannovskii, however, was willing to leave the last word to the navy.

It is easy to see why Witte was vehemently opposed to this project. It undermined the fundamental concept behind his China policy which consisted of basing Russian influence on a special relationship with Peking. The Finance Minister feared quite rightly that St Petersburg's claims to be a friend wishing only to protect would sound hollow if the big brother to the north resorted to the same rough tactics as the other great powers. Murav'ev, on the other hand, was inclined to the Wilhelminian line of reasoning: historical experience showed that the rulers of China, like all 'eastern peoples', were impressed by sheer power and strength (*mogushchestvo i sila*), not friendship. Only those means which the

24. Romanov, *Russia*, pp. 133ff.; Malozemoff, pp. 93ff.; text of the lease: *Russko-kitaiskie otnosh.*, pp. 78ff.; Sladkovskii, pp. 430ff.

25. For the Russian documents: *KA* 58, pp. 150–5, *KA* 87, pp. 19–63; for German documents: *GP* 14/1, chap. 90. Cf. H. Altrichter, *Konstitutionalismus u. Imperialismus* (Frankfurt, 1977); A.J. Irmer, *Die Erwerbung von Kiautschou 1897–1898* (Cologne, 1930); A. Vagts, *Deutschland u. die Vereinigten Staaten in der Weltpolitik* (New York, 1935), pp. 1006ff.

Germans had 'used so successfully' in Kiaochow would work.[26] The imitative tendency which dominated Russian diplomacy was accepted so unquestioningly that Witte let himself be persuaded to undertake an attempt, as risky as it was futile, to persuade the German Kaiser to renounce a lengthy stay in Shantung.

The seizure of Port Arthur demonstrates that the Tsar and his Foreign Minister did not act simply as Witte's assistants but pursued important China policies of their own over Witte's head. One should not overestimate Witte's resistance, however, despite indications in his memoirs to the contrary.[27] He did not pursue his offer to resign and managed rather successfully to adapt to the setback which he had suffered. In any case he registered no further complaint when it became evident that his concerns would receive further attention in the ensuing negotiations with Peking and that the Siberian-Manchurian railway network would now acquire an outlet on the Yellow Sea in Kwantung. Witte had his financial agents in Peking sweeten the agreements for leases and concessions with the customary deposits into private accounts.[28]

The circumstances surrounding the creation of a Russian preserve on the southern tip of the Liaotung Peninsula make it clear that St Petersburg was not inclined to treat its Chinese ally with excessive kindness in the race for the spoils of the Middle Kingdom. In late 1897 and early 1898, Murav'ev did not hesitate to make it known in Berlin that Russia considered not only Chinese Turkistan and 'toute la Mantchourie' but also the province of Chihli as a 'sphére d'action exclusive' in which it would tolerate no outside political influence.[29] Thus for the first time a claim was made on Peking and Tientsin; a daring move which prompted the German Kaiser to match this 'tasty bite' with a sphere of interest of his own: 'Shantung including the Yellow River'.[30] More than anything, however, the Russian coup and the ambitions it exposed could not fail to startle the British Government and make it think in terms of an Anglo-Japanese *rapprochement*. The usually hesitant Salisbury re-

26. Foreign Minister Murav'ev to Nicholas II, 11 (23) Nov. 1897, in *KA* 52, pp. 103–08.
27. Vitte, *Vospominaniya* 2, pp. 132–48.
28. Excerpts from the text in Krahmer, *Rußland*, pp. 19f.
29. 'Russisches Promemoria 2.1.1898', *GP* 14/1, pp. 134f.
30. A note of Bülow's, 2 Jan. 1898, ibid., p. 136. On German interests see: J.E. Schrecker, *Imperialism and Chinese Nationalism. Germany in Shantung* (Cambridge, Mass., 1971); V. Schmidt, *Die deutsche Eisenbahnpolitik in Shantung, 1898–1914. Ein Beitrag zur Geschichte des deutschen Imperialismus in China* (Wiesbaden, 1976).

sponded with unwonted alacrity in order to preserve the much vaunted 'European balance in Chinese waters'. The Japanese abandoned Weihaiwei (not without a prior understanding with London) and the British promptly occupied it.[31]

One wonders why the autocracy was so confident that it could not only lay claim to an unlimited expansion of its zone of influence in the Far East but also take concrete steps in this direction. Such a zone could not be secured economically or militarily so long as Russia's trade with China was minimal, her Pacific fleet unimpressive and the future path of her railway not even explored. The promise inherent in Russia's strategically advantageous position would have to wait for the future. Not only in foreign capitals did the prophylactic leap to Port Arthur and Dairen leave the impression that Russia was beginning to overextend herself by precipitous and ill-considered actions — St Petersburg also apparently understood that it was time to send out signals (especially to Tokyo and London) that moderation would be exercised.[32]

This may be the reason why Russian diplomats under Murav'ev set out in the spring of 1898 to defuse the Russo-Japanese confrontation in Korea. The Russo-Korean Bank which had just been founded was liquidated, Russian military and financial advisers were withdrawn from Seoul, and Japanese commercial and industrial interests were recognised explicitly in the Nishi-Rosen agreement of 25 April 1898. Thus considerable good-will was shown to Tokyo although St Petersburg did not accept Japanese offers to award Manchuria to Russia while taking Korea for Japan.[33] The next year an opportunity arose to arrive at a similarly vague *modus vivendi* with the English. A Russo-British agreement of 28 April 1899 dissipated the autocracy's fear that its old rival would sweep over the Great Wall of China. St Petersburg promised in return to curb the ambitions of the Russo-Chinese Bank and respect British claims on the Yangtse valley.[34] Witte, however, was very reluctant to retreat. He was concerned about the confidence of his French creditors, while the success of the bank he directed led him to

---

31. L.K. Young, *British Policy in China 1895–1902* (Oxford, 1969), pp. 69ff.; I. N. Nish, *The Anglo-Japanese Alliance. The Diplomacy of the Two Island Empires 1894–1907* (London, 1966), pp. 53ff.; cf. the notes of the British ambassador to Japan, Sir E. Satow (1895–1900): G.A. Lensen, *Korea and Manchuria Between Russia and Japan 1897–1904* (Tallahassee, Flo., 1966).
32. For the following see: Romanov, *Russia*, pp. 151ff.; Malozemoff, pp. 109ff.
33. Krupinski, pp. 74ff.; text of the treaty in Krahmer, *Russia*, pp. 185f.
34. A Popov, 'Anglo-Russkoe soglashenie o razdele Kitaya 1899 g.', *KA* 25, pp. 111–34; L.K. Young, pp. 93ff.; text: *Sbornik dogovorov*, pp. 315ff.

believe that it could compete effectively in Chinese exports and on the Shanghai silver market with the very efficient Hongkong and Shanghai Banking Corporation.[35] The widespread desire in St Petersburg for a period in which to extend Russian power without outside interference is plainly evident in Russia's acceptance of a concession for the Shankaikwan-Hsinmintun railway that placed Peking's connection to southern Manchuria into British hands.

The agreements with Japan and England also show that St Petersburg wished to concentrate on cutting off its 'Informal Empire' in Manchuria for a time from international economic competition. In comparison with the other great powers (especially England and Germany) 'Russian trade was nil'[36] with East Asia, and St Petersburg was forced to insist most stubbornly on the exclusivity of its zone. In September 1899 American policy under John Hay became to persuade the great powers to agree to the 'open door' principle in China in order to keep markets open to American economic imperialism. Russian diplomats contented themselves with paying ambiguous lip service to this idea and pointing to the free port of Dairen.[37] This had been very adroitly declared *porto franco* because the Russians could not obtain sufficient shipments from home to build up their position in Manchuria and were consequently forced to rely on direct imports.

St Petersburg had sought the agreements of 1898 and 1899 in order to lessen the risk of conflict with Japan and England. However, after Port Arthur was seized, the feeling began to spread that the divine peace evoked up by the Tsar's disarmament proposals at the Hague was less likely in the near future than a passage of arms, especially with 'apes who behave like Europeans'.[38] In order to convey the extent of the dangers which the Empire faced during the next few years, I shall return now to Russia's internal problems.

Expansion as far as the Great Wall of China and the Gulf of

35. E. Agahd, *Großbanken u. Weltmarkt* (Berlin, 1914), pp. 124ff.
36. *GP* 14/1, p. 141. For the extent of Russian trade with China see below.
37. For American policies toward China see: H.U. Wehler, *Der Aufstieg des amerikanischen Imperialismus. Studien zur Entwicklung des Imperium Americanum 1865–1900* (Göttingen, 1974), pp. 259ff.; T.J. McCormick, *China Market, America's Quest for Informal Empire 1893–1901* (Chicago, 1967); M.B. Young, *The Rhetoric of Empire. American China Policy, 1895–1901* (Cambridge, Mass., 1968); M. H. Hunt, *Frontier Defense and the Open Door. Manchuria in Chinese-American Relations 1895–1911* (New Haven, 1973); E.H. Zabriskie, *American-Russian Rivalry in the Far East. A Study in Diplomacy and Power Politics, 1895–1914* (Philadelphia, 1946); Chang Chung-tung, *China's Response to the Open Door, 1898–1906* (Michigan State Univ., 1973).
38. Alexander III's wording (Dec. 1891) in *Dnevnik Lamzdorfa*, 2, p. 216.

Chihli was risky, and its consequences had not been adequately considered. Witte's financial and economic policy came under additional pressure, especially because of the increased pace at which Far Eastern railways had to be built and the military's insistence, not without reason, on increases in the defence budget. In the year in which Port Arthur was seized, the naval chiefs also succeeded in extracting from the Finance Minister an expensive build-up of the fleet (for which there was some justification in view of Japanese rearmament). The demands of Kuropatkin, the new Minister of War, were no less insistent than those of the navy. To make matters worse, international capital markets proved unusually reluctant at this time to accede to St Petersburg's requests for loans. The enquiries made by Murav'ev, Kuropatkin and Witte in Paris in the autumn of 1898 were not promising, and St Petersburg was also put on notice that France did not wish to see its treaty obligations to Russia extended into East Asia.[39]

Russian policy in Asia around the turn of the century was by no means exhausted by the grand schemes in Manchuria. Far from being supplanted by Far Eastern endeavours, Russia's traditional interests in Central Asia, Persia and Ottoman Turkey were instead stimulated. The opportunities detected by St Petersburg can be seen in a report from the Foreign Minister approved by the Tsar in January 1900.[40] Murav'ev recommended that as much pressure as possible be put on the British Empire, already in difficulty because of the Boer War. In Central Asia this should be done by entering into diplomatic relations with Kabul and strengthening Russia's military position in Turkistan and Transcaspia (it was assumed that Britain's authority over 'the freedom-loving tribes of India' was weakening). In Persia, Russia should strengthen her trade and economic position and use a loan to extract a commitment from the Shah not to grant railway concessions to non-Russian candidates. At the same time exploration by Russian engineers should be accelerated and the resulting plans prepared for concessions on Persian railways.[41] The Sultan should also be urged not to permit railways near the Black Sea coast, and Russia should insist that no Turkish fortifications be built on the Bosporus.

Murav'ev's ministerial colleagues were far from unanimous in

39. Anan'ich, *Rossiya*, p. 191.
40. *KA* 18, pp. 4–18.
41. For Persian policies see: Kazemzadeh, *Russia*, pp. 302ff.; Ananyich, *Rossiiskoe samoderzhavie*, pp. 18ff.

their response to this plan.[42] The Minister of War and the Navy Chief deeply regretted that the existing situation made a surprise military action aimed at conquest (*zakhvat*) of the Bosporus impossible. However, the armaments and operational planning necessary to bring this traditional goal within reach should not, they believed, be neglected. Plans were considered to fall back on the 'art of diplomacy' in order to gain control of the Straits — much in the way Kwantung had been acquired — although such plans were immediately dismissed by Murav'ev as illusory. Both Kuropatkin and Admiral Tyrtov found good reason in this catalogue of foreign projects for new financial demands of their own. Their rationale alone meant that Witte was forced to urge great caution in his presentation and point out Russia's limitations. Above all he warned against provoking 'wealthy England' and creating a crushing burden on the national Treasury and the people's ability to pay taxes. Witte begged the ministers to consider the huge sums which would be necessary in order to provide Russia's East Asian positions with military and transport protection. He failed to mention that he himself had initiated Russia's costly entry into world imperialism.

Military leaders were also not immune from the fear that, in vastly extending her role in Asia, Russia might overextend herself, even though she aimed at preserving the peace. Even before the Boxer Rebellion and its associated international consequences put Russian policy through the severest of tests, Kuropatkin had analysed in detail the general principles and limitations of Russian policy.[43] His exposé expressed grave concern that the need to reinforce Russia's advances in East Asia would not only perpetuate her military inferiority *vis-à-vis* Germany and Austria but also increase that inferiority in a most dangerous way.[44] According to Kuropatkin the most important task of military policy was to overcome Russia's weakness on her western frontiers. The new naval programme, which promised to surpass Japanese efforts by 1903, should not under any circumstances be at the expense of the army; the inevitable increase in troop levels in the Far East should no longer detract from Russia's ability to defend her European

42. *KA* 18, pp. 18ff.
43. Extensive excerpts from the War Minister's memorandum (14 [27] Mar. 1900) in: *General Kuropatkin, Memoiren. Die Lehren des Russisch-Japanischen Krieges* (Berlin, 1909), pp. 47ff. *passim.*
44. Kuropatkin, pp. 53ff., 79, 106.

borders. Behind these warnings stood the fact that Witte had been prepared to grant an increase of only 160 million rubles in special funds in the five-year budget of the War Ministry for 1899 to 1902 and not the 565 million which Kuropatkin considered essential if Russia's borders and her positions in East Asia were to be defended.[45] Russia's dire financial straits revealed once again that the Empire remained in a position of continual and increasing overextension of resources as a result of its own international policies and those of foreign governments.

Under the circumstances the Minister of War recommended 'extreme caution in our foreign relations'. In the Far East this meant: renouncing the annexation of Manchuria so that eastern Siberia could be preserved as a land for future Russian settlement and saved from submersion beneath 'the surging waves of the yellow race'; renouncing any railway projects south of the Great Wall and particularly in the Yangtse valley; securing influence by extending the Manchurian railways as quickly as possible and building up trade and economic relations; undermining local provincial authorities and closing northern China to foreign advisors. Kuropatkin's call for self-restraint was related above all to the looming conflict with Japan. He recommended caution in Korea in order to avoid such a conflict — at least so long as the Amur and Kwantung areas were insufficiently defended and the Russian fleet remained inferior to the Japanese. It would take six or seven years, the Minister thought, before Russia could think of expelling the Japanese from East Asian waters (hopefully with the help of the Germans, French and British) and creating a 'weak, independent Korea under our protectorate'.[46]

These views brought Kuropatkin very close to Witte, although the two ministers continued to disagree about financial priorities. The Minister of War did not take a back seat in his high hopes for the future. Russia's international policy in the twentieth century would not aim at border amendments and annexations, but 'systematic, unflinching efforts at gradual, peaceful conquest' of the Asiatic periphery. Nor did he shrink from sweeping visions of the tasks that would occupy 'future generations' — furthering Russian preeminence through the peaceful conquest not only of Persia, northern China and Korea but also the approaches to the Black Sea and to

45. Ibid., pp. 119ff.
46. Ibid., pp. 74f., 124.

the Indian and Pacific Oceans. 'When Russia has in her hands a railway between the Baltic Sea and the Pacific Ocean, and when she reaches her feelers down to the Bosporus and on to the Indian and Pacific Oceans, then with her inexhaustible supply of natural resources she will offer all the powers of the world awesome economic competition.'[47]

Such remarks serve as a reminder that the Russian military was no stranger to modern, imperialist lines of thought and argument. Kuropatkin did not disagree fundamentally with Witte's dictum that Russia had to assert herself as a 'metropolis' despite of her backwardness. The Finance Minister was of course inclined to measure Russia's backwardness in terms of production and capital reserves rather than cruiser tonnages, numbers of automatic weapons and military strength. The report which he presented to the Tsar in February 1900 was no less depressing than Kuropatkin's warning about the military superiority of Russia's presumed opponents. Despite an extraordinary rate of industrial growth Russia had not been able to make up the developmental advantage of the industrialised states. By 1898 per capita production of pig-iron had reached 1.04 poods, but Great Britain produced the equivalent of 13.1 poods, the United States 9.8 poods, Belgium 9.0 poods, Germany 8.1 poods and France 3.06 poods. The discrepancy was even greater so far as coal was concerned: Russia produced 5.8 poods per capita, while Great Britain produced 311.7 poods, Belgium 204 poods, the United States 162.4 poods, Germany 143.8 poods and France 50.7 poods. Russia's enormous disadvantage was similarly apparent in every other branch of manufacturing. The volume of foreign trade in Russia reached only 10 rubles per capita, compared with 75 rubles in France and Germany and 164 rubles in Great Britain.[48]

Witte concluded from these figures that it was essential to speed up the rate of industrial expansion as much as possible. Russia's economic independence had finally to be secured if she was to fulfil her political tasks in the world.

International competition will not wait. If energetic measures are not taken now to enable our industry over the next decades to produce goods which cover Russia's needs and those of the Asiatic countries which are or will be brought under our influence, then rapidly expanding foreign

47. Ibid., pp. 77f.
48. Report of the Finance Minister (Feb. 1900) in: *IM* 2/3 (1935), pp. 131ff.

industries will break through our tariff barriers and penetrate our home-land like the Asiatic countries mentioned. Those foreign industries will then gradually pave the way for even more dangerous foreign political influences, because mother countries now assert their rule over colonies much more by force of trade than force of arms. Your Majesty's humble servant fears that the slow growth of Russian industry could make it more difficult for your Majesty to fulfil the great political tasks that await you, that the continuing industrial captivity [*plenenie*] of the Russian people will sap its political strength, and that insufficient economic development could engender both political and cultural backwardness.[49]

Witte clearly knew in his own mind that Russia could not yet compete with the imperialist powers. The Foreign Minister, Finance Minister and Minister of War all wished to avoid conflict (although for different reasons), and they were prepared to compromise, as evidenced by the agreements with Japan and England. Nevertheless, one must not forget that the Russian desire to be a world power had not diminished and that partial retreats were never understood as being final. The long-term project of 'peaceful conquest' had no limits. Behind the notion of 'open door' policies (which Witte supported in China in so far as they did not threaten Russia's own sphere of influence) lay an expansionary drive just as virulent as that exhibited by the American State Department in the declarations of principle it had been announcing to the world since 1899.

There was a great difference, however, between Russian imperialism and the imperialism of the great industrial and commercial powers. Unlike the case of the United States, a chasm separated Russian pretensions and capabilities. In Russia, expansion was an expression of economic weakness, not exuberant strength. It resulted in part from a compensatory psychological need to at least appear to be a great national power, and this did not enhance St Petersburg's ability to judge the limits of Russian capabilities in the real world. Russian policies in Asia also led to the creation of zones of influence territorially contiguous with the Empire. The construction of railways in Manchuria tended to create *de facto* integration of Russia's northern Chinese colony within the continental Empire. Therefore, if foreign powers erupted into this Russian zone, the territorial integrity of the Empire itself was threatened. This situation, together with Russia's general backwardness, helps one to understand the attitudes, fluctuating between fear and extravagant

49. Ibid., p. 133.

ambition, which underlay Russian policy in East Asia.

9.2   *From the Boxer Rebellion to the Russo-Japanese War*

The Boxer Rebellion (the course of which will not be related here) made the extravagance of Russian expansionism clear to all.[50] For St Petersburg, the problems raised by rebellion against the 'foreign devils' could obviously not be reduced to how best to relieve the besieged embassy quarter in Peking. Witte's entire colonisation effort was imperilled when the Boxers, supported by regular troops, attacked the Russians in the summer of 1900. The Finance Minister had originally hoped to prevent the destruction of railway areas in northern China with the help of the contingent of protective troops under his command. However, his hopes were soon dashed when insurrection swept across Manchuria as far as the Amur. Almost the entire Chinese Eastern Railway with the exception of the junction at Harbin was lost as well as a large part of the southern railway including Mukden. By the autumn of 1900 about 170,000 Russian troops had been sent to pacify the area. Manchuria was thus occupied by the greatest military force ever sent from Europe to the Far East. Only a handful of Russian batallions, which mopped up in the province of Chihli and in the coastal areas after General Linevich had captured Peking, were ever assigned to the allied supreme commander, Count Waldersee.

Witte, seeing his projects in East Asia in extreme danger, insisted that Russia's policies toward China be de-coupled as quickly as possible from the rigid European alliance of convenience. His grievances about the brutal Russian military regime in Manchuria merely described what had happened as a consequence of his own policies.[51] Vice-Admiral E.I. Alekseev extracted virtually unlimited power of command from the Chinese governor of Mukden late in 1900,[52] and St Petersburg then focused on the negotiation of

50. On the Boxer Rebellion see Chester C. T'an, *The Boxer Catastrophe* (New York, 1955); V.C. Purcell, *The Boxer Uprising* (Cambridge, 1963); Fan Wŏn-lan, pp. 447ff.; G.A. Lensen, *The Russo-Chinese War* (Tallahassee, 1967); Russian diplomatic documents in *KA* 14, pp. 8–49; for the influence of Russian imperialism on Chinese reform movements see: D.C. Price, *Russia and the Roots of the Chinese Revolution 1896–1911* (Cambridge, Mass., 1974), pp. 64ff., 164ff.

51. Cf. Witte's letters to the Minister of the Interior, D.S. Sipyagin (1900/01), in *KA* 18, pp. 30–48; for the Finance Minister's attitude to the Boxer Rebellion see also: 'Dnevnik Polovtsova', *KA* 46, pp. 129ff. (13 Aug. 1900).

52. Wording of the agreement in Romanov, *Russia*, pp. 427f.; cf. as well L.K. Young, pp. 269ff.

binding guarantees in separate discussions with the central government in Peking. It was hoped that Witte's old partner, Li Hung-
chang, would prove amenable. Beneath the cover of diplomatic notes
which paid lip service to the integrity of the Chinese Empire,
St Petersburg intended to sue for far more than a mere return to the
status quo ante. The proposed treaty, approved by Witte, Kuropatkin and the new Foreign Minister, Lamzdorff, at the end of
January 1901, linked the continuing presence of Russian troops not
only to the restoration of peace and security but also to an array of
unspecified reparations that would widen the opportunities of the
Russian government, the Chinese Eastern Railway Company and
the Russo-Chinese Bank. Until the railway was laid and regular
trains were running, Chinese troops would be excluded from Manchuria; local authorities and unarmed local police would serve at the
pleasure of the occupying power. Beyond Manchuria in Mongolia
and Sinkiang, Russia also demanded exclusive rights to railway
concessions, exploitation of raw materials, the creation of industry,
as well as an agreement that a branch line be built 'in the direction of
Peking'.[53]

The other powers in China watched the Russian regime in Manchuria with growing disquiet. They all considered the Russian
programme presumptuous and likely to stir up conflict. The negotiations with Li did not progress, and London and Tokyo moved
closer together in their attempts to check Russian imperialism.
St Petersburg meanwhile vastly overestimated Russia's strength and
did nothing to appease the Japanese. Russian arrogance oozed from
every line of the conditions for a Korean treaty presented to the
Japanese statesman Ito in November 1901. No reasonable exchange
was offered along the lines of Korea for Manchuria; instead, Russian
freedom of action would be total in northern China while the
Japanese would be subjected to restrictions in Korea.[54] The Russians also considered it self-evident that once their railway and
rearmament campaign had been completed, 'weak, independent
Korea' would become a protectorate of the Russian Empire.

Japan responded at the end of January 1902 with a carefully
prepared alliance with Great Britain, which suddenly underscored

---

53. Ibid., pp. 209ff.; Krupinski, p. 94.
54. Romanov, *Russia*, pp. 236f.; Malozemoff, pp. 171f. For Russo-Japanese
relations in 1900–01, see the diplomatic correspondence in *KA* 63, pp. 7–54; for the
negotiations with Ito in St Petersburg, see ibid., pp. 44f.; for Japanese policies: Nish,
The Anglo-Japanese Alliance, pp. 196ff.

Russia's isolation.[55] The anxiety induced by this treaty forced the Russian government to climb down from the slender branch of imperialist illusion and prepare to compromise. St Petersburg was also forced to be more realistic because Germany was not prepared to go beyond assurances of neutrality; the United States supported Chinese resistance and protested against Russian claims to monopoly rights; and most important, Russia's French ally was interested at the time in seeking a *rapprochement* with London and made no effort to promise Russia effective help. The Franco-Russian declarations of March 1902 established the principles which France wished to see underlying St Petersburg's policies: independence for China and Korea and open door for all nations in the region.[56] The treaty which Russian diplomats concluded with China on 26 March (8 April) 1902 seemed to follow these principles. Russia agreed to evacuate Manchuria in three stages within eighteen months if this was not prevented by new rebellions or the actions of other powers.[57] It was already doubtful at the time, however, whether this promise would be kept.

In order to understand why Russian policy-makers proved unable, in the next two years, to continue along the path of sober compromise, one must re-examine the economic weakness of Witte's Far Eastern empire. The Finance Minister had wagered that opening the East Asian frontiers would so stimulate economic development in Russia that the industrial expansion which the state had fostered would finally prove self-propelling — thanks to the huge markets, the exploitation of rich deposits of raw materials and the re-routing of inter-continental trade through Russian treaty ports and railways. During the years of economic growth Witte had succeeded in making this vision seem so credible that his projects won the approval of the Tsar and the interest of foreign investors. Witte benefitted especially from the fact that his concept did not seem very different than the autocracy's traditional imperial principles and seemed to further the ambitions of Russian policy in the Far East. However, the Finance Minister had only been able to justify the

55. Nish, pp. 204ff., 216ff.; L.K. Young, pp. 295ff.; G. Monge, *Ursachen u. Entstehung der englisch-französischen Entente 1900–1907* (Seeheim, 1969), pp. 57ff.
56. *Sbornik dogovorov*, pp. 322f.; German text of the declaration in C.V. Zepelin, *Der Ferne Osten* (vol. 1, Berlin, 1907), pp. 38f. For the French position see P. Renouvin, *La question d'Extrême Orient* (Paris, 1946), pp. 214f.; C. Andrew, *Théophile Delcassè and the Making of the Entente Cordiale 1898–1905* (London, 1968), pp. 237f. *passim*.
57. Malozemoff, p. 175; text of the Manchurian agreement in *Russko-kit. otnosh.*, pp. 91ff.; Sladkovskii, pp. 435ff.

costs of his enormous plan by promising future profits and by identifying his project with Russia's diplomatic and strategic interests.

According to Witte's own calculations, between 1897 and 1902 state expenditures for the Far East reached the impressive sum of 1,141 million rubles, a total barely less than the entire state budget of 1903 (1,296 million rubles). Receipts from tariffs and from railway and ship freightages covered only about one-tenth of the amount required. If the payments on interest and principal of state loans (1903: 289 million rubles) are added to the annual sums required by Russian policies in the Far East, the resulting figure is roughly equivalent to the annual budget allotted to war and the navy (1903: 456 million).[58] The vast amounts of money involved reveal why the financing of Russian policy in East Asia made Witte politically more and more vulnerable when the pressure began to mount following the economic depression which had been spreading since the turn of the century. Everyone realised with growing alarm that for the foreseeable future, Russia could not escape the crushing costs of the Finance Minister's projects in the Far East.

Witte himself had to admit that for the most part only speculators had been attracted by the great opportunities for the Russian economy which he had foreseen in northern China. As the dubious activities of the Bezobrazov group showed, the most attractive plans for concessions could not be brought to fruition without massive state aid, even when they enjoyed the personal approval of the Tsar and investments from his private purse. Bezobrazov had hoped to use an East Asian Company, together with timber concessions on the Tumen and Yalu rivers, to subvert Witte's railway and banking monopoly in the Far East, but he did not get very far.[59] It quickly became apparent that Russia's northern Chinese sphere of influence was far from an inexhaustible market for Russian exports. Apart from vodka and tobacco, most wares in Manchurian cities came from Europe and America, primarily by way of Chinese middlemen. The materials to develop Port Arthur and Dairen came for the most part from Japan and other foreign suppliers, not Russia. The same is true of equipment for the Manchurian railways. Finally, official trade statistics reveal that, apart from Kwantung and the railway strip, the 'economic conquest' of China never occurred.

58. Malozemoff, pp. 188f.
59. For the interest group centred on A.M. Bezobrazov, the Secretary of State at the time, see: Romanov, *Russia*, pp. 267ff.; Malozemoff, pp. 177ff.; J.A. White, *The Diplomacy of the Russo-Japanese War* (Princeton, 1964), pp. 31ff.; Vitte, *Vospominaniya* 2, pp. 238ff.

By the time of the war with Japan, trade between Russia and China (including Sinkiang) had grown only slightly. The total value of Russian exports to her eastern neighbour stood at only 5,047 million rubles in 1895. This figure had hardly increased by 1900 (6,702 million) and did not spiral upwards until Russia occupied Manchuria and her army needed to be maintained (1902: 9,315 million rubles, 1903: 22,441 million). Russia had always run a large deficit in the balance of trade between the two countries, and this continued. At the turn of the century, about half of China's tea exports went to Russia. The total value of Chinese exports to Russia between 1895 and 1903 rose from 41,567 million rubles to 56,498 million rubles.[60]

Witte set his tariff policies with the intention of attracting transcontinental shipments of freight onto the Chinese Eastern Railway, opened in 1901. However, the railways faced stiff competition from steamship lines, such as Norddeutscher Lloyd, which could offer much lower rates. By 1903 the railway had only acquired about half the Chinese tea trade (to the extent that it was being shipped at all over the old caravan route to Kyakhta).[61] Early in 1901 the free port of Vladivostok was closed, and the effects point to how dubious the Finance Minister's tariff measures really were. The inclusion of Transbaikal within Russia's protective tariff system (a measure Witte took in order to promote Dairen, which he favoured) crippled private initiative in the Russian Far East and almost destroyed the east Siberian branches of the Russo-Chinese Bank.

Financial colonisation now shifted to northern China and created hectic activity in Harbin (Manchuria) where speculators hoped to earn spectacular profits thanks to orders from the railway and the army of occupation.[62] However, Russian industry in Manchuria did not strike deep roots, with the exception of some mills that flourished thanks to continuing Chinese regulations which forbade the export of wheat. Witte founded a Manchurian Mining Company to block non-Russian interests, but it failed to survive the planning stage. Wherever Russian commerce flourished with China before the war, it was based not on strong private initiative but on financial and military intervention by the state (which further hindered colonisation in eastern Siberia). By 1904 private Russian investment in Manchuria had still not exceeded 15 million rubles, while con-

60. Figures cited in Sladkovskii, pp. 337–43.
61. Malozemoff, pp. 186ff.; White, pp. 11ff.
62. Agahd, *Großbanken*, pp. 124–37.

struction of the Chinese Eastern Railway and supplies for Port Arthur and Dairen had cost almost 500 million.[63] This gave Witte yet another reason to insist on exclusive rights within Manchuria, Mongolia and Sinkiang. Here too superior competition had to be kept out and territories secured (as had happened on a smaller scale in Persia) so that the state's financial investments would at least appear to have been justified from an economic point of view. Any thought of profitability had to be left to an uncertain future.

As the concept of peaceful penetration appeared less and less viable, Russian efforts in northern China were increasingly exposed as an expression not of commercial interests but of the imperial self-image of political élites, the norms of international prestige, the strategic interests of the military, and the ideology of *kul'turtregerstvo* which helped dampen a rising sense of frustration and anxiety. St Petersburg's policy in East Asia finally reverted to traditional style alliances and military agreements as a result of the international tensions following the occupation of Manchuria — in particular the danger that Russia and Japan would come to blows. When it became apparent in 1903 that the Chinese Government was no longer prepared to offer preferential treatment in return for the complete evacuation of the occupied provinces, Russia's policies in China became an appendage of her conflict with Japan.

Korea occupied centre stage on the eve of the war because of the unsolved problem in Manchuria and the laxity of the decision-making process in St Petersburg. Every weakening of Russia's position in northern China endangered Port Arthur and increased Russia's interest in keeping Japan out of northern Korea at least. After the first phase of evacuation had been completed in October 1902, St Petersburg tried in vain to arrive at an agreement with Peking on new arrangements which would solidify Russia's position in Manchuria.[64] After a series of internal conferences, the course of which reflected the government's lack of direction, the autocracy finally decided in April 1903 to leave the troops where they were until China decided to accede to Russia's wishes. The Russian proposals were modified once more in September before Peking, encouraged by the other powers, abruptly rejected them. Russia then found herself in an untenable international position. To make matters worse, St Petersburg proved incapable of formulating a clear programme to guide Russian actions in Manchuria and to

63. Sladkovskii, p. 333.
64. For what follows see Romanov, *Russia*, pp. 292ff.

respond to the one problem that now dwarfed all others — the Japanese rival.

No one was able to mould the various opinions within the autocracy into a well-considered plan for negotiations with the Japanese. In April 1903 the Tsar finally decided simply to limit Bezobrazov's self-glorifying agitation between the Yalu and Kwantung, which was alarming the Japanese and undermining Witte's full authority. Nicholas also approved the sending of Kuropatkin to Tokyo in June, but all the Minister of War could do was demonstrate that Russia had no substantial compromise to offer. Foreign Minister Lamzdorff was, as always, concerned but unable to rally support around a general plan. Witte, whose influence was waning, returned from a trip to the Far East inclined to think that Russian troops should be withdrawn from Manchuria and the defence of Russian property assigned to the railway police whose numbers would be increased to 25,000. Kuropatkin proposed that Russia prepare for the approaching conflict by renouncing, if possible, Kwantung and the Southern Manchurian Railway and preparing to annex the northern provinces in order to improve her strategic position. The leadership of the navy and the Far Eastern command in Port Arthur under Admiral Alekseev were content to vastly overestimate its own strength and argue that a Japanese landing in Korea should not be tolerated.[65]

When Tokyo presented precisely formulated demands in August 1903 which would have compelled St Petersburg to confirm the integrity of China and recognise Japanese domination of Korea,[66] Russian policy-makers were extremely disorganised and unable to take decisions. Nicholas II was in the process of freeing himself from the dominant influence of Witte in order to yield to the revolt which had been gathering steam for about a year around Bezobrazov, his uncle Grand Admiral Aleksei Aleksandrovich, and Minister of the Interior Pleve. On the Tsar's orders, a Far Eastern governorship was created on 1(14) August under Admiral Alekseev in Port Arthur, a step which deprived both Witte and Kuropatkin of all direct authority in the Far Eastern area of crisis and even involved the governor in diplomatic relations with Japan.[67] Two weeks later

---

65. White, pp. 50ff. Cf. 'Dnevnik Kuropatkina' (17 Nov 1902 to 7 Feb. 1904), *KA* 2, pp. 6–117; also the excerpts from the War Minister's memorandum of 25 Nov. 1903 on the Manchurian question in: Kuropatkin, *Memoiren*, pp. 155ff., 173ff.
66. White, pp. 102ff., 351.
67. Text of the Tsar's edict in Zepelin, *Der Ferne Osten*, 1, p. 44.

Nicholas offered the deeply offended Finance Minister the power-less honourary position of President of the Council of Ministers, and appointed the ailing E.D. Pleske, a banker with no political reputation, as the new Minister of Finance. The triumvirate of Witte, Lamzdorff and Kuropatkin, which had proved reasonably capable of arriving at a consensus and of taking decisions, was no more. In Japan, the impression grew that Russia had determined on a collision course.

The new direct relationship between the Tsar and his representa-tive in the Far East dangerously increased the structural weaknesses within the autocratic leadership. Nobody expected that the Tsar, personally inclined to react by denial, would be able to manage the East Asian conflict through his 'personal rule'. The decision-making process disintegrated into a confused system of consultation and communication in which the various personalities and institutions involved impeded one another. At this time of great political tension the Tsar spent weeks visiting his relatives in Hesse. Lamzdorff required almost eight weeks to negotiate Russia's first answer to the Japanese proposals and forward them to Tokyo by way of Port Arthur. Alekseev's regime in Kwantung and along the Yalu river was as dilettantish as it was incontrollable, and it helped aggravate the already strong suspicions of the Japanese. This lack of direction in Russian policy was partly based on the illusion that St Petersburg could play for time in its confrontation with Japan. In addition, Japanese strength and determination were vastly underestimated. Nicholas fooled himself into believing that he could influence Japanese policy simply by voicing the standard claim that he as Tsar did not want war.[68]

This is not the place to describe in detail the four exchanges of notes between August 1903 and January 1904 which preceded the Japanese attack on the Russian fleet in Port Arthur.[69] St Peters-burg's negotiators were fixated on the illusory hope that Russia could maintain all her rights in Manchuria while limiting Japan's freedom of movement in Korea by precise stipulations. Tokyo insisted more and more bluntly that the integrity of the Chinese Empire had to be guaranteed and that Japan had to be granted ac-cess to the Russian sphere of influence. Kuropatkin, meanwhile,

68. 'Dnevnik Kuropatkina', *KA* 2, pp. 40 (22 Mar. 1903), pp. 77f. (14 Oct. 1903), 80 (28 Oct. 1903); for Russia's underestimation of Japanese war readiness see the excerpts from the Russian press in Zepelin, *Der Ferne Osten* 1, pp. 64f.
69. Wording of the notes: White, pp. 362ff., Romanov, *Ocherki*, pp. 235ff.

steadfastly maintained that northern Korea (as far as the thirty-ninth parallel) must be neutralised, a demand which the Japanese stubbornly rejected and which the Russians did not apparently drop until the order for the torpedo attack on Port Arthur had already been given.[70] In its final diplomatic response on 3 February 1904 St Petersburg refused to satisfy the fundamental Japanese demand that Russia 'respect the independence and territorial integrity of the Chinese . . . Empire'.

Taken by themselves it is hard to see how St Petersburg's counter-proposals could have motivated the Japanese to go to war. What did probably provoke the decision to strike a massive preventive blow was probably the evasions and delays which were typical of St Petersburg's style of negotiation. The Japanese 'war party' feared, not without reason, that it would be totally impossible to force the Russians to make concessions when their railway by Lake Baikal had been completed and their fleet further strengthened.[71] It is not easy to determine accurately to what extent the autocracy's behaviour toward the Japanese was based on calculation and to what extent it can be ascribed simply to the astonishing lack of direction in the Russian decision-making process. Sometimes 'firmness' was thought best to preserve the peace, sometimes St Petersburg simply trusted that there would be no war because Russia did not want it and Japan had reason to fear it. Russian analysis of the situation did not extend far beyond the unhelpful observation that 'time is Russia's best ally' because 'every year makes us stronger'.[72] The Russians also took comfort from the thought that Tokyo would suffer international blame for an attack and would be isolated. As a result, the Japanese would seek an accomodation with Russian demands.

Finally, one must remember that not only the self-deluded Russians overestimated their strength: the power of the Russian Empire was hypostasised in the capitals of Europe as well. The resulting spectrum of views influenced St Petersburg and helped dissipate many concerns. Most foreigners believed that Russia had no reason to fear defeat at the hands of the Japanese because of her size and the immensity of her resources, even if the newcomer did enjoy some initial successes. The autocracy no doubt held a similar view. The political and military dilettantism of Alekseev and Vice-Admiral

70. Cf. 'Dnevnik Kuropatkina', *KA* 2, pp. 95f. (15 Dec. 1903).
71. For Japan's position: White, pp. 125ff.
72. Nicholas II, 15 Dec. 1903: 'Dnevnik Kuropatkina', *KA* 2, p. 95.

Abaza (who sat on the 'Special Committee for Far Eastern Concerns' and acted as conduit between the Tsar and his representative) doubtless had a great deal to do with the fact that Nicholas did not summon up the will to state clearly Russia's readiness to seek an understanding. St Petersburg in any case did not have a consistent strategy in case of conflict. Even after the Japanese ambassador was recalled (25 January/7 February 1904), the Russians were indecisive, failing to mobilise and being content merely to issue directions that the landing of an enemy in Korea should be considered a *casus belli* only if it occurred on the western coast facing Kwantung north of the thirty-eighth parallel.[73]

No less ominous than their misjudging of the Japanese was the inability of the Tsar and his advisors adequately to understand what the internal political effects of a war would be. The weakness of the autocratic leadership was reflected in the instability of the whole regime. This was not only a result of the decline in quality of the social élites. More important, the conflict in East Asia occurred just at a time when the entire system was in danger of being toppled by the economic, social and political damage which the Empire had endured. Unlike the difficult years 1878 to 1881, this crisis would involve the entire population, not just 'society'.[74] While the university disturbances of 1899 and the workers' strikes of the 1890s still seemed like isolated events which could be contained, indications had been accumulating since the turn of the century that 'a volcano now existed beneath Russia' which could 'erupt at any minute'.[75] The peasant disturbances of 1902 made it plain that the hungry Russian masses in rural areas would no longer remain passive. They revolted against a series of poor harvests, heavy taxation and the hopelessness of their impoverished existence. The following year a strike movement spread all too quickly, adding to the unrest. It highlighted the dissatisfaction of the working class and the ability of that class, under the influence of Social Democracy, to organise itself effectively. Not least inclined to express their revolutionary fervour were the students, with their continual willingness to protest and demonstrate. They succeeded in gaining broad sympathy within urban intellectual circles with a further wave of terrorist attacks on ministers and governors-general.[76] In April 1902, after

73. Ibid., pp. 106f. (25 Jan. 1904), 108f. (26 Jan. 1904).
74. Cf. chaps. 4 and 5.
75. *Dnevnik A.V. Bogdanovicha* (Moscow/Leningrad, 1924), p. 269 (24 Dec. 1901), cited in Solov'ev, *Samoderzhavie i dvoryanstvo*, p. 156.
75. On the peasant revolts and strike movements in 1902–3 see A. Pershin,

Education Minister N.P. Bogolepov had been murdered, one of
Witte's few friends, Minister of the Interior D.S. Sipyagin, was also
assassinated. His successor, V.K. Pleve, struck many observers as
'the last card' the regime had to play in its efforts to contain the
crisis.[77] Rebellious students were drafted into the army by former
Minister of War Vannovskii, who had retired in 1898 but was now
placed in charge of education.

The revolutionary ferment was also to be seen in the rapid
proliferation of political opposition, with very different motivations
and sources of social support. These voices made themselves heard
in the administrations of the zemstvos and the cities, in noble
associations and professional organisations, reflecting the re-
emergence of a movement which began to give rise to the coalescing
of a broad spectrum of political groups — moderate constitutionalists, radical-democratic intellectuals and Slavophile aristocratic circles opposed to the bureaucracy. They created the basis for a
'movement of national liberation' against the despotism of official-
dom personified by Minister of the Interior Pleve.[78] After the turn
of the century the nationalities question also bubbled up once more
as a result of restrictions imposed on Finnish autonomy. Not the
least important reason for the public mood of disgust and dissatisfaction was the serious economic stagnation which had become
firmly entrenched at the turn of the century. Industry was depressed because the nation's lack of capital had provoked a rapid
decline in the number of state contracts. Landowners dependent on
exports were frustrated by the Ministry of Finance's inability to
grant credits or offer assurances that tariffs would be reduced.[79]

The common opponent, the object of much displeasure and even
sheer hatred, was the bureaucracy: The political opposition suffered

---

Agrarnaya revolyutsiya v Rossii, vol. 1, *Ot reformy k revolyutsii* (Moscow, 1966),
pp. 63ff., 226ff.; L. I. Emelyakh, 'Krest'yanskoe dvizhenie v Poltavskoi i Khar'kovskoi guberniyakh v 1902 g.', *IZ* 38, pp. 154–75; A.K. Wildam, *The Making of a
Workers' Revolution. Russian Social Democracy 1891–1903* (Chicago, 1967); on the
return of terrorism: M. Hildermeier, *Die Sozialrevolutionäre Partei Rußlands* (Cologne, 1978).

77. *Dnevnik A.A. Kireeva*, 14 Sept. 1902, cited in Solov'ev, *Samoderzhavie i
dvoryanstvo*, p. 163.

78. On the 'social movement' see S. Galai, *The Liberation Movement in Russia
1900–1905* (Cambridge, 1973); see also G. Fischer, *Russian Liberalism: From Gentry
to Intelligentsia* (Cambridge, Mass., 1958); V. Leontovitsch, *Geschichte des Liberalismus in Rußland* (Frankfurt, 1974²), pp. 277ff.; L. Bazylow, *Polityka wewnętrzna
caratu i ruchy społeczne w Rosji na początku XX wieku* (Warsaw, 1966), pp. 177ff.;
V. Zilli, *La rivoluzione russa del 1905. La formazione dei partiti politici, 1881–1904*
(Naples, 1963), pp. 307ff.

79. Cf. chap. 7.

from the oppressive police system, and 'society' from the paralysing self-importance of the authorities. For Russia's rural and industrial economy, the evil was the traditional dependence on the state, which only grew worse during the agricultural crisis and the depression. Conflict stemming from the dynamic changes engendered by the economic upswing of the 1890s ran right through society. These changes posed a danger to the established order because the autocracy had not been affected and continued to rest on the reactionary foundations left by Alexander III.

Russia's rulers did not fail to discern the crisis generated by a rising number of dangerous situations. Socialist Revolutionary terrorism which threatened the lives of senior government officials could not be overlooked. The repressive state apparatus was also mobilised against striking workers, peasant agitators and rebellious students — so brutally and resolutely that even the Minister of War felt increasingly uncomfortable sending soldiers to act as security police and ordering them 'to shoot at a defenceless crowd'.[80] Faced with rebellion the government had no other answer but police and soldiers (unless one believes that the attempt to use 'police socialism' to divert working-class organisations was a viable alternative).[81] A critical observer in Court circles wrote: 'The Russian people is sinking further and further towards wretched slavery thanks to the unchecked whims of functionaries, thoughtless, bureaucratic minds with their almost comic mania to bring everything under official control, and the absence of any healthy, predictable policies. The people's patience is wearing thin, the ground for anarchy is becoming more and more fertile. . . . Russia will suffer great harm.'[82] The peasants' collective responsibility for taxes and impositions was abolished, but this was the only innovation produced by years of discussing the peasant problem.[83] No further reform was attempted which might have

80. 'Dnevnik Kuropatkina', *KA* 2, pp. 13 (8 Dec. 1902), 40 (1 Apr. 1903).
81. A.P. Korelin, 'Russkii "politseiskii sotsializm"', *VIst* (1968/10), pp. 41–58; Korelin, 'Krakh ideologii politseiskogo sotsializma v tsrarskoi Rossii', *IZ* 92 (1973), pp. 109–52; A.V. Vovchick. *Politika tsarizma po rabochemu voprosu v predrevolyutsionnyi period 1895–1904 gg.* (Lw'ow, 1964), pp. 107ff.; D. Pospielovsky, *Russian Police Trade Unionism* (London, 1971); J. Schneiderman, *Sergei Zubatov and Revolutionary Marxism* (Ithaca, 1976); W. Sablinsky, *The Road to Bloody Sunday* (Princeton, 1976), pp. 56ff.
82. 'Dnevnik Polovtsova', *KA* 3, p. 161 (22 Sept. 1902).
83. For the agrarian policies, especially abrogation of collective responsibility, see: M.S. Simonova, 'Otmena krugovoi poruki', *IZ* 83 (1969), p. 159–95; idem, 'Politika tsarizma v krest'yanskom voprose nakanune revolyutsii 1905–1907 gg.', *IZ* 75 (1965), pp. 212–42; idem, *Agrarnaya politika samoderzhaviya v nachale XX v.* (Moscow, 1975); cf. S.M. Sidel'nikov, 'Zemel'no-krest'yanskaya politika samoderzhaviya v preddumskii period', *ISSSR* (1976/4), pp. 124–35.

indicated the autocracy's ability to innovate or even its appreciation that an extensive campaign of stabilisation was essential if the system was to be preserved. Nicholas II seemed unmoved even by the incessant appeals of his extremely reactionary uncle, Grand Duke Sergei Aleksandrovich, who saw 'our police state' sinking into chaos and anarchy.[84] The barbarism of the Tsarist regime was brought to the attention of the whole world as a result of the bloody Jewish pogrom in Kishinev (1903).[85]

If the Russo-Japanese War is examined from within Russia, one is immediately inclined to wonder about the extent to which government behaviour overseas was influenced by the dangerous internal situation. When warning that war had to be averted because of mounting tensions within Russia, concerned voices from within the Tsar's inner circle referred, virtually without exception, to the fragility of national finances. The Tsar too finally grew weary of hearing Witte make this point. However, the social convulsions shaking Russia were included only occasionally, and with great reservation, in the catalogue of arguments advanced by the Minister of War in favour of a defensive attitude. Individual ministers like Kuropatkin or Justice Minister Murav'ev admitted only in private conversation or in their diaries that internal policies 'cannot continue much longer as they are', that the army was likely to be permeated with politically unreliable elements if the 'whole Russian people is not cured', or that setbacks in a war could lead to 'serious outbreaks of violence'.[86] This could never be pointed out to the Tsar.

One cannot therefore really claim that the government's ability to manage foreign policy was impeded by fear of revolution. Equally insignificant for the decision-making process were views such as those formulated by Pleve in private conversation that Russia needed 'a small, victorious war' in order to escape revolution because 'a war would distract the attention of the masses from political questions'.[87] There are no firm indications in the source

84. Excerpts from the private correspondence of the Grand Duke in: Solov'ev, *Samoderzhavie i dvoryanstvo*, pp. 153ff.; for the sense of crisis in government circles see L.G. Zakharova, 'Krizis samoderzhaviya nakanune revolyutsii 1905 g.', *VIst* (1972/8), pp. 119–40.
85. On Minister of the Interior Pleve's policy toward Jews and on the wave of pogroms in 1903 see H.D. Löwe, *Antisemitismus u. reaktionäre Utopie*, chapter V.
86. 'Dnevnik Kuropatkina', *KA* 2, pp. 12 (3 Dec. 1902), 20 (5 Jan. 1903), 44 (24 July 1903), 52f. (10 Aug. 1903).
87. Pleve's comments: ibid., p. 94 (11 Dec. 1903); cf. also the oft-quoted response in: Vitte, *Vospominaniya* 2, p. 291.

materials that discussions during the winter of 1903–04 gave serious consideration either to the domestic political situation or to hopes that conflict with Japan could be used to squash rebellion. At most, the Tsar had an ominous feeling that the autocracy was running out of options, both in domestic and foreign policy. The result of such misgivings can possibly be seen in his desperate attempts to create change, at least within his inner circle, by dismissing Witte, reining in Bezobrazov and establishing a direct relationship with the viceroy in the Far East. However, the Tsar's habitual uncertainty and indecisiveness persisted. His ingrained attitudes and fatalistic assurance soon embroiled him in war.

St Petersburg did not have a strategic plan which took even the military implications of the situation into account, not to mention an analysis of the connection between the external and internal threats. In contrast to the Balkan crisis of the 1870s the public was not aroused and did not demand that Russian interests and the 'honour' of the Empire be resolutely defended. Society was domestically-orientated, concerned (despite all differences of opinion) with internal political and social change. There was little interest in warding off the 'Yellow Peril', about which Wilhelm II had been importuning his cousin for years, or in pursuing a 'mission' in East Asia, which had been used to provide ideological justification for Witte's imperialist policies.[88] Consequently the autocracy stood alone on the eve of the Russo-Japanese War.

88. Cf. Gollwitzer, *Die gelbe Gefahr*, pp. 206ff.

10

War and Revolution

This is not the place to discuss the history of the war, the string of Russian defeats culminating in the destruction of the Baltic squadron, which, after a long and trying voyage, went to the bottom off Tsushima in May 1905 with flags still flying.[1] Instead, attention will focus on the connection between imperialist policies, social revolution and the economic crisis — a nexus which attracted everyone's attention after 'Bloody Sunday' (9/22 January 1905).[2] The events of the war will be included only to the extent to which the military fiasco in East Asia can help explain the destabilisation of autocracy in Russia. Three questions arise above all: firstly, it is necessary to determine to what extent the course of the war affected the governmental crisis. Secondly, an investigation will be made into the factors in the internal revolutionary situation which caused the Tsar to sue for peace in the summer of 1905. Finally, the impact of military defeat on the regime's struggle for survival in the face of revolution and its own financial bankruptcy will be examined.

Firstly, as we have seen, dissatisfaction, protest and revolt had begun to spread in Russia well before the danger of war arose, let alone the military defeats. Destabilisation had grown since the turn of the century as a result of a widespread crisis — caused by economic depression, the increasing distress of the rural population, aggravated by poor harvests, and the government's inability to push ahead with determined reform policies in order to shore up its crumbling legitimacy. The brutal regime of Interior Minister Pleve

---

1. D. Walter, *The Short Victorious War. The Russo-Japanese Conflict 1904–1905* (London, 1973); for an official history of the war see *Russko-yaponskaya voina 1904–05 gg. Rabota Voenno-istoricheskoi kommissii po opisaniyu russko-yaponskoi voiny* (9 vols., St Petersburg, 1910).
2. W. Sablinsky, *The Road to Bloody Sunday* (Princeton, 1976).

played an important role in depriving the bureaucratic police state of support, even in places where modest concessions on the part of the autocracy would have awakened confidence and a readiness to co-operate — in the zemstvo union for instance, whose representatives desired only to be freed from administrative strangulation and to have their work approved by the Tsar. Instead, Pleve demonstrated at every turn that the government had no intention of allowing even its loyal subjects greater liberty. Such intransigence benefitted activist circles among the liberal intelligentsia who, during these years, politicised the climate at the level of local self-government and especially at the professional congresses of doctors, lawyers and agronomists. The 'Union of Liberation' (*soyuz osvobozhdeniya*), founded in the summer of 1903, began to make constitutional demands and campaign for the creation of a united national front, thus helping to develop sympathy and support even for socialist groups struggling for political freedom.[3] The rural agitation and strikes of 1902 and 1903 understandably raised the morale of those in exile or the underground. The Socialist Revolutionaries responded with a sensational renewal of terrorism, combined with a campaign for agrarian socialism pitched at the expectations and level of understanding of the peasantry.[4] The Social Democrats also grew more confident that the debilitating internal struggle between Bolsheviks and Mensheviks could be smoothed over and the working masses drawn onto the streets in ever-increasing numbers.[5]

Foreign policy attracted little interest in the face of all these united fronts, incipient campaigns, and attempts at formulating programmes. Even during the months when the Russo-Japanese conflict was at its worst, there was only scattered comment criticising the autocracy's long-term involvement in the Far East. In July 1903 the Union of Liberation's journal, *Osvobozhdenie* (published in Stuttgart), accused the government of risking Russia's friendship with France, inciting England and America against Russia and criminally neglecting Russia's 'natural' sphere of influence in the

3. Besides the literature mentioned in chap. 9, note 78, cf. G. Freeze, 'A National Liberation Movement and the Shift in Russian Liberalism, 1901–1903', *SR* 28 (1969), pp. 81ff.; also K. Fröhlich, *The Emergence of Russian Constitutionalism 1900–1904* (The Hague, 1981).
4. Essential: M. Hildermeier, *Die Sozialrevolutionäre Partei Rußlands 1900–1914*, (Cologne, 1978).
5. D. Geyer, *Lenin in der russischen Sozialdemokratie 1890–1903* (Cologne, 1962), pp. 247ff.; J. Keep, *The Rise of Social Democracy in Russia* (Oxford, 1963), pp. 70ff.

Near East by setting out on a collision course with Japan.[6] The legal opposition press considered it highly unlikely, however, that the 'mighty Saint Bernard' (Russia) could lose to the 'little pug' (Japan).[7] *Revolyutsionnaya Rossiya*, the voice of the Socialist Revolutionaries, continued to aver, only a few days before the outbreak of hostilities, that the empty treasuries in St Petersburg and Tokyo were signs that peace would be preserved. The ruling camarilla was, allegedly, sorely tempted to resort to military adventures in order to distract the people from their grievances, but 'Tsarist, plutocratic Russia', in search of new markets for her capitalist industry, would not wish to run such a risk in the end.[8]

The Socialist Revolutionaries had evidently not yet included the possibility of war in their strategic plans, and had only casually considered the possibility that war could prepare a bloody *coup de grâce* for the 'cannibals of national chauvinism'. Social Democratic groups had also not been overly excited by the idea that the looming conflict could bring about 'the beginning of the end of Russian absolutism'.[9] After the Japanese attack on Port Arthur however, a more accurate analysis of the situation was inevitable. Both Social Democrats and Socialist Revolutionaries concentrated on spreading the watchword 'war on war', and adopted resolute defeatism as part of the revolutionary struggle.[10] That the war was actually beginning to foment revolution was realised only after the impact of Bloody Sunday had made itself felt.

Liberal groups, with their broadly based demands for a constitution, were much more profoundly affected by the outbreak of war, for they now found themselves caught up in a crisis of identity never previously imagined.[11] Patriotic fervour spread throughout the zemstvo milieu and the organs of local government in the cities. For a few months opposition activities came to a standstill and old hostilities declined as the feeling emerged that government and

6. P. Struve in: *Osvobozhdenie* 3/27, (19 July [1 Aug.] 1903), pp. 33ff. For Struve see: R. Pipes, *Struve. Liberal on the Left, 1870–1905* (Cambridge, Mass., 1970).
7. Cited by M. Pavlovich 'Vneshnyaya politika i russko-yaponskaya voina', *ODR* 2/1, p. 19.
8. 'Voina i mir?', *Revolyutsionnaya Rossiya* 39 (1 Jan. 1904), pp. 8f.
9. Parvus (Helphand), 'Der Anfang vom Ende?', in *Aus der Weltpolitik. Sozial-dem. Zeitungen-Korrespondenz* 5/49 (30 Nov. 1903), pp. 1–10.
10. Cf. A. Fischer, *Russische Sozialdemokratie u. bewaffneter Aufstand im Jahre 1905* (Wiesbaden, 1967), pp. 29ff.
11. For what follows: S. Galai, 'The Impact of War on the Russian Liberals 1904 bis 1905', *Government and Opposition* 1 (1965), pp. 85–109; Galai, *The Liberation Movement*, pp. 196–272. The authoritative Soviet version: E.D. Chermenskii, *Burzhuaziya i tsarizm v pervoi russkoi revolyutsii* (Moscow, 1970).

society should call a truce in the face of the external threat. Patriotic desires to defend the motherland were strongest in those circles which clung to the Slavophile hope that Russia would be cured of all evils when ruler and people were united with each other in a harmony based on mutual confidence and when this spiritual relationship was no longer hampered by tight administrative control and the arbitrary actions of officials. Through expressions of devotion to the Tsar, offers to support the Red Cross, and other helpful activities these circles hoped to increase their own influence and coax Nicholas II into summoning representatives of society to his side.

The zemstvo-constitutionalists, who were dedicated to further reforms and the transformation of Russia along the lines of a liberal constitutional state, were also swept up in the wave of patriotic fervour after the war broke out. They considered it their national duty to help fight the external enemy. Although they did not entirely abandon tough criticism of the regime's policies in East Asia, many felt that in the end the war would compel the Tsar to let Russia regenerate herself on a constitutional basis. Early defeats at the front reinforced their view that catastrophe could only be avoided if elected representatives of the people helped determine the destiny of the motherland. Even in radical circles patriotic sentiments were not without influence in the spring of 1904, as can be seen in divergent statements emanating from the Union of Liberation. Its adherents continued to proclaim that only an alliance of all freedom-loving forces could create a 'free Russia', but many were worried that unconditional defeatism would isolate them from 'society'. Thus Peter Struve, the editor of *Osvobozhdenie*, was drawn to making artificial distinctions in his early articles on the war, lending his support to the Tsar's army while, at the same time, arguing that Russia had more to fear from Pleve than the Japanese. It took some time before vehement protest brought the *Osvobozhdentsy* back to clearly defining the overthrow of autocracy as the liberation movement's foremost war aim.[12]

This process of clarification was furthered both by military defeats and the harrassment which Pleve inflicted on the organs of

12. P. Struve, 'Voina', in *Osvobozhdenie* 17/41 (5 [18] Feb. 1904); Struve, 'Voina i patriotizm', ibid. 18/42 (19 Feb. [3 Mar.] 1904), p. 319; (P.N. Milyukov), 'Voina i russkaya oppozitsiya', ibid. 19/43 (7 [20]/3/1904), pp. 330ff.; cf. Galai, *Liberation Movement*, p. 203f. For Milyukov's political biography see: T. Riha, *A Russian European. Paul Miliukov in Russian Politics* (Notre Dame, 1968).

local self-government. The patriotic emotion of the first weeks of the war was quickly exhausted, and the high-flown declarations in the government press could not sustain complete confidence in victory. By early May 1904 zemstvo leaders realised that their hopes for a new era of trust and co-operation had been dashed. During the summer months, opposition in Russia began to gather once more under the influence of news from the front, anti-government demonstrations in Warsaw and Helsingfors, and the terrorist activities of Socialist Revolutionary groups who assassinated the Governor-General of Finland on 3 June 1904 and the hated Minister of the Interior himself on 15 July. With its radical slogans combining 'down with the autocracy' with anti-war statements and its intensified struggle for a constituent assembly the Union of Liberation found increased sympathy even among those who would have preferred to avoid illegal forms of social protest. Thereafter, the development of the reform movement and the differences within it stood in close interrelation with the autocracy's attempts to halt its rapid loss of authority by making half-hearted promises and currying favour. The revelations of the war and the mass disturbances which soon broke out had a large impact on the patterns of behaviour that were to re-appear regularly in the next few years in the course of the conflict between government and opposition.

After Pleve's murder it was obviously impossible for the Tsar to restore confidence by means of gestures alone. On 11 August, a few days after the débâcle of the Pacific squadron off Port Arthur, Nicholas issued a manifesto promising to abolish corporal punishment as well as outstanding redemption payments, but even the so-called 'Slavophiles' gathered around the chairman of the Moscow zemstvo, D.N. Shipov, were unimpressed. Better received was the naming of Prince P. D. Svyatopolk-Mirskii to the post of Minister of the Interior shortly after the defeat at Liao Yang (21 August). He hoped to introduce better conditions and to improve the strained relations with the zemstvos.[13] Although Mirskii's governmental renewal was much praised, it met with little support. The Union of Liberation had meanwhile expanded and at the end of September signed democratic resolutions in Paris together with socialist and other revolutionary groups.[14] Its leaders did not succeed in imposing this programme on All-Russian congress of zemstvo represen-

---

13. Leontovitsch, pp. 286ff.; Bazylow, *Polityka*, pp. 296ff.
14. Galai, *Liberation Movement*, pp. 214ff.; G. Fischer, *Russian Liberalism* pp. 167ff.; Pipes, *Struve*, pp. 363ff.

tatives, but the constitutional front formed here in November 1904 could not be satisfied by the weak Minister of the Interior. While the congress demanded that the government permit a freely elected national assembly, the Tsar refused even Svyatopolk-Mirskii's modest proposal for reform of the Council of State.[15]

At the same time the liberal and democratic potential of the intelligentsia was being mobilised by a banquet campaign, newly created professional unions, and newspapers which had grown rebellious and critical of the regime. The movement was bursting the bounds of moderate constitutionalism. The popularity of 'fourfold' (universal, free, secret and direct) suffrage and calls for a constitution 'from below' could no longer be contained by such apolitical concessions as those granted by the Tsar on 12 December.[16] With their explicit condemnation of the zemstvo movement, whose lawlessness was supposedly pleasing the 'enemies of the motherland', the authorities succeeded in silencing even those people who longed for a credible sign of confidence from the Tsar, if only for the sake of internal peace.

The fall of Port Arthur on 20 December 1904 helped lay bare both the senselessness of the war and the helplessness of the government. While the supreme authorities dispatched more and more cannon fodder east to fight for Russia's 'honour and glory' and the empire in the Pacific, strikes and disturbances began to overwhelm the large industrial centres. These signalled the start of a protest movement which considered the zemstvos superfluous. When, in the first days of January, the workers of St Petersburg could no longer be contained in their factories and the demonstration led by Father Gapon was mowed down in front of the Winter Palace, no one remained to applaud the government in the name of 'society'.[17] Neither through the Shidlovskii commission investigating the grievances of the workers nor in contacts with groups of entrepreneurs could the government see a way to contain the mass agitation.[18] The demand for political reform had become general.

15. Galai, *Liberation Movement*, pp. 226ff.; Leontovitsch, pp. 289ff.; L.G. Zakharova, 'Krizis', pp. 119–40.
16. For detailed presentation of the discussions about the law of 12 Dec. 1904 see Leontovitsch, pp. 295ff.; Chermenskii, pp. 40ff.
17. Sablinski, pp. 143ff.; 172ff., 198ff., 229ff.
18. S.M. Schwartz, *The Russian Revolution of 1905* (Chicago, 1967), pp. 75–128; Chermenskii, pp. 52ff.; R.A. Roosa, 'Russian Industrialists, Politics, and Labor Reform in 1905', *Russian History* 2 (1975), pp. 124–48; G.E. Snow, 'The Kokovtsov Commission. An Abortive Attempt at Labor Reform in Russia in 1905', *SR* 31 (1972), pp. 780–96; A.Ya. Avrekh, *Stolypin i Tret'ya Duma* (Moscow, 1968), pp. 153ff.

The constitutional movement was now carried along on the wave of a revolution which had originated in urban Russia and the Polish areas of the Empire and which soon engulfed the villages as well. In the black earth zone and border areas there were frenzied riots directed at the large landowners. In the spring of 1905 everything, for the constitutionalists, came down to the question of how the rebellious masses could be won over to the 'peaceful path' of reform. Fear spread that the revolutionary parties would draw the people away from 'moderate forces' if the latter's constitutional programme was not linked to some decisive social demands which benefitted workers and peasants.[19] The constitutional movement tended therefore to radicalise its position while fearing at the same time that a revolution could destroy not only the autocracy but society as well. On 18 February 1905 the Tsar announced in a rescript to the new Minister of the Interior, Bulygin, that he would 'call together worthy men elected with the confidence of the whole population to engage in the preparation and discussion of proposed legislation'. However, only a minority of the organised opposition considered this offer adequate.[20]

The war obviously continued to play a role in the escalation of the political crisis and the regime suffered another grave humiliation at Mukden at the end of February. However, it would be a mistake to imply that the revolution of 1905 took shape essentially as an anti-war movement. Among socialists and liberals, constitutional reform and socio-political change took precedence over the question of peace. Despite all the differences in their strategy, and in their understanding of the revolution Socialist Revolutionaries, Mensheviks and Bolsheviks alike all focused on a popular armed insurrection against the autocracy.[21] They did not fail to decipher the connection between war and revolution, and they saw in the military defeats which tsarism was suffering in the Far East a guarantee that they would emerge victorious. However, very few

19. For the revolutionary movement in the spring of 1905, see the Soviet collection: *Revolyutsionnoe dvizhenie v Rossii vesnoi i letom 1905 g.* (Moscow, 1957); for the present state of Soviet research into the first Russian revolution: G.M. Derenkovskii, A.E. Ivanov et al., 'Osnovnye itogi izucheniya istorii pervoi russkoi revolyutsii za posled.ie 20 let', *ISSSR* (1975/5), pp. 42–60.
20. German text of the edict: A. Palme, *Die Russische Verfassung* (Berlin, 1910), p. 76.
21. Hildermeier, *Die Sozialrevolutionäre Partei*, chap. 5; A. Fischer, *Russische Sozialdemokratie*, pp. 41ff.; Keep, pp. 149ff.; for the revolution in Poland: G.W. Strobel, *Die Partei Rosa Luxemburgs, Lenin u. die SPD* (Wiesbaden, 1974), pp. 207ff., 220ff.; M.K. Dziewanowski, 'The Russian Revolution of 1904–05 and the Marxist Movement in Poland', *JCEA* 12 (1953), pp. 259–75.

Russian socialists saw as much revolutionary potential in the war as Lenin. He argued openly in favour of a Japanese victory after the fall of Port Arthur because he believed that the defeat of Russian absolutism in the war was essential for the 'struggle for socialism by the international and Russian proletariats'. The Japanese bourgeoisie was engaged in a progressive struggle against tsarism; 'progressive Asia' (in the guise of Japan) was dealing a decisive blow to 'backward Europe' (in the guise of tsarism); this 'historic war' was therefore playing 'an enormous revolutionary role'. 'The war is far from over, but every step that prolongs it brings us closer to an immense new war, the struggle of the people against the autocracy, the proletariat's struggle for freedom.'[22] No one else insisted so openly that war, not peace, was the elixir of revolutionaries.

Such a line of reasoning doubtlessly struck the constitutionalists as perverse. However, views to the contrary, envisaging a final victory of Russian arms had lost much of their value. Only a few isolated voices, such as that of the Kharkov professor, P.P. Migulin, an old critic of Witte's financial policies, still thought after the defeat of Port Arthur that defending Kwantung and Korea was essential for the inner renewal Russia needed. Even the enthusiasm of businessmen's associations and stock exchange committees had ebbed away.[23] Migulin's appeals in support of rampant imperialism remind one of Max Weber and Friedrich Naumann. It was claimed that no state, Russia included, could forego a worldwide presence at this time. Restraint would keep the country's internal life mired in the reactionary past. The successful assertion of Russian interests in East Asia and the Pacific would, however, produce an internal awakening, release creative forces and 'cosmopolitan ideas', and finally help overcome Russian passivity and self-preoccupation — 'our eternal curse, *oblomovshchina*'.[24]

In the spring of 1905, however, such appeals could no longer restrain the zemstvo movement's vehement opposition to the war. Among the opposition groups the liberal democratic views of the Union of Liberation were the most widespread, and the Union succeeded at the All-Russian zemstvo congress (22 to 26 April) in mobilising a broad though inconsistent majority in favour of a democratically elected Constituent Assembly.[25] As before, the

22. The fall of Port Arthur in: Lenin, *PSS*, vol. 9, pp. 151–9.
23. Chermenskii, pp. 52ff., 74ff.
24. P.P. Migulin, *Voina i nashi finansy* (Kharkov, 1905) — foreword, 7 Jan. 1905.
25. Galai, *Liberation Movement*, p. 250; Chermenskii, pp. 64ff.

constitutionalists hoped that the unceasing string of military catastrophes would help their cause, and the destruction of the fleet off Tsushima (14//27 May) raised hopes for a quick end to the 'useless war'. However, far more attention was paid to internal developments than to the war. The views of the zemstvo union and other organisations were apparently not much influenced by the government's readiness after the end of May to seek a negotiated peace with Japan.

A more important factor during the summer was the rising fear of elemental forces shaking society. Many worthy constitutionalists were afraid that if the autocracy fell, the foundations of civil society would also disappear. Faced with events which seemed to be leading in the direction of chaos and anarchy, some brave friends of freedom began to falter. Early in June leading representatives of the constitutional movement once more sought the ear of the Tsar. Nicholas gave the liberal petitioners, attired in dress-coats and medals, a gracious reception but little else. A few days later he could be seen encouraging a delegation of extremist enemies of reform in their crusade in support of autocracy.[26]

The revolutionary convulsions — peasant uprisings, mutiny on the armoured cruiser Potemkin, and bloody battles in Odessa and elsewhere — continued to influence the internal divisions within the Union of Liberation as well. Caught between the radical-democratic intelligentsia, the 'Union of Unions' and the moderate zemstvo men, the '*Osvobozhdentsy*' began to disintegrate. At the heart of the struggle was the question of whether to seek reconciliation or confrontation. Even the idea of a general strike received some support at the conferences of professional unions in July and August.[27] In such an atmosphere, the problem of war or peace seemed of little consequence.

The extent to which the revolutionary process had become independent could be seen during the peace conference (27 July to 23 August). Witte's negotiations with the Japanese were completely overshadowed by the heated controversy unleashed in all political camps by an edict announcing the creation of an advisory Imperial Duma and an accompanying system of suffrage.[28] The wave of

26. I.P. Belokonskii, *Zemstvo i konstitutsiya* (Moscow, 1910), pp. 167ff.

27. Galai, *Liberation Movement*, pp. 258ff.; Galai, 'The Role of the Union of Unions in the Russian Revolution of 1905', *JGO*, 24 (1976), pp. 512–25; cf. L. K. Erman, *Intelligentsiya v pervoi russkoi revolyutsii* (Moscow, 1966).

28. G.E. Snow, 'The Peterhof Conference of 1905 and the Creation of the Bulygin Duma', *Russian History* 2 (1975), pp. 149–62.

strikes and rebellions could not be stemmed by the Treaty of Portsmouth, and the climax of the domestic conflict was still to come when the government sought to save its skin by publishing the October Manifesto (17(30)October).[29]

Secondly, there is no doubt that the revolutionary situation within Russia was the decisive factor in Nicholas's decision, after the fleet had been destroyed, to accept the offer of the American president to mediate a peace. However the internal pressures which were threatening to overwhelm the nation's resilience and topple the autocracy cannot be considered in isolation. The internal disruption not only aggravated the psychological impact of military defeat but also endangered Russia's international position. Foreign sources of capital dried up so that a continuing war could no longer be financed — unless, of course, there was a willingness to risk national bankruptcy and the consequent loss of Russia's status as a great power. In May 1905 the internal and external threats to the regime began to accumulate into a crisis which left the Tsar only one choice — peace.

It is not easy to say exactly when the Tsar realised the extent of the dangers which he faced and the effect that they would have on the war. For a long time Nicholas seemed to resent the presumptuousness of those wanting him to have some understanding of the effects of the revolution. Only after his uncle the Grand Duke Sergei Aleksandrovich was murdered on 4 February 1905 did Nicholas gradually seem to realise that a revolution in Russia was not only possible but 'already in progress' as the Minister of the Interior put it.[30] Even then, however, the Tsar failed to draw any serious consequences. His rescript to Bulygin promised 'society' a form of political participation which appears highly suspect on close analysis. Autocratic government was to remain as solidly entrenched as the intention to continue the war until victory had been achieved. Nothing would indicate that the Tsar felt inclined to heed the advice of his most obtrusive correspondent, the German Kaiser — to go to the Kremlin in Moscow and there, surrounded 'by the clergy with banners, crosses, incense and the pictures of saints', proclaim to the people that the Tsar proposed for the sake of the 'holy war' to go to

29. See note 30, pp. 183ff.
30. Cited in *Istoriya SSSR*, vol. 6 (Moscow, 1968), pp. 124f.

the side of his brave army.[31] Nicholas was neither willing nor able to make such a grand gesture, though it would have pleased many a Slavophile heart. The Tsar also seemed unaffected by the deep pessimism Witte was experiencing in late February 1905 when he described the hopelessness of the situation to Commander-in-Chief Kuropatkin. According to Witte, terrible new bloodbaths and catastrophes could well result from the decline in Russia's international prestige, the incredible costs and casualties of the war, 'the most demented war the world has ever seen', the incompetence of the universally despised government, and the excited state of all levels of the population.[32] After the defeat at Mukden (27 February) the hopes of Nicholas and his entourage had focused on the Baltic squadron. Since the autumn of 1904 it had been steaming toward East Asia with the eyes of the world on it in an attempt to change the fortunes of war and put an end to Japanese mastery of the seas. That the fighting strength of this new armada, plagued by a series of embarrassing incidents, could not be high was clear to all serious observers, but official St Petersburg chose to see and hear nothing.[33] Hence it was not until after Tsushima that the Tsar finally realised that Russia could not continue with the war.

Before the spring of 1905 Nicholas was not even alarmed by the financial problems attendant upon the war — like so many other calamities they could be ignored with a little effort. The Minister of Finance, V.N. Kokovtsov,[34] had evidently long sheltered the Tsar from such worries with the connivance of the financial committee of the Council of State. In any case there was no sign of panic at Court. Russia had been able to maintain the iron-clad principle that her currency was backed by gold. Behind this firm commitment, however, was the sobering fact that for a long time the government had only been able to function, both internally and externally, thanks to Russia's international creditworthiness. The costs of the war were therefore necessarily covered for the most part with foreign credits. It was large state loans (under the circumstances available only in Paris or Berlin) which made it possible to preserve Russia's gold reserves, purchase military equipment and service the current debt.

31. Cf. the letters of 21 Feb. and 3 June 1905 in: *GP* 19/2, pp. 383ff., 419ff.
32. Witte to Kuropatkin, 27/2/1905 in: *KA* 19, pp. 73ff.
33. Cf. the memoirs of the Finance Minister, V.M. Kokovtsov, *Iz moego proshlogo. Vospominaniya 1903–1919 gg.* (Paris, 1933), vol. 1. pp. 65f.
34. For a recent study of the Finance Minister's policies see G.E. Snow, 'Vladimir N. Kokovtsov. A Case study of an Imperial Bureaucrat 1904–1906', PhD thesis, Indiana Univ., 1976.

The financial history of the Russo-Japanese War has been thoroughly researched.[35] At the outbreak of war Russia's financial circumstances were far from hopeless, despite her high foreign debts (ca. 4,200 million rubles in 1904). Payments on interest and principle were covered by the budget, as they had always been. Thanks to a demonstrable surplus in the national Treasury (ca. 500 million rubles), the Finance Minister had sufficient funds available to get over the first months of the war. However, long-term plans had to be laid, and new foreign loans became a burning issue as early as the spring of 1904.[36] Additional financing required irksome negotiations with the large French and German banks, and St Petersburg had to assume that the governments would bring political pressures to bear, as they had done during peace time. Nevertheless, the problems were not insurmountable, as the first year of the war demonstrated. In April 1904 the French cabinet closed its mind to the possibility that Russia would suffer defeat at the hands of the Japanese and did not move to reject Russian requests. With Witte and Kokovtsov threatening to turn to Berlin if necessary, Paris approved a loan negotiated by Noetzlin and Hottinguer. The conditions for this loan of 800 million francs (300 million rubles) were well suited to Russia's straightened circumstances, i.e. they were not very favourable. Treasury bills were set at 5 per cent to mature in five years and divided into two lots, with a high commission for the banks (1.5 per cent) and a low issue price of 94. Such conditions made it clear that France did not intend to allow her ally any easy money.[37] However, the loan was placed readily, without the reductions in the rate which had been feared. The French government's demands for further industrial orders and the completion of strategic railway lines (Bologoe-Siedlce) turned out in practice not to be feasible. German firms received about two-thirds of Russia's foreign orders in 1904–05.[38]

35. Sources: B.A. Romanov (ed.), *Russkie finansy i evropeiskaya birzha 1904–1906* (Moscow, 1926); A.L. Sidorov (ed.), 'Finansovoe polozhenie tsarskogo samoderzhaviya v period russko-yaponskoi voiny i pervoi russkoi revolyutsii', *IA* (1955/2), pp. 120–49; idem, 'Denezhnoe obrashchenie Rossii, 1904–1907', ibid. (1956/3), pp. 88–123; also: Romanov, *Russia in Manchuria*, pp. 323–68.

36. Cf. Kokovtsov's report on the financial situation, 17 Mar. 1904, in *Russkie finansy*, pp. 31–62, as well as Kokovtsov to Lamsdorff, 11 Apr. 1904, ibid., pp. 92ff.

37. For the loan of 29 Apr. [12 May] 1904: ibid., pp. 77ff., 375f.; cf. Anan'ich, *Rossiya*, pp. 107ff.; Girault, *Emprunts*, pp. 393ff., 402ff.

38. B. Vogel, *Deutsche Rußlandpolitik*, pp. 189ff.; J.W. Long, 'The Economics of the Franco-Russian Alliance 1904–1906', PhD thesis, Univ. of Wisconsin, 1968, pp. 34ff., 40ff.; Girault, pp. 450ff., Poidevin, pp. 286ff.

The Russian Minister of Finance had been spared further pilgrimages to Paris for the time being, while St Petersburg profited once more from Franco-German rivalries. After the commercial treaty with Germany was finally signed by Witte and Bülow in July 1904, Kokovtsov knew that he could count on the German loan which had long been withheld. Complaints in the Moscow press that the commercial treaty was an 'economic Sedan' for Russia were therefore greatly exaggerated.[39] When representatives of Crédit Lyonnais came looking for new business in the autumn of 1904, the Russian Finance Minister was even forced to tell them that in view of the forthcoming influx of German capital they would have to wait until the following spring. Kokovtsov would later have warm memories of the negotiations with the Mendelssohn bank in Berlin which were approved by the Tsar in mid-December.[40] The loan, issued at 4.5 per cent over eighty years, tallied with Berlin's policy of keeping Russia involved in the war and preparing her possibly to join a continental league against England. The 500 million *Reichsmark* loan (231 million rubles) went through in the first weeks of the new year with the additional participation of Russian banks.[41]

The Russian Treasury's extreme dependence on foreign credits posed no problem for the time being because loans had apparently been obtained without effort. However, this only papered over the high risks involved in financing the war. After the military setbacks of 1904 the Finance Ministry was faced with a war whose duration could not be foreseen and whose costs far surpassed all earlier estimates. The two loans mentioned above did not even come close to covering Russia's expected financial requirements for 1905. In October 1904 Kokovtsov was already making it known in Paris that he planned to place 500 million rubles worth of State Treasury notes on European capital markets in the following spring. He still felt strong enough, though, to spurn French demands that the new loans be coupled with industrial contracts — Rafalovich informed the French Ministry of Finance that Russia was 'neither Turkey nor Bulgaria' and would not accept treatment as a 'second-class power'.[42] Everything changed, however, after the events of Bloody Sunday in St Petersburg. France closed her ears to Russian requests for more

---

39. Cited in Pavlovich, 'Vneshnyaya politika', p. 24.
40. Kokovtsov, *Iz moego proshlogo*, 1, pp. 60f.
41. For the German loan see Anan'ich, *Rossiya*, pp. 113ff., Vogel, *Rußlandpolitik*, pp. 85f.; *Russkie finansy*, pp. 114–30, 376ff.
42. Long, 'The Economics', p. 65.

loans, despite the ever increasing sums of money which the Parisian press were receiving from Kokovtsov's agents.[43]

Coolness in relations had been normal between the partners in the Franco-Russian Alliance, but they now turned ice cold as a result of the brutal excesses of the tsarist regime. The indignant French public put pressure on their government. Sudden falls in the value of Russian securities revealed that the autocracy's war on its own people had begun to undermine Russia's foreign prestige. The new French cabinet, under former Minister of Finance Maurice Rouvier, was accused during excited debates in the Assembly of sustaining a 'government of murderers' and 'butchers of the Russian people'. With the help of Russian émigrés, the entire left as far as the Radicals worked to mobilise a large part of the French public in a vehement campaign against tsarist despotism.[44]

However, despite poor relations the coolly calculating world of French banking did not reject Kokovtsov's request for a loan out of hand. A very solicitous Edouard Noetzlin had an audience with the Tsar in mid-February 1905, although promising first impressions were quickly dissipated. Nevertheless, on 27 February (12 March) Noetzlin and Hottinguer agreed in St Petersburg on conditions for a new contract — it would be a credit of 600 million francs spread over eight years at a fixed rate of interest of 6 per cent. On the very day agreement was reached with Kokovtsov, however, the two intermediaries were summoned back to Paris, to the great consternation of their Russian partners. Rouvier let it be known that in the wake of the Russian defeat at Mukden the French cabinet did not wish to grant new loans for the time being. Paris then announced that it no longer simply wanted the Russians to undertake reforms. Peace would also have to be made — partly because the Moroccan crisis was beginning and a badly shaken Russia was not of much value as an ally.[45]

The recalling of the French bankers (which was taken in St Petersburg as an affront and gave rise to claims that Russia had been stabbed in the back) must have made the Tsar begin to realise the extreme seriousness of Russia's financial situation. More and more foreign observers remarked that Russia was fast approaching bankruptcy. Even Witte now pleaded with the Tsar to make peace, and did not hesitate to predict 'terrible catastrophes' and 'huge

43. *Russkie finansy*, pp. 131ff., 154ff.; Long, 'Economics', pp. 77ff.
44. Long, 'Economics', pp. 69ff.
45. *Russkie finansy*, pp. 161ff.; Long, 'Economics', pp. 83ff.; Anan'ich, pp. 129ff.

outbreaks of violence' if the Tsar demanded more sacrifices from his country. 'In order to continue the war, enormous sums of money and many new recruits are needed. But further expenditures will ruin the Empire's financial and economic position. . . . The poverty of the people and with it the darkening and embittering of the public mood will increase. Russia will lose prestige, and foreign holders of our securities (including the entire French middle class) will grow hostile to us. . . . The army is very much needed now in Russia herself.'[46] Nicholas, who had always disliked Witte's dramatic appeals, did not respond to this request.

As a result, Kokovtsov's financial policies floundered even more. The Minister had great difficulty finding urgently needed sources of new funds. Early in March he explained to Nicholas in a lengthy memorandum that the national Treasury was scarcely able to cover the foreign commitments that were coming due, that foreign loans could at best be acquired under ruinous and intolerable conditions, and that the national bank's gold reserves could not be touched if 'complete destruction of our monetary system' was to be avoided. Military defeats and internal disturbances had also lowered Russia's credit-worthiness to dangerous levels.[47] All that Kokovtsov was able to arrange were extremely risky internal loans (200 million rubles at 5 per cent) and the floating of short-term bill credits at 7 per cent which Mendelssohn negotiated in April for a period of nine to twelve months (150 million rubles). These were emergency measures which by no means guaranteed that the war could be continued.[48] When Russia's remaining hopes for a shift in the fortunes of war sank with the fleet off Tsushima, the time had clearly come to draw some speedy conclusions. European capital markets would no doubt remain closed until peace had been concluded with Japan. The autocracy had either to deal with these facts or face bankruptcy and its own collapse. At the end of March the German Kaiser was still advising the autocracy to persevere in the war until the enemy was exhausted and vigorously to combat the threatened revolution through a mixture of reform and repression. Now, however, the Kaiser abandoned his theory of 'bogging down the war' and emphatically urged his cousin to seek peace.[49]

46. Witte to Nicholas II, 28 Feb. 1905 in: Vitte, *Vospominaniya* 2, p. 573.
47. Cited in B.A. Romanov (ed.), 'Konets russko-yaponskoi voiny', *KA* 28, pp. 188f.
48. Anan'ich, *Rossiya*, pp. 140ff.
49. Wilhelm to Nicholas, 3 June 1905 in: *GP* 19/2, pp. 419ff. For the idea of 'bogging down' the war: Bülow to Speck v. Sternburg (Washington), 22 Mar. 1905,

It is impossible to judge whether Nicholas still needed the Kaiser's words in order to persuade him to accept the good offices of Theodore Roosevelt. The Tsar's decision to enquire into the Japanese conditions for peace seems to have been taken before the War Council met on 24 May (6 June) on the eve of an audience with the American envoy. Grand Duke Vladimir Aleksandrovich, speaking for his nephew Nicholas, claimed that this step had to be taken above all because internal circumstances posed a threat to the entire system. The situation had become so serious 'that we have all lost our way (*sbity s tolku*); we cannot continue like this'. Russia was in 'such a desperate or at least difficult situation that our internal well-being (*blagosostoyanie*) is more important than victory. . . . We are living under abnormal conditions, and it is essential that security be re-established within Russia'. The military situation also made peace seem advisable, according to the Grand Duke, especially in view of the fact that Vladivostok, Sakhalin and Kamchatka could not be defended without a fleet. He did not wish to count any longer on possible victories for Russian arms — even if Commander-in-Chief Linevich's requests for fresh contingents of troops could be met. Any further defeat would make the Japanese conditions so much worse that 'no Russian could accept them'.[50]

The discussions in the War Council revealed not only the regime's dilemmas but also that the military establishment experienced great difficulty in comprehending the hopelessness of the situation. Minister of War Sakharov described the difficulties which would be encountered in recruiting more soldiers but thought the humiliation (*pozor*) of ending the war 'without a single victory', 'without the least bit of success' was unacceptable. Such a peace would expel Russia for a long time from the circle of great powers and would not bring security.[51] The military command in the Far East was in complete agreement with this plea to reject a 'shameful peace'. Linevich and Kuropatkin continued with their assurances that the enemy's strength was beginning to wane and that Russian troops were straining at the leash in their eagerness to do battle.[52] Admiral Dubasov maintained that the war had to be continued

ibid., pp. 583ff.; see in general: B. Vogel, 'Die deutsche Regierung u. die russische Revolution von 1905', *Deutschland u. die Weltpolitik im 19. u. 20. Jh. Fs. für F. Fischer* (Düsseldorf, 1973), pp. 222–36.

50. Minutes of the War Council meeting of 24 May 1905 in: *KA* 28, pp. 191–204, here: 198, 200f.

51. Ibid., p. 202.

52. Cf. Kuropatkin to Witte, 25 May 1905 in: *KA* 19, pp. 77f.

because Russia had no choice but to defeat her enemy: 'Our eastward expansion is an elemental drive, a movement to natural borders. We cannot retreat here'. The high command had evidently lost touch with reality in the wake of Russia's military disasters. Others complained that it was not yet known 'what Russia thinks', or whether the people could be roused to 'national enthusiasm'. They wanted to discover if the people were prepared to make any and all sacrifices for the war 'as we now see in Japan'. The gentlemen of the War Council envied Japan her 'truly national war'. It is therefore not surprising that an idea with Slavophile overtones emerged from these irritated circles — that the 'views of the people' could be articulated by a *zemskii sobor* or national assembly.[53]

The Tsar was evidently in no mood, however, either to consult 'the people' or to allow the War Council to decide on matters of war and peace. His decision to enter into negotiations so long as there was still a chance of 'peace with honour' could not be postponed. Assurances that the war would be continued, and that Russians would 'die willingly and joyfully' if Japanese conditions proved an affront to their honour,[54] were no more than a placebo for humiliated patriots. It is academic now to wonder whether the Russian army would have been able to continue the war if necessary. One should not lend much credence though to Kuropatkin's attempts to cover up his own failure as commander of the army with the excuse that Russia had been stabbed in the back.[55] The view that Russian military power was 'undefeated in the field' came to be the officially accepted version, but such phrases could not hide the reality of the situation.

As we have seen, a closely interwoven web of factors induced Russia to sue for peace at Portsmouth. The threat of revolution hanging over the regime, the prospect of bankruptcy and the senselessness of waiting for military victories to restore the autocracy's prestige left the Tsar no other choice. The notion that political reform might awaken national enthusiasm for the war was absurd during the summer of 1905. Whatever concessions Nicholas offered his subjects, political participation would clearly have strengthened opposition to an unpopular war, not weakened it. On the other hand, it was very doubtful whether ending the war would do anything to quell the internal crisis, and the prognoses offered the

53. *KA* 28, pp. 200ff.
54. Ibid., p. 201.
55. Cf. the justification written by the former commander-in-chief: Kuropatkin, *Memoiren* (Berlin, 1909), *passim.*

Tsar in this respect were contradictory and full of uncertainty.

The gains which the autocracy could expect to make in its negotiations with the Japanese were not insignificant. In view of the concert of international powers St Petersburg's diplomats could reasonably hope to prevent financial collapse and deliver Russia from her débâcle in Far East with her dignity still intact.[56] There were numerous indications that the powers involved in China (especially the United States) were intent on limiting Japanese claims in East Asia. Roosevelt's encouragement, the Kaiser's expressions of affection and, last but not least, the *entente* signed by Delcassé between England and France showed that the antagonisms within the international system could be exploited to Russia's benefit. That Russian interests were not furthered by an alliance such as the one Wilhelm II pushed the Tsar in Björkö in July 1905 dawned only slowly on both emperors. Russia's status as a great power could only be preserved if the government took the *entente cordiale* into account. It was neither possible nor desirable for a weakened Russia to try to break up this combination by means of an anti-English continental league dominated by Germany. Before anything though, a relatively acceptable peace had to be arranged.[57]

Peace was not a panacea for internal disorder of course, but it did afford the regime a new chance to survive the revolution. A fundamental prerequisite would have to be the lifting of the financial blockade which, in the summer of 1905, was still almost total. When the Russian peace delegation under Sergei Witte set out for America, its strategy was directed primarily at restoring the government's financial freedom of action and preparing the way for new loans. Beyond all the matters hotly disputed at Portsmouth, the securing of new loans was St Peterburg's primary objective in the negotiations. Prospects that this would actually occur began gradually to restore the government's confidence. This was detectable only a few days after the Russo-Japanese Treaty was signed, when the long delayed statutes and electoral regulations governing the Bulygin Duma were published (6/19 August).[58] However, concerted

56. For the diplomatic history of the conclusion of peace see Romanov, *Ocherki diplomaticheskoi istorii*, pp. 409ff.; White, *The Diplomacy*, pp. 227ff.; Zabriskie, *American-Russian Rivalry*, pp. 107ff.

57. For the German offer of an alliance in 1904/05 see Vogel, *Rußlandpolitik*, pp. 201ff., 216ff.; J. Steinberg, 'Germany and the Russo-Japanese War', *AHR* 75 (1970), pp. 1965–86; Romanov, *Ocherki*, pp. 458ff., for French policies: E.M. Rozental', *Diplomaticheskaya istoriya russko-frantsuzskogo soyuza nachala XX v.* (Moscow, 1960), pp. 113ff.

58. Text: F. I. Kalinychev (ed.), *Gosudarstvennaya duma v Rossii v dokumentakh*

attempts to restore stability in Russia on the basis of the peace treaty and this pseudo-constitutional reform failed. Public opinion reacted to the Portsmouth agreements with virtual indifference. Little attention was paid to Russia's renunciation of Kwantung and the Southern Manchurian Railway, her approaching retreat from Manchuria and the abandonment of the southern part of Sakhalin Island. The government did not even get much credit for Witte's great success in the negotiations,[59] in resisting Japanese demands for reparations.

Instead, interest focused almost exclusively on the internal disagreements which intensified as a result of the new Duma law. Liberals, torn between conflicting emotions of disappointment, outrage and fear of revolution, found no more satisfaction in an imperial Duma constituted along the lines of the zemstvo act of 1864 than they did in the plan to restrict this new institution to a consultative role. Widespread violence shook the countryside, dashing the government's hopes for a loyal peasant majority in the Duma. In October a general strike not only closed down the transportation system but confronted the regime in St Petersburg and elsewhere with an organised, revolutionary counterforce: soviets of worker delegates who gave pointed expression to the radically democratic demands of the working population.[60]

Thirdly, it must be said that this is not the place to describe the history of the mass revolutionary disturbances which were barely affected by the Tsar's October Manifesto[61] and which did not reach their climax until December 1905. What will be outlined, however, is the connection between revolution, the financial crisis, and international politics. The immediacy of the danger facing the autocracy was not fully apparent until the end of the war, and the govern-

---

i materialakh (Moscow, 1957), pp. 30ff.; also Leontovitsch, pp. 328ff.; Galai, *Liberation Movement*, pp. 257ff.; Chermenskii, pp. 105ff.; Davidovich, *Samoderzhavie*, pp. 240ff.

59. Treaty of Portsmouth (23 Aug. [5 Sept.] 1905): Romanov, *Ocherki*, p. 494; White, *The Diplomacy*, pp. 247ff., 359ff.; L.N. Kutakov, *Portsmutskii mirnyi dogovor* (Moscow, 1961); text: *Sbornik dogovorov*, pp. 395ff.; for the effect on Anglo-Japanese relations see Nish, *The Anglo-Japanese Alliance*, pp. 323ff.

60. Much literature exists on this, eg.: O. Anweiler, *Die Rätebewegung in Rußland 1905 bis 1921* (Leiden, 1958), pp. 39ff.; A. Fischer, *Russische Sozialdemokratie*, pp. 137ff.

61. For an extensive account of the October Manifesto and Witte's government see: H.D. Mehlinger and J.M. Thompson, *Count Witte and the Tsarist Government in the 1905 Revolution* (Bloomington, Ind., 1972); also: G.S. Doctorow, 'The Government Program of 17 October 1905', *RR* 34 (1975), pp. 123–36.

ment's margin for manoeuvre in foreign policy was severely limited until the spring of 1906. Of great importance in this respect is the fact that the internal convulsions affected the financial system down to its very roots. Pacifying the population and warding off national bankruptcy were related parts of the same problem. Substantial loans were needed to liquidate the war debt, but they could not be secured so long as foreign countries doubted that conditions could be stabilised. On the other hand, law and order could hardly be maintained so long as financial collapse seemed imminent. Huge new sums of money were needed to combat the revolutionary ferment, and the return and demobilisation of Russia's Far Eastern armies would not bring the national Treasury any relief in the short term.

The general strike of October 1905 underlined how directly the revolution was hindering government attempts to re-establish normal international relations. Probably of least concern was the fact that diplomatic attempts to reduce Anglo-Russian tensions were not initially successful. More important was the general air of insurrection which pervaded the international loan negotiations Witte had organised in St Petersburg and to which he had invited the British banker Lord Revelstoke, Edouard Noetzlin from Paris, the American J.P. Morgan and Alfred Fischel from the Mendelssohn bank in Berlin.[62] The Imperial Bank on the Nevskii Prospekt was surrounded by strikers. Kokovtsov had to have his alarmed guests led under police escort from the cold, unlit Hôtel de l'Europe to the Ministry of Finance. On the day the October Manifesto was issued (17/30 October) they escaped turbulent St Petersburg on board a chartered Finnish ferry. Promises to renew negotiations 'as soon as circumstances allow' brought cold comfort.[63] Witte was just about to be named as head of government, and the role he played in the cancellation of the talks is not known. In the message he gave Noetzlin to take back to Paris, the former Minister of Finance let it be known that Russia would support France in international affairs (meaning first and foremost in the Moroccan crisis). Witte also pointed out to the French that they too stood to 'lose everything' if the autocracy fell to a 'real revolution' and the constitutional

---

62. For the remainder: Long, *Economics*, pp. 112ff.; Girault, *Emprunts*, pp. 430ff.; Romanov, *Ocherki*, pp. 5, 99, 599ff.; Ananyich, pp. 149ff.; *Russkie finansy*, pp. 206ff.; Kokovtsov, *Iz moego proshlogo* 1, pp. 96ff.
63. Cf. Kokovtsov to the representatives of the bank syndicate, 18 (31) Oct. 1905, in: *Russkie finansy*, pp. 225f.

reforms which he had introduced failed.[64] Hopes that France would feel enmeshed in the fate of the autocracy because of the approximately 10,000 million francs she had loaned Russia turned out to be justified. The linkage between state reform, loyalty to the alliance and financial aid began to be felt.

The October Manifesto and the end of the great October strike did not settle the disturbances in Russia. Nobody knew whether the formal promise of a constitution would create new confidence in the regime. At Witte's urging, Nicholas had promised his subjects 'the solid foundations of civil freedom': personal inviolability of the individual, freedom of conscience, speech and association, universal suffrage, the right of the future imperial Duma to approve legislation, and the right of peoples' representatives to participate in a legal review of the actions of the state authorities. In October the Constitutional Democratic Party (*Kadety*) still included the activist wing of the zemstvo liberals and the professional intelligentsia and did not propose to wait for Witte to assume 'the leadership of the liberation movement' and isolate the 'extremists'.[65] The Kadets demanded far more than the October Manifesto promised: a legislative national assembly on the basis of 'fourfold' suffrage, parliamentary government, sweeping agricultural reforms with forced expropriation of the large estates and the restoration of autonomy in Poland and Finland. The only group content with the Tsar's constitutional promises was that part of the zemstvo movement which was frightened by the spectre of revolution. It soon constituted itself as a separate political party — the 'Union of the Seventeenth of October' (*Oktyabristy*).[66]

More important at first were the continuing calls for mass revolutionary action with which the Social Democrats and Social Revolutionaries answered the October Manifesto, thus keeping the general unrest alive. A sure sign of this was the financial panic which reached its preliminary peak in December 1905. Massive withdrawals of

64. For this see Noetzlin's report in: *DDF* 2/VII, no. 110, pp. 149ff.
65. Witte to Nicholas II, 9 Oct. 1905, in: *KA*11, pp. 53ff.
66. J.E. Zimmerman, 'Between Revolution and Reaction: The Russian Constitutional Democratic Party (1905–1907)', PhD thesis, Columbia Univ., 1967; G.N. Rhyne, 'The Constitutional Democratic Party from Its Origins Through the First State Duma', PhD thesis, Univ. of North Carolina, 1968; U. Liszkowski, *Zwischen Liberalismus u. Imperialismus. Die zaristische Außenpolitik vor dem Ersten Weltkrieg im Urteil Miljukovs u. der Kadettenpartei 1905–1914* (Stuttgart, 1974), pp. 10ff.; E. Birth, *Die Oktobristen 1905–1913. Zielvorstellungen u. Struktur* (Stuttgart, 1974); L. Menashe, 'Alexander Guchkov and the Origins of the Octobrist Party: The Russian Bourgeoisie in Politics', PhD thesis, New York Univ., 1966, pp. 84ff., 117ff.; Chermenskii, pp. 158ff.

savings and the cashing in of letters of credit further decimated the gold reserves of the Imperial Bank and Treasury. A similar response was created by the so-called financial manifesto of the St Petersburg Soviet of Workers' Deputies (2/15 December) which called on the population to close savings accounts and withhold taxes.[67] The rapid flight of capital accompanied by a general run on the banks, joined the paper money flowing back from Manchuria in halting the free convertibility of gold for internal payments. In addition, Berlin demanded that part of Russian gold reserves be put on deposit in the *Reichsbank* to cover short-term currency credits.[68]

By the end of the year the government was faced with bankruptcy. I.P. Shipov, the new Finance Minister introduced by Witte, thought the situation so desperate that the issue laws would have to be changed. Between 16 October and 8 December, gold reserves had shrunk by almost 250 million rubles to 1,076 million rubles, while the supply of paper money in circulation had soared on account of the war to about 1,250 million rubles. In addition, payments of about 400 million gold rubles were falling due. Backing for the currency, the fundamental tenet of St Petersburg's financial policy, had therefore already melted away in actual fact.[69] However, the Finance Committee hesitated formally to abrogate the credit ruble's convertibility into gold coin, partly because a public admission that the Russian Empire was bankrupt would only add fuel to the fires of revolution. Rather than handing the enemies of the state 'such a sharp insurrectionary weapon' the autocracy preferred to wait until the rebellions in Moscow and the Baltic region had been quashed. The financial steps which had to be taken could then be seen as an 'act of wise foresight on the part of the state' and not as yet another success for the forces of revolution.[70]

It was important that Witte was also strongly opposed to abrogating the gold standard. The new President of the Council of Ministers was banking on extracting another large emergency loan by exploiting the fear of foreign creditors (especially the French)

67. G. Garvy, 'The Financial Manifesto of the St. Petersburg Soviet 1905', *IRSH* 20 (1975), pp. 16–32; Anweiler, *Rätebewegung*, pp. 68ff.

68. On the financial crisis: Long, *Economics*, pp. 118ff., Anan'ich, pp. 153ff.; for Germany see R. Martin's pamphlet: *Die Zukunft Rußlands u. Japans. Die deutschen Milliarden in Gefahr* (Berlin, 1905).

69. For the Finance Minister's suggestions for protecting Russia's gold reserves (end of 1905) see: *IA* (1955/2), pp. 132ff.

70. Report of the financial committee to Nicholas II (14 Dec. 1905) in: *IA* (1955/2), pp. 127ff.; for the defeat of the revolutionary movement see Mehlinger and Thompson, pp. 106ff., 124ff.

that Russia might otherwise prove unable to pay her debts. However, even Witte could not keep his equanimity in the face of this race against time. The estimated budgetary deficit for 1906 was running at between 700 and 800 million rubles. The Finance Committee had recourse to emergency decrees at the end of the year, but they could hardly be expected to pull the regime through the winter.[71] When Kokovtsov went to Paris early in January 1906, French capital markets proved obdurate because of the Moroccan crisis and because the French public still did not feel sure that the autocracy would be able to consolidate itself. In order to buttress the Russian gold standard Rouvier was only willing to grant short-term emergency help, limited to about 100 million rubles (267 million francs).[72] Larger accords would depend on an improvement in the internal situation within Russia and a satisfactory outcome for France at the Algeciras Conference. St Petersburg did manage to arrange a moratorium with Mendelssohn which delayed the repayment of German bill credits until the end of 1906, but even this did not really give the regime an opportunity to catch its breath.[73] Witte asked Noetzlin to come to St Petersburg in February, when he informed his guest that Russia's minimal needs had risen to 2,750 million francs (1,000 million rubles).

It had become clear in the meantime that French *haute finance* was not prepared to make any binding commitments before the end of the Moroccan conference. Neither the British nor French cabinets were willing to back such extensive financial deals. To make matters worse, a change in government in France had brought Poincaré and Clemenceau to the helm in a coalition betraying no sympathy for tsarism. It soon became apparent that Russia was not strong enough to influence German policy either, or even to play the mediator between Berlin and Paris.[74] In vain did Witte beg the

---

71. Cf. the decision about limiting military expenses, 29 Dec. 1905, in: *IA* (1955/2), pp. 140ff.

72. *Russkie finansy*, pp. 229ff.; Long, *Economics*, pp. 146ff.; idem, 'Russian Manipulation of the French Press', *SR* 31 (1972), pp. 343–54; Rozental', *Diplomaticheskaya istoriya*, pp. 162ff., 199ff.; Anan'ich, pp. 163ff.; Mehlinger and Thompson, pp. 218ff.

73. For Kokovtsov's visit to Berlin (14 Jan. 1906), see the report to the finance committee (11 [24] Jan. 1906) in: *Russkie finansy*, pp. 252–68.

74. For the connection between the loan and the Algeciras conference see Long, *Economics*, pp. 159ff.; on the Moroccan crisis: Andrew, *Delcassé*, pp. 268ff.; G. Monge, *Ursachen u. Entstehung der english-französischen Entente*, pp. 232ff.; A. Moritz, *Das Problem des Präventivkrieges in der deutschen Politik während der ersten Marokko-Krise* (Berne, 1974), pp. 53ff.; Rozental', pp. 182ff.; A.I. Astaf'ev, *Russko-germanskie diplomaticheskie otnosheniya 1905–1911 gg.* (Moscow, 1972), pp.

German Kaiser to attempt to find a quick solution to the Moroccan question so that the Russian revolutionaries could be defeated and rebellion prevented from spilling across Russia's borders 'like the French Revolution'.[75] Wilhelm II had no desire to demonstrate sympathy for St Petersburg either without receiving any concrete quid pro quo.

Nervous tension was high among officials along the Neva. Not only was the diplomatic conference lengthy, delaying effective financial aid, but the approaching meeting of the imperial Duma was creating a new internal situation. The Kadets had been highly successful in the election, and the assembly was likely to be refractory.[76] Witte, as the new Prime Minister, must therefore have been all the more anxious to secure the loan and avoid having to put it to the vote of such an 'undisciplined and politically inexperienced bunch'.[77] The pressure of time was still a factor when the powers finally did reach an agreement in Algeciras on 18/31 March 1906. The problem of the Russian constitution now turned out to be one of the toughest hurdles remaining in the finalising of St Petersburg's financial arrangements. French Finance Minister Poincaré demanded guarantees that the loan be made in accordance with the constitution and that the Duma not be allowed to revise Russia's foreign commitments. The autocracy pointed to the budgetary rules of 8 March 1906 which excluded any intervention by the future parliament, but the French were not satisfied.[78]

There was good reason for Poincaré's stalling tactics. The Russian loan had become one of the hotly debated issues in the French election, and the cabinet was confronted with loud demands from its own camp that no aid be given 'bloody tsarism' in its struggle against the people. Prominent Russians, from Maxim Gorky to representatives of the Duma majority warned against loaning French gold to help put autocracy back on its feet. In conversations with ministers in Paris, the liberals Maklakov and Dolgorukov predicted that a regenerated tsarism would once again revert to undemocratic practices. The reaction to Kokovtsov's loan negotiations in the

32ff.; B.F. Oppel, 'The Waning of a Traditional Alliance. Russia and Germany after the Portsmouth Peace Conference', *CEH* 5 (1972), pp. 318–29.

75. Cited in Anan'ich, p. 171.

76. For the elections to the Duma see: Mehlinger and Thompson, pp. 273ff.; R. Rexheuser's analysis, *Dumawahlen und lokale Gesellschaft. Studien zur Sozialgeschichte der russischen Rechten vor 1917* (Cologne, 1980); W. B. Walsh, 'The Composition of the Dumas', *RR* 8 (1949), pp. 111–16.

77. Anan'ich, p. 171.

78. H. Landauer, *Das Budgetrecht in Rußland* (Berlin, 1912).

Russian press left no doubt that the political representatives of the new Russia were deeply opposed to any support for the ruling regime.[79]

Policy-makers in Paris had two main interests: preventing the collapse of Russian securities held by Frenchmen and maintaining imperial Russia as a reliable partner in the Alliance. These concerns far outweighed any sympathy republican France may have felt for democracy in Russia. *Realpolitik* based on capitalism drove back any idealistic impulses to the recesses of private sentiment. So autocracy's dependence on foreign capital helped to save its skin, while France contributed to retarding parliamentary government in Russia. When the French cabinet could no longer postpone taking a decision on Russian credits, expert opinion and Witte's official statements sufficed to allay the concerns of the lenders. Full authority over loans, it was said, was invested solely in the Finance Committee appointed by the Tsar and not in the representative bodies.[80]

The loan was finalised on 3 (16) April 1906. The Russian Government received a credit of 2,250 million francs (844 million rubles) at 5 per cent interest spread over forty years. French high finance covered more than half of this amount (1,200 million francs), and the remainder came from banks in England (330 million), Austria (165 million), Holland (55 million) and Russia (500 million). The extremely low issue price (83.5 per cent) and non-convertibility for ten years highlighted the extremely difficult position in which the autocracy found itself. The government had in addition to agree not to seek any new loans during the following two years and to use the loan only to cover the budgetary deficits of 1905 and 1906.[81]

The political consequences of these developments should not be underestimated. The German Kaiser was deeply offended by Russian behaviour over the Moroccan question and forbade Berlin

79. Long, *Economics*, pp. 198ff.; idem, 'Organized Protests against the 1906 Russian Loan', *CMRS* 13 (1972), pp. 24–39; O. Crisp, 'The Russian Liberals and the 1906 Anglo-French Loan to Russia', *SEER* 39 (1960), pp. 479–511; B.V. Anan'ich, 'Vneshnie zaimy i dumskii vopros 1906–1907 gg.', *IZ* 81 (1968), pp. 199–215; Chermenskii, pp. 246ff. For the effects of the loan on discussions within Russia: K. Ferenczi, *Außenpolitik u. Öffentlichkeit in Rußland 1906–1912* (Husum, 1982), chap. 2.

80. Long, 'French Attempts at Constitutional Reform in Russia', *JGO* 23 (1975), pp. 496–503.

81. Final negotiations and terms of the loan in: Long, *Economics*, pp. 181ff.; Mehlinger and Thompson, pp. 227ff.; Girault, *Emprunts*, pp. 435ff.; *Russkie finansy*, pp. 378ff.

banks to participate in the loan.[82] In the international arena St Petersburg would henceforth remain bound to the Anglo-French *entente*. The military repercussions could already be foreseen before the loan was publicised (9/22 April). The Russian and French chiefs of the general staff, Generals Palitsyn and Brun, met secretly and thoroughly revised the military convention of 1892. The anti-British clause, introduced in 1901 at Delcassé's insistence, was dropped at French request. Henceforward the mutual obligations would relate solely to the German Empire and its allies.[83]

---

82. For the attempts to get German banks to participate see the correspondence between Mendelssohn and Witte in: *Russkie finansy*, especially pp. 315ff.

83. Long, *Economics*, pp. 192ff.; Anan'ich, *Rossiya*, p. 173; Rozental' pp. 215ff.

PART III

Between the Wars 1905–1914

War and revolution left Russia deeply scarred. After the defeat in the Far East had been sealed and the revolutionary uprisings quashed, the *ancien régime* proved unable to restore the old conditions. The Fundamental Laws of 23 April 1906 had set the autocracy on a constitutional path,[1] and the government of Stolypin which took over in July from the transitional cabinets of Witte and Goremykin, had to seek a consensus, however fragile, with politically organised society. Only under fairly stable conditions could agricultural reforms be introduced which would bring a long-term solution to the social crisis and give the country new hope for development.

The autocracy had difficulty in drawing appropriate conclusions from the experience of war and revolution. Political concessions were denigrated as a product of duress and were not accepted as a new beginning in their own right. From the start, influential forces were intent on restricting Duma constitutionalism to Prussian levels. They were acceptable at most as a mere ornament to bureaucratised autocracy.[2] Stolypin made a daring attempt to accommodate the Duma in the construction of his bureaucratic regime, but within a few years found his path blocked on many sides.[3] After parliament had twice been dissolved prematurely, the *coup d'état* of 3 (16)

1. G.S. Doctorow, 'The Fundamental State Law of 23 April 1906', *RR* 35 (1976), pp. 33–52; Mehlinger and Thompson, pp. 289ff., 336ff.
2. For the first two Dumas of 1906–07 see: S.M. Sidel'nikov, *Obrazovanie i deyatel'nost' Pervoi Gosudarstvennoi Dumy* (Moscow, 1962); A. Levin, *The Second Duma* (New Haven, 1940); Chermenskii, *Burzhuaziya*, pp. 211ff., 338ff.
3. Hosking, *The Russian Constitutional Experiment. Government and Duma, 1907–1914* (Oxford, 1973), *passim*; A. Ya. Avrekh, *Tsarizm i tret'eiyun'skaya sistema* (Moscow, 1966); Avrekh, *Stolypin i Tret'ya Duma* (Moscow, 1968); L. Bazylow, *Ostatnie lata Rosij carskiej. Rządy Stol'ypina* (Warsaw, 1972); A.M. Davidovich, *Samoderzhavie v epokhu imperializma* (Moscow, 1975), pp. 248ff., 301ff.; M. Hagen, 'Der russische "Bonapartismus" nach 1906. Genese u. Problematik eines Leitbegriffs in der sowjetischen Geschichtswissenschaft', *JGO* 24 (1976), pp. 369–93; A. Levin, 'P.A. Stolypin: A Political Re-appraisal', *JMH* 37 (1965), pp. 445–63; M.S. Conroy, *Peter A. Stolypin* (Boulder, Col., 1976).

June 1907 succeeded in forcing through a restrictive franchise and in decimating the previously dominant Left in the Duma.[4] However, the new majority of Octobrists, Nationalists and moderate Right soon lost its coherence. The extreme Right, which knew how to use its support at the Court to full advantage, soon arranged for the Prime Minister's reform policies to fail.[5] The authoritarian tsarist state with its constitutional embellishments quickly proved incapable of far-reaching reform.

In foreign policy the regime had no more success in freeing itself from the past.[6] The huge loan of 1906 made it clear that St Petersburg was neither willing nor able to abandon international politics. Russia's French ally and creditor wanted her to remain a reliable partner, at least in Europe. First steps in this direction were taken when Russia's unpopular adventure in the Far East was liquidated by the new Foreign Minister Izvolskii. The settlement reached with Japan and Great Britain in the summer of 1907 tied what remained of Russian *grande politique* to the interests of the Anglo-French *entente*.[7] St Petersburg's traditional diplomacy of freely playing off Paris against Berlin was henceforth of limited and

4. A. Levin, *The Third Duma. Election and Profile* (Hamden, Conn., 1973); Levin, 'June 3, 1907: Action and Reaction', *Essays in Russian History* (Hamden, Conn., 1964), pp. 233–73; for the new electoral law: Palme, pp. 194ff.

5. Birth, *Die Oktobristen, passim*; B.C. Pinchuk, *The Octobrists in the Third Duma 1907–1912* (Seattle, 1974); R. Edelman, *Gentry Politics on the Eve of the Russian Revolution: The Nationalist Party 1907–1917* (New Brunswick, 1980); for the extreme right, primarily: H. Rogger, 'The Formation of the Russian Right 1900–1906', *CSS* 3 (1964), pp. 66–94; Rogger, 'Was There a Russian Fascism? The Union of the Russian People', *JMH* 36 (1964), pp. 398–415; H. Jablonowski, 'Die russischen Rechtsparteien 1905–1917', *Rußland-Studien. Gedenkschrift für O. Hoetzsch* (Stuttgart, 1957), pp. 43–55; D.C. Rawson, 'The Union of the Russian People 1905–1907. A Study of the Russian Right', Ph.D. thesis, Univ. of Washington, 1971; for recent work on the whole question: R. Rexhauser, *Dumawahlen und lokale Gesellschaft* (Cologne, 1983); T. Emmons, *The Formation of Political Parties and the First National Election in Russia* (Cambridge, Mass., 1983).

6. A modern overview of Russian foreign policy from 1905 to 1914 which includes the specialist research remains to be written. A presentation of internal political discussion on foreign policy can be found in: I.V. Bestuzhev, *Bor'ba v Rossii po voprosam vneshnei politiki 1906–1910* (Moscow, 1961); Bestuzhev, 'Bor'ba v Rossii po voprosam vneshnei politiki nakanune pervoi mirovoi voiny (1910–1914)', *IZ* 75 (1965), pp. 44–85; K. Ferenczi, *Außenpolitik und Öffentlichkeit in Rußland 1906–1912* (Husum, 1982); see also the general surveys: I.V. Bovykin, *Ocherki istorii vneshnei politiki Rossii. Konets XIX v.–1917 g.* (Moscow, 1960); P.N. Efremov, *Vneshnyaya politika Rossii 1907–1914 gg.* (Moscow, 1961); a valuable contribution was made recently by D.C.B. Lieven, *Russia and the Origins of the First World War* (London, 1983).

7. Monge, *Ursachen u. Entstehung der englisch-französischen-russischen Entente*; Kazemzadeh, *Russia and Britain*, pp. 447ff.; V.A. Marinov, *Rossiya i Yaponiya pered pervoi mirovoi voinoi, 1905–1914 gody. Ocherki istorii otnoshenii (Moscow, 1974)*; S.S. Grigortsevich, *Da'lnevostochnaya politika imperialisticheskikh derzhav v 1906–1917 gg.* (Tomsk, 1965).

often only symbolic value.

Interest in maintaining Russia's status as a great power did not depend on encouragement from outside. Where the *'Wille zur Weltgeltung'*[8] ('will to world domination') had begun to fail in the wake of military humiliation, it was quickly restored. Russia's annihilated fleet and the terrible condition of her army may have condemned her for a time to a defensive strategy of preserving the *status quo*, but this did little to hinder expansionist views for the future. The Russian military, the diplomatic corps and, last but not least, the Tsar were not inclined to abandon Russia's historic mission to raise her gaze to grandiose objectives beyond the Empire itself. The strategic elites' feeling of self-importance continued to be bound up with Russian hegemony, and a hegemonistic power had to make its presence felt on the world stage.

The internal conferences which preceded the treaties with Tokyo and London reveal how difficult it was for the Russians to appreciate the real limitations on their power.[9] The Foreign and Finance Ministers had to try very hard to convince not only the general staff but also the Ministers of Trade and Industry that Russia would long have to share Manchuria with Japan and Persia with England. Naval commanders whose fleet had been destroyed were naturally most reluctant to accept a position in the Pacific and the Persian Gulf which apparently held little promise for the future.

There was no doubt that Russia's military capacity should quickly be built up again in accordance with her claims to great power status.[10] By the summer of 1906 naval headquarters considered the principle firmly established that the backbone of new fleet would be the most modern battleships of the dreadnought class. The fleet would then be used not only to protect the coasts but also to project in strength wherever this seemed to be in the imperial interest.

8. K. Wernecke, *Der Wille zur Weltgeltung. Außenpolitik u. Öffentlichkeit am Vorabend des Ersten Weltkrieges* (Düsseldorf, 1969).

9. 'K istorii anglo-russkogo soglasheniya 1907', *KA* 69/70, pp. 3–39; 'Anglo-russkaya konventsiya 1907 g. i razdel Afganistana', ibid., pp. 10, 54–66.; cf. Bestuzhev (1961), pp. 127ff., 156ff.

10. Of seminal importance for Russian rearmament policies after 1906, especially with regard to the fleet, is the research of K.F. Shatsillo: *Russkii imperializm i razvitie flota nakanune pervoi mirovoi voiny, 1906–1914 gg.* (Moscow, 1968); idem, *Razvitie vooruzhennykh sil Rossii nakanune pervoi mirovoi voiny. Voennye i voenno-morskie programmy tsarskogo pravitel'stva v 1906–1914 gg.*, (Avtoref. diss.), (Moscow, 1968); idem, *Rossiya pered pervoi mirovoi voinoi. Vooruzhennye sily tsarizma v 1905–1914 gg.* (Moscow, 1974), as well as the preliminary work of the same author in: *IZ* 69 (1961), pp., 73–100; *IZ* 75 (1965), pp. 86–121; *IZ* 83 (1969), pp. 123–36.

While Izvolskii diplomats worked away secretly at revising the Straits Conventions in Russia's favour,[11] the chiefs of staff of the army and navy, Palitsyn and Brusilov, elaborated a plan to secure Russia's long-term interests in the Black Sea.[12] The suggestive power of the old clichés about Russia's 'historic mission' had not been lost. Russia's 'drive for the open sea' and her goal of seizing the Straits and establishing a dominant position in the eastern Mediterranean and Asia Minor had to be satisfied. This could be achieved in the long run, it was said, 'not by international treaties but solely by means of the struggle and the presence of well-armed forces'. For the time being, of course, Russia could not bring her potential to bear in this conflict. The vulnerability of Russian military power meant that Russia's big power policies would have to rely on the skills of diplomats rather than an anemic army or the wasted remains of the fleet.

In the meantime St Petersburg was being seriously affected by a variety of crises in the international system. The permanent state of crisis in the Ottoman Empire, nationalist developments in the Balkans, German penetration of the Near East and Vienna's Balkan policies — all created tremendous challenges and temptations for the Russian leadership after 1908.[13] All the more bitter then was the repeated experience that Russia, because of her military weakness, could often only pretend to pursue great power policies. When Turkish troops occupied a number of Persian border towns in January 1908, voices in Russia demanded military sanctions. Stolypin, however, begged his colleagues not to fall victim to 'febrile delirium' and to adhere to a strictly defensive policy. In a few years, he said, Russia might be able 'to once more to speak her earlier language'.[14] The policy of *attentisme* to which St Petersburg was

11. See W. M. Carlgren, *Iswolsky u. Aerenthal vor der bosnischen Annexionskrise. Russische u. österreichisch-ungarische Balkanpolitik 1906–1908* (Uppsala, 1955); Bestuzhev (1961), pp. 179ff.; K. B. Vinogradov, *Bosniiskii krizis 1908–1909 gg. — prolog pervoi mirovoi voiny* (Leningrad, 1964); Astafyev, *Russko-germanskie diplomaticheskie otnosheniya*, pp. 137ff.; for the discussions about the Sanjak railway and the Danube–Adriatic Railway see: W.S. Vucinich, *Serbia between East and West, 1903–1908* (Stanford, 1954), pp. 210ff., 229ff.

12. Report by the head of the central administration of the general staff and the head of the navy general staff, 24 Dec. 1906, in: Shatsillo, *Russkii imperializm*, pp. 318–21.

13. For Russian policies towards the Ottoman Empire, see the work of M. Hiller, *Krisenregime Nahost: Russische Orientpolitik im Zeitalten des Imperialismus 1900–1914* (Frankfurt, 1985). From the Soviet side and from the point of view of German expansion see the following: B.M. Tupolev, *Ekspansiya germanskogo imperializma v Yugo-Vostochnoi Evrope v kontse XIX–nachale XX veka* (Moscow, 1970).

14. Bestuzhev (1961), p. 151.

driven only increased the desire to keep up in the arms race. Within a decade, it was hoped, Russia would be able to take the offensive in asserting her interests.[15]

It is important from the point of view of domestic politics to realise that not only people in government wanted the Russian Empire to make her presence felt as a great military power once more. Agreement on this score extended far into the constitutionalist camp. Even the oppositionist Kadets were forced to support the great power mentality of the ruling elite if they did not wish to be seen as lacking in patriotism.[16] A broad national consensus seemed unlikely in most aspects of internal policy, but it might possibly arise out of a successful foreign policy. Thus one of the great 'national challenges' of the post-war period came to be created by the huge discrepancy between pretensions and capabilities. Expensive plans to rebuild the fleet and equip the army were incompatible with the deplorable state of national finances, the weakness of the national economy and Russia's structural backwardness. This problem could be overcome only by long-term programmes of reform and development.[17] 'Russia cannot be a great power with an economy in ruins.' This pithy dictum offered by Finance Minister Kokovtsov to military leaders serves to underline the fundamental dilemma facing Russian policy: namely the tension between the needs of internal restabilisation and the costs to the nation of pursuing imperial interests.[18]

The regime was not unaware of this state of affairs. Foreign policy, naval policy and military planning all posed a financial and economic problem, not only in the internal struggles between the ministries but also in the relations between the government and the imperial Duma. National defence and foreign policy remained the prerogatives of the Tsar. However, according to budgetary stipulations in the constitution, that irksome relic of the revolution, the Duma had to approve naval construction and any increases in the size of the army. The Duma's budgetary committee and the com-

15. For the problem in general see V.R. Berghahn, *Rüstung u. Machtpolitik. Zur Anatomie des 'Kalten Krieges' vor 1914* (Düsseldorf, 1973).
16. Liszkowski, *Zwischen Liberalismus u. Imperialismus*; J.F. Hutchinson, 'The Octobrists and the Future of Imperial Russia as a Great Power', *SEER* 50 (1972), pp. 220–37; also the work of Birth, Pinchuk and Hosking.
17. For general financial and economic policies see: J. Nötzold, *Wirtschaftspolitische Alternativen*; A.P. Pogrebinskii, *Gosudarstvennye finansy tsarskoi Rossii v epokhu imperializma* (Moscow, 1968).
18. Cf. the attitude of the Finance Minister in the special deliberations about the navy programme (3 Aug. 1909) in: Shatsillo, *Russkii imperializm*, pp. 327ff.

mittee on national defence became important check points which the government could not avoid. Ruling Russia was therefore made more complicated by the need to find a parliamentary majority in budgetary matters.[19] However, the Duma movement with its concern for Russia's great power status was sympathetic to rearmament policies. Sometimes extra budgetary requests from the Ministers of War and the Navy were approved by the Duma faster than the Council of Ministers.[20] Nationalism embraced the competing interests of a divided public and made it possible for the government to give priority to increasing Russia's military power. However, nationalism also reduced the government's ability to use its limited financial resources in a productive way and to adhere in the long run to the defensive policy of the post-war years. The results of these relationships will be discussed later in greater detail.

19. A. Martiny, *Parlament, Staatshaushalt u. Finanzen in Rußland. Der Einfluß der Duma auf die russische Finanz- u. Haushaltspolitik 1907–1914* (Bochum, 1977); S.L. Levitsky, 'Interpellation u. Verfahrensfragen in der russischen Duma', *FOG* 6 (1958), pp. 170–207.
20. See W.A. Sukhomlinov, *Erinnerungen* (Berlin, 1924), p. 225, where he says that the Duma 'never failed to approve money for the army'.

11

Armaments, Financial Policies and the Economy

The demand of the Russian élites, as well as of broad sections of 'society', that their country should be a great power was therefore an integral part of the political system in imperial Russia. This created problems above all for state financing, and financial policy came under heavy pressure again after 1906. During the period of war and revolution the Russian gold standard had almost collapsed. The budgetary deficits of 1905 and 1906 completely exhausted the great liquidating loan which had been secured to prevent a débâcle and to preserve Russia's solvency. By 1907 the residual costs of the war against Japan had swallowed the enormous sum of 2,316.8 million rubles for extraordinary needs alone — a sum almost exactly equivalent to total regular state expenditure for 1908.[1] Under such circumstances the Finance Minister had one aim which took precedence over all others: the monetary system and the national budget had to be restored to good health.

This objective clearly could not be realised by the traditional method of taking out loans on domestic and foreign capital markets. A serious financial policy could not possibly increase the already enormous volume of state debt. In 1907 more than 16 per cent of state expenditure went on payments on interest and principal; in 1913 the figure was still 13.7 per cent. It was equally clear that revenues could not be increased by imposing an even heavier financial burden on the Russian people. The years of revolution had shown that the regime could no longer test its subjects' tolerance level with impunity. At this time the national Treasury drew approximately 60 per cent of its normal revenues from indirect taxes

---

1. Pogrebinskii, *Gosudarstvennye finansy*, pp. 50ff.; Shatsillo, *Russkii imperializm*, pp. 202ff.; A.L. Sidorov, *Finansovoe polozhenie Rossii v gody pervoi mirovoi voiny* (Moscow, 1960), pp. 14ff.; cf. the relevant table and the ensuing data.

and almost a third from its monopoly on alcohol alone. Substantial change would result only from national economic recovery, rapid industrial growth, increasing productivity of agriculture and an increase in mass purchasing power. Financial policy depended therefore on the success of Stolypin's agrarian reforms as well as on overcoming the depressed state of the economy.[2]

This explains why Kokovtsov (who had once more taken over the Ministry of Finance under the new conditions of a constitutional budget and a unified cabinet) viewed all demands for increased military expenditure with great caution.[3] This experienced individual, seeking to assert the traditional importance of his office, became the chief proponent in Stolypin's government of policies which aimed at curbing the demands of the army and navy. Already in the autumn of 1906 he was opposing the requests of the Ministries of War and the Navy in grave memoranda to the Prime Minister replete with sober analyses of the situation. According to Kokovtsov, stability, and security depended on overcoming Russia's financial and economic problems, and unchecked rearmament would only ruin the country. The demands placed on the state must not surpass the capacity of the Russian people. Without solid budgetary policies, the banks and the public would not regain the necessary confidence. Kokovtsov therefore insisted that the Empire had to be protected primarily by diplomatic means and by an 'appropriate orientation in our foreign policy'.[4]

The chiefs of staff of the army and navy were vigorously opposed of course to any reduction in military expenditures or to any decrease in Russia's peacetime strength. The General Chief of Staff, F.F. Palitsyn, pointed out that even the largest military budget cost less than a lost war.[5] However, the military usually had a very difficult time with Kokovtsov. In 1909 Russia entered a period of

---

2. For the kind of research being done see: A. Moritsch, 'Neuere Literatur zur Stolypinschen Agrarreform', *JGO* 24 (1976), pp. 230–49; the older standard work of W.D. Preyer, *Die russische Agrarreform* (Jena, 1914) is still indispensable; the standard Soviet overview is S.M. Dubrovskii, *Stolypinskaya zemel'naya reforma* (Moscow, 1963[3]). For peasant colonisation of Siberia during the agrarian reforms see: Treadgold, *The Great Siberian Migration*; also L.F. Sklyarov, *Pereselenie i zemleustroistvo v Sibiri v gody stolypinskoi agrarnoi reformy* (Leningrad, 1962); L.M. Goryushkin, *Agrarnye otnosheniya v Sibiri perioda imperializma (1900–1917 gg.)* (Novosibirsk, 1976), pp. 133ff., 157ff., 298ff.

3. For the new cabinet system see N.G. Koroleva, 'Reforma Soveta Ministrov Rossii v 1905 g.', *Sovetskie arkhivy* (1972/1), pp. 85ff.

4. Kokovtsov to Stolypin, 14 Nov. 1906, in *Russkie finansy*, pp. 349–66; cf. also the Finance Minister's note written on 6 Sept. 1906, ibid., pp. 336–40.

5. Shatsillo, *Russkii imperializm*, pp. 327–9.

economic expansion in the wake of good harvests, and state revenues rose. Nevertheless, the Finance Minister stuck to his tight
monetary policy and tried his best to gain reductions in the ambitious ten-year plan for the army and navy.[6] According to
Kokovtsov, the armed services should confine themselves to defence and forget about ambitious projects. Russia needed neither
'command of the seas' nor a battle-fleet to satisfactorily guarantee
the security of the Empire. Ambitions directed at the world political
scene struck Kokovtsov as pure adventurism in the context of
Russia's financial straits. 'If the whole world really was our enemy,
we should only have a single escape: a kind of self-interment in the
cemetery.'[7] The demands of his ministry forced him to try to keep
the level of unproductive expenditures down and to see to it that the
growing volume of money in circulation (together with Russia's
foreign debts) were consistent with a currency backed by gold.
Kokovtsov was reluctant to see the nation's gold reserves run down
for the sake of battleships and guns; gold should be saved for times
of crisis. Kokovtsov's resistance to plans for large-scale rearmament
did not diminish until the period between 1911 and 1914 when, as
successor to the assassinated Stolypin, he frequently succumbed to
pressures emanating from the military. The international crisis also
played a role in frustrating a long-term strategy to heal the economy.

Since the end of 1907, the Duma majority had been fundamentally loyal but wilful. Kokovtsov had to be wary of it in budgetary
matters and also in respect to taxation law. The right of the people's
representatives to play a hand in Russia's dealings with European
high finance remained a delicate question. During his time in office,
Kokovtsov spent about half of his fourteen-hour working day on
Duma matters.[8] Although he was not a minister in parliament, he
had to concern himself both with party politics and the variety of
opinions in the politically relevant parts of society. When
Kokovtsov allowed himself to get carried away in the Duma in 1908
and cried out that Russia had 'no parliament yet, thank God', his
resignation had to be seriously considered in view of the public
outrage.[9]

6. For the economic cycle, see the data in: Khromov, *Ekonomicheskoe razvitie*,
pp. 296f. *passim*; see also: B. Löhr, *Die 'Zukunft Rußlands'. Perspektiven russischer
Wirtschaftsentwicklung und deutsch–russische Wirtschaftsbeziehungen vor dem Ersten Weltkrieg* (Wiesbaden, 1985).
7. Kokovtsov, 3 Aug. 1909, cited in: Shatsillo, *Russkii imperializm*, pp. 327–9.
8. See the exchange of letters between Kokovtsov and Noetzlin in: *Russkie
finansy*, pp. 332ff.; Kokovtsov, *Iz moego proshlogo* 1, p. 287.
9. Kokovtsov 1, pp. 307ff.

Table 10: State revenues 1900–1914 (in mill. of rubles)

Budgetary year	Ordinary revenues	Direct taxes	Indirect taxes	Tariffs	Tolls & fees	State monopolies	Monopoly on alcohol	State assets	State railways	Extraordinary revenues	State loans
1900	1,704	132	505	(204)	89	329	(270)	474	(362)	33	(29)
1901	1,799	131	470	(219)	95	439	(379)	494	(379)	164	(158)
1902	1,905	133	429	(225)	101	546	(485)	524	(408)	202	(199)
1903	2,032	135	440	(241)	107	606	(542)	571	(453)	171	(41)
1904	2,018	135	419	(219)	104	614	(543)	572	(455)	385	(383)
1905	2,025	127	409	(213)	100	686	(609)	553	(431)	794	(790)
1906	2,272	163	494	(241)	113	777	(698)	603	(491)	1,084	(1,077)
1907	2,342	183	510	(260)	123	791	(707)	636	(510)	143	(135)
1908	2,418	194	526	(279)	137	794	(709)	648	(513)	201	(189)
1909	2,526	199	530	(274)	152	814	(719)	708	(568)	163	(149)
1910	2,781	216	593	(301)	170	866	(767)	797	(626)	24	—
1911	2,952	224	630	(328)	190	890	(783)	888	(708)	3	—
1912	3,106	243	650	(327)	199	943	(825)	938	(742)	2	—
1913	3,415	273	708	(353)	231	1,025	(899)	1,044	(814)	14	—
1914	2,898	281	661	(304)	209	647	(504)	965	(733)	1,604	(1,595)
1900–14	36,193	2,769	7,974	(3,988)	2,120	10,767	(9,439)	10,415	(8,193)	4,987	(4,745)

Source: Khromov, *Ekonomicheskoe razvitie*, pp. 504–13

Table 11: State expenditures 1900–1914 (in mill. of rubles)

Budgetary year	Ordinary exp.	Min. of the Int.	Min of Fin.	Monopoly on alcohol	Min. of Ed.	Min. of Trans.	Min. of Trade & Ind.	Main. Agr. Admin.	Min. of War	Min. of the Navy	State credit	Railway debts	Extraordinary exp.*
1900	1,599	88	280	(112)	34	367	—	41	332	89	267	(112)	284
1901	1,665	89	308	(145)	33	389	—	41	335	93	277	(126)	209
1902	1,802	94	334	(158)	37	446	—	43	343	100	290	(129)	365
1903	1,883	100	366	(171)	39	456	—	52	351	114	289	(136)	225
1904	1,907	106	350	(166)	42	449	—	47	372	113	298	(136)	831
1905	1,925	114	339	(169)	43	449	—	47	378	117	307	(132)	1,280
1906	2,061	136	353	(178)	44	477	32	36	393	112	357	(135)	1,152
1907	2,196	140	429	(221)	46	508	32	47	406	88	374	(133)	387
1908	2,388	147	432	(212)	53	571	33	58	463	93	398	(137)	273
1909	2,451	156	460	(196)	64	551	39	71	473	92	395	(135)	156
1910	2,473	160	409	(188)	80	537	39	86	485	113	409	(138)	124
1911	2,536	168	403	(188)	98	543	42	104	498	121	399	(133)	310
1912	2,722	179	425	(199)	118	555	54	120	528	176	394	(133)	449
1913	3,094	185	482	(235)	143	641	65	136	581	245	424	(142)	289
1914	2,927	207	446	(208)	154	705	60	146	427	214	366	(119)	1,938
1900–14	33,629	2,069	5,816	(2,746)	1,028	7,644	396	1,075	6,365	1,880	5,244	(1,976)	8,272

Source: Khromov, *Ekonomicheskoe razvitie*, pp. 524–9.

*Extraordinary expenses include: debt repayment 1900–14: 842 mill. rubles; China policies, the Far Eastern War and its aftermath 1900–09: 2,787 mill. rubles; expenses for the military and rearmament 1908–14: 2,301 mill. rubles.

Most of the budget was 'iron-clad', that is secure against intervention from the Duma, because of earlier budgetary laws. However, this did not make the Finance Minister's task any easier. The annual budgetary debates were always very hard on him. Not only was criticism from the left usually biting, but the conservatives had many complaints as well. One of Kokovtsov's most important legislative proposals aimed at introducing progressive income tax and reducing the favourable treatment accorded the wealthy in the way in which the fiscal burden was distributed (only about 7 per cent of state revenues came from direct taxes in Russia compared with over 30 per cent in England). However, this project had no hope of being approved by the majority of deputies in the Duma, not to mention the senators in the Council of State.[10] In addition, the Ministers of War and the Navy could usually counter Kokovtsov's recalcitrance with the argument that the legislative bodies looked favourably upon extra funds for rearmament. The Tsar also stood firmly on the side of the admirals and army commanders.

A glance at the evolution of the national budget between 1905 and 1914 shows that the military's demands for more money forced the Ministry of Finance increasingly onto the defensive. Kokovtsov could not avoid realising that the regime's claim to be a great power forced it to keep up in the international arms race. Between 1907 and 1913 regular military expenditure rose continuously: by 43.1 per cent for the army (from 406 million to 581 million rubles) and by as much as 178.4 per cent for the navy (from 88 million to 245 million rubles). If both services are taken together, then growth in these years reached 67.2 per cent, while ordinary expenditure in the national budget rose only by 40.9 per cent.[11] The accelerating element within Russian rearmament was clearly the fleet and the naval syndrome revealed by the Russian elites. Although expenditure on Stolypin's agrarian reforms and on general education also increased sharply before the war, the increases in these backward sectors — more than threefold — barely began to make an impact (Main Agricultural Administration: 47 million rubles in 1907 and 146 million in 1914; Ministry of Education: 46 million and 154 million rubles).

10. On the constitutional role of the Council of State see O.W. Gerus, 'The Reformed State Council 1905–1917. A Phase in Russian Constitutionalism', PhD thesis, Toronto, 1970.
11. For these calculations see table 11.

In judging the costs to the nation of rearmament, one could argue that, although the military budget increased rapidly in absolute terms, its share of the expanding total budget only increased by slightly less than 3 per cent (from 23.8 to 26.7 per cent). However, actual costs can only be calculated when high extraordinary expenditures on the army and navy are included. Detailed calculations cannot be entered into here, but already in July 1907 the costs of the 'small naval programme', including the construction of four dreadnoughts, were assessed at 120.7 million rubles. A ten-year programme, decided upon in February 1910, promised the army 71.8 million rubles in annual special expenditures and the navy 69.8 million. Further demands from the two services soon produced more large increases. Kokovtsov had always steadfastly refused to take out loans to cover such expenditures; however, he was now forced instead to consider increasing state prices for spirits and taking other fiscal measures. In the spring of 1911, Minister of the Navy I.K. Grigorovich was already busy elaborating new proposals which would channel 512.6 million rubles to the Baltic fleet in the ensuing five years and 102.2 million rubles to the previously neglected Black Sea fleet. Minister of War Sukhomlinov's programmes to strengthen the army, approved in July 1913 and June 1914, required 433 million rubles in additional expenditures until 1917.[12] Between 1908 and 1914 a total of 2,301 million rubles were set aside in the national budget for armaments and military costs under the heading of extraordinary expenditure — a gigantic sum, almost exactly equal to the huge costs of the war from 1904 to 1907. To this must be added monies spent on building strategic railways and roads. In December 1909 Kokovtsov estimated at 500 million rubles the costs of building the urgently needed Amur railway and double-tracking the Trans-Siberian Railway alone.[13]

Kokovtsov was just as aware as his predecessors of the problems generated by Russia's financial dependence. The experience of 1905 had underlined the high risk of relying on foreign countries to finance Russia's wars and the lesson remained vivid. If at all possible, the budget should therefore be balanced without the help of

---

12. Data cited in Sidorov, *Finansovoe polozhenie*, pp. 51–82; cf. Sidorov (ed.), 'Iz istorii podgotovki tsarizma k pervoi mirovoi voine', *IA* (1962/2), pp. 132ff.; Shatsillo, *Rossiya*, pp. 86ff. In Germany the relationship between the army and navy budgets was, from 1909 to 1912 about 2:1, after 1913 about 3:1 (on account of the large army proposals); cf. P.C. Witt, *Die Finanzpolitik des Deutschen Reiches, 1903–1913* (Lübeck, 1970), pp. 380f. (Tab. XIV b).
13. Kokovtsov, 14 Dec 1909, in: Shatsillo, *Russkii imperializm*, pp. 342ff.

foreign loans. This principle proved very difficult to uphold, however, as was evident during preliminary work on the budget of 1909 when a deficit of about 150 million rubles could not be closed. In addition, the short-term war loan which St Petersburg had taken out with France in 1904 had to be amortised in the spring of 1909 and this required 300 million rubles (800 million francs).[14] The Finance Minister had been seeking a combined solution to the problem since the summer of 1908: war bonds at 5 per cent interest would be exchanged for long-term bonds at a lower rate of interest and tied to loans which were to be used to balance the budget. Although early contacts showed that the French banks were not opposed to such a plan, later negotiations took an unpleasant turn when Finance Minister Caillaux demanded that French firms be given the battleship contracts in the 'small naval programme' of 1907 and that the agreement already reached with the Hamburg shipyard of Blohm & Voss be cancelled.

The pressure was made even worse by an unfavourable international situation. Izvol'skii's secret diplomacy in the Bosnian annexation crisis had irked France. The Parisian press cast doubt on St Petersburg's desire for peace and urged that no new loan be granted. The Russian Ministry of Finance found itself under pressure, and toward the end of 1908 Kokovtsov recommended a deal to the finance committee and the Duma, the involuntary nature (*vynuzhdennyi kharakter*) of which he himself could not deny. Kokovtsov's defiant dictum, 'alliance et amitié ne sont pas synonyme de joug et servitude',[15] did not apply apparently to financial affairs. On 1 (14) January 1909 a loan was signed for 525 million rubles (1,400 million francs) at 4.5 per cent interest, running until 1959 with an issue price of 89 per cent. Bankers' commissions and taxes reduced the actual amount received by a further 6 per cent. The response in both the press and the Duma was frosty, and liberal critics in particular emphasised the tributary nature of Franco-Russian financial relations. Kokovtsov's trip to Paris was even compared with the humiliating treks of the old Russian princes to the seat of the Golden Horde.[16]

Not until the economic upswing, beginning in 1909, was the Ministry of Finance able to survive for a few years without new

14. For this and the following see: Anan'ich, *Rossiya i mezhdunarodnyi kapital*, pp. 219ff., 233ff.; Girault, *Emprunts*, pp. 487ff.
15. Kokovtsov to Rafalovich, 31 Aug. 1908, cited in Anan'ich, *Rossiya*, p. 228.
16. A.I. Shingarev in the Duma debate of 16 Feb. 1909, ibid., p. 252.

loans. Increased state revenues made it seem as if even the great arms programme of 1910 could be financed, despite Kokovtsov's strong reservations. However, after Russia's French ally insisted that work progress faster on the strategic railway network in Poland, the national Treasury soon began to run dry. Kokovtsov, now promoted to Prime Minister, was testing international capital markets again in April 1912.[17] The only practical method of acquiring funds this time was to float government-backed Russian railway bonds in Paris. Once again, however, the Empire was subjected to untoward demands. Verneuil, president of the Parisian stock-brokers' syndicate, arrived in St Petersburg in June 1913 on a semi-official mission and quickly made it clear that the French government would only approve a loan if St Petersburg consented to make substantial increases in the peace-time strength of the army and immediately begin construction on the agreed railway lines.[18] The Russian government had actually already planned on increasing the size of the army by 360,000 men in view of the big German military bills of 1912 and 1913.[19]

Kokovtsov was opposed above all to a commitment to lay fixed stretches of track whose usefulness had been determined solely by the military. However, the French were not satisfied with his attempts, in the ensuing negotiations, to promise only general measures 'to improve the capacity of our railway network'. Conditions for the loan were finally settled at the Quai d'Orsay on 28 October (10 November) 1913. But Kokovtsov's partners refused to budge and pointed to the report of a general staff conference which had received the Tsar's approval in the meantime and which laid down in detail Russia's strategic railway programme for the next four years.[20] The Prime Minister refused to accept the French conditions until December, when a change in the French cabinet from Barthou to Doumergue threatened to delay the loan further. The agreement was signed on 17 (30) January 1914, just two weeks before Kokovtsov was dismissed. The railway bonds which the French accepted were fixed at 4.5 per cent interest, were guaranteed by the Russian national treasury and received a nominal value of 665

17. Ibid., pp. 267ff. For the Franco-Russian military negotiations see: V.I. Bovykin, *Iz istorii vozniknoveniya pervoi mirovoi voiny. Otnosheniya Rossii i Frantsii v 1912–1914 gg* (Moscow, 1961), pp. 73ff.
18. Anan'ich, *Rossiya*, pp. 271ff.; Girault, *Emprunts*, pp. 564ff.
19. Witt, *Die Finanzpolitik*, pp. 337ff., 356ff.
20. DDF 3/VIII, no. 79; *Materialy po istorii franko-russkikh otnoshenii za 1910–1914 gg.* (Moscow, 1922), pp. 716ff.

million francs (249.4 million rubles). Agreements of a similar magnitude were planned for the years to come.[21]

Although it is true that the Russian Empire could not have continued as a French ally prior to the First World War without financial help, one should not forget that Russia's own financial strength was never greater than during the economic upswing of 1909 to 1914. Without this boom and the resultant rapid increase in state revenues, St Petersburg's military policies could hardly have been financed at all. Armaments remained an economic problem, closely connected to industrial growth and rising agricultural production as well as to the mounting international engagement of Russian banks.[22] Foreign observers — military men, economic experts and politicians alike — viewed Russia at the time as a promising giant stepping into the future with enormous strides. It was commonly thought that the Empire had overcome the shock of military defeat and revolution and was rapidly modernising. In Germany and Austria advocates of a preventive war were supported by the impression that Russia was accumulating immense power and was a nation to be feared. Such images and anxieties were felt elsewhere as well: In England, France and even the United States respected voices foresaw a great future and an important international role for imperial Russia. They did not contemplate such a prospect with unmitigated joy.[23]

If one confines oneself to economic statistics then the impression of rapid industrial expansion in Russia will doubtless be confirmed. Rates of growth in the most important sectors were only slightly lower than those of the 1895 to 1899 period. This was true above all for the manufacture of capital goods, the total value of which rose by 84 per cent between 1908 and 1913, from 1,349.9 million rubles to 2,489.4 million (with the metallurgical industry alone experiencing an increase of 88.9 per cent). The output of the young chemical industry was worth 35.3 million rubles in 1908, and had almost quadrupled by 1913. The production of consumer goods also benefitted from the boom, though at a more modest rate: on the eve of

21. Anan'ich, *Rossiya*, pp. 279ff.; Girault, *Emprunts*, p. 566f., Bovykin, *Iz istorii*, pp. 102ff.

22. I.F. Gindin, *Russkie kommercheskie banki* (Moscow, 1948), pp. 153ff.; Gindin, 'Moskovskie banki v period imperializma', *IZ* 58, pp. 38–106; Shepelev, *Aktsionernye kompanii*, pp. 233ff.

23. See R. Ropponen, *Die Kraft Rußlands. Wie beurteilte die politische u. militärische Führung der europäischen Großmächte in der Zeit von 1905 bis 1914 die Kraft Rußlands?* (Helsinki, 1968), especially pp. 181ff., 196ff.

the First World War it still constituted 62 per cent of total industrial production. Consumer goods increased in value by 32.8 per cent, from 3,062.2 million rubles in 1908 to 4,060.5 million rubles in 1913. The increase in the textile industry amounted to 46 per cent.[24]

The upswing was given added momentum by uniformly excellent harvests (except in 1911) which boosted mass purchasing power. Increased agricultural production not only strengthened the industrial boom but also augmented the national Treasury's revenues, thanks to taxes on consumption and, last but not least, increased the volume of Russian exports. The Treasury derived about 30 per cent of its revenues from state monopolies and these monies rose by almost one-third between 1908 and 1913. The balance of foreign trade was clearly positive (though the surplus was declining) as increased receipts from exports sufficed to cover rising imports sucked in by the industrial boom. The chronic deficit in the balance of payments remained, however. The surplus in foreign trade (1908 to 1913: 2,274.1 million rubles) was offset by a deficit in the balance of foreign exchange payments (3,485.6 million rubles) which could only be covered by loans and bond issues, i.e. by further increases in the national debt. The Finance Ministry increased the nation's gold reserves but could not keep pace with the rising tide of debt.[25]

Such impressive statistics on the rapid growth of Russian industry cannot, however, conceal the structural problems underlying these apparently prosperous times. The economic upswing was not entirely 'home-made', and it reflected the Russian economy's international ties. Rapid increases in the amount of direct foreign investment between 1908 and 1914 are the most telling sign of the importance of imported capital.[26] A careful study of apparently contradictory data and estimates show that early in 1914 foreign sources accounted for 48 per cent (5.119 million rubles) of the share capital of Russian joint-stock companies and companies with foreign investment compelled by law to publish their results. Foreign participation in new capital formation far exceeded this proportion. One can say therefore that 'foreigners did not just invest in an economic upswing that was already under way — as happened for

24. Calculations by Bovykin in: 'Probleme der industriellen Entwicklung Rußlands' in Geyer (ed.), *Wirtschaft u. Gesellschaft*, p. 203.

25. Sidorov, *Finansovoe polozhenie*, pp. 29ff., 82ff.; A.I. Bukovetskii, 'Svobodnaya nalichnost' i zolotoi zapas tsarskogo pravitel'stva v kontse XIX–nachale XX veka', in *Monopolii i inostrannyi kapital v Rossii* (Leningrad, 1962), pp. 359–76.

26. Shepelev, *Aktsionernye kompanii*, pp. 231ff.; Girault, *Emprunts*, pp. 122ff., 422ff.; McKay, *Pioneers*, pp. 33ff.

instance in the United States and Canada — but helped initiate the upswing or at least its individual phases.'[27]

The share of foreign capital in total productive expenditure in Russia reached almost 55 per cent between 1908 and 1913 (1,420 million rubles), a figure clearly surpassed only during the Witte era (63.5 per cent) and during the initial phase of Russian industrialisation between 1861 and 1881 (84.9 per cent).[28] Foreign investors had always concentrated on the railways, heavy industry and other developing sectors. Mining, smelting, metallurgy and machine-building attracted French and Belgian investors in particular. In the spring of 1917, 54.1 per cent of these shares were in foreign hands, while 45 per cent of the chemical industry and as much as 61.8 per cent of construction companies and municipal services were owned by foreigners. The involvement of international capital reached its peak with the monopoly production and sale of oil. In 1914 about 55 per cent of total investment in this branch of industry came from outside Russia, 37 per cent from Great Britain alone. The electrical industry was dominated by subsidiaries of the German companies Siemens and AEG, and in 1914 Russian capital held less than a 15 per cent share.[29]

Russia's financial position clearly benefitted from direct foreign investment. The participation of international companies in Russian industry did not have such a harmful effect on the balance of payments as new foreign loans would have had. Only part of the profits were removed from the country and substantial sums were reinvested. Although the dividends paid by Russian companies were at levels above the European average, they should not be exaggerated. Between 1909 and 1913 foreign companies paid from 5.1 to 7.2 per cent in dividends — just a little more than the average 5.0 to 6.6 per cent of all joint-stock companies active in Russia. Annual dividends of from 20 to 30 per cent (like those paid out by the principal shareholder in the gold-producing company, Lena Goldfields Ltd.) were most unusual.[30] The entrepreneurial experience and know-how which Russian industry gained as a result of foreign

27. Bonwetsch, 'Das ausländische Kapital', pp. 412–25, here: pp. 416, 418.
28. Bovykin, 'Probleme', p. 197
29. Bonwetsch, 'Das ausländische Kapital', pp. 423ff.; V.S. Dyakin, *Germanskie kapitaly*, pp. 6ff.; for British capital investments see: A.I. Ignat'ev, *Russko-angliiskie otnosheniya nakanune pervoi mirovoi voiny* (Moscow, 1962), pp. 13–57.
30. Bonwetsch, 'Das ausländische Kapital', p. 422; McKay, *Pioneers*, pp. 26f. In Germany, F. Krupp for instance paid out 8 per cent in dividends in 1910, 10 per cent in 1911, 12 per cent in 1912 and 14 per cent in 1913. Cf. H. Jaeger, *Unternehmer in der deutschen Politik 1890–1918* (Bonn, 1967), pp. 206ff.

participation must also be taken into account. The benefits of this were incalculable for rapid industrial progress in high technology.

The well-established theory that Russia sank to semi-colonial status before 1914 is based primarily on this penetration of Russian industry by foreign capital and technology. However, the percentage share of foreign investments was far higher between 1861 and 1881 than just before the war. In addition, foreign capital was far from exercising direct dominance over industrial development in pre-war Russia.[31] The large Russian banks were always present on the boards and directorates of the international consortia which handled most industrial financing. Laws governing the operation of joint-stock companies also played a role in preventing foreign capital from becoming 'independent' with a free hand in Russia.[32]

Moreover, the 'capitalist international' supposedly at work in Russia cannot be distinguished by national criteria. Capital in Russia did not generally or co-operate along national lines, and foreign governments were unable to direct it. The large share of foreign capital in French hands did repeatedly lead to closely interconnected political, military and economic relations. However, pressures from the French cabinet were related primarily to the Russian national Treasury's need for loans, and this is why political concessions could not always be avoided. Direct investments, on the other hand, had virtually no impact on Russian foreign policy. Capital knew no homeland. The political implications of Russia's dependence on foreign countries and her technical and industrial underdevelopment were more clearly apparent in the rearmament campaign than anywhere else. There is no doubt that large arms contracts contributed a great deal after 1909 to the modernisation and expansion of industry. It was common practice at meetings of the Council of Ministers for the army and navy to point out the positive economic effects of their proposals in order to make them seem more palatable to the Minister of Finance. The armed forces thus tried to portray their arms policies as a way to promote industry and to free them from the reputation of being 'unproductive' expenditures.

The shipyards and workshops under navy control had become old and unprofitable, and saving them seemed to be an especially urgent task. Private industry was also quick to make its voice heard

31. See the balanced view presented in McKay, *Pioneers*, pp. 268ff.
32. For laws governing the stock market see: Shepelev, *Aktsionernye kompanii*, pp. 251ff.

Table 12: International involvement of the Russian economy 1 January 1914 (in mill. rubles)

Foreign loans and investments		Russia's foreign assets	
State loans	3,971	State assets in China	300
Municipal loans	420	Chinese Eastern Railway &	
State-guaranteed railway		Russian property in China	328
loans	975	Outer Mongolia	11
Bonds of state land		Persia	110
credit banks	230	Gold of the Imperial Bank	
Foreign capital in		outside the country	167
joint-stock companies	2,602	Debts of Turkey, Greece &	
Foreign investment in other		Bulgaria	152
forms	247		
	8,445		1,068

Source: Data from A.L. Vainshtein, *Narodnoe bogatstvo i narodnokho-zyaistvennoe nakoplenie predrevolyutsionnoi Rossii*, (Moscow, 1960), pp. 444f.

when in 1907 the first new battleships were to be built and the Minister of the Navy prepared to award the contract to the British firm of Vickers. The 'Board of the Congress of Representatives of Russian Trade and Industry' demanded from the government 'that only Russian, not foreign, enterprises should be called upon in such important matters to the whole nation as the re-birth of the Russian navy'. In November 1907 the Council of Ministers agreed that ships of the line would be built only 'in Russian yards, from Russian materials and by Russian workers'. This did not settle the matter however: after the call for tenders neither Vickers nor a Russian firm received the contract but Blohm & Voss in Hamburg. Not until the French protested, with the backing of Prime Minister Clemenceau and Finance Minister Caillaux, did St Petersburg move in the autumn of 1908 to adopt a policy of not assigning government contracts to foreign countries.[33]

Thereafter, St Petersburg attempted to stick to this policy. The French, English and American offers which poured into government offices were refused, though the Foreign Ministry often urged officials to accede to the wishes of Russia's ally, France.[34] The

33. Shatsillo, 'Inostrannyi kapital i voenno-morskie programmy Rossii nakanune pervoi mirovoi voiny', *IZ* 69 (1961), pp. 73–100, here pp. 75f., 77f.; for the connection between reinforcing the fleet and encouraging industry see: Shatsillo, *Russkii imperializm*, pp. 202ff.
34. G.M. Derenkovskii, 'Franko-russkaya morskaya konventsiya 1912 g. i anglo-

Minister of the Navy, however, was not impressed even by the remonstrances of Poincaré who went to St Petersburg in 1912 to seek participation for French firms. In the end, only two orders for light cruisers were placed outside Russia — in Germany, on the eve of the war. Both ships were not ready until after the war had broken out, and although St Petersburg had already paid for them in part, they were incorporated into the German navy.[35]

Clearly, far from excluding foreigners, the policy of channelling armament orders to Russian industry required the participation of foreign capital and the co-operation of foreign firms. All large private industries and shipyards in receipt of armament contracts were connected with big Russian banks in which European companies held a sizeable share.[36] This was especially true of the two most important financial syndicates in the Russian arms trade: the Russo-Asiatic Bank (created in 1910 by combining the Russo-Chinese Bank and the Northern Bank) and the St Petersburg International Bank of Commerce. The Russo-Asiatic Bank was dominated by Parisian syndicates (Société Générale, Banque de Paris et des Pays-Bas, Union Parisienne and others) which held 65 per cent share of the stock. Germans held more than 30 per cent of the stock and bonds of the International Bank of Commerce. Armaments and warships were therefore financed internationally. This also meant that firms working for the Ministries of War and the Navy were represented on the boards of the great finance companies. The high degree of concentration and monopolisation which existed in the Russian arms and shipbuilding industries can thus be understood.

All private producers of artillery and about half the munitions manufacturers belonged to financial syndicates with ties to the Russo-Asiatic Bank. All the light cruisers and fourteen of the thirty-six torpedo boats ordered for the Baltic fleet were constructed in shipyards financed by these groups. After 1912 the industrial heart of the Russo-Asiatic Bank was the Putilov works which produced 43 per cent of Russian weapons and now also accepted warships. By 1914, the financial-industrial complex associated with Russian, French and Belgian banks had taken over other important shipyards, weapons producers and engineering works

russkie peregovory nakanune pervoi mirovoi voiny', *IZ* 64 (1959), pp. 82–135.

35. Shatsillo, 'Inostrannyi kapital', pp. 83f.
36. For the following: Bovykin, 'Banki i voennaya promyshlennost' Rossii nakanune pervoi mirovoi voiny', *IZ* 64 (1959), pp. 82–135.

(Nevskii Shipbuilding Russo-Baltic Company, Tallinn Shipyards etc.). It even took over the Tula Blast-Furnace Company and began putting together its own metallurgical base.

While the Russo-Asiatic Bank concentrated on St Petersburg and the Baltic coast, the International Bank of Commerce and the St Petersburg Credit and Discount Bank (*Uchetnossudnyi bank*) co-operating with it were active primarily in the south where they dominated the expansion of the Black Sea fleet, begun in 1912. In May 1914 French syndicates played a large role in uniting the only two shipbuilding companies in southern Russia, 'Naval' and 'Russud' in Nikolaev. Both companies had been close to bankruptcy before the naval programme was approved, but now they were modernised and greatly expanded. Respected engineering, iron and cable works (L. Nobel, G.A. Lessner, Phoenix etc.) were associated with this new consortium as well as an artillery factory in Tsaritsyn.

The international system which provided the financing for most of Russia's war industry involved not only foreign capital but highly developed western technology as well.[37] Almost all Russian firms active in the armaments business had either foreign suppliers or co-operation. Not just equipment was imported but also engineers, mechanics and skilled workers. Warships in particular could not have been built without this transfer of technology. Turbines, diesel motors, manufacturing installations, optical equipment etc. were ordered in vast quantities. Licences were often purchased and copies made. The French arms manufacturer Schneider et Cie (Creuzot), the English companies Vickers and John Brown, as well as Krupp, Blohm & Voss, AEG, Vulkanwerft, Škoda and many other large and small firms in industrialised Europe participated in the Russian arms boom. In the few years preceding the war, the Naval shipyards in Nikolaev alone handed out contracts to no fewer than 100 foreign companies, especially in Germany and England. The technological backwardness of Russian industry thus created a dependence that was no less real than the dependence on international capital. When the flow of German supplies was cut off after the war began, the great Russian shipyards could only be saved from ruin by state sequestration.

Although Russian industry expanded rapidly in the economic upswing before the war, that expansion was clearly not sufficient to

37. For what follows see: Shatsillo, Inostrannyi kapital', pp. 78ff.

reduce the sway held by other countries over Russia's policies as a great power. This is clearly evident in the armaments business, one of the most powerful engines of industrial progress. Quantifying research has shown conclusively that the structural weaknesses in the Russian economy were not overcome by the industrial boom, induced primarily by Russia's desire to be a great world power. Agriculture remained the dominant sector and here the rate of growth lagged behind that of industry, despite the high rates of investment (1913: 11.6 per cent of national income) which were surpassed only by those of the United States and Germany (c., 13 to 14 per cent).[38] Stolypin's land reform was intended to create a prosperous peasant middle class by dissolving communal tenure, re-allocating land and creating new settlements. However, reform ground to a halt in the final few years before the war, and there was no further modernisation of agriculture. Productivity grew at a very slow rate (c. 0.3 per cent per annum compared with 2.7 per cent in industry). Since agriculture employed 72 per cent of the workforce and produced 53 per cent of the goods, such a slow rate was a tremendous drag on the over-all increase in per capita income. Socio-economic development in Russia before 1914 was still at a level reached in central and western Europe before the era of 'modern economic growth'. In 1912 per capita income in Russia was only about one-quarter of the levels in Germany and England, and only a little more than half the Italian level. It was almost 60 per cent less than in Germany in 1873.

Since western economies were growing at a far faster pace, attempts before the war to reduce Russia's relative backwardness were totally thwarted. Despite all the efforts undertaken since the time of Witte, Russia's relative underdevelopment increased instead of decreasing when compared with the great industrial nations which the Russian élites considered as their rivals for a place in the sun. Per capita income in Russia had stood at about one-half the western average around 1860, but by 1913 it was only one-third of the western average. There really was no strategy for 'catching up'.

38. The following figures are cited in P. Gregory, 'Wirtschaftliches Wachstum u. struktureller Wandel im zaristischen Rußland', in Geyer (ed.), *Wirtschaft u. Gesellschaft*, pp. 210–27ff.; P. Gregory, 'Some Empirical Comments on the Theory of Relative Backwardness: The Russian Case', *Economic Development and Cultural Change* 22 (1974), pp. 645–55.; idem, 'A Note on Relative Backwardness and Industrial Structure', *QJE* 88 (1974), pp. 520–7; idem, 'Russian National Income in 1913', ibid., 90 (1976), pp. 445–59. For national income in Russia (without international comparisons), see the calculations of A.L. Vainshtein, *Narodnoe bogatstvo i narodnokhozyaistvennoe nakoplenie pred revolyutsionnoi Rossii* (Moscow, 1960).

12

Foreign Policy and Military Planning

Although preserving Russia's international status was not the sole reason why the government strove to promote industrial expansion using foreign capital and technology, it was certainly the most important one. The huge sums directed towards armaments before the war starved all other developmental programmes. During a time of relative domestic peace the political and military elites' ingrained fear of revolution was overshadowed by a feeling that the real danger was external. The autocracy believed that its ultimate success or failure would ride on its ability to shoulder the approaching international burdens and avoid a new Tsushima. To this extent, there was an anti-revolutionary streak to the autocracy's great power policies, and rearmament could be seen as a strategy for maintaining the system. The government also knew that its basic foreign policies had the support of large sections of the Duma.

This strategy would probably not have seemed so plausible if it had not been developed against a background of continually escalating international conflict. St Petersburg had been humiliated by the Bosnian annexation crisis, and the autocracy's sense of danger naturally centred on the foreign threat.[1] Fears that Russia was either not equipped or very ill-equipped to defend her interests successfully mushroomed into such a trauma that Europe seemed in permanent danger of going to war. In the light of these fears all

1. Besides Bestuzhev's work see: H. Jablonowski, 'Die Stellungnahme der russischen Parteien zur Außenpolitik der Regierung von der russisch-englischen Verständigung bis zum Ersten Weltkrieg', *FOG* 5 (1957), pp. 60–92; M. Wolters, *Außenpolitische Fragen vor der vierten Duma* (Hamburg, 1969); also the party histories by Birth and Pinchuk as well as — for the Kadets — Liszkowski, *Zwischen Liberalismus u. Imperialismus*. A detailed analysis is presented by: K. Ferenczi, *Außenpolitik u. Öffentlichkeit in Rußland 1906–1914* (Husum, 1982).

sacrifices for the sake of armaments seemed reasonable and necessary.

During the Balkan wars of 1912–13, Russian confidence in the ability of the various alliances to keep the peace completely evaporated.[2] The feeling became widespread that a clash with Germany and Austro-Hungary was inevitable and had to be accepted as a historical necessity. What the Russian government wanted under the circumstances was to postpone the 'decisive battle' until Russia's military strength was equal to the enormous exactions of such a war. The arms programmes for the army and navy were calculated to match the military build up of potential opponents and, if possible, to prepare Russia for war by 1917. This strategy was not based, as we shall see, on any plans to launch an offensive and thus initiate a great war.[3] The government's basic attitude remained one of *attentisme*. St Petersburg thought it prudent to prepare for the inevitable 'struggle between peoples' but was unwilling to take the calculated risk of a preventive first strike.

This is not the place to delve into the diplomatic history of the prewar years and to describe in detail how Russian foreign policy reacted to the international crises of 1908 to 1914.[4] There is no doubt, however, that both Foreign Ministers in this period, A.I. Izvol'skii (1906–10) and S.D. Sazonov (1910–16), preferred to avoid war. They adopted a defensive strategy for securing Russian interests and thus tried to take into account the Empire's limited military margin of manoeuvre.[5] I shall discuss later in a separate analysis why these principles were increasingly undermined after the winter of 1913–14 but would first like to look more closely at

2. O. Bickel, *Rußland u. die Entstehung des Balkanbundes 1912* (Berlin, 1933); E. C. Thaden, *Russia and the Balkan Alliance of 1912* (Pennsylvania, 1965); E.C. Helmreich *The Diplomacy of the Balkan Wars 1912–1913* (Cambridge, Mass., 1938); J.M. Miller Jr., 'The Concert of Europe in the First Balkan War, 1912–1913', PhD thesis, Clark Univ., 1969; R.J. Crampton, 'The Decline of the Concert of Europe in the Balkans 1913–1914', *SEER* 52 (1974), pp. 393–419; Bovykin, *Iz istorii*, pp. 124–78; A.V. Ignat'ev, *Russko-angliiskie otnosheniya*, pp. 145ff., 168ff.; Bestuzhev (1965), pp. 60ff.

3. A work still essential for Russian military strategy and planning is: A.M. Zayonchkovskii, *Podgotovka Rossii k imperialisticheskoi voine. Ocherki voennoi podgotovki i pervonachal'nykh planov* (Moscow, 1926); more recently, see the collective work of the Institute of War History of the Soviet Department of Defence: *Istoriya pervoi mirovoi voiny 1914–1918* (Moscow, 1975), vol. 1, pp. 95ff., 185ff.

4. There is no comprehensive history of Russia's role in the period leading up to the First World War which takes the most recent research into account. The best account of the Russian diplomatic apparatus has been given by D.C.B. Lieven, *Russia and the Origins of the First World War* (London, 1983).

5. Cf. the autobiographical comments of the Foreign Minister in: *The Memoirs of Alexander Isvolsky* (London, 1920); S.D. Sasonoff, *Sechs schwere Jahre* (Berlin, 1927).

the capacity of the Russian leadership in the prewar period to engage in conflict and endure the strain. This approach leads us firstly, to examine the connection between foreign and military policy and to examine the goals which the government set itself in order to ensure Russia's international status. I shall then investigate how and with what consequences the nexus of diplomatic and military policies pertained to the domestic conditions on which the stability of tsarist Russia depended.

Although Russian diplomats and military figures had many differences of opinion on individual aspects of foreign policy, they were in agreement on the essentials.[6] Russia's fundamental policies as a great power did not need to be discussed. No one in St Petersburg doubted that Russia's 'historic right' to the Straits meant that no other great power could be allowed to dominate Constantinople. Russia's 'historic vocation' as the power responsible for the fate of the Balkan peoples was incompatible with any change in the status quo. Along the Asian periphery of the Empire Russian positions in the Far East, Central Asia and Persia had to be defended, although risky expansionist goals could be renounced for the time being. An understanding with Japan and Great Britain, such as that arranged by Izvol'skii in the summer of 1907, was an important prerequisite for such a policy. In view of the weakness of the Empire, the task of 'preserving Russia's honour and dignity' was assigned first of all to the art of diplomacy rather than to the military. On this point too there was no dissent. It was also understood that doubt could not be cast on the fundamental justifications for the Franco-Russian Alliance. This alliance, intimately related to St Petersburg's dependence on capital imports, was Russia's only guarantee of security in the face of far superior German military strength. There could be no serious thought of a volte-face in the alliance system along the lines of the unfortunate agreement of Björkö. This is not to deny that forces still existed high up in the government which were opposed to closer ties with England in particular and which proposed renewing the special relationship with Germany that had prevailed at the time of Bismarck.

Certainly, Izvol'skii and Sazonov had to take into account such conservative sentiments nourished by fear of revolution. They themselves had good reason to strive for a reduction in tensions

---

6. For the original differences see the minutes of the special deliberation of 7 Sept. 1906 in *KA* 56, pp. 59–64; also A. Iswolsky, *Au service de la Russie. Correspondence diplomatique* (Paris, 1937), vol. 1, p. 378; Bestuzhev (1961), pp. 129ff.

with Germany and even for friendly relations. The Ministry of War was also anxious to avoid military conflicts on the western frontier. The periodic meetings of the two Emperors as well as the Potsdam agreement of 1910–11 on the Baghdad Railway and on Russian positions in Persia conformed therefore to these principles.[7] However, the series of Russo-German contacts should not lead one to conclude that St Petersburg could have chosen 'between England and Germany' after 1907 or balanced itself between the two powers and thus gained a free hand in foreign policy. To accept this often expressed view would be to fall prey to a tactical ploy by which official St Petersburg customarily used to hide (even from itself at times) the fact that it had no real alternative. Although it is well known that Russian attempts to appear to be playing Germany off against the West were often a cause for concern in London and Paris, the *entente* powers were not sufficiently impressed to adopt Russian interests as their own — in the Near East for example.[8]

The Bosnian crisis was not the only event to underscore the limited success enjoyed by Russian diplomacy in defending prime imperial interests. Little was gained from the secret convention signed with Italy in October 1909 whereby Rome promised to look favourably on Russian ambitions in the Straits and St Petersburg promised the same with regard to Italian interests in Tripoli and Cyrenaica.[9] The Russian Empire did not acquire any valuable gains during the Italo-Turkish War of 1911. Finally, although Sazonov had hoped in the spring of 1912 that the League of Balkan States would enhance Russian prestige by making her the dominant power in the Near East, the alliance got caught up a few months later in snares of its own making.[10] The Foreign Ministry and both armed services agreed that Russia could not practise big power policies without modern equipment for her army and navy.

Despite all the set-backs and disappointments, the consensus between military and diplomats on basic questions of international

7. Astaf'ev, *Russko-germanskie diplomaticheskie otnosheniya*, pp. 187ff., 219ff.; Kazemzadeh, *Russia and Britain*, pp. 593ff.
8. For this see the recent work of H. Lemke, 'Großbritannien u. die deutsch-russischen Verhandlungen über Persien u. die Bagdadbahn nach der Zusammenkunft in Potsdam (1910/11)', *JGSLE* 18/2 (1974), pp. 115–45; H. Mejcher, 'Die Bagdad-bahnals Instrument deutschen wirtschaftlichen Einflusses im Osmanischen Reich', *GuG* 1 (1975), pp. 447–81.
9. *Sbornik dogovorov*, pp. 402ff. For the internal conditions behind Italian colonial policies see: W. Schieder, 'Aspekte des italienischen Imperialismus' in W.J. Mommsen (ed.), *Der moderne Imperialismus*, pp. 148–71.
10. Thaden, *Russia and the Balkan Alliance*, pp. 99ff. *passim.*

policy held until the First World War. After some initial resistance
the high command of the army and navy had accepted the 'return to
Europe' effected by Izvol'skii and now supported the idea. The
territorial agreements in the Far East made it possible for the general
staff to concentrate once again on defence against Germany and
Austria. In April 1906 the alliance with France had been recast and
the anti-English clauses of 1901 were now void.[11] In this respect as
well the general staff and the Ministry of War conformed to the new
foreign policy. At the same time, however, Russia's military leaders
realised more than ever that the Alliance served French interests
more than Russian. In the case of a conflict with Austria (as might
have happened in 1908–9 over Aehrenthal's annexation policies and
the German 'ultimatum') Russia could not automatically expect
French help.[12] St Petersburg, on the other hand, was directly
implicated in every increase in tension between France and Germany and had little opportunity to influence the conflict.

The imbalance in the Alliance resulted from Russia's weakness,
and an acceptable degree of equilibrium could be achieved only
through massive increases in Russia's military potential. So long as
this was impossible, Izvol'skii's and Sazonov's efforts to maintain
the line to Berlin could only meet with the approval of the general
staff. The army and navy's lack of preparedness for war could be
seen time and again in St Petersburg's dealings with Austrian
policies and on the question of the Straits. The strategy of falling
back on diplomacy to preserve the peace was therefore justified. As
the status quo in the Balkans increasingly disintegrated, the military
insisted on this basic principle of Russian policy just as deter-
minedly as the Foreign Minister who had to bear the heavy burden
of St Petersburg's diplomatic defeats.

It would be wrong to deduce from this unanimity of view that the
diplomatic and military leaders co-ordinated all their actions and
plans. The Prime Minister's ability to direct events remained limited. The armed forces and diplomacy formed two arcane fields well
separated from one another, and the Council of Ministers had little
leverage on activities not concerned with matters of state. The Tsar
was not the kind of man to ensure adequate integration of foreign
policy and military strategy, although according to the constitution
this task fell to him alone. Izvol'skii was responsible only to the

11. Cf. p. 188.
12. L. Neiman, 'Franko-russkie otnosheniya vo vremya bosniiskogo krizisa
1908–1909 gg.', *FE* (1958), pp. 375–406.

Tsar; otherwise he enjoyed remarkable independence. It is true that at the Tsar's direction imperial decisions were prepared at special inter-ministerial conferences, especially during times of crisis. Under the chairmanship of the Prime Minister, the Ministers of War and the Navy spoke their minds on foreign affairs and the Minister of Foreign Affairs responded with maxims on military strategy. The Council of Ministers was also advised in advance of the Foreign Minister's rare appearances before the Duma. For the rest, however, the Foreign Minister decided for himself how much he wished to tell his colleagues. Izvol'skii's behaviour in the Bosnian crisis (when he and Aehrenthal prejudiced fundamental Russian interests at Buchlau without informing Stolypin) provides a good example of how the Minister could freely and unilaterally decide even highly sensitive foreign policy matters. This situation was not gradually remedied until after 1909 when Stolypin put his brother-in-law, Sazonov, in charge of the Foreign Ministry and an extensive re-shuffle occurred among top diplomatic personnel.[13]

Policy was even more difficult to coordinate in the armed forces than in foreign affairs. Besides the Ministries of War and the Navy there were separate general staffs for the army and navy which were not subject to ministerial control until 1909. In addition, an Imperial Defence Council was left over from the Japanese war and this concerned itself with questions of planning and armaments under the chairmanship of the Tsar's uncle, Nikolai Nikolaevich. Until its dissolution in 1908 this body dealt primarily with smoothing over disputes between the services. As in Germany and elsewhere, antagonism between army and navy remained an enduring fact of life.[14] The two chiefs of staff usually consulted each other only when compelled to by tight finances, and regular co-operation was out of the question. The Tsar and his Foreign Minister supported the admiral's struggle to make naval rearmament the top priority because, as Izvol'skii said, a strong fleet was essential for any state which desired 'to remain among the great powers' and not sink to the level of a 'second-class power'.[15] In the meantime, however, the War Ministry had great difficulty in getting approval for the army's financial needs. During the crisis years before 1914 the towering

13. For the reforms in the Foreign Ministry see Bestuzhev (1961), pp. 58ff.
14. For German naval policies see primarily: V.R. Berghahn, *Der Tirpitz-Plan. Genesis u. Verfall einer innenpolitischen Krisenstrategie unter Wilhelm II* (Düsseldorf, 1971).
15. Izvolskii, 14 Dec. 1909, in the special session on the naval programme in: Shatsillo, *Russkii imperializm*, p. 346.

figure of Admiral I.K. Grigorovich always had the ear of the Tsar and he succeeded effortlessly in making the navy Russia's top priority — despite the undoubted fact that Russia was a land power whose military strength was determined by the state of her army and not the number of battleships in her possession.[16]

The question of the degree to which foreign policy and military policy were coordinated must therefore take into account the lack of communication between army and navy. The strategy behind the costly naval programmes was unclear for a long time and was only loosely related to the plans of the War Ministry and army general staff for mobilisation and military operations. After the shocking events of Tsushima the Russian naval authorities were in disarray and soon became caught up in improvised projects for reconstruction without any overall plan. All that concerned the admirals was to have another proud armada at their disposal as soon as possible and save the Ministry's shipyards and workshops from wrack and ruin. These were the considerations behind the plan (already agreed to in 1906 by the Tsar and Minister of the Navy A.A. Birilov) to build four dreadnoughts for the Baltic fleet in the next five to seven years.[17]

Chiefs of staff Admiral Brusilov and General Palitsyn were instructed to examine this proposal in December 1906 and they came up with very different priorities: During the next ten to twenty years they thought it would be best to concentrate on coastal defence in the Baltic Sea (if possible along the line between Reval and the Åland Islands). Instead of giving priority to battleships in the Baltic, a Black Sea fleet should be built strong enough to protect 'our rich southern flank' and to fulfil Russia's 'historic mission' in the Straits, Asia Minor and the Aegean.[18] Birilov's successor, Admiral Dikov, adopted these plans with particular verve, encouraged by Izvol'skii's support and the backing of exposés written by young naval officers. In October 1907 Dikov expressed the view to the Foreign Minister that the navy consider 'moving into the Straits as an unshakeable goal'. It was also anxious 'to secure for the Black Sea fleet a station at the outlet to the Mediterranean, near the Dardanelles'.[19] In order to give this plan

16. For the disproportion between army and navy rearmament see idem, 'O disproportsii v razvitii vooruzhennykh sil Rossii nakanune pervoi mirovoi voiny', *IZ* 83 (1969), pp. 123–36.
17. Idem, *Russkii imperializm*, pp. 52ff.
18. Report on the 24 Dec. 1906, ibid., p. 318ff.
19. Ibid., pp. 92f.

added weight, Dikov advanced reasons which were not only historic in nature but which also reflected modern imperialism and trade: the Russian economy's interest in exports made it imperative to bring not only grain but also southern iron ore and coal to world markets — into the ports of southern Europe, Africa and Asia Minor, and through the Red Sea to Abyssinia, Arabia and the Indian Ocean. It need not be emphasised that this vision of the future tallied very nicely with Izvol'skii's plans (though the latter's secret diplomacy in Buchlau, with its obsessive concern for revising the Straits conventions, would soon run aground).

By 1907 it was apparent that no real coordination existed between foreign and naval policy. In the spring the Imperial Defence Council had made large cuts in an enormous naval construction programme proposed by the navy general staff. At its most grandiose this programme had called for four large modern squadrons, each with eight battleships, four heavy and nine light cruisers, as well as thirty-six torpedo boats and smaller units. Two of these squadrons were to operate in the Pacific. Thus naval general staff sitting at the drawing board designing a world strategy with little relation to reality. They grotesquely overestimated Russia's financial resources and were oblivious to the decision already taken to halt expansionism in the Far East and seek a *modus vivendi* with Tokyo and London. The parameters of the 'small naval programme' passed in July 1907 were far more modest, though still ambitious enough: four dreadnoughts would be built to form the core of the Baltic fleet with a few ships added. The Black Sea fleet went unmentioned. The new battleships were not laid down until 1909, and when the World War erupted three of them were ready for service.[20]

Although such construction programmes must by their very nature reflect anticipated and not present needs, one is still struck by the imitative nature of Russia's naval programme. It was typical of the times. The matching of German naval armaments was inevitable, though one cannot say that Russian 'Mahanism' was as obsessed by Admiral Tirpitz's proposals as the plans of the German *Reichsmarineamt* were obsessed by the English navy.[21] What the

20. Ibid., pp. 57ff.; *Istoriya pervoi mirovoi voiny* 1, pp. 268f.
21. See Berghahn, *Der Tirpitz-Plan*, pp. 173ff. *passim*; idem, *Rüstung u. Machtpolitik*, pp. 70ff. The Russian decision to build battleships followed the general 'dreadnought leap' of 1906. The basic works of the American naval historian A.T. Mahan (*The Influence of Sea Power Upon History, 1660–1783* [Boston, 1890]; *The Influence of Sea Power Upon French Revolution and Empire, 1793–1812* [Boston, 1893]) had accelerated naval imperialism. They were already available in Russian translation in 1894 and 1898 respectively.

new Russian navy would actually do was not evident at first. All that was clear was that navy planners had forced the army to develop more slowly. The hesitant Minister of War, Rediger, did not succeed until July 1908 in obtaining even part payment of the amount the general staff reckoned was necessary for the army to catch up. While 2,100 million rubles was the estimated sum, the army was promised a mere 300 million rubles, to be paid in instalments until 1915.[22] In view of the pitiful state of Russia's land forces, this was a mere drop in the ocean.

Although Kokovtsov had been insisting on coordination ever since 1906, the first joint financial plan for the army and navy was not ready for approval until 1910.[23] Even then, this ten-year plan only saw the light of day because of the depressing experience of the Bosnian crisis. When Berlin let it be known in March 1909 that it no longer intended to restrain its Austrian ally from taking sanctions against Serbia, the Minister of War declared that the army was not prepared for war and could not even assume a defensive role.[24] Nevertheless, General Sukhomlinov (Rediger's successor) was still refused a significant budget increase during discussions in the summer of 1909 about the budget for the following year. The Council of Ministers thought the upper limits of the state's financial resources had been reached.[25] However, the topic of increased funding did not disappear: the navy had meanwhile surfaced with demands for yet more thousands of millions. In the next few months Stolypin had to spend as much time soothing his Minister of Finance as he did calming the quarrels between army and navy. Kokovtsov raged over the flagrant lack of coordination and the absence of a persuasive strategic concept, and demanded carefully justified and heavily reduced cost estimates.[26]

It was therefore fiscal constraints and not concerns related to foreign policy or military strategy which led to limited agreements between army and navy. What was finally decided on and passed by

22. Shatsillo, *Rossiya*, pp. 38ff. Cf. the minutes of the Council of Ministers' discussion about navy and army budgets for 1908 in *IA* (1962/2), pp. 124–31 (1 Feb. 1908).
23. For the financial history of the rearmament plan: Sidorov, *Finansovoe polozhenie*, pp. 57ff.
24. Sukhomlinov, p. 221; cf. the reports of the German military plenipotentiary Captain v. Hintze in: G. Graf v. Lambsdorff, *Die Militärbevollmächtigten Wilhelms II. am Zarenhofe 1904–1914* (Berlin, 1937), pp. 309ff..
25. Sidorov, *Finansovoe polozhenie*, p. 62.
26. For this see the minutes of the special sessions of 3 Aug., 21 Aug., 14 Dec. 1908 and 2 Jan. 1910 in Shatsillo, *Russkii imperializm*, pp. 322–51.

the Council of Ministers on 24 February 1910 was a plan to provide both ministries with essentially equal slices of funding over the next ten years — about 70 million rubles each per annum.[27] Thus the imbalance between the services was not in the least mitigated. The Ministry of War had to use the promised special credits to cover the army's most urgent needs if it was to catch up with the west: forts and roads, new types of artillery, new equipment etc. The Naval Ministry meanwhile enjoyed much wider horizons: the Baltic fleet would be expanded to eight dreadnoughts with the attendant cruisers and torpedo boats. It would thus be able to impose Russian 'rule in the Baltic' and threaten the German coast if the allies were gracious enough to draw at least part of the German fleet out of the Baltic. The naval high command was of the opinion that it could preserve Russian superiority over the Turks in the Black Sea by relatively modest increases in the existing fleet. In the Far East, only Vladivostok and Nikolaevsk could be defended. Additional cover was provided by a secret convention with Japan, signed on 21 June (4 July) 1910, which confirmed the division of Manchurian interests as agreed to in 1907 and appended to the existing convention an agreement to consult.[28]

A striking imbalance between naval and army equipment could be discerned in the programme for 1910. This once more confirmed that the regime did not propose to stop cutting into the present needs of conventional land-based defence in order to prepare a global naval presence. We shall not seek to determine for the moment whether Russia's concentration on the Baltic contained the seeds of a strategic concept with some connection to the broad outlines of foreign policy. Before attention became focused on the eastern Mediterranean as a result of the war in Tripoli, the Agadir crisis and Turkish naval plans, the new Minister of the Navy Grigorovich had proposed further projects in April 1911: a five-year programme to strengthen the Baltic fleet and to draft 'legislation on the Imperial Russian Fleet' which would have ensured

27. Minutes of the meeting of the Council of Ministers on 24 Feb. 1910 in: *IA* (1962/2), pp. 132–42, as well as the bill to be debated in the Imperial Duma on 25 Mar. 1910, ibid., pp. 142–51.
28. E.B. Price, *The Russo-Japanese Treaties of 1907–1916 Concerning Manchuria and Mongolia* (Baltimore, 1933), pp. 39ff., 113f.; Grigortsevich, *Dal'nevostochnaya politika*, pp. 257ff., 293ff.; Marinov, *Rossiya i Yaponiya*, pp. 59ff. For the connection with alliance relations between England and Japan see I.H. Nish, *Alliance in Decline. A Study in Anglo-Japanese Relations 1908–1923* (London, 1972); P. Lowe, *Great Britain and Japan 1911–1915. A Study of British Far Eastern Policy* (London, 1969).

continuous naval expansion into the 1930s.[29] These new projects went far beyond the ten-year plan which had been passed the previous February. Grigorovich required 512.6 million rubles in additional funds for 1911–15 (or 1912–16), i.e. an approximately 70 per cent increase in the budget approved in 1910. He wished to add four new heavy cruisers, four light cruisers, thirty-six destroyers and twelve submarines to the four battleships of the 'Sevastopol'' class which had been laid down in 1909. This complement would be extended, beginning in 1914–15, to include four more battleships and another five light cruisers. Thus by 1919 at the latest the Baltic fleet would consist of two squadrons operating independently.

Although the deliberations of the Council of Ministers and inter-ministerial commissions proceded at a snail's pace, it was already apparent by the spring of 1912 that the maritime pressure groups could not be held in check. Despite exhorbitant estimates from domestic shipyards and suppliers which were far in excess of international price levels, the authorities decided that the ships could not be built outside the country under more favourable conditions. Their concerns about cost were mitigated by the link in Russia between rearmament and industrial expansion. In June 1912 the Duma approved most of the sum requested: 421.1 million rubles for shipbuilding and additional sums later for harbours and state shipyards.

What distinguished Grigorovich's naval policies from those of his predecessors was an approach which took into account much more than before future developments in international politics. The Minister was primarily concerned with making the Russian navy a worthwhile partner for France and England within the *entente* — that, at least, was the plan. From his 'workshop' in the Baltic Grigorovich began building powerful formations which could also be used in other trouble spots. He was attempting in the long run to create an imperial presence in the eastern Mediterranean, which had taken on a new interest in the light of the Italo-Turkish War and of Russian ambitions in the Straits. When the Straits were blockaded because of the war and Russian exports of grain were left to rot in the southern ports in April 1912, Grigorovich's plan seemed more plausible.[30] However, the Liman von Sanders crisis and two Balkan

---

29. For the following: Shatsillo, *Russkii imperializm*, pp. 70ff.
30. The blockading of the Straits in April 1912: Bestuzhev (1965), pp. 57ff.

wars would soon demonstrate how far removed these plans were from the actual challenges which Russian policy would have to face in the last remaining years before the Great War.

The expensive naval programmes bore rather meagre fruit. Grigorovich succeeded only for a very short time in gaining influence within the Franco-Russian Alliance. At Russian insistence a naval convention was signed with France on 3 (16) July 1912 in Paris, but at the time this did not have a great deal of military value and was not much more than a matter of prestige for the Minister. Both sides concurred in principle that the French fleet would operate in the Mediterranean, the British in the North Sea, and the Russian in the Baltic.[31] However, such banalities could not hide the emptiness of the agreement. The naval staffs also turned their minds to how Russian dominance in the Black Sea could be guaranteed. They parted in the hope that London could be persuaded to arrive at a naval agreement with St Petersburg which would complement the Anglo-French naval convention about to be signed. This would formally confirm the Triple Entente. As is well known, by the time the First World War erupted such an agreement had not been concluded. The tortuous negotiations, handled in part by Sazonov, finally foundered on British reluctance. Russian hopes of obtaining commitments in the Baltic from the Home Fleet or, in case of war, of undertaking a common landing with the British in Pomerania remained illusory. Such proposals did, however, lend additional weight to arguments in Germany for a preventive war.[32] Nothing came of the grand design which would have bound together Russian diplomacy and naval policy and make tsarist Russia an equal partner with Britain on the world political stage. When London did go to war, it was not for Russia's sake but because the Schlieffen plan had been put into effect.

Finally, Russia's naval rearmament was almost useless from a military point of view. Despite huge investments the Baltic fleet was unable to extend its coastal defence farther west than the protective barrier between Narva and the Porkkala Peninsula in Finland. When war came, the navy defended only St Petersburg and contributed little to covering the Russian flank or securing the army's lines

---

31. Derenkovskii in *IZ* 29, pp. 80ff.; Bovykin, *Iz istorii*, pp. 76ff.
32. Derenkovskii, pp. 111ff., 116ff.; A.V. Ignat'ev, *Russko-angliiskie otnosheniya*, pp. 200ff. Evidence of the German reaction to the secret naval negotiations with untenable conclusions in E. Hölzle, *Der Geheimnisverrat u. der Kriegsausbruch 1914* (Göttingen, 1973); Hölzle, *Die Selbstentmachtung*, pp. 241ff.

of supply.[33] During the two Balkan wars and the ensuing Liman von Sanders crisis, when the old idea of taking action in the Straits arose once more, Grigorovich's contribution to the government's effectiveness was even smaller.

Nothing substantial had been done by 1911 to strengthen the Russian fleet in the Black Sea. The ten-year programme of February 1910 had planned on 50 million rubles to modernise three aging heavy cruisers and build nine torpedo boats and six submarines.[34] This modest beginning seemed sufficient at the time to maintain the old principle that the Russian fleet should always be superior to the Turkish fleet including any Romanian contribution. Soon afterwards, however, St Petersburg got wind of the first contracts signed by the Young Turks with British shipyards to propel the Ottoman Empire into the dreadnought era. This caused the Council of Ministers, at Sazonov's insistence and despite the delaying action of the naval authorities, to decide to increase the previous estimates. The relevant act came into effect in May 1911. It assigned 150.8 million rubles over five years to improve the decaying harbours and shipyards and build three new battleships, in an effort to strengthen the Black Sea fleet. Nevertheless, Grigorovich's Baltic programme remained the top priority, as was evident in the naval proposals of 1912. The Minister would not be swayed, even by the temporary blockade of the Straits in April 1912, which so upset the Ministry of Trade and southern Russian exporters. Grigorovich wished to postpone until 1917–19 the old question of when and how the Straits could be brought under Russian control, and even then thought that this 'historic goal' could probably be attained only in the context of a great European war.

St Petersburg had therefore to rely on diplomacy during the ensuing events. An unsuccessful effort was made to subvert the Turkish contracts with Vickers and Armstrong and persuade the British government to delay the planned delivery in 1913 of the first of three battleships. St Petersburg apparently had little appreciation of the fact that Great Britain and France wished to support the Ottoman Empire against German eastward expansion. The situation took an alarming turn in the fall of 1912 when the the League of Balkan States, which Sazonov had skilfully patched together, was torn asunder and the Bulgarian army soon after began to approach Constantinople. Russia's defiant assurances that Bulgaria would not

33. *Istoriya pervoi mirovoi voiny* 1, pp. 267ff.
34. For the following: Shatsillo, *Russkii imperializm*, pp. 90ff., 121ff.

be permitted to establish herself firmly in the vicinity stood in stark contrast to the means which St Petersburg actually had at its disposal to prevent this danger. In early 1913 a maritime operation was to be mounted to protect the Russian embassy, but all that could be found in Odessa was a transportation ship for 750 men. There could be no real pressure on Turkey of the kind which Sazonov's representative Neratov and the Russian ambassador in Constantinople Charykov had considered exerting during the Agadir crisis and the Tripoli War. Nothing could persuade the Sultan to allow Russian warships to enter the Sea of Marmara 'to defend the prevailing status of the Straits'. Grigorovich considered dispatching the Black Sea squadron, but in the end such a risky operation was not undertaken.[35] All that remained was for the Russians to offer the Porte diplomatic support against Sofia, a tactic which interred for good what remained of the League of Balkan States. Sazonov, Sukhomlinov and Grigorovich also agreed to prepare systematically for a landing so that in five years time Russia would be able to assert her mastery of the Bosporus and Dardanelles.

The alarm which gripped St Petersburg when the German general Liman von Sanders was named commander of the military region of Constantinople in December 1913 should be seen in the context of the Russian Empire's serious military deficiencies. Turkey quickly agreed under pressure from Berlin to seek accommodation, but not because she was intimidated by the strength of Russia's Black Sea fleet. The politicians in St Petersburg knew full well that the limits of their power would quickly be reached if Britain and France did not come to the rescue. The military maintained that Russia was completely equipped for a 'duel' with Germany or Austria, but the solidity of the alliance between Berlin and Vienna made conflict with only one enemy seem unlikely. St Petersburg appreciated the fact that military action directed at the Straits would inevitably lead to a large European war; however, no one knew whether such a war was desirable or whether Russia would gain possession of the Straits. No firm guarantees were forthcoming from Paris and London where the governments were more inclined to test Russian stability and wait to see what St Petersburg decided. The debate within the Russian leadership became caught up in contradictions,

35. Thaden, *Russia*, pp. 38–57; Thaden, 'Charykov and Russian Foreign Policy at Constantinople in 1911', *JCEA* 16 (1956), pp. 25–44; Bovykin *Iz istorii*, pp. 128, 136ff.; Shatsillo, *Russkii imperializm*, pp. 100ff. For the debate between the ministers involved see: Ya. M. Zakher, 'Konstantinopol' i prolivy', *KA* 6, pp. 48ff., *KA* 7, pp. 32ff.

and in the end nothing was resolved. All that was understood was that even a landing in the Bosporus would take a considerable amount of time to prepare. Kokovtsov drew the only appropriate conclusion when he said that war at the present time would be the 'greatest misfortune that could befall Russia'.[36]

This example illustrates just how narrow the Russian Empire's margin for manoeuvre was. After the Liman von Sanders crisis had dissipated the most urgent concern facing Russian policy in the Straits was the balance of forces in the Black Sea. The Turkish fleet, under the command of a British admiral would have two modern dreadnoughts at its disposal by the summer of 1914, while the Russian fleet would have none. Russian naval attachés therefore busied themselves during these critical months scotching Turkish enquiries in Brazil, Argentina and Chile concerning the purchase of another battleship. There is nothing to indicate that the Russian admirals had reason to insist on a great war in order to gain control of the Straits.[37]

If the navy did therefore support the defensive tactics of Russian diplomacy right through until 1914 because it had good reason to want to postpone a conflict, one must then ask what tasks the army could fulfil as part of Russia's great power policies. The nexus of problems that occupied the Ministry of War and the general staff can be reduced to three critical areas.

Firstly, the army had to prepare for a war which would almost certainly be waged against the allied armies of Germany and Austria. Measures also had to be taken against Turkey in the Caucasus and in eastern Anatolia and against Romania.

Secondly, the army had to face the fact that the advantage enjoyed by its potential opponents, especially Germany, in weaponry and overall military capacity could not be made up in the foreseeable future because of short finances and lack of industrial capacity.

36. For the discussions in St Petersburg about the Liman v. Sanders crisis see M. Pokrowski, *Drei Konferenzen. Zur Vorgeschichte des Krieges* (Hamburg, 1920), pp. 32ff.; E.A. Adamov (ed.), *Konstantinopel u. die Meerengen*, vol. 1, pp. 77ff.; *Die internationalen Beziehungen* I/1, no. 295; Zakher in: *KA* 6, pp. 69ff., *KA* 7, pp. 35ff.; cf. F. Fischer, *Der Krieg der Illusionen* (Düsseldorf, 1969), pp. 490ff.; A.S. Avet'yan, *Germanskii imperializm na Blizhnem Vostoke. Kolonial'naya politika germanskogo imperializma i missiya Limana fon Sandersa* (Moscow, 1966); Bovykin, *Iz istorii*, pp. 168ff.; Ignat'ev, *Russko-angliiskie otnosheniya*, pp. 175ff.; Bestuzhev (1965), pp. 72ff.; for Liman's role in the war: U. Trumpener, *Germany and the Ottoman Empire 1914–1918* (Princeton, 1968). Recently, on German policies toward Turkey before 1914: A.S. Silin, *Ekspansiya germanskogo imperializma na Blizhnem Vostoke nakanune pervoi mirovoi voiny (1908–1914)* (Moscow, 1976), here: pp. 207ff.
37. For this in detail see: Shatsillo, *Russkii imperializm*, pp. 134ff.

Thirdly, the army command was faced with the problem of how to meet the demands of Russia's French ally that the Russian army be placed at a maximum level of preparedness for war. This meant that the army would have to be strong enough to undertake an offensive that would immediately tie up large German forces.

Russia's military leaders realised that the country could not bear these numerous demands and impositions or was at best only inadequately prepared for them. The grave problem this posed hung over the Russian armed forces until the war. Russian diplomats were not able to detach Germany from Austria and ease the burden on the army. The prospect therefore of having to face a German-Austrian military coalition in case of war forced military planners to make difficult choices. Above all, Russia had to avoid an enemy pincer movement out of East Prussia and Galicia which would cut off the Russian army corps in the Vistula provinces from the hinterland. It was all the more essential to provide for such dangers, as Russia was unlikely to be able to mobilise her troops as quickly as her enemies mobilised theirs. Since the time of Milyutin, the general staff had tried to compensate for this serious disadvantage by concentrating as many troops as possible near the border. However, this strategy was inherently risky and the Far Eastern War ruled it out for the immediate future.

The Ministry of War's own view of Russian military strength was very pessimistic, as can be seen in its strategy and plans for mobilisation.[38] In 1909, shortly after he had taken over as War Minister, Sukhomlinov officially abandoned the plan to concentrate most of Russia's land-based forces in the Vistula area in peacetime. The field armies would be deployed instead about 200 versts further east — behind the lines Kovno, Białystok, Brest-Litovsk, Kamenets-Podolsk. This would also alleviate the problem of bringing in adequate reserves and supplies, which had proved so difficult throughout Russian military history. The decaying fortifications in Congress Poland were accordingly abandoned (with the single exception of Novogeorgievsk, though this seems to make little strategic sense), and a new defensive belt was prepared further east, near the new deployment areas and supply camps. This was the reason for the very high proportion of funds directed toward fortifications in the rearmament programme of 1910 (372.6 million rubles out of a total of 715 million). The Minister of War also hoped to modernise the army by

38. A.M. Zayonchkovskii, *Podgotovka Rossii*, pp. 50ff., 68ff.

undertaking a thorough reform of its decrepit structure, and in this he was largely successful.[39]

Mobilisation order number 19 came into effect on 1 September 1910 after a long period of preparation. It was based on the premise that the enemy armies would quickly thrust over the Russian frontier, even though most of Germany's strength would have to be directed against France in a two-front war. In directives sent to the army commanders by the general staff, it was assumed that the enemy would take advantage of his ability to concentrate his forces more quickly and that Russia would not be able to halt the advance until the area around Białystok and Brest-Litovsk. Russia's decisive counter-offensive would then be mounted from deep in the deployment areas which had been drawn back into the Empire. The provinces in Congress Poland were viewed as a forward area which would be lost after delaying actions during the early stages of the war and only reconquered as part of a massive counter-attack. The strategy of temporary retreat was the price to be paid for the relatively slow pace of Russian mobilisation.[40]

Army commanders were not uncritical in their reaction to this plan, and more precise instructions about where the Russian counter-offensive would be concentrated and the direction of the attack were not forthcoming until one and a half years later. A new deployment plan, given the royal assent on 1 May 1912, took the Schlieffen plan into consideration in that it assumed that the main strength of the German army would be directed against France. However, the general staff continued to base its strategy on the premise that the more agile enemy would open the war with an offensive thrust deep into Russia. Plans for the Russian counter-attack allowed for two variations: in plan A the Russian attack would be concentrated against Austria-Hungary and in plan G against Germany. After the Russian deployment had been completed in plan A, the 'armies of the German front' (the First and Second Armies) would defeat the German corps in East Prussia, lay siege to Königsberg and keep the Prussian fortifications on the Vistula under surveillance; meanwhile the 'armies of the Austrian front' (Third, Fourth and Fifth Armies) would advance toward Lemberg and Przemy'sl and destroy the enemy along the eastern edge of the Carpathian Mountains. Two

39. Ibid., pp. 83ff.; Sidorov, *Finansovoe polozhenie*, p. 65; Shatsillo, *Rossiya*, pp. 43ff.

40. A.M. Zayonchkovskii, pp. 211ff.

armies on the flanks would secure the area near the imperial capital and the Baltic coast (the Sixth Army) and the area by Romania and the Black Sea coast (the Seventh Army). According to plan G, the expected enemy advance would be parried, and the main Russian offensive consisting of three armies (the First, Second and Fourth) would then be directed against East Prussia. Only two armies would be stationed along the Austrian front, and these would merely provide cover for operations against East Prussia. They were expected to hold the area around Brest-Litovsk at all costs and to prepare a relief attack against Lemberg.[41]

In assessing this strategy, one should be aware of two facts: firstly, the general staff immediately concentrated on plan A, that is on a strategy which foresaw offensive operations against both East Prussia and Galicia but which, according to the disposition of forces, accorded priority to defeating the Austrian armies. Secondly, the directives of 1912 were revised and replaced in the autumn of 1913 by mobilisation plan number 20. However, Russian deployment in July 1914 followed the old plans of 1912 and not the new ones because of delays incurred in adopting the latter.[42] In order to understand the political relevance of Russian strategy during the prewar years, one must look at these military plans in the context of the obligations which France and Russia owed each other under the Alliance.

The chief flaw in the military convention (according to the Russian general staff) was that Russia was not assured of French assistance in case of war against Austria. The mechanics of the alliance only came into effect if Germany mobilised. France was interested solely in what Russia could contribute to containing German forces in the east (although that was not very much after 1905). By 1909 no further agreement about military operations had been reached at the annual conferences of the general staffs — the Russians, handicapped by their own unreadiness for war, could hardly have made any.[43] The French obviously insisted that Russia proceed as quickly as possible with rearmament and substantially reduce the period required for mobilisation. In 1910, when Sukhomlinov's reorganisation and restructuring of the army was only beginning, the Russians still found meetings with the French very embarrassing, even though Russia would probably have to face only

41. Ibid., pp. 256ff.
42. Ibid., pp. 302ff.
43. Ibid., pp. 175ff.

three to five German army corps and some reserve divisions. French military commanders were promised that Russia would turn two-thirds of her forces against Germany and would attempt to give the impression even during peace time that the enemy would have to face a serious offensive between fifteen and thirty days after mobilisation had begun.[44]

General Zhilinskii had to face the extreme displeasure of his French colleague at the next year's conference on 18 (31) August 1911 in Krasnoe Selo — a meeting overshadowed by the Agadir crisis. The Russian plans for deployment led General Dubail to doubt (with good reason) whether the Russians were prepared for a quick offensive the timing of which had been coordinated with France. Zhilinskii could only assure the French that he would continue to concern himself with loyally fulfilling Russia's treaty obligations. He also pointed to the growing danger Russia faced from Austria-Hungary, and stated bluntly that the Tsar's armies would 'not be prepared in the next two years to wage a war on Germany with the least prospect of success'. The army would not have its full complement of heavy field artillery until 1913 at the earliest, it would not have modern automatic weapons until 1914 and would not even have an adequate supply of munitions for the infantry until 1916.[45]

When the chiefs of the general staff met in Paris in July 1912 the new Russian plans for mobilisation were already in effect. The eastward movement of the deployment areas suited the sluggishness of the Russian army but did not suit French demands for quick, mass attacks on the German front. Zhilinskii claimed that already by the fifteenth day after mobilisation Russia would make the enemy 'feel the strength of her armies', but his own calculations for internal circulation did not support these assertions. The Russians continued to concern themselves mainly with the Austrian front where they thought 'the effect on morale' of any setbacks would be 'devastating'. Zhilinskii also pointed out that Russia had to maintain strong border forces in Asia Minor and in Finland. General Joffre, however, was not sympathetic. The French chief of staff advised against splitting up the army and insisted that priority be given to an offensive towards Allenstein and possibly further, in the direction of Posen and Berlin.[46]

44. Ibid., pp. 198f.
45. Minutes of the general staff conference (18 [31] Aug. 1911): *Der diplomatische Schriftwechsel Iswolskis* 1, pp. 137ff.
46. Minutes (14 July 1912): ibid. 2, pp. 181ff.; *DDF* 3/III, no. 200.

Russia's lack of preparedness for war also explains why Joffre now began to insist that the network of strategic railways had to be extended. This would indeed probably have increased the speed of Russian mobilisation. The French also demanded at the conference of general staffs in August 1913 that Russian plans for deployment be changed and large forces concentrated in the province surrounding Warsaw.[47] The government's decision, taken one month earlier, to increase the peace-time strength of the army by 360,000 men favoured such a request. Under permanent threat of war and faced with substantial German army proposals, the Russian government now clearly strained every sinew to overcome Russia's relative underdevelopment for the expected 'decisive battle'. While Kokovtsov sought to arrange a large loan to finance the strategic railway, the new mobilisation plan of September 1913 proposed that a new army corps be created and stationed along the Vistula. All these preparations were overtaken by the actual outbreak of war.

47. Minutes (August 1913): ibid. 3, pp. 272ff.; *DDF* 3/VIII, no. 74.

13

Internal Political Conflicts and the Decision to go to War

In the previous chapters St Petersburg's great power policies were described primarily from economic, military and strategic points of view. Attention will now focus on how policies intended to ensure Russia's status were related to the internal political interests and conflicts which tsarist Russia had to face.[1]

Government prestige in Russia was obviously not very high after 1905. The state could not even count on the unquestioning confidence of those people on whose loyal service it relied. The democratic-minded majority in the first and second Dumas did not give the government a chance gradually to grow accustomed to the new constitutional order. Stolypin could not effectively govern Russia until after the *coup d'état* of June 1907. To the extent that the regime did not rely simply on administrative repression, it had to deal with extremely heterogeneous political forces which did not necessarily provide secure majorities for the government's reform plans. In domestic politics it was hard to find a common denominator which would unite the potential governing parties — the Octobrists, Nationalists and the moderate Right. The experience of revolution kept alive a general desire for peace and order, but few long-term programmes can be based on such sentiments. The continuing traditions of the zemstvo movement, a desire for the rule of law, and aversion (for a variety of reasons) to the bureaucratic police state could not easily be forged into a strong political vision. On the

1. For the following sketch of the situation, cf. above all: Hosking, *The Russian Constitutional Experiment*; Birth, *Die Oktobristen*; Pinchuk, *The Octobrists*; Liszkowski, *Zwischen Liberalismus u. Imperialismus*; Avrekh, *Tsarizm*; idem, *Stolypin*. For the impact on the public and the internal political function of foreign policy see: Bestuzhev (1961, 1965); Wolters, *Außenpolitische Fragen*; Jablonowski, *Die Stellungnahme der russischen Parteien*. I thank K. Ferenczi for references and material from his thesis, now published as *Außenpolitik u. Öffentlichkeit* (Husum, 1982).

other hand, there was little desire to steer a collision course with the cabinet. Only the Octobrists continued to risk conflict in their attempt fully to exploit the possibilities offered by the constitution. However, although they wished to offer those parts of society with spokesmen in the Duma effective representation in the political process, they were generally not very successful. The interests and expectations of the local notables represented by those Duma parties willing to co-operate were just too different and too diffuse. Their common loyalty to nationalism and a powerful state seemed to be the most likely source of consensus.

Views may have differed as to what was meant by 'the people' and 'the nation', by 'Russian' and 'Slavic', by the spiritual nature of Statehood (*gosudarstvennost'*) and the uplifting power of the Orthodox faith. Russians were united, however, in the belief that if the Russian Empire's 'historic mission' was to be fulfilled she would have to rise again renewed vigour and might after such a period of deep humiliation.[2] This sense of nationalism, expressed in timeworn clichés, reflected the opinion of what might be called loyal society. Most large landowners, businessmen in trade and industry, officers and bureaucrats were motivated by such sentiments. The ideology of individual leaders and groups had various accents, as it always had, but this did not hamper the ability of a revived nationalism to unite the nation. In turning to traditional values, these social classes sought reassurance of their identity and confirmation that there was still a place for them in a united, indivisible Russian Empire. In this respect there was little conflict between the national liberalism common among the Octobrists and the national conservatism of the moderate right. The potential for conflict was small even in those areas where an imperial, centralist view of the state and nation clashed with ideologies coloured by Pan-Slavism and Social Darwinism. Democratic and federalist undercurrents which had been at the root of 'Neo-Slavism', did not offer an alternative. It was taken for granted that Russia still had a 'historic responsibility'. Such traditional views explain the undoubted primacy of Balkan politics, including the entire Turkish question.

It should be noted that proponents of national unity were not at all inclined to accept government foreign policy uncritically. The spectre of Tsushima was evoked time and again in the Duma, and a cloud of guilt hung over the government benches in the Tauride

2. For these national values cf. Birth, pp. 130ff.

Palace. Octobrist criticism concentrated on proving that rational great power policies were impossible unless the people's representatives were allowed to thoroughly reform the central administrative system. The Octobrists insisted that the Duma also make use of its rights in questions of foreign and military policy.[3] In time of crisis the Octobrists were almost as much inclined to chauvinism as the nationalist parties. They often decried as weak and ignoble St Petersburg's hesitant diplomacy which strove above all to avoid conflict, and they demanded strong policies. Russia, they said, should not be hampered by alliances or the traditional arrangements of the European powers, and she should never hesitate to demand that her own interests be recognised. In the years just before the war, however, there seemed to be one imperative which swept all else before it: the duty to arm for the 'inevitable struggle with the Germanic races', with the Dual Monarchy and Wilhelminian Germany, in order to thwart the *Drang nach Osten*.[4] During the Balkan wars it became apparent that growing Russian chauvinism would not be satisfied with the defensive *Realpolitik* Sazonov was practising with the support of the armed forces.

This nationalist mood held the Duma majority together. Even the Kadets were by no means immune — as illustrated by the history of this party of lawyers and professors, originally formed to fight the good fight for parliamentarism and social reform. The strictly oppositionist Kadets, accused of lacking patriotism and being susceptible to revolution, were unwilling, for the most past, to see themselves scorned as Russia's own '*vaterlandslose Gesellen*'. It was bad enough not to be considered socially acceptable, and they had absolutely no desire to be expelled beyond the pale of 'respectable' society to where the Social Democrats and Socialist Revolutionaries considered it honourable to stand. Both these groups had little representation in the Duma, although even the radical–democratic wing of the Socialist Revolutionaries had a public voice in the form of the small Trudovik faction. The pressure on the Kadets to conform resulted during the prewar years in the development of a policy of national liberalism and the defection of the left-orientated factions.

Although the 'right-wing Kadets' wished to maintain their freedom

3. Pinchuk, pp. 63ff.
4. For this see also: W. Markert, 'Die deutsch-russischen Beziehungen am Vorabend des Ersten Weltkrieges', in Markert (ed.) *Osteuropa u. die abendländische Welt* (Göttingen, 1966). pp. 166–86, 212–21.

to criticise, they were prepared to co-operate with the Duma majority. They certainly found it easier to admire the statesmanship of the Octobrist leader, A.I. Guchkov, than to abandon the security which came with being included in the national consensus. The glory and lustre of the plans for Russian power had a strong appeal for these tamed liberals as well, and they could even find social and political alibis to justify their keenness to praise Russia's alliance with England and France. Many Kadets began to accept the thesis that foreign policy was of prime importance, a theory defended by Peter Struve in his apotheosis, 'Great Russia' (*Velikaya Rossiya*).[5] The atmosphere of 'intellectual anti-militarism' which had originally dominated the party melted away.[6] Although its scholarly leader, P.N. Milyukov, was strongly opposed to Russian or Pan-Slav chauvinism, even he was impressed by the argument that there should be no party wrangling in foreign policy when the good of the nation demanded solidarity.[7] As early as the Bosnian crisis, Milyukov had insisted that the Kadets should do their best to adopt 'a broadly national viewpoint'. In their pronouncements they should seek to cloak the fact that Russia was unprepared for war 'because such statements about our weakness reduce our opportunities in foreign countries'. Even when it came to 'Slavic policies' he did not wish to see his party excluded: 'The Slavic collective we are actually witnessing in Europe amounts to an alliance with us and is directed against Germanic civilization.'[8]

There certainly were Kadets who cultivated a pacifist and cosmopolitan position and who saw peace and disarmament as the great motive force of the epoch. However, such visions remained well-concealed when the time came to propose real political alternatives.

---

5. P. Struve, 'Velikaya Rossiya. Iz razmyshleni o russkoi revolyutsii', in idem, *Patriotitsa. Politika, kul'tura, religiya, sotsializm. Sbornik statei za pyat' let, 1905–1911 gg.* (St Petersburg, 1911), pp. 73–96 (first appeared in: *Russkaya Mysl'* 1, 1908).

6. The term appears in A.I. Guchkov, *Rechi po voprosam gosudarstvennoi oborony i obshchei politike 1908–17 gg.* (Petrograd, 1917), p. 78 (speech of 7 May 1912).

7. For a detailed presentation of Milyukov's position see: Liszkowski, *Zwischen Liberalismus u. Imperialismus*; see also the collection of Milyukov's essays, *Balkanskii vopros i politika A.P. Izvol'skogo* (St Petersburg, 1910) and, more generally, the memoirs of P.N. Milyukov: *Vospominaniya, 1859–1917* (New York, 1955), vol. 2, pp. 14ff.; see too the political biography: T. Riha, *A Russian European. Pavel Miliukov in Russian Politics* (Notre Dame, 1969); also: H. Giertz, 'Die außenpolitische Position Miljukovs am Vorabend u. während der bosnischen Krise', *JGSLE* 18/2 (1974), pp. 77–113.

8. Milyukov before the Kadet Central Committee on the 1 Mar. 1909, cited in the minutes of the meeting, *CGAOR*, F. 523, ibid. 1, d. 30, 1. 2f. (information from K. Ferenczi).

Although leading Kadets wished their party to have a strong profile, little room was available for manoeuvre. During the Balkan crisis of 1912–13 Milyukov's views were very close to those of Sazonov — much closer in fact than those of the tough talking nationalist agitators who feigned readiness for battle. The liberal faction in the Duma was caught up in its own way in the thought processes of great power politics, and the positions it adopted were already present in the government. Thus one can see emerging once again the entire spectrum of nationalist attitudes and expectations upon which the pseudo-constitutional system rested.

The Praetorian Guards of the extreme Right together with influential cliques from the Court strengthened the arch-conservative camp in its rejection of the new order of 1907. This very heterogeneous group also wanted a strong national state, but with some peculiar variants of its own. The arch-conservatives were dedicated to the 'holy traditions' of autocracy and orthodoxy — Russia's only reliable line of defence in time of chaos. They insisted that capitalism, stock exchanges, banks, Freemasons and the Jewish plutocracy were closely linked to the hydra of revolution. Constitutionalism was considered a fateful erosion of all that was intrinsically Russian in the country. Out of their reactionary sentiments arose a desire to return to the idyllic world of the conservative, hierarchical, autocratic, agrarian state where aristocrats defended the throne.[9] People of intelligence on the extreme Right realised that this dream was useful for agitational purposes but of no use in formulating real policies. In the Council of State and on the periphery of the court camarilla, the arch-conservatives devoted their energies to thwarting the reforming policies introduced by Stolypin. In foreign affairs they argued in favour of reconstituting a league of anti-revolutionary monarchs in the tradition of the Holy Alliance and the *Dreikaiserbund*.[10] They opposed all that comprised the fundamental national consensus: the alliance with republican France, the pro-English naval policy, and the ingrained aversion to Germany and Austria-Hungary. These arch-conservative views were not without influence in the government, and the Tsar himself had a soft spot for such reactionary mystifications. The arch-conservatives also had links with the nationalists.[11]

9. H.D. Löwe, *Antisemitismus u. reaktionäre Utopie*, chapter X.
10. Jablonowski, 'Die Stellungnahme', pp. 69ff.
11. Cf. the psychic profile of the Tsar in v. Hintze's reports (1908–10) in: Lambsdorff, *Die Militärbevollmächtigten*, pp. 300ff. *passim*.

Almost all political factions which supported Russian nationalism and Russia's role as a great power were represented in the upper echelons of government — from Octobrists to unyielding monarchists. The result was that the government's 'national policy' had a curious vagueness about it. Stolypin's cabinet had to withstand strong internal pressures from a conservative group gathered around State Comptroller P.C. Schwanebach and Minister of Agriculture A.V. Krivoshein.[12] A highly flexible political vocabulary was therefore devised. Official pronouncements aimed to please both the Duma and a public infected by nationalism. The grinding conflicts which occasionally even derailed government policy were therefore caused more by internal problems than by the broad outlines of foreign policy. 'Society' was interested above all else in itself. In the Duma, the political Right was permeated with a hierarchical agrarian conservatism which succeeded in severely restraining moderate innovation. Its members strove to prevent the government from yielding to the Octobrists and developing a need for parliamentary legitimation. The Octobrists tried to prepare the way for Stolypin's reform proposals, although at times they did so more vigorously than the Prime Minister would have liked. They considered themselves the unofficial governing party of constitutional, law-abiding Russia, and they longed to see this status recognised when they proffered their criticisms to ministers. However, the Octobrists were not strong enough to live up to such claims and after 1912 in particular could no longer even pretend to consistency. This loose band of fellow-travellers was simply too heterogenous and the entire pseudo-constitutional regime was in consequence steadily losing its capacity to function.

In his confrontations with the Duma and the Council of State, Stolypin was careful to do all he could to gloss over the conflicting interests and achieve his ends by means of shifting majorities and ploys of doubtful constitutionality. He knew full well how important it was to align his policies with the fundamentally nationalist mood of the country and to suggest to the public that Russia's national interests were in good hands. It was very difficult, however, to solve internal political conflicts by means of a relatively relaxed, non-fanatical great Russian nationalism. The nation's finan-

---

12. For a biography of the Minister of Agriculture see the recent book by his son, K.A. Krivoshein: *A.V. Krivoshein (1857–1921). Ego znachenie v istorii Rossii nachala XX veka* (Paris, 1973); H. Heilbronner, 'P. Kh. von Schwanebach and the Dissolution of the First Two Dumas', *CSP* 11 (1969), pp. 31–55.

cial squeeze and military weakness meant that vehement demands for demonstrations of Russian might continually had to be restrained and held in check pending a more advantageous future. Since those sections of the population that supported the state had only a vague understanding of Russia's foreign policy problems, they usually expected stronger demonstrations of Russian power than St Petersburg's diplomats (and the military) could provide.

This discrepancy created long-lasting problems for the government. The outcome of the Bosnian crisis was deplored by an aroused public opinion as a 'diplomatic Tsushima'[13] and a sense of deep humiliation became widespread. Izvol'skii announced that he wished the Duma to judge his conduct, but even this did not suffice to restore his injured reputation, especially since the Tsar restricted his appearances before parliament. The Foreign Minister, who liked to pose as an enlightened man of the world, wanted to improve the public image of Russian diplomacy with the help of a new press division headed by an Octobrist,[14] but it was not easy to popularise the policy of self-restraint which had been forced upon the government. Dissatisfaction and suspicion refused to melt away. In 1910, as a result of an interview in Potsdam, a fragile demarcation between Russian and German interests in Persia was arranged. A broad band of opinion felt that the Foreign Ministry had proved subservient to the German Kaiser, tended to distance itself too much from England and France and to fritter away Russian interests.[15] In 1912 and 1913 Izvol'skii's successor, Sazonov became entangled in all the contradictions of the Balkan League which he himself had patched together, and the failure of the attempt to create a great Slavic order also became apparent. The government was further embarrassed by a wave of anti-Austrian feeling which swept through the chauvinist camp and stirred up irrational Germanophobia. There was less and less confidence in St Petersburg's ability adequately to defend the 'Slav cause', especially the interests of Russia's Serbian and Montenegrin 'brothers'. Sazonov repeatedly had to seek personal conversations with party leaders in the Duma favourable to the government in order to rally their support.[16]

One should nevertheless bear in mind that the noisy nationalist campaigns (in which some voices could even be heard calling for

13. The wording comes from P. Milyukov, *Balkanskii vopros*, pp. 133ff.
14. Cf. Bestuzhev (1961), pp. 67ff., 101ff. *passim*.
15. Ibid., pp. 331ff.; Liszkowski, *Zwischen Liberalismus u. Imperialismus*, pp. 149ff.
16. Bestuzhev (1965), pp. 62ff.

war with Austria) did not create a political force capable of offering a credible alternative to the Tsar. Neo-Slavism was much discussed, but it was neither well-organised nor consistent, and the hypnotic effect of chauvinistic slogans was greater than the political skill of those who mouthed them.[17] Even in spheres where the aggrieved sense of national pride found smoother, calmer, more statesmanlike expression and where protest was limited to expressions of 'national mourning', impatience with St Petersburg's diplomacy was increasing.[18] The cumulative effect of repeated frustrations helped to spread the fatalistic feeling that only a war could resolve the series of humiliations that Russia had suffered. As seen already, such senti-ments also infiltrated the government after the wars in the Balkans, although ministers in St Petersburg knew better than the public how very risky the predicted 'struggle between peoples' would really be.

Dissatisfaction with the government's policies of restraint might seem comprehensible in the light of all the money being spent on armaments. Although the right-wing parties found it offensive that the Duma should consider military matters and although the con-servative majority in the Council of State even forced a government crisis over navy credits in the spring of 1909, the Duma itself always did its 'patriotic duty' in matters of national defence.[19] Apart from disputes about individual items in the budget (when intense shadow boxing developed over parliament's right to interfere) the Duma always willingly granted the War Ministry's budgetary requests. After the ten-year programme of 1910, the government even began to encourage the view that imperial Russia was returning to the ranks of the great military powers. Early in 1911 Stolypin praised the Duma's patriotic work on the budget which had 'put a sword back into the hands of unarmed Russia'.[20] The question of whether adequate attention was being paid to the effectiveness of Russian arms policies remained unanswered however.

17. Liszkowski, 'Zur Aktualisierung der Stereotype "Die deutsche Gefahr" im russischen Neoslawismus', in *Rußland und Deutschland. Fs. für G. v. Rauch* (Stuttgart, 1974), pp. 278–94; W. Zeil, 'Der Neoslawismus', *JGSLE* 19/2 (1975), pp. 29–56; C. Ferenczi, 'Nationalismus u. Neoslawismus in Rußland vor dem Ersten Weltkrieg', *FOG*, 34 (1984), pp. 7–127.

18. 'Difficult days of national sorrow' was Guchkov's expression in his budgetary speech on the 19 Mar. 1909 when referring to the outcome of the Bosnian crisis in: Guchkov, *Rechi*, p. 49.

19. Pinchuk, pp. 63ff.; Hosking, pp. 74ff.; Bazylow, *Ostatnie lata*, pp. 306ff.; E. Chmielewski, 'Stolypin and the Russian Ministerial Crisis of 1909', *CSS* 6 (1967), pp. 1–38; R. Edelman, 'The Russian Nationalist Party and the Political Crisis of 1909', *RR* 34 (1975), pp. 22–54.

20. Cited in Birth, p. 143.

The Duma found it no easier than the government to understand why a battle fleet was needed. The Navy Ministry (which did not shed the stigma of being the 'Tsushima Department' until the energetic Admiral Grigorovich took charge) was wholeheartedly in favour of course, but this feeling was not widespread.[21] The public's idea of imperial grandeur was based on the conventional view that Russia was a land-based power, and society never developed an enthusiasm for the fleet to compare with that of Wilhelmine Germany. Although naval uniform appears in the pictures of the little crown prince, it never became the kind of patriotic boys' wear that it did in Germany.[22] Russian society was far more impatient for a robust army than for floating fortresses of the dreadnought class. Nevertheless, the Duma did approve Grigorovich's mammoth proposal in June 1912, even though a majority had opposed the 'small naval programme' back in the spring of 1908.

At first there was little confidence, especially among the Octobrists, in efforts to strengthen the army. The lack of urgency in the War Ministry's approach to its 'holy mission' seemed inconsistent with the dangers posed by the international environment. Guchkov, the temporary president of the Duma (1910–11) who had made a name for himself as a military expert on the defence committee, repeatedly took offence after 1908 at the 'same old sins' of the War Ministry: the ponderousness of the military bureaucracy, the technical backwardness of Russian artillery, the 'chaotic' administration of the supply department.[23] The Octobrists' leader could claim that, together with ministerial aide General Polivanov, he had worked to reduce nepotism, rationalise the military chain of command and improve the conditions in which the officer corps lived.[24] By the time of the first Balkan war Guchkov, a critical thinker who had supported the generals in their opposition to building battleships until the last, was more optimistic than before about Russia's military potential. During the debate on the budget in May 1912 he spoke of how the Empire had been delivered from a 'state of

---

21. For the Duma's view of naval policies: Shatsillo, *Russkii imperializm*, pp. 163ff.

22. For the comparison with Germany see: Berghahn, *Der Tirpitz-Plan*; J. Meyer, *Die Propaganda der deutschen Flottenbewegung 1897–1900* (Berne, 1967); W. Deist, *Flottenpolitik u. Flottenpropaganda. Das Nachrichtenbureau des Reichsmarineamtes 1897 bis 1914* (Stuttgart, 1976).

23. Guchkov, *Rechi*, p. 77 (7 May 1912).

24. Evidence in the memoirs of A.A. Polivanov, *Iz dnevnikov i vospominaniya po dolzhnosti voennogo ministra i ego pomoshchnika 1907–1916* (Moscow, 1924), vol. 1.

powerlessness and inability to defend herself'.[25] Finally, in the two years before the war most of public opinion felt that Russia was militarily strong enough to adopt a more offensive posture in defending her national interests. As a result. St Petersburg's *attentisme* met with even less comprehension. Chauvinist spokesmen suffered no loss of credibility in 1913 when they raged about 'another Mukden', after Sazonov sought an agreement from Vienna on rearranging the fragments of the Balkan League.

Faced with these problems, Kokovtsov's government did not have much to offer the nationalist movement by way of suitable domestic distractions. Such a tactic had been easier under Stolypin. The former Prime Minister, murdered in September 1911,[26] had repeatedly used manipulatory techniques to gain elbow-room, and had intentionally directed great Russian nationalism against the 'foreign peoples' living within the Empire.[27] Thus the desire of the Polish National Democrats for reconciliation (*ugoda*) was rapidly exhausted. Public opinion and a majority in the Duma were very susceptible to Stolypin's call to 'secure the west'.[28] The glory of the Russian nation still seemed threatened in the western borderlands, above all by Poles and Jews, but also by the struggle of the Ukranians, White Ruthenians and Lithuanians for an autonomy which had once again been crushed in the years after 1907. Nationalist stirrings among Latvians and Estonians, the Germans in the Baltic provinces and, last but not least, the Finns' 'constitutional struggle' stoked the fear that 'Great Russia' was in danger so long as Russian culture and religion had to contend with competing nationalisms.[29]

25. Guchkov, *Rechi*, p. 77 (7 May 1912).

26. On the assassination of Stolypin see: Avrekh, *Stylopin*, pp. 367ff.; Bazylow, 'Zagadka 1 sentyabrya 1911 g.', *VIst* (1975/7), pp. 115–27; Bazylow, *Ostatnie lata*, pp. 427ff.; also: B. Yu. Mayski, 'Stolypinshchina i konets Stolypina', *VIst* (1966/1), pp. 134–44, 2, pp. 123–40.

27. There is no modern compendium of Russian policy towards national groups from 1905 to 1917 and no comparative analysis of nationalist movements within the Russian Empire. For a brief summary see: G. v. Rauch, *Rußland. Staatliche Einheit u. nationale Vielfalt* (Munich, 1953), pp. 277ff., 171ff. See the contemporary view of O. Hoetzsch, *Rußland. Eine Einführung auf Grund seiner Geschichte von 1904 bis 1912* (Berlin, 1913), pp. 437ff.; extensive overviews from an opposition point of view: A.I. Kastel'yanskii (ed.), *Formy natsional'nogo dvizheniya v sovremennykh gosudarstvakh* (St Petersburg, 1910), pp. 577–653.

28. E. Chmielewski, *The Polish Question in the Russian State Duma* (Knoxville, Tenn., 1970); Z. Łukawski, *Koło Polskie w rosyjskiej dumie państwowej w latach 1906–1909* (Wrocław, 1967); M. Wierzchowski, *Sprawy Polski w III i IV dumie państwowej* (Warsaw, 1966).

29. M. Hagen, 'Die Deutschbalten in der III. Duma. Zwischen nationalem Abwehrkampf, Autonomiestreben u. Klassenkampf', *ZfO* 23 (1974), pp. 577–97; J.H.

This feeling was largely a reaction to the tendency of young people to assert their national identity — signs of which could be seen all the way from the revolution of 1905 to the situation among the Moslem Turkic peoples. The Russians had a vague feeling that the historical trend toward modernisation would lead to a burgeoning sense of self among the various peoples in their multi-national empire and to an erosion of the state (as was already happening in the Austro-Hungarian Empire to the great satisfaction of all 'true Russians'). This led to the defiant belief that everything had to be done to preserve one of the traditional fictions of Russian nationalism — that the nation and the state were as one under the aegis of the Almighty. Stolypin created an outlet for these feelings in the practice of administrative Russification, usually promoted as a means of improving national security. His restrictive electoral law of 1907 cut non-Russian representation in the Duma from 105 to 32 seats, thus pleasing the nationalists. In 1909 the area around Kholm was annexed to the province of Kiev and in 1911 zemstvo institutions were introduced into the western provinces. (The latter move was intended to neutralise the large Polish landowners by strengthening the Orthodox peasantry.) Such steps were certain to please the Octobrists, the nationalists and the moderate Right — that informal coalition which formed the social foundation of Stolypin's regime. When the conservative majority in the Council of State rejected the bill passed by the Duma, Stolypin was willing to undertake a small coup for the sake of his zemstvo act.[30] He knew that he was invincible so long as he kept the nationalist camp strong and on his side. This compact collapsed, however, under Stolypin's successor, partly because Kokovtsov was not the man to whip up public demands and partly because his cabinet relaxed its repression of non-Russian nationalities.[31] Yet this and the failure of Sazonov's Near Eastern diplomacy in the two Balkan wars cannot fully

Hodgson, 'Finland's Position in the Russian Empire 1905–1910', *JCEA* 20 (1960), pp. 158–73; Avrekh, *Stolypin*, pp. 44ff.; Bazylow, *Ostatnie lata*, pp. 338ff.; Hosking, pp. 106ff.

30. Idem, pp. 116ff.; Bazylow, *Ostatnie lata*, pp. 391f.; E. Chmielewski, 'Stolpin's Last Crisis', *CSS* 3 (1964), pp. 95–126; M.S. Conroy, 'Stolypin's Attitude towards Local Self-Government', *SEER* 46 (1968), pp. 446–61; M. Hagen, 'Die Russische Presse zur Regierungskrise im März 1911', *Das Vergangene u. die Geschichte. Fs. für R. Wittram* (Göttingen, 1973), pp. 403–28; Avrekh, *Stolypin*, pp. 92ff., 349ff.; E.D. Chermenskii, *IV Gosudarstvennaya duma i sverzhenie tsarizma v Rossii* (Moscow, 1976), pp. 33ff.

31. In general see: D.R. Costello, 'Prime Minister Kokovtsov and the Duma. A Study in the Disintegration of the Tsarist Regime 1911–1914', PhD thesis, Univ. of Virginia, 1970, pp. 47ff. *passim*.

explain the government's continual loss of authority. The most important reasons for the decline of the 'moderate Right' which Stolypin had managed to forge together can be found instead in the changes occurring in Russian society during these years of tense international relations and apparent economic prosperity.

The general trend rightwards, which could be seen in the outcome of the elections to the fourth Duma in the autumn of 1912, was engendered by a changing climate already visible under Stolypin.[32] An equally significant indication of this development was the spreading decomposition of the Octobrist party. With its close ties to the government, it could no longer pretend to be a thorn in the flesh of immobile conservatism. The grass-roots of the party, heterogeneous and lacking in dynamism, slid into a lazy kind of patriotic loyalty. The Octobrism of 1905–7 shrivelled away in the contented midst of a society that was turning to particularist interests and could no longer be rallied to the banner of constitutionalism.

The Kadets, only a little further to the Left, also suffered under the paralysing impact of political stagnation and the 'crisis of political parties'.[33] Left-leaning dissidents sought contact with the Social Democrats and the populist intelligentsia, but most liberals insisted that the party had to continue playing its role as the loyal opposition. During this period of stifling reaction both the right wing of the party and the centre around Milyukov found it impossible to breathe fresh air back into Russian politics. St Petersburg sank into a morass of resignation.

The forces of monarchism and conservatism were in the strongest position to disrupt Kokovtsov's plans. There were no more reform policies like those of Stolypin, which aimed at creating a state that, though still authoritarian, was able to modernise. The Ministers of Justice and the Interior gave free rein to the anti-Semitism of the extreme Right with the spectacular trial of Mendel Beilis for ritual murder and steered a generally reactionary course, at odds with the policies the Prime Minister was trying to pursue.[34] The authorities were able to manage the bureaucratic routine of government, but this did not create enthusiasm which might have been communicated to society. The government found itself confronted instead

32. For a short description of the political groups in the IVth Duma see: Wolters, *Außenpolitische Fragen*, pp. 34ff.
33. Avrekh, *Stolypin*, pp. 430ff.
34. H. Rogger, 'The Beilis Case: Anti-Semitism and Politics in the Reign of Nicholas II', *SR* 25 (1966), pp. 615–29; Löwe, *Antisemitismus u. reaktionäre Utopie*, chap. X. 4.

with worsening social tensions which could not even be hidden, let alone solved. This was the reason for the lack of direction in internal policy. Vehement criticism of Russia's defensive foreign policy, which crystallised into an ideology of hyper-nationalism, should also be seen against this background of internal frustration and immobility.

Let us examine the causes in more detail. Firstly, it should be noted that the widespread sense of public discontent seems to stand curiously in contrast with the economic boom then underway.[35] In fact, various aspects of this prosperity provoked new fears, deep dissatisfaction, and strong conflicting interests. The 'shower of gold' prompted by the economic upswing only touched an extremely thin layer of privileged society. While strata connected to the St Petersburg world of finance, heavy industry, and defence enjoyed rich profits, other sectors of the economy continued to suffer from increasing competition, declining markets and heavy risks in the hectic atmosphere of the prewar period. The boom years, accompanied by widespread economic concentration, were far from unanimously viewed as a time of assured progress. Instead, commerce and industry tended to become more acutely aware of how lop-sided rapid economic growth had been.

Even the haute bourgeoisie, which prospered as a result of the boom, was not free from worry. Although the government managed to create opportunities for profit, it could not secure peace in labour relations. The rapid growth of heavy industrial centres had attracted even more job-seekers out from the over-populated rural areas and into the cities. Between January 1910 and July 1914 the total number of factory workers rose by almost one-third, of which the St Petersburg area and the metal-working industry in particular absorbed a disproportionately high share.[36] The teeming labour market and difficult social conditions made these workers, who had grown up in the slums or been imported from the countryside, susceptible to the kind of radical, incendiary talk offered in particular by Bolshevik and neo-populist circles.

In the spring of 1912, the blood-bath in the Lena goldfields focused attention once more on social tension and government brutality. Once again the proletariat showed its readiness to go on

---

35. Cf. chap. 11.
36. For a recent Soviet view see: G.A. Arut'yunov, *Rabochee dvizhenie v Rossii v period novogo revolyutsionnogo pod"ema 1910–1914 gg.* (Moscow, 1975), pp. 28–64.

strike.[37] A tide of labour unrest swept over Russian industry, directed not only at securing the everyday interests of the working class but also at manifesting fierce opposition to the state authorities. The wave of strikes continued right through to July 1914, and when Poincaré visited St Petersburg just two weeks before war broke out, conditions in the working-class areas of the capital were reminiscent of a general strike.[38] The government did not even enjoy the full confidence of the captains of industry, as can be seen from the activity of A.I. Konovalov, leader of the small Progressive Party controlled by influential entrepreneurs. Early in 1914 Konovalov tried to establish contacts as far left as the Bolsheviks in order to make it possible to stabilise the situation from below — a plan necessarily inimical to the state authorities.[39]

There is no doubt that the renaissance of the Russian labour movement after 1912 helped stir up new fears within society and disgruntlement with the authorities. Society was once more suffused with feelings of insecurity and purposelessness. Such sentiments prepared people psychologically for that combination of fatalism and ideological susceptibility which produced the chauvinism of the few years preceding the war. Not only extreme chauvinists sought distraction through an aggressive foreign policy; frustrated politicians in the Duma, hemmed in between radicalism on the one side and reaction on the other, saw the 'paralysis' of the regime as the real reason for Russia's defeats in the Balkans and were gradually recruited to the nationalist cause. In November 1913 Guchkov predicted before the Octobrists an approaching period of chaos, anarchy and enormous convulsion which would prove highly detrimental to the cause of the bourgeoisie, whose wealth depended 'on the peaceful evolution of the state'. The only hope (supposedly) lay in 'marshalling those social circles and groups of the population whose political faith lies primarily in Russia's role as a great power'.[40] Thus Guchkov too looked to Russian nationalism, with its hunger for

37. For the effects of the massacre on the government see: Costello, pp. 91ff.
38. For an extensive description of the wave of strikes see: Arut'yunov, pp. 138ff. *passim*, pp. 307ff.
39. Cf. L.H. Haimson, 'The Problem of Social Stability in Urban Russia 1905–1917, in *Slavic Review*, 23 (1964), pp. 619ff.; ibid., 24 (1965), pp. 1ff.; for the genesis of the Progressive Party see: V.N. Seletskii, 'Obrazovanie partii progressistov. K voprosam o politicheskoi konsolidatsii russkoi burzhuazii', *VMU-Ist* (1970/5), pp. 33–48; V. Ya. Laverychev, *Po tu storonu barrikad. (Iz istorii bor'by moskovskoi burzhuazii s revolyutsiei)* (Moscow, 1967), pp. 92ff.; Chermenskii, *IV Gosudarstvennaya duma*, pp. 53ff.
40. Guchkov, *Rechi*, pp. 95–111, here p. 105 (8 Nov. 1913), English translation in *RR* 3 (1914), pp. 141–158.

displays of imperial might, to save the country from the feared catastrophe.

Much of the internal tension resulted from the fact that during the phase of industrial expansion most of the landowning class had no sense at all that they were headed toward a hopeful future. Throughout the economic cycles, the landed classes cultivated the traditional feeling that private agriculture had been neglected by the government and made to bear the costs of a dubious kind of progress which at best served the interests of Jews and Germans. Such complaints were voiced by those still wrapped in a feudal cocoon, by discouraged or dispossessed landowners and by representatives of big business, whose profits depended on exports and strong markets. The conflict between industry and agriculture, which had been fought out in the era of Witte and Vyshnegradskii and firmly entrenched by the protective tariff, gained new significance during this period of economic expansion. The mood among landowners swung between depression and outrage and was not improved by the fact that they, unlike industry, did not have well-organised groups to defend their interests.[41] Agriculture was organised by region and could not compete with industry's powerful sectoral and umbrella groupings. The venerable aristocratic associations, which channelled expressions of their conservatism through a 'Nobles' League', did not offer a satisfactory substitute.[42] An aggressive interest group inclusive of peasant elements like the German 'Farmers' League' would have been unthinkable in Russia.

Efforts to modernise agricultural associations intensified in the years immediately before the Great War, largely as a result of discussions about revising the trade agreement with Germany.[43] In 1912 an All-Russian Chamber of Agriculture was founded. A little later, representatives of the agrarian movement found opportunities

41. For a new study that includes the Russian research see: J.H. Hartl, *Die Interessenvertretungen der Industriellen in Rußland 1905–1914* (Vienna, 1978); see also R.A. Roosa, 'The Association of Industry and Trade 1906–1914', PhD thesis, Columbia Univ., 1967, and the essays: idem, 'Russian Industrialists Look to the Future. Thoughts on Economic Development 1906–1914', in *Essays in Russian and Soviet History* (Leiden, 1963), pp. 189–208; idem, 'Russian Industrialists and "State Socialism" 1906–1914', in *SS* 23 (1972), pp. 395–417 (with the answer of J.D. White, ibid. pp. 414–21); G. Guroff, 'The State and Industrialization in Russian Economic Thought 1909–1914', PhD thesis, Princeton Univ., 1970.
42. Cf. G.W. Simmonds, 'The Congress of the Representatives of the Nobles' Associations. A Case Study in Russian Conservatism', PhD thesis, Columbia Univ., 1964; I.D. Vaisberg, *Sovet Ob"edinennogo dvoryanstva i ego vliyanie na politiku samoderzhaviya 1906–1914* (Moscow, 1 Cand. thesis MGU, 1956).
43. For the following: Bonwetsch, *Kriegsallianz u. Wirtschaftsinteressen*, pp. 18ff.; Bestuzhev (1965), pp. 48ff., 74.

to discuss their interests at regional meetings encouraged by the Chamber of Exports, and they once more expressed (in pointed terms) the resentment they had always felt over the industrial protectionism of Russian Finance Ministers. The thesis that official tariff and trade policies discriminated against agriculture in order to benefit industry was a familiar complaint of agrarian Russia. Under these conditions, it is easy to see how Germanophobic nationalism could help reinforce the protest against high or even higher tariffs. Protective tariffs had been an integral part of Russo-German trade relations since the time of Bismarck, and the question of the terms under which the treaty of 1904 would be renewed caused the agricultural lobby to take up a position directed as much against Germany as against Kokovtsov. The old accusation that Berlin, with the help of Russian industrial circles, had forced St Petersburg to accept an unequal treaty to end the Far Eastern War was now revived. Some spokesmen even went so far as to claim that the Russian Empire had sunk to the level of a German colony and that the existing treaty was leading 'without fail to the destruction of the national economy'.[44]

The continual expansion of the powerful German economy, Russia's most important trading partner, doubtless contributed to the anti-German hysteria. German exports to Russia increased between 1905 and 1913 by more than 150 per cent.[45] The Russians noted with anger that German grain had taken over traditional Russian markets in Scandinavia while inside the Empire (in Finland and the Vistula provinces) it was also selling better than Russian produce. Moreover, it was not difficult to portray the German economy's massive penetration of Asia Minor and the Russian zone of interest in Persia as a continual provocation. Influential Russian newspapers pointed, with ever increasing urgency, to the danger that Germany would gain control of the Straits and halt Russian exports. Inflammatory 'proof' of this thesis was not difficult to find in the jungles of German publishing.

Kokovtsov continued Russia's traditional industrialisation policies and considered high tariffs essential. He therefore was not in a position to mitigate agrarian protest. He was also averse to emotional Germanophobia — especially since Russia's rearmament programmes depended on untroubled relations with the German

44. Cited in Bonwetsch, *Kriegsallianz*, pp. 21f.
45. Cf. Bonwetsch, 'Handelspolitik u. Industrialisierung', pp. 288ff.

economy and because neither France nor England could have played the role which Germany had always played in the modernisation process. In February 1914, pressure arising from a revolt which centred around Minister of Agriculture Krivoshein, forced the Prime Minister to step down, defamed as a friend of Germany and a promoter of Jews. The Nationalists cheered Kokovtsov's dismissal as a seventy-five-year old, I.L. Goremykin, became Prime Minister.[46] However, Kokovtsov's successor as Finance Minister, P.L. Bark, also proved unable to score impressive gains for Russian agriculture, despite the fact that majorities favourable to the agricultural lobby could have been found both in the Council of State and the Duma.[47] The problems the government faced were firmly embedded in the very foundations of the Russian economy. They reflected the structural contradictions in the plans for development which had encouraged rapid industrial progress and in so doing had destroyed the traditional norms and fabric of Russian society. Ever since the emancipation Russians had felt that they were living in a time of dissolution and change, and this was especially true of the segmented society which emerged after the big drive to modernise in the 1890s. However, the array of problems facing Russia between 1912 and 1914 produced a crisis which was felt to be unusually profound and hopeless.

In order to understand how internal conditions made the Russians more susceptible to pervading nationalism, the following factors must be considered together: the disintegration of pseudo-constitutionalism, an atmosphere of catastrophe charged with strong social tension, the turbulence of a period of economic boom, dissatisfaction in agricultural circles, and the declining ability of the government to assert its authority. The Russian view of international conflict was also partly determined by the hopelessness of the internal situation. A good portion of the press encouraged the feeling that Russia was under threat, and this increased the temptation to take up chauvinist ideologies in order to escape the social crisis of identity. Deep-seated fears were projected onto a foreign enemy which could easily be identified as the 'German menace'. Many were convinced by the Germans' own apparent determination to confirm the hostility imputed to them. The notion inherent in both German and Russian nationalism that there would be an

46. Costello, pp. 202ff.; Kokovtsov, *Iz moego proshlogo*, vol. 2, pp. 259ff.
47. Bonwetsch, *Kriegsallianz.*

inevitable, decisive show-down between Slavs and Teutons was advanced at great length on both sides, as evidenced in the 'newspaper war' of the spring of 1914. In Russia this belief still went hand in hand with bitter denunciations of government timidity.[48]

To these observations should be added an enquiry into how internal tensions affected the decisions taken by the Russian authorities during the July crisis of 1914. A subtly differentiated answer is clearly required here, and I shall look first at the small number of decision-makers who normally dealt with military and foreign policy problems. By the time of the Liman von Sanders crisis (at the latest) Sazonov, Sukhomlinov and Grigorovich had agreed that the collapse of the Ottoman Empire was imminent and that Russia had to arm herself to seize the Straits by force when this happened. The ministers expected military clashes with Austria-Hungary, provoked by a conflict between Austria and Serbia (or again between Serbia and Bulgaria), in which Russia would have to support the Serbs against Vienna. The Russians no longer thought that war could be limited to the Near East and conceived the approaching conflict as a 'great European war'. The ministers also agreed that the Empire would not be able to support such a huge effort until two or three years hence. Until then Russia should consolidate her interests but avoid military sanctions, especially when the support of England and France was not guaranteed.[49] The ministers hoped that by agreeing to more rapid military rearmament and strategic preparations, they would be in a position by about 1917 no longer to have to act defensively, with the accompanying losses in prestige. At the same time they wished to strengthen Russian military power in relation to Germany, in order both to counter-balance the effects of the large German military programme and to increase Russia's influence within the *entente*. They also hoped to induce Paris and London to include Russia's essential interests in the Near East within the terms of the alliance. This uniformity of views was not contradicted by the fact that the Minister of War intervened in the mounting Russo-German press feud in the spring of 1914 to declare self-confidently that Russia did not fear such bluster and was prepared for war. Sukhomlinov's statement was merely a paraphrase of declarations emanating repeatedly from Germany which

---

48. For the 'newspaper war' in the spring of 1914 see: K. Wernecke, *Der Wille zur Weltgeltung*, pp. 249ff.; F. Fischer, *Der Krieg der Illusionen*, pp. 542ff.; Liszkowski, *Zwischen Liberalismus u. Imperialismus*, pp. 229ff.
49. Cf. the literature mentioned in chap. 12, note 36.

he did not wish to leave unanswered, especially as he felt personally slighted by the lack of confidence in the Ministry of War. Public agitation had to be appeased.[50]

Since the spring of 1914, Sazonov had directed his efforts at securing the period of grace which the military considered essential. The Foreign Minister tried of course to improve Russia's position in case of war, but he had few successes to incline him to optimism. The relationship with Paris was strengthened and many outstanding disagreements cleared up; however, conversations with London about an Anglo-Russian naval convention, desired as much by Paris as St Petersburg, were of no avail — Sir Edward Grey on the British side personified London's traditional aversion to continental commitments. In addition, the eternal annoyances inherent in the Anglo-Russian relationship in Persia could be mitigated only with the greatest of effort.[51] Sazonov's attempts to revive the League of Balkan States (including Constantinople) this time reached a disappointing conclusion, as did the efforts to firmly establish the status quo sketched out in the peace offers of 1913. St Petersburg had great difficulty in curbing its two closest allies, Serbia and Montenegro. When an international naval display was organised to force the stubborn King Nicholas to open up Scutari, Russian ships did not participate — arresting proof that St Petersburg had little margin for manoeuvre in its competition with Austria.[52] Sazonov succeeded neither in strengthening Russia's position in Bulgaria nor in resolving the Macedonian question; the explosiveness of Serbia's relationship with Austria could not be reduced and attempts to draw the Porte closer to Russia remained equally fruitless. Sazonov's diplomatic pressure to create an autonomous Armenia, gain a foothold for Russia in the debt administration of the Ottoman Empire and shield the border areas in Asia Minor (e.g. from foreign railway concessionaries) did not succeed. By the summer of 1914 neither Turkish nor Bulgarian neutrality was guaranteed in case of

50. The unsigned article by the Minister of War appeared under the heading, 'Russia wants peace but is prepared for war' in *Birzhevye vedomosti*, 27 Feb. (12 Mar.) 1914; on the occasion of the debates in the French assembly about three-year military service; the article by Sukhomlinov in the same newspaper on 31 May (13 June) 1914 fulfilled a similar function: 'Russia is prepared and France must also be prepared!'. Cf. Bovykin, *Iz istorii*, pp. 113f., Bestuzhev (1965), p. 78; Sukhomlinov, p. 252.
51. Kazemzadeh, *Russia and Britain*, pp. 510ff., 581ff.; D.W. Spring, 'The Trans-Persian Railway Project and Anglo-Russian Relations 1909–1914', *SEER* 54 (1976), pp. 60–82. Cf. chap. 14.
52. Cf. E.C. Helmreich, *The Diplomacy of the Balkan Wars*, pp. 294ff.

war, nor was Romanian neutrality despite repeated contacts.

In addition, the government could not be at all sure of the loyalty of the various nationalities living within the Russian Empire. Unlike Vienna, St Petersburg had succeeded in repressing 'national movements which undermine the mechanism of state'. However, the mounting danger of war prompted some ministers to express concern, especially in regard to the Polish question. In January 1914, after the Council of State had rejected a languages regulation, Sazonov dared to suggest in a report to his Imperial Majesty that 'the question be once more examined of the extent to which the reasonable wishes of Polish society could be gradually granted in respect to self-administration, language, schools and the church'.[53] He hoped that 'unified and consistent' policies toward national minorities would immunise the Poles against the increasing attractiveness of an Austro-Polish solution. This initiative, too, went for naught.

An examination of all these facts makes it clear that the Russian political elite had no reason to desire a great war in July 1914. St Petersburg did not have a strategy of preventive war, either in reaction to the tense internal situation or similar to Berlin's policy of 'calculated risks'.[54] Fear of a German 'pincer attack' had indeed increased, as well as awareness of the mounting danger of war. All the relevant sources show however that the autocracy continually tried to avoid a clash with the Central Powers, even after Austria had declared war on Serbia. It was St Petersburg's diplomacy of conflict avoidance which accounted for Belgrade's willingness to make extremely broad concessions in response to Austria's ultimatum. In addition, St Petersburg received no encouragement from London, whose hesitant behaviour long cast doubt on British willingness to come to Russia's help.[55]

Three factors were primarily responsible for the order for general mobilisation, which the Foreign Minister, under heavy pressure from his generals, wrested from the Tsar on the afternoon of 17 (30) July:[56] firstly, the realisation, justified by a number of indications,

53. Sazonov to Nicholas II (7 [20] Jan. 1914), in *IB* I/1, no. 52.
54. For this concept cf. A. Hillgruber, 'Riezlers Theorie des kalkulierten Risikos u. Bethmann Hollwegs politische Konzeption in der Julikrise 1914' in W. Schieder (ed.), *Erster Weltkrieg. Ursachen, Entstehung u. Kriegsziele* (Cologne, 1969), pp. 240ff.
55. From a Soviet point of view: A.L. Narochnitskii, 'Velikie derzhavy i Serbiya v 1914 g.', in *VIst* (1976/4), pp. 22–32.
56. See the daily record of the Foreign Ministry, 17(30) July 1914, in *IB* I/5, no. 284.

that Berlin was not serious about preventing Austria-Hungary from taking further military action after Belgrade had been bombarded; secondly, the conviction that Russia could not leave Serbia, exhausted by the Balkan Wars, to her fate. That would have destroyed the last fairly reliable pillar of Russian policy in the Near East; thirdly, the fear of Sukhomlinov and his Chief of General Staff, Yanushkevich, that Russia would never catch up with rapid German mobilisation if the military remained suspended in the 'pre-mobilisation phase' (*predmobilizatsionnyi period*) ordered on 12 (25) July after Austria had declared war on Belgrade, the 'partial mobilisation' phase (ordered on 16 (29) July) of the military districts of Kiev, Odessa, Kazan' and Moscow and of the Baltic and Black Sea fleets, and the confusion of the general mobilisation ordered on the same day but rescinded a few hours later.

These three factors together — the feeling that Germany was purposely being deceitful, that St Petersburg might lose its last card in the Balkans and that Russia might become bogged down in the technical deficiencies of her own military organisation — produced an extremely tense atmosphere which the general staff in particular could no longer bear. Partial mobilisation against Austria weakened the front against Germany, and news that the Germans had secretly begun mobilising increased the pressure to arrive at a decision. Wilhelm II offered to mediate in Vienna, but the Russians had lost all confidence. St Petersburg's minimal demand that Austria eliminate from her ultimatum those points 'that infringe on Serbia's rights as a sovereign state' had apparently been rejected, judging by the statements of German Secretary of State von Jagow.[57] Notification from the German ambassador Pourtalès on 18 (31) July that Austria had accepted German advice and declared that she would not 'infringe Serbia's territorial integrity or harm Russia's legitimate interests' came too late to stop the general mobilisation ordered again the previous day.[58] In any case, no one in St Petersburg could guarantee the authenticity of this second-hand promise.

In view of the solid research that has built up since the seminal work of Fritz Fischer, one can forgo a closer examination of the reactions of Germany and other nations to the July crisis.[59] Instead,

---

57. Ibid., no. 278, p. 305.
58. Ibid., no. 334.
59. For a research paper containing extensive discussion of the literature see K. Hildebrand, 'Imperialismus, Wettrüsten u. Kriegsausbruch 1914', *NPL* 20 (1975), pp. 160–94, 339–64; W. Schieder, 'Der Erste Weltkrieg', *SDG* 6 (1972), pp. 841ff. For the Soviet view see especially: N.P. Poletika, *Vozniknovenie pervoi mirovoi voiny*

the behaviour of the Russian leadership will be studied once more in the context of the internal crisis. The government and the imperial court cannot have been overwhelmed by the feeling that they were faced with a revolutionary situation. Statements can be found, like the oft cited memorandum of arch-conservative P.N. Durnovo in February 1914, which allude to the danger of a social revolution if war should erupt. Some spokesmen on the extreme right worried that a war would destroy the Russian state and seal the triumph of Social Democracy: 'these Attilas will devour all of humanity until they themselves are devoured by the anarchists. . . .'[60] However, one cannot say that the internal situation produced an atmosphere of alarm within the government. The Tsar and his ministers and generals did not view their decision to order a general mobilisation and stand firm by Serbia's side in the context of counter-revolutionary crisis management. Nicholas had disavowed those who proposed anti-revolutionary solidarity among the old 'eastern monarchies' and who would have preferred 'a little alliance with Germany to the great friendship with England'.[61] In this memoirs Sazonov reports that he pointed out to the hesitant emperor, in their decisive conversation on 17 (30) July, that 'Russia [would] never forgive the Tsar' if he capitulated to the German demands and thereby 'heaped shame on the good name of the Russian people'.[62] The tone of this statement reflects a very traditional style of argument, not the kind of panic engendered by revolution sweeping through the streets and squares of the capital. Moreover, the general strike of the previous few days (7 to 15 July) had now ended and St Petersburg was once more fairly calm and quiet.[63]

(*iyul' skii krizis 1914 g.*) (Moscow, 1964); the book is a revised version of the first edition of 1935. Poletika's starting-point is that the war was 'provoked' by Austria and 'unleashed' by Germany, while France pushed (*podtalkivat'*) Russia to enter the war; with her 'provocative policy' of 'non-interference' England also promoted the outbreak of war. Bovykin, *Iz istorii*, p. 70, emphasises that Russia's lack of equality in the Alliance with France was used 'as an instrument' by imperialistic circles in England and France in order to draw the Russian Empire into the war against Germany.

60. The quote about 'Attilas' comes from the extremist right-wing deputy E.N. Markov in May 1914, and is quoted by Jablonowski, 'Die Stellungnahme', p. 74; the analysis of the debates in the Duma during 1913–14 in Wolters, *Außenpolitische Fragen*, pp. 77ff., shows that reactionary speakers' predictions of revolution were in response to similar comments by Social Democratic deputies. Durnovo's memorandum is contained in: *Krasnaya nov'* (1922/6), pp. 182ff.

61. E.N. Markov, 10(23) May 1914, cited in Jablonowski, 'Die Stellungnahme', p. 70.

62. Sasonoff, *Sechs schwere Jahre*, p. 251.

63. In *Rabochee dvizhenie*, p. 373, Arut'yunov gives 15(28) July as the last day of

One should not overestimate Nicholas II's warning to the Kaiser that Austria's declaration of war on Serbia had provoked such 'enormous outrage' in Russia that it would be 'a very difficult task to calm those people here who want war'. The Tsar's pronouncement simply reflected the conventional practice of pleading the mood of one's own people.[64] Russian diplomacy (and much else besides) had for many years been quick to make use of 'the perception of apparent discord' between official policy and public opinion in order, as Sazonov once wrote, 'to persuade the cabinets that... we should have to fight off the pressure of public opinion'.[65]

Even if the government had believed that internal stability was in danger, who was there at the centre of power in the old regime with the will to implement a Bonapartist strategy of diversion or pacification? There is no evidence that such a man existed.

An examination of domestic tension also does not reveal any convincing proof that Russia in the summer of 1914 was close to a 'revolutionary situation', the maturing of which was interrupted by the war.[66] If the situation is compared with the experience of 1904–5, one can detect no comparable accumulation of social protest and rebellion with the potential to destroy the system. True, there was a similarly explosive climate in the industrialised centres, but no concentrated disorder in the countryside and, above all, no common vision which could have united the labour movement and society, at least for a short period of time. This was due, not least of all, to the fact that what consensus there was among the wealthier classes rested on a heterogeneous kind of nationalism which did not extend to the working classes. Ten years earlier, on the other hand, a united front against the police state and the 'senseless war' and in favour of constitutional guarantees and substantial social reforms had generated the quickly accelerating whirlpool which threatened to sweep away the regime. The zemstvos, the professional intelligentsia, the petty bourgeoisie, the proletariat and finally the peasant masses of 'starving Russia' had joined in the general revolt.[67] In 1914, however, there were no common aims capable of overcoming

---

the 'general strike'; however, as the strike statistics show, the climax of the movement had already passed on 11(24) July.

64. Nicholas II to Wilhelm II, 17(30) July 1914, in *IB* I/5, no. 276.

65. Cf. Sazonov, 18(31) Oct. 1912, ibid., III/4.1, no. 100; Liszkowski, *Zwischen Liberalismus u. Imperialismus*, p. 61.

66. See Haimson's discussion of the problem in: Geyer (ed.), *Wirtschaft und Gesellschaft*, pp. 304ff.

67. See chap. 10.

class barriers and uniting the people.

Loyalty to the government was stronger than the will of the opposition to resist, although the opposition could have won broad support for a liberal, democratic alternative and gained credibility in the eyes of the people with demands for a 'national' and possibly parliamentary government.[68] One should also not overestimate the importance of the renaissance of Freemasonry or the development of an organisation reaching from Kadets and Progressives as far as Social Reformists, Populists and Social Democrats. It is very doubtful whether these minority groups could have broken out from their exclusive circles and risen to lead the people if war had not broken out and chauvinism not became ingrained. There is no reason at all either to see the beginnings of an anti-militaristic common front against the government in the Kadets' rejection of the large rearmament programme.[69] Unlike the years 1904 to 1905, when Russia was in the throes of extensive reorganisation, the political will to resist was not very widespread in the society of 1914. The emotional nationalism to which public opinion escaped reveals a lack of political vision and a sense of fear, largely of revolution. Premature comparisons with the situation during the third winter of war in 1916–17, when the February revolution was in incubation, are misguided.

Those social tensions which existed did not hold any potential for revolution in July 1914, and no one with any power in the government was trying to use general mobilisation as a tool of domestic pacification. This does not mean, however, that the Tsar and his ministers acted in a vacuum, unaffected by Russia's domestic problems. They were steeped in those concepts of national power and prestige which ascendant nationalism was proclaiming from the roof tops, and their understanding of Russia's interests and her historic mission was not far removed from that of most of the public. Although Russian diplomacy was free from emotional chauvinism, it was as much concerned as the chauvinists were about the Empire's position as a great power and Russia's role 'among the Slavic peoples, conferred by history'.[70] Aggressive adventurism had not infected the military command, but the view that Russia's

---

68. Cf. H. Rogger, 'Russia in 1914', in *1914. The Coming of the First World War* (New York, 1966), pp. 229–53; Haimson, pp. 318ff., seems to me to overestimate the opposition's ability to resist.
69. Liszkowski, *Zwischen Liberalismus u. Imperialismus*, pp. 240f.
70. Sazonov, 7(20) Jan. 1914, in *IB* I/1, no. 52.

imperial position and the honour of her army made it impossible to leave Serbia to meet her fate alone or to let Constantinople fall to others had become axiomatic.

Internal conflict within Russia was not instrumental in the decision which the governing élite finally took. The fear that further hesitation would provoke internal convulsions was not so strong as the belief that the decision to go to war would gain public approval during this period of high tension. The government found comfort in the knowledge that going to war for Serbia's sake would bring the Tsar and society closer together and would not generate internal political conflict. The common people too, it was thought, would support emperor and motherland as they prayed for a Russian victory. In this limited but by no means marginal sense, the nationalism whish was rooted in Russian society was partly responsible for the outbreak of war.[71]

The nationalist ideology which insisted that Russia must be a great power was a social product of frenetic modernisation. Again in 1914 it demonstrated its ability to unite the nation, apparently able to integrate an old society riven by economic, social and political divisions. In a unanimity of view based for the most part on ideology alone, the wealthy and educated classes put themselves at the service of the government.

The capacity of nationalism to mitigate internal conflict allowed Tsarist Russia to go to war, but nationalism could not be stronger than society itself. This became clear when the government proved unable to satisfy nationalist expectations during the long and costly years of war. War quickly exposed the fissures and fractures in Russian society and finally helped to unloose the tidal wave of soldiers, workers and peasants which swept the old society away. This explains why the Revolution of 1917 wiped out not only tsarism but the entire society (nationalists included.)

71. For the patriotic outburst when war erupted see: Chermenskii, *IV Gosudarstvennaya duma*, pp. 68ff.; V.S. Dyakin, *Russkaya burzhuaziya i tsarizm v gody pervoi mirovoi voiny, 1914–1917* (Leningrad, 1967), pp. 45ff.; Wolters, *Außenpolitische Fragen*, pp. 106ff.; Liszkowski, *Zwischen Liberalismus u. Imperialismus*, pp. 262ff.

14

The Asian Periphery

This is not the place for a more detailed discussion of the relationship between the war and the Revolution, and the events of 1917 lie outside the framework of this book. In the final chapter I shall highlight instead some problems which, though they have only been touched on so far, are very much part of the structure of Russian imperialism. A description will be made of the colonies lying within the borders of the Empire, the methods and function of colonial rule in the Asian borderlands, and finally the impact which this colonial 'periphery' had on tensions within the heartland. In addition, the Russian zones of influence beyond the eastern borders of the Empire will be reviewed once more, in order to highlight the connection between 'internal' and 'external' colonial policies. The history of Russian conquests in Central Asia and the expansion in the Far East has already been sketched out. The following summary can therefore refer back to earlier chapters and concentrate on the problems which existed in the years immediately prior to the World War.[1]

Before 1914, tsarist Russia exercised colonial rule in the strict sense only within its own borders. After her holdings in America had been liquidated with the sale of Alaska in 1867, no more Russian colonies were separated from the motherland by land or sea. Russian imperialism was therefore a continental phenomenon and in this respect, unique.

It is not easy to determine just which regions within the Russian Empire should be considered as internal colonies. The Empire had been created by a process of continual colonisation which had still not been completed by the beginning of the twentieth century even in European Russia. 'New Russia' and the Crimea, the central Volga, the Tatar homelands as far as the Urals as well as the Russian

1. Cf. chaps. 4 and 9.

north — all evinced colonial features, although otherwise these 'borderlands' (*okrainy*) had little in common. The multinational structure of the Empire also poses some difficulties. So far as movements for independence and autonomy are concerned, the tsarist 'peoples' prison' bore the stigma of being a colonial system. Unlike the Austro-Hungarian monarchy, however, the *ancien régime* in Russia never seriously considered far-reaching solutions to the nationalities problem.

Neither the historical process of colonisation nor the suppression of national groupings suffices to justify comparisons with the 'colonialism' of the great powers of Europe. Economic criteria, which define colonialism in simple terms as the exploitation of underdeveloped peripheral regions by the metropolis are also unsatisfactory. According to this definition rural Russia would have been a colony of Russian industry and tsarist Russia as a whole a colonial dependent of finance capital from Europe.

The decision to confine Russian colonialism before 1914 to the Asian frontiers of the Empire, to Siberia, Central Asia and the Caucasus, is based on pragmatic considerations, not categorical definitions. Many of the features typical of Russia's internal colonies could indeed have been found (though with substantial gradations) in Russian Asia: economic and socio-cultural inferiority relative to the metropolis, economic exploitation, special administration determined by military needs, and segregation of the local population from Russians of all estates and classes. Such similarities should not, however, cause us to overlook the great differences, both within these colonies and between them.

Unlike the Caucasus and Central Asia, Siberia was firmly established before the war as a colony for Russian settlement. Its development was heavily influenced by the problems caused in European Russia by industrialisation and the structural crisis in agriculture. Between 1861 and 1914 this 'land of the future' received four million peasant colonists from the zones of rural over-population. Between 1905 and 1911 about 2.5 million people were attracted to Siberia by Stolypin's settlement programme — though this was still far too few to draw off the annual population surplus of Russian villages. The territories beyond the Urals were included in the plan for agrarian reform, that is in the government's attempts to reduce rural poverty in European Russia and dispel the threat of revolution in the countryside. The indigenous nomads and hunters of Siberia, described in official jargon as 'aliens' (*inorodtsy*), had long since become a minority in their own homeland. Russians (including Little and White Russians) comprised almost 85 per cent of the Siberian population by 1911. Only the far eastern Amur province (*priamurskoe general-gubernatorstvo*) was still receiving non-Russian immigration from beyond the Mongolian and Manchurian frontiers.[2]

State-controlled colonisation with its emphasis on western Siberia, the Altai region and the Kirghiz Steppe around Semipalatinsk was accompanied by large-scale measures intended to open up the transportation routes concentrated on the Great Siberian Railway. As mentioned earlier, both economic and strategic factors played a role in its construction.

The huge investments required by the Trans-Siberian Railway gave a strong impetus to industrial expansion in European Russia during the 1890s. Siberia's untapped mineral resources offered an inexhaustible supply of raw materials for Russian industry, and rising gold production was already contributing to the balance of payments. The railway was also the vehicle carrying Sergei Witte's 'economic imperialism' beyond the borders of Transbaikal. The result was the 'peaceful penetration' of Manchuria and Russia's unfortunate participation in the scramble for China. Although defeat in the war against Japan had clipped Russia's ambitions in eastern Asia, her policies in Siberia were far from being confined to peasant colonisation. Double rail extension of the Siberian Railway and the completion in 1916 of the stretch from Nerchinsk to Khabarovsk (i.e. the connection to Vladivostok over Russian territory) were among the great national development programmes of the prewar period. The cost was only a little less than the cost of re-equipping the fleet.

The opening of more transportation routes doubtless remained the most pressing task for the future. Developmental planners in St Petersburg dreamed of a flourishing agriculture in Siberia, but even this would have had great difficulty in competing on the internal Russian market because of the enormous transportation costs. The customs barrier at Chelyabinsk underlined the problem. Using Siberia's rivers as a route for exports was at best a distant goal. The

---

2. Treadgold, *The Great Siberian Migration*; Sklyarov, *Pereselenie i zemleustroistvo*; L.M. Goryushkin, *Sibirskoe krest'yanstvo na rubezhe dvukh vekov. Konets XIX–nachalo XX v.* (Novosibirsk, 1967); Goryushkin, *Agrarnye otnosheniya v Sibiri*; also the numerous maps in the atlas published by the Russian resettlement authorities: *Atlas Aziatskoi Rossii* (Moscow, 1914).

idea that Siberia could supply food to Transbaikal and to the Amur province was of little value at first because competition from Chinese, Japanese and American imports could not easily be overcome. Vladivostok's status as a free port was cancelled, and in 1909 tariffs were placed on imports coming over the Manchurian border, but these measures were not very effective, especially as Chinese border trade was not included until 1913. Finally it was thought that the Siberian surplus could be sold in Russian Central Asia, and the plan to build a southern Siberian railway to Semipalatinsk (eventually to be connected with the Turkistan railway by way of the Kirghiz Steppe) was closely related to this project.[3]

No other colony on the periphery of the Russian Empire was as intimately connected as Siberia with the developmental problems of the metropolis before 1914, and no other was so deeply marked by the conditions and internal contradictions there. The new settlers were placed on state and 'cabinet' lands as well as on the old territories of the Cossacks. They had the right to work the land granted to them but did not own it.[4] Most simply reproduced, under Siberia's tough climatic conditions, the same small, impoverished subsistence farming — financially squeezed, exploited by rapacious commodity buyers and profiteers, by 'business plutocrats and usurers'. The muzhiks often became paupers in Siberia even if they had not arrived as such. The number of immigrants who returned was not insignificant, about 20 per cent at the height of migration — a sign too that the authorities were becoming overwhelmed by the wandering stream of people. The relatively prosperous kulaks who shipped Siberian butter as far as western Europe formed a thin upper stratum, much as they did in Russian villages. Social tensions and antagonisms were if anything stronger in the colony than in European Russia, not only between the new settlers and long-term Siberians, but also in the urban context. Last but not least, the grossest forms of early capitalist exploitation and wage slavery were brought to Siberia via the railway, the small and medium-sized enterprises which often served the railway and the mining companies (gold mining in particular). The Siberian proletariat

---

3. For the government's thoughts see the joint report written by Stolypin and Krivoshein after their visit to Siberia in 1910: (German version) *Die Kolonisation Sibiriens. Eine Denkschrift* (Berlin, 1912); see also Hoetzsch, *Rußland. Eine Einführung*, pp. 393ff., 399ff.; O. Goebel, *Volkswirtschaft des Ostbaikalischen Sibiriens um 1909* (Berlin, 1910).
4. Goryushkin, *Agrarnye otnosheniya*, pp. 249ff., 289ff.; G.P. Zhidkov, *Kabinetskoe zemlevladenie, 1747–1917 gg.* (Novosibirsk, 1973), pp. 194ff.

and sub-proletariat first developed some movement during the revolution of 1905 and made their presence felt as part of the Russian working class.[5]

Colonialism in Siberia did not follow the classic pattern in that cities, farming communities and Cossack encampments all had a Russian character. The special administrations which existed before 1914 in Yakut, Buryat, Khalka and Siberian Kirghizia were modelled after peasant districts in Russia. They established the minority status of the 'ethnic' population and were coupled to an administrative system which fundamentally differed from the administrative system of the motherland only in the lack of zemstvos (and in Transbaikal through more militarisation).[6]

Asiatic Russia, with its coastal and border provinces in the Far East, remained the strategic foundation on which the Empire's East Asian policy rested. As mentioned earlier, Russian ambitions and the financing for them were much more modest after 1905. However, the understanding with Japan did not mean that military defence of Vladivostok and of the lengthy coast as far north as Kamchatka could be forgotten. The governor-general of the Amur region had insufficient means at his disposal, and the impressions which Kokovtsov and Sukhomlinov brought back from official visits in 1909 and 1911 respectively, were depressing. Construction of the Amur railway held out the promise of long-term relief, and the Pacific coastal flotilla and harbour fortifications at Vladivostok and Nikolaevsk on the Amur had been gradually strengthened since 1910. However, such measures were not sufficient even to permanently secure Russia's Far Eastern territories, let alone put the Empire in a position to practise grand international politics. Consequently St Petersburg insisted all the more vehemently on maintaining the legacy left by Witte's Manchurian policies after they had been pruned back at Portsmouth — namely the Chinese Eastern Railway, the extra-territorial corridor slicing through three north

---

5. *Istoriya Sibiri*, vol. 3: *Sibir'v epokhu kapitalizma* (Leningrad, 1968), pp. 251ff., 340ff.; V.F. Borzunov, *Proletariat Sibiri i Dal'nego Vostoka nakanune pervoi russkoi revolyutsii* (Moscow, 1965); A.A. Mukhin, *Rabochie Sibiri v epokhu kapitalizma 1861–1917gg*. (Moscow, 1972), pp. 119ff.; G. K. Rabinovich, *Krupnaya burzhuaziya i monopolisticheskii kapital v ekonomike Sibiri kontsa XIX–nachala XX v.* (Tomsk, 1975). The total numbers working in mines, industry and transportation in Siberia are estimated at 250,000 in 1905 and 500,000 in 1913. The statistics for mining alone are more precise: 69,000 in 1905 and 87,800 in 1913, of whom 45,800 and 53,700 respectively worked in gold mining (Mukhin, *Rabochie*, pp. 139, 149).
6. E. Amburger, *Geschichte der Behördenorganisation Rußlands von Peter dem Großen bis 1917* (Leiden, 1966), p. 284; *Istoriya Sibiri* 3, pp. 423ff.

Manchurian provinces and linking Vladivostok with the Trans-Siberian Railway.[7]

Russia's withdrawal into northern Manchuria and to a sphere of interest recognised by Japan did not of course mean that St Petersburg was able to install a protectorate there. The old vision of the Informal Empire could not be recaptured, and Russian rule remained confined to the railway with its head office in Harbin. This head office was responsible in matters concerning policing and the courts for about 60,000 Russian subjects, including the officers and soldiers of the protective troop guarding the railway corridor. Attempts to establish organs of Russian municipal government in Harbin and other cities in the corridor met with resistance from the Chinese provincial authorities and foreign consulates.

The economic life of the northern Manchurian provinces was affected by the Russian presence only to the extent that the railway employed about ten thousand Chinese workers and local business supplied some of the needs of the colonial Russians. For the rest these settlements remained isolated from the Chinese environs. A greater concentration of Russians could be found only in Harbin (c. 30,000 including the garrison), served by bank branches, businesses, workshops, mills and schools administered by Russians as well as a steamer connection on the Sungari from Harbin to Blagoveshchensk. Like most Russian enterprises the lumber and coal concessions mostly served the needs of the railway. Economic initiatives with a further import did not take root.

Russian trade with China showed the same negative balance it always had. The value of Russian exports exceeded 30 million rubles only once (in 1911) while Chinese exports to Russia, mostly tea, reached two to three times this amount.[8] The Russians were not especially disturbed by the imbalance, less so than by Chinese trade in the Far Eastern border areas which proved very difficult to control even after the free passage of goods was abolished in 1913. Although the Chinese Eastern Railway's share of trade with Russia was growing, it still produced high deficits which had to be absorbed by the state Treasury in St Petersburg — over 50 million rubles between 1909 and 1914, more than the large rearmament programme

7. For what follows see: Goebel, pp. 189ff.; Kindermann, *Der Ferne Osten*, pp. 132ff.; Price, *The Russo–Japanese Treaties*; Grigortsevich, *Dal'nevostochnaya politika*, pp. 121ff., 257ff., 272ff., 293ff.; Sladkovskii, *Istoriya torgovo-ekonomicheskikh otnoshenii*, pp. 314ff.
8. Sladkovskii, pp. 337ff.

of 1910 had provided for the Pacific flotilla (34.3 million). The far lower freight rates of the southern Manchurian Railway and the Japanese open port in Kwantung (Dairen) hurt the profitability of the Russian railway. Despite the difficulties, Russia knew that she was not alone in her desire to see the status quo preserved in Manchuria. Japan too insisted on it, and Tokyo promised its support in the treaties of 1907 and 1910. The Russo-Japanese accord gained added strength from the fact the Japanese were increasingly impeded by American policies toward China, especially after the annexation of Korea in 1910. This also caused a strain in Japan's alliance with Great Britain. International banking consortia were anxious to gain a foothold in Manchuria, and Washington openly demanded that the Japanese and Russian railways be internationalised. A railway project supported by the State Department seemed particularly threatening: a competing line would be built from Chinchou to Aigun with the help of European banks.[9] Such pressures persistently convinced Russia and Japan to co-operate and to offer joint resistance. Partnership with Japan helped compensate for the Russian Empire's lack of mobility and contributed to the preservation of Russian interests in East Asia before 1914.

This accord also proved its value before 1914 in respect to Outer Mongolia. Russia's 'special interests' in this nomadic territory had already been recognised in the Russo-Japanese Treaty of 1907. When the Lamaist regime of the 'living Buddha' in Urga exploited the revolutionary chaos in China in the autumn of 1911 to loosen its traditional ties with Peking, St Petersburg could not remain indifferent, especially since Peking asked Russian diplomats to intercede and the Mongolian secessionists also requested Russian help. In this situation, Tokyo did not hesitate to grant the Russians a free hand in Urga and set about demarcating the respective spheres of influence in the Mongolian territory as well (the convention of 25 June/8 July 1912).

A little later, Sazonov decided formally to recognise the autonomy of Outer Mongolia. In a protocol of 21 October (3 November) St Petersburg promised the Mongolian government support in maintaining this autonomy. Urga rewarded the Russians for this assurance by confirming those trade and consular rights which

---

9. Zabriskie, *American–Russian Rivalry*, pp. 131ff., 161ff.; P. Lowe, *Great Britain and Japan*; Nish, *Alliance in Decline*; M.N. Hunt, *Frontier Defense and the Open Door. Manchuria in Chinese–American Relations 1895–1911* (New Haven, 1973); Marinov, *Rossiya i Yaponiya*, pp. 108ff.; Grigortsevich, pp. 310ff., 443ff.

Russia had enjoyed in this outer Chinese region since 1881. In February 1913 St Petersburg granted a credit of two million rubles and offered seventeen officers and forty-two non-commissioned officers to organise a Mongolian brigade. The young Chinese Republic had nothing but protests with which to meet this challenge. By the end of 1913 Peking was finally forced to declare that it would respect Mongolian autonomy and make further use of St Petersburg's good offices.[10]

One should not exaggerate the fruits Russia hoped to gain from her new role as protector. The special relationship between Russia and Mongolia was certainly in line with St Petersburg's general attempts to shield the strategic approaches to Russia's Asian holdings against foreign influences and to continue to act as a great power in East Asian affairs. However, Peking proved to be very sensitive about the Mongolian question, and the Russians found it best to proceed very cautiously and restrain ambitions to create a Greater Mongolia. Russia's interests in Manchuria were much more important, and this alone was reason enough to avoid long-lasting conflict with the new China.

In addition, the kind of economic profit which would have excited Russian businessmen was not possible in this thinly settled country. Caravans often took more than two months on the unpaved routes between Urga and Kyakhta. Mongolian traders brought wool, horses, cattle and animal products over the border while the Russians exchanged cotton goods, linen and sugar. When, in the autumn of 1913, imaginative merchants in Irkutsk hit upon the idea of urging that a state railway be built to Urga, Sazonov declined. (However, he did have an agreement drawn up giving St Petersburg control over any future railway projects.) The Ministry of Finance prepared to grant subsidies to help start a branch of the Siberian Bank known as the National Bank of Mongolia. In the summer of 1914 it again became apparent that the artificially constructed regime in Urga could be maintained only by Russian weapons and a further three million ruble loan. A council of Russian advisors controlled the Mongolian budget so that the Tsar's protectorate appeared firmly established.[11]

If all these developments are taken together, there is no indication before 1914 that economic motives were driving the Russian Empire

10. Kindermann, pp. 156ff.; Grigortsevich, pp. 370ff.; P.S.H. Tang, *Russia and Soviet Policy in Manchuria and Outer Mongolia 1911–1931* (Durham, N.C., 1959).
11. Grigortsevich, pp. 413ff. See also the pertinent documents in: *IB* I/1–4.

to pursue an East Asian policy of clinging to or reinforcing her traditional positions in Manchuria and Outer Mongolia. These policies were motivated by strategic considerations. Unlike in the Witte era, grandiose prophylactic schemes to secure markets in Russian areas of influence beyond the Empire's Far Eastern frontier did not play a determining role. The government was still far more interested in these areas than individuals were. It dragged and carried them along in order to satisfy what turned out to be the long-term rationale for Russian imperialism in Asia: to protect distant, underdeveloped regions of the Empire which — like Siberia and the Transbaikal — had remained Russian colonies. To this extent, Russia's East Asian policies before 1914 were an appendage of internal colonial policies and of attempts to open up and exploit Russian Asia in order to mitigate the social and economic problems threatening the regime in its own heartland. An examination of Russian Turkistan, the Caucasus and Russia's position in Persia will make even clearer the connection between Russia's internal colonies and attempts to gain influence for strategic reasons.

The severest forms of colonial rule before 1914 were practised not in the Far East but in the Central Asian regions of the Empire. With the governor-generalship of Turkistan, three times as large as the German Empire, and the protectorates of Khiva and Bukhara, this colonial area comprised the conquests of the 1860s and 70s — the steppes, deserts and oases from the eastern shore of the Caspian Sea to the Pamirs. It was bordered to the south by Persian and Afghan provinces and to the north by the huge 'Steppe governor-generalship' settled by Kasakhs (officially called 'Kirghizes') and Russian colonists. In Turkistan, the colonial administration run by the military ruled over Islamic peoples and tribes. The population of the governor-generalship is estimated in 1913–14 at about 6.7 million (1897: 5.28 million). Here the Russians comprised an 'ethnic' minority of about 6 to 7 per cent of the population (1897: 197, 420; 1910: 382, 688). The old Uzbek trading centre of Tashkent was the capital of the colony with approximately 270,000 inhabitants, of whom about 80,000 were Russians in 1914. Tashkent had organs of municipal government modelled on Russian ones, in which a few native deputies participated. Turkistan had only one representative in the imperial Duma in St Petersburg in 1906, and none after the new electoral law of 1907 came into effect.[12]

12. R.A. Pierce, *Russian Central Asia*; E. Allworth (ed.), *Central Asia*; M. Sarkisyanz, 'Russian Conquest in Central Asia', pp. 248–88; B. Hayit, *Turkestan*

Unlike Siberia before the First World War, Turkistan was not a colony where Russians settled but a big 'military base', destined to become an economic exploitation zone for the metropolis.[13] It was hoped primarily that Turkistan would supply the Russian cotton industry with a secure source of raw materials. The production in Central Asia of silk, wool, fruit, oil and coal was of lesser importance to the Russian economy. The idea of also directing some of the overflow from Russia's rural population into Turkistan was scuttled by the climatic conditions and by the indigenous society and culture which was inimical to the Orthodox mentality of the Russian peasantry. Substantial numbers of peasant settlers only became established in the north-east, around Semirech'e during Stolypin's time. By 1910 only about 188,000 people had come, little more than one-tenth the number that Minister of Agriculture Krivoshein hoped would settle in Central Asia in the long term.

The political compromise with England regarding Persia, Afghanistan and Tibet diminished the military and strategic importance of the colony. Thereafter economic efforts focused on rapid expansion of the cotton crop, concentrated around Fergana. Substantial progress was made in this respect in the 1890s, parallel to the extension of the Transcaspian colonial railway to Tashkent. Late 1905 saw the completion of the line between Orenburg and Tashkent, originally begun with an eye to imperial confrontation with England. The new connection with the internal railway network brought an undreamed-of boom in cotton from Turkistan. The amount of land under cultivation more than tripled between 1902 and 1913 and comprised about one-fifth of all irrigated land. Russian banks, entrepreneurs and businesses became increasingly involved, attracted by costs of transportation which had sunk immeasurably since the old caravan days, and by hopes for high speculatory profits.[14]

---

zwischen Rußland u. China (Amsterdam, 1971), pp. 151ff.; for the problems inherent in the population statistics see: I.M. Matley, in Allworth, pp. 92ff.

13. It was Krivoshein who called Turkestan a 'military camp' in a report on the results of his tour of inspection: *Zapiska glavnoupravlyayushchego zemledeliem i zemleustroistvom o poezdke v Turkestanskii krai v 1912 g.* (St Petersburg, 1912), pp. 78f.

14. J. Whitman, 'Turkestan Cotton in Imperial Russia', *SEER* 15 (1956), pp. 190–205; A.M. Aminov and A. Kh. Babakhodzhayev, *Ekonomicheskie i politicheskie posledstviya prisoedineniya Srednoi Azii k Rossii* (Tashkent, 1966), pp. 70ff., 83ff.; I.M. Matley, 'Agricultural Development, Industrialization' in Allworth (ed.), pp. 266ff., 309ff.; V.A. Suvorov, *Istoriko-ekonomicheskii ocherk razvitiya Turkestana. Po materialam zheleznodorozhnogo stroitel'stva 1880–1917 gg.* (Tashkent, 1962); J. Stadelbauer, *Bahnbau u. kulturgeographischer Wandel.*

Enterprising individuals nevertheless faced all sorts of obstacles. Water and property rights were unclear in many areas and detracted from the credibility of large scale projects. The price of property was driven up by a shortage of arable land. Nevertheless, about half the needs of Russia's internal textile industry already came from the colony by the time war broke out, even though raw American cotton could overcome high tariffs and still sell more cheaply in Moscow than raw cotton from Turkistan. In the interests of national autonomy, the Ministry of Agriculture in St Petersburg sought vigorously to further the spread of cotton, whose varieties were similar to American imports, by means of irrigation. However, opening up new land was very expensive, and Krivoshein's exhorbitant plans for investment never materialised.

The destruction of Turkistan's traditional economic structure by the expanding cultivation of cotton could be seen on all sides, not just in the fact that the colony's dependence on grain imports from Russia increased and Russian textiles ruined the local trade. More and more peasants were torn from their familiar, natural surroundings and sacrificed to the profiteering of moneylenders and middlemen.[15] Rigid capitalism was implanted in pre-modern, oriental surroundings, and the lower strata of the population drawn into the colonial economy became impoverished. Although even the Russian functionaries realised the consequences of such exploitation, their memoranda, aimed for the most part at securing administrative reforms, did not do much to change the deplorable conditions. The military nature of the administration had to be maintained if Russian interests were to be permanently preserved. The introduction of zemstvo institutions could not seriously be considered in a land where Russian settlements and military bases were islands lost in a foreign sea. The reverberations of the revolution of 1905 and of the Young Turk movement initiated a local struggle for autonomy, and this only increased the feeling that the colony should be left in the hands of the generals.[16]

In the two vassal states of Bukhara and Khiva a kind of indirect

---

15. Cf. the treatise by O. Hoetzsch written as a result of a trip: 'Russisch-Turkestan u. die Tendenzen der heutigen russischen Kolonialpolitik', *Schmollers Jahrbuch* 37 (1913), pp. 903–41, 1427–73.

16. Krivoshein, *Zapiska*, opposes suggestions that a civilian administration be introduced, as was proposed in the auditor's report of Senator Pahlen — *Otchet revizii Turkestanskogo kraya* (23 vols., St Petersburg, 1909–11). See also R.A. Pierce (ed.), *Mission to Turkestan. Being the Memoirs of Count K.K. Pahlen 1908–1909* (New York, 1964).

rule was practised, similar to the regime Russia had developed in her Persian sphere of influence. In Bukhara, the Central Asian core of the Islamic world, a political agent with diplomatic status controlled the emir's costly household and made certain that any reform movements which appeared were tightly contained. The influence of the Young Turks therefore succeeded neither in breaking up the traditional feudal system nor in endangering the interests of its protectors. In the khanate of Khiva, one of the most backward of the Central Asian areas under Russian protection, the military commander of the neighbouring district of Amu-Darya assumed control. In 1912 only about 6,000 Russians lived here, alongside 550,000 to 800,000 natives whose Turkoman subproletariat repeatedly revolted in the last few years before the war against the Uzbek ruling class.

Despite much temptation, St Petersburg refrained from annexing the emirate of Bukhara for reasons related to the Anglo-Russian Pamir agreement of 1895 which remained valid after the settlement of 1907. When the Transcaspian Railway cut through Bukhara the emirate, with its population of about 2.5 million (of whom only ca. 50,000 were Russians, including the military), was fully exposed to the economic interests of the metropolis. The tariff barrier had already fallen in 1895, and the prewar cotton boom, which attracted branches of the large Russian banks into Bukhara, strengthened economic ties with the Empire. Khiva was also affected, though less severely, by these developments.[17]

If one considers the methods of Russian rule in Turkistan, St Petersburg's brand of imperialism in Central Asia seems closest to British colonial policies in India. The way in which informal influence was secured in Bukhara and Khiva is also very similar to Britain's long-term practices in Afghanistan. These similarities are even stronger in the case of Persia. However, unlike the English in India, the Russians did not succeed in substantially influencing the political culture of the Islamic intelligentsia. Emancipatory projects in the colony were inspired by pan-Turkic and pan-Islamic ideals, not by the weak rallying calls emanating from the Russian liberals

17. S. Becker, *Russia's Protectorates in Central Asia*; H. Carrère d'Encaussee, *Réforme et révolution chez les musulmans de l'Empire russe: Bukhara 1867–1924* (Paris, 1966); A.S. Sadykov, *Ekonomicheskie svyazi Khivy s Rossiei vo vtoroi polovine XIX nachale XX v.* (Tashkent, 1965); T.G. Tukhtametov, *Russko-bukharskie otnosheniya v kontse XIX–nachale XX v.* (Tashkent, 1966); Tukhtametov, *Rossiya i Khiva v kontse IX–nachale XX v. Pobeda khorezmskoi narodnoi revolyutsii* (Moscow, 1969).

under the pseudo-constitutional regime of 1907. The influence of the Socialist Revolutionaries and Social Democrats was also confined almost entirely to the Russian areas, primarily to workers living along the railway.[18]

Like Turkistan, Caucasia was an administrative product of Russian military expansion and not a peripheral territory which could be Russified by inflows of peasant settlers or by cultural assimilation. The governor (*namestnik na Kavkaze*) in Tiflis had to keep pacified a region divided along ethnic, religious, historical and geographical lines. Here the Russian conquest had not been completed until 1864, after more than sixty years of struggle. In the south the governors secured the borders which had been established with Persia and the Ottoman Empire in 1828 and 1878 respectively. In the north they joined the territory of the 'Cossack armies' to Terek and Kuban and by 1899 had added the province of Stavropol'. Strategic military considerations (increasingly including questions of internal security) were the determining factor in why Caucasia had not been taken into the general administration of the Empire by the time imperial Russia collapsed.[19]

While the regions to the north of the mountain chain (the northern Caucasus) remained part of the governorship as a strategic hinterland, the system of internal colonial rule became most severe in multi-ethnic 'Transcaucasia' (*Zakavkaz'e*). These territories, administratively part of Asian Russia and numbering about 6.5 million people in 1912, included the provinces of Baku, Tiflis, Erivan, Elizavetpol' and Kutais, the regions (*oblasti*) of Kars and Batum and the districts (*okrugi*) of Zakataly and Sukhum. A separate 'Military Tribal Administration' was established to deal with the mountain peoples whose 'holy war' against the Russian army of the Caucasus had aroused liberal and democratic sympathies all over Europe. The largest national groupings in Transcaucasia were the Muslim Azerbaijanis and Christian Georgians and Armenians; a few Russians could be found only in the larger cities.[20] By 1914 peasant colonisa-

---

18. Pierce, pp. 234ff., 249ff. Soviet historians already speak about the period between 1905 and 1907 as the 'union of the movement of national liberation among the peoples of Central Asia with the revolutionary movement of the Russian working class'; see Aminov and Babakhozhdayev, pp. 104ff. as well as L. Tillett's critique of ideology: *The Great Friendship. Soviet Historians on the Non-Russian Nationalities* (Chapel Hill, N.C., 1969), pp. 358–81.

19. For the history of administration in Caucasia see: Amburger, pp. 412ff.

20. A. Bennigsen, 'The Muslims of European Russia and the Caucasus', in Vucinich (ed.), *Russia and Asia*, pp. 135–66; V. Gregorian, 'The Impact of Russia on the Armenians and Armenia', in ibid., 167–218; D.M. Lang, 'A Century of Russian

tion from European parts of the Empire had brought only about 12,000 families to Transcaucasia, scarcely 100,000 individuals in all. Four-fifths of the population lived in the countryside, still mostly in semi-feudal dependence, despite the agrarian reforms proclaimed between 1864 and 1870. The redemption of peasant lands did not become obligatory until the end of 1912. Village life was characterised by poverty, backwardness and over-population.

The population of the cities grew extremely rapidly, especially Tiflis (1912: 306,000 inhabitants) and Baku (1913: 334,000 inhabitants). This derived for the most part from immigration from the over-populated countryside. Between 1876 and 1912 there was an almost fivefold increase in the population of Tiflis, the old Georgian royal residence and a centre of trade and administration as well as the headquarters of the Transcaspian Railway. The business life of the city was dominated by the Armenians who in 1897 already comprised 71 per cent of the merchants and 45 per cent of the small and medium-sized shopkeepers.[21] Baku, the oil capital of Russia, had been attracting workers of all nationalities and religions since the mid-1880s. Between 1897 and 1913 alone over 83,000 people poured into the city from European Russia, almost 80,000 from the Transcaspian provinces, and over 40,000 from Persian Azerbaijan. The workers of Baku were similarly diverse. Among the employees of the oil industry 39 per cent were Azerbaijani, 24.7 per cent Russians, 20 per cent Armenians and 8.7 per cent Daghestanis — a truly heterogeneous proletariat whose labour struggles repeatedly beamed signals to the strike movement within Russia, for the last time in the summer of 1914.[22]

Transcaucasia's economic importance to the Russian economy rested above all on oil production and the supplying of Russian industry with liquid fuels. In 1913 more than 80 per cent of naphtha produced in imperial Russia came from Baku and Grozny alone. Everything else produced by this area, even the copper and manganese ore mines, were of relatively little importance. Oil syndicates dominated by foreign firms (Nobel, Russian General Oil, Shell

Impact on Georgia', in ibid., 219–47; E. Sarkisyanz, *Geschichte der orientalischen Völker Rußlands bis 1917* (Munich, 1961), pp. 53ff., 82ff., 138ff., 154ff.

21. L.D. Megrian, 'Tiflis During the Revolution of 1905', PhD thesis, Univ. of California, 1968, chap. 1.

22. B. Ya. Stel'nik, *Bakinskii proletariat v gody reaktsii 1907–1910 gg.* (Baku, 1969), pp. 31ff.; A.N. Guliev, *Bakinskii proletariat v gody novogo revolyutsionnogo pod"ema* (Baku, 1963); G.A. Arutyunov, *Rabochee dvizhenie v Zakavkaz'e v period novogo revolyutsionnogo pod"ema, 1910–1914 gg.* (Moscow and Baku, 1963); Arutyunov, *Rabochee dvizhenie v Rossii*, pp. 349ff.

Petrol) controlled about 85 per cent of the share capital. On the Russian market they enjoyed an undisputed monopoly. In response to the economic depression, they had been cutting back production in Baku since the turn of the century (1901: 671 million poods; 1913: 407.8 million), a decline which could not be compensated for by the development of oil-fields in Grozny (1901: 34.8 million poods; 1913: 73.7 million). Rising profits were generated nevertheless thanks to a strictly controlled price cartel which managed to create several severe fuel shortages in Russia before 1914. The oil industry also owned a large share of the steamship lines on the Caspian Sea and the Volga. The value of goods passing through the port of Baku in 1910 exceeded that of all other Russian ports, including St Petersburg, and 85 per cent of these goods consisted of petroleum products.[23]

The military security of Transcaucasia never became a particular problem before 1914 as a result of international politics. The governors and diplomats in St Petersburg had only to deal with the Armenian question in Eastern Anatolia and railway projects in Asia Minor. Even the thorny issue of action in the Straits, about which the Russian government was constantly concerned after 1913, did not prompt St Petersburg to strengthen substantially the Caucasian army and adopt a strategy permitting more far-reaching operations. The military complained that the railway connection with the Russian interior went by way of large detours (Erivan–Tiflis–Baku–Vladikavkaz). Neither the long discussed mountain line parallel to the old Georgian military road nor the projected section along the Black Sea coast had been completed. Only one macadamised road, leading in the direction of the fortress of Erzerum, headed towards the Turkish border. After 1908 the military district responsible for pacifying Russia's north Persian zone of influence was served only by a branch line of the Transcaucasian Railway as far as the Persian border (Dzhulfa). From here unruly Tabriz, the capital of Persian Azerbaijan, could be reached by a paved road.[24]

23. Khromov, *Ekonomicheskoe razvitie*, p. 459; L. Eventov, *Inostrannyi kapital v neftyanoi promyshlennosti Rossii* (Moscow, 1925); P.V. Volobuev, 'Iz istorii monopolizatsii neftyanoi promyshlennosti dorevolyutsionnoi Rossii', *IZ* 52 (1955), pp. 80–111; B. Yu. Akhundov, *Monopolisticheskii kapital v dorevolyutsionnoi bakinskoi neftyanoi promyshlennosti* (Moscow, 1959); M. Ya. Gefter, 'K istorii toplivno-metallicheskogo goloda v Rossii', *IA* 1951/6, pp. 49–80; M. Ya. Gefter et al. (eds.), *Monopolisticheskii kapital v neftyanoi promyshlennosti Rossii 1883–1914 gg.* (Moscow, 1961); R.W. Tolf, *The Russian Rockefellers. The Saga of the Nobel Family and the Russian Oil Industry* (Stanford, 1976).
24. A.T. Sagretyan, *Istoriya zheleznykh dorog Zakavkaz'ya 1856–1921 gg.* (Ere-

In the years before the First World War, governors usually had to devote more attention to internal security than to the outside world. Transcaucasia had been deeply affected by the revolution of 1905, and the administration remained shaken by the experience. Organisations led by Social Democrats found many recruits in the oil-producing areas, along the railways and even among the Georgian nobility. The Caucasian committees were strong and played an even more direct role in the all-Russian labour movement than the Siberian committees. No less unsettling was the explosiveness of the various nationalist movements, especially the militant Armenian *Dashnaktsutyun*, in their resistance to Russian rule and their bitter feuds with one another. Social tensions were virulent and widespread in this multinational area, whether between the stratum of Armenian merchants and the impoverished, Muslim peasants or between the Georgians and Armenians. Thus the governors' regime found its *raison d'être* not least of all in the repression of social or national revolutions in Transcaucasia. The problems facing the Russian state were therefore not much different here than in the western territories, in Poland or the Baltic provinces.

As has been indicated, the colonial regime in Transcaucasia was coloured by the tasks which Russia had set herself in Persia. In no other outpost of Empire, not even in Manchuria, did Russian power express itself in such crude forms of 'indirect' rule as here. The treaty of partition signed with London in 1907 had turned the northern provinces of Persia over to Russian rule, and during the pre-war years they were not far removed from the status of an internal colony of the Russian Empire. What distinguished the zone under Russian protection from Khiva or the emirate of Bukhara was scarcely more than the former's continuing ties with the Persian state. It was only thanks to the internal needs of the Anglo-Russian cartel that Persia itself continued to exist, at least as a fiction of international law, and that St Petersburg and London pledged themselves to maintain her 'integrity and independence'. The Russian rulers in northern Persia only felt compelled to observe some limitations and restrictions because of the tense relations which characterised the Anglo-Russian partnership even after 1907.

The need for consensus usually inhibited British policies more than Russian ones for reasons which are not hard to discover.

---

van, 1970). Cf. the contemporary views in M. Friederichsen, *Die Grenzmarken des Europäischen Rußlands, ihre geographische Eigenart und ihre Bedeutung für den Weltkrieg* (Hamburg, 1915), pp. 99ff.

Persia's very geographical proximity conferred advantages which the Russians were able to exploit. Tehran, the political centre of Persia, lay within the Russian sphere of influence. The brigade of Cossacks commanded by Russian officers was ubiquitous, and regular troops could be summoned quickly. Russia could easily hold on to northern Persia from the Caucasus, the Caspian Sea and Turkistan in a way that Britain could not imitate, either in her southern sphere of interest or in the so-called 'neutral zone'. This was as true of the commercial and financial penetration of Persia as it was of political subversion and a strong military presence. Faced with St Petersburg's massive interference in Persian affairs before the war, London could only seek to mitigate the problem or at best claim some choice morsels as compensation.[25]

This imbalance distinguished the Anglo-Russian relationship in Persia from the Russo-Japanese relationship in the Far East. What affected both partnerships in a similar way was the challenge to their condominium from third parties: ambitious American commercial imperialism in northern China and advancing German economic power in the Near and Middle East. In both cases the threat of external competition served to dampen conflict between the partners and forced them to support each other despite continual friction.

Russian policy toward Persia was upset most of all before the war by the arrival of the Baghdad Railway. The German push into the Near East threatened the policy, effective since 1889, of closing Persia's northern provinces to foreign concessionaries and cast a new light on Russia's customary reluctance to build railways. In the Potsdam agreement of 1910 St Petersburg was first forced to recognise that Persia could no longer be excluded from the railway age. In this agreement, signed in August 1911, Germany recognised Russia's special interests in her own north Persian sphere of influence and St Petersburg promised not to interfere with the continuing construction of the Baghdad Railway. In addition, the outline of the impending revolution in communications was established: St Petersburg undertook to acquire the concession for the railway between Tehran and Chaniki and to build it within a certain period of time so as to meet with a branch line of the Baghdad Railway on the border between Persia and the Ottoman Empire.[26]

25. For what follows: Kazemzadeh, *Russia and Britain*, pp. 510ff., 581ff.; B.C. Bush, *Britain and the Persian Gulf 1894–1914* (Berkeley, 1967).
26. Astaf'ev, *Russko-germanskie otnosheniya*, pp. 187ff., 219ff.; idem, *Sbornik*

It is not surprising that the Potsdam agreement immediately reawakened older Russian railway projects which had previously lain dormant: the connecting link between the Transcaucasian line and Tehran and plans for a great trans-Persian line as far as the borders of British India. The driving force behind the discussions which now began was a syndicate of large Russian banks. Confident of state support and the participation of French and British capital, the syndicate concentrated on the trans-Persian line after 1911. Both these initiatives and the Russo-German agreement deeply affected St Petersburg's relations with London. Sazonov and the Russian bankers wished to see the railway built by way of Kerman and Karachi, but they met with stubborn resistance in London. British policy opposed opening up the route to India. Instead of St Petersburg's plan, Grey argued for a line ending in Bender Abbas on the Persian Gulf which would compete with the Baghdad Railway. The Anglo-Russian talks dragged on for years in a deadlocked position, thus contributing substantially to the irritable atmosphere and to a dispute-prone partnership.[27]

When the opening of Persia to the railways became inevitable, there could be no more doubt about Russia's dominant place in the economic life of the country. The northern sphere of influence in particular had become a Russian colony in the economic sense as well before 1914. Unlike the situation in Manchuria, the penetration strategy introduced by Witte had made Russian dominance apparently inevitable. The financial instrument which guaranteed this position was the 'Persian Loan and Discount Bank', already acquired by the Russian national bank in 1894 and taken over by the national Treasury in 1903. It raised millions in loans and advances in order to keep the Tehran government at heel and, in conjunction with the British-run Imperial Bank of Persia, administered Persia's national debt. It controlled the income from tariffs and taxes in the northern provinces, was the chief stockholder in the postal and telegraph services, owned concessions for roads, ports and shipping, and financed (at times with the help of inexpensive French loans of capital) a substantial amount of Persian business, especially export companies. Early in 1913 the Persian Loan and Discount Bank acquired the rights to build the railway to Tabriz and to exploit the

---

dogovorov, pp. 405ff.; also Mejcher, 'Die Bagdadbahn', pp. 447–81; A.S. Silin, *Ekspansiya,* pp. 165ff.
27. D.W. Spring, 'The Trans-Persian Railway Project and Anglo-Russian Relations 1909–1914', in *SEER* 54 (1976), pp. 60–82.

broad railway corridor.[28]

Russia was not only Persia's most important creditor but also her largest trading partner. About 70 per cent of Persian exports, primarily raw cotton and agricultural products, passed over the Russian border between 1909 and 1914. Russian sugar, supported as always by export subsidies, held a market share of about 80 per cent, while the Russian textile industry supplied approximately 40 per cent of all cotton products imported by Persia. Persia ran a deficit in its trade with Russia. The volume of this trade far exceeded Anglo-Persian trade and the gap was widening. In 1913–14 exports to Persia from Great Britain and India reached only half the value of Russian exports (32 million rubles compared to 64 million); British and Indian imports from Persia were less than one-fifth of Russian imports (10.3 million rubles compared to 54.3 million).[29]

Despite these impressive figures, 'ruble imperialism' in Persia remained a costly drain on the Russian national Treasury. As in the Far East, Russia's private sector remained heavily reliant on government help, and the Loan and Discount Bank in Tehran was no exception. When it experienced liquidity problems late in 1913 and the Ministry of Finance wanted to refuse subsidies, Sazonov painted a dramatic picture of the consequences. If the bank collapsed, he said, 'all Persia' would fall 'into the hands of the English and Germans'. This would impose 'economic servitude (*poraboshchenie)*' on Russian competitors.[30] The powers of the state thus still had to be applied with an eye to securing Russian dominance and in disregard of questions of profitability.

Russian policy in Persia could not relax for a moment in the prewar years. Not only did St Petersburg continually have to assert its pre-eminence over English and German rivals, but political instability and unrest in the protectorate also caused concern. Many factors were involved: the movement for constitutional reform among Persian merchants and the Shiite clergy who, in October 1906, had forced through a constitution and parliament against the wishes of the highly indebted regime run by the corrupt Qajar dynasty; mounting protests against the Russian protector; the regionalism of feudal tribal leaders who resisted the Court in Tehran; the revolt of the impoverished lower social strata against the indi-

28. B.V. Anan'ich, *Rossiiskoe samoderzhavie i vyvoz kapitalov*, pp. 122ff.; P. Luft, 'Strategische Interessen', pp. 530ff.
29. Entner, *Russo-Persian Commercial Relations*, pp. 39ff.
30. Anan'ich, p. 189.

genous caste of landowners. In addition, Azerbaijani itinerant work-men, the Armenian *Dashnaktsutyun* and Caucasian Social Democrats introduced the experience of the Russian Revolution into the north-ern provinces and created links with the sources of unrest in Transcaucasia.[31]

The internal crisis in Persia continually gave the Russian govern-ment reason to underline its interests with displays of military force. In the summer of 1908 this was still done indirectly through the Cossack brigade, which acted in the name of Shah Mohammed Ali when it blew up the parliament and began a murderous campaign of revenge against the reformers. When insurrection reached Tabriz, however, St Petersburg decided on armed intervention. Regular Russian troops pacified this centre of resistance in April 1909, and the Shiite shrine of Meshed in the province of Khorosan was occupied. In the end an Anglo-Russian compromise arrived at in July 1909 saw the abdication of Shah Mohammed Ali as the lesser evil. The new constitutional government was required to stabilise internal conditions so that Persia would once again be able to pay her debts and business would not suffer any more damage.

However, this experiment too was not very successful. When the American financial consultant Morgan Shuster took steps in 1911 to reduce the dependence of the Persian budget on the financial imperatives of London and St Petersburg, the protecting powers feared they would lose their exclusive rights.[32] Again St Petersburg intervened with troops, although this step did not delight its British partner. Under the pressure of such an ultimatum, Shuster was dismissed in January 1912, parliament was dissolved and reform policies suffered a severe setback. The miserable failure of an at-tempt, undertaken shortly before, to restore Mohammed Ali, St Petersburg's favourite, to the throne explains in part the harshness of the Russian reaction. The military regime of occupation which Russia established in the northern provinces of Persia in the winter of 1911-12 was never abandoned in the years that followed.

31. Sch. Ravasani, *Sowjetrepublik Gilan. Die sozialistische Bewegung im Iran seit Ende des 19. Jhs. bis 1922* (Berlin, c. 1975), pp. 112ff.; G.S. Arutyunyan, *Iranskaya revolyutsiya 1905–1911 gg i bol'sheviki Zakavkaz'ya* (Erevan, 1956); M.S. Ivanov, *Iranskaya revolyutsiya 1905–1911 gg.* (Moscow, 1957).
32. M. Shuster, *The Strangling of Persia* (London, 1912).

PART IV

Conclusions

I shall now conclude this overview with a short summary and review of the sources of conflict in international politics. Russian imperialism before 1914 had ample opportunity for expansion through Russia's internal colonies and Asian protectorates. The problems the government experienced in providing for the strategic defence of these domains precipitated the rough suppression and exploitation which they suffered. Further integration of the Asiatic periphery into the Russian economy had long presented itself as a grand task for the future. Some colonial areas along the periphery had already been assigned economic functions which affected more than merely regional or individual interests. Cotton from Turkistan and oil from the Caucasus played an important role in the industrial expansion of the Empire. Plans for the Russian railway system included the Caucasus, Persia, Central Asia and Siberia. The railway promised to open up inexhaustible supplies of raw materials and new markets for central Russian industry, the products of which could not otherwise compete with those of other nations. Russian banks, with their links to European high finance, could find many long-term outlets for their capital in the Asian periphery and make the Russian Empire one of the twentieth century's greatest zones of development.

One cannot say that such a perspective would have impressed only those interest groups which used state protection to become established in Russia's colonies and zones of influence. The politically conscious public had also completely absorbed the Asian periphery into its understanding of the Russian Empire. However, neither the government nor those segments of society on which it rested found Russia's colonial mission so absorbing that Asian policy could have become the focal point of Russian imperialism. Russian ambitions remained directed at what had come to be accepted as the 'really vital interests' of the Empire: gaining control over the Straits, securing influence in the Balkans and preparing for the great 'decisive struggle' with the Teutons. The string of international crises which occurred before 1914 were very much of a nature to keep Russian policy firmly orientated toward these traditional goals.

We have already seen how poorly prepared the Russian Government was to accomplish its 'historic mission' in the Near East. Nowhere was Russian weakness clearer than when it came to influencing the affairs of the Ottoman Empire. The manifest interest which Russia took in this strategic area stood in curious contrast with what she could actually hope to gain. The means and methods which brought tsarist Russia some measure of success along the Central and East Asian periphery of the Empire were of no use in Turkey. The Ottoman Empire had long since become a domain of the large European banking syndicates and, aligning themselves with the policies of the concert of powers, they created a broad breech for modern financial imperialism.[1] Russia was unable to keep even in this race, and the disadvantages from which she suffered could not be offset with military threats or even actions — St Petersburg still had good reason to avoid war.

Russia did not of course enjoy a clearly defined sphere of interest in the Ottoman Empire similar to her position in Persia or Manchuria. Russian power could not even implant itself in eastern Anatolia, close to the borders of the Caucasian governorship and the protectorate in northern Persia. Russia had the sympathy of Turkish Armenians and their Church, but this was no basis for lasting influence. In January 1914 Russian diplomats negotiated administrative regulations on behalf of the concert of powers, but even this did not come close to giving St Petersburg special privileges in the provinces of eastern Anatolia.[2] The only privileges which Russia enjoyed in Asia Minor resulted from a promise that had been wrung from the Sultan in August 1900 by means of a treaty. The Porte had agreed to grant railway concessions in eastern Anatolia exclusively to 'Russian capitalists'. However even this exclusionary clause, much like Russia's veto over railways in Persia, lost its validity during the last few years before the war. After 1909

1. The most recent summary is Schölch, *Wirtschaftliche Durchdringung*, pp. 404–46; also the general survey in M.S. Anderson, *The Eastern Question 1774–1923* (London, 1966), pp. 287–309.
2. For Russian documents on the Armenian question and administrative regulations in eastern Anatolia: *IB* I/1 *passim*. Cf. the recent work: S. Stepanyan, *Armeniya v politike imperialisticheskoi Germanii* (Erevan, 1975), pp. 67ff., 94ff.

French capital worked to free the Young Turk government from this old commitment.[3]

Russia's limited margin for manoeuvre in Asia Minor can be seen in her inability to get into the railway business, unlike her success in Persia at about the same time.[4] Sazonov could only try to gain political favours in return for accepting Franco-Turkish agreements, and he did not get much. Bold hopes to link railways to a revised status for the Straits had already proved empty during the war over Tripoli. Even the more modest goal of winning French help in order to gain participation in the 'dette publique ottomane' failed because of German demands for compensation. By the time the Franco-Turkish railway and loan agreements were ready to be signed in the spring of 1914, Sazonov had only achieved one important condition: the contracting parties promised not to start building the railway east of the Trebizond–Karput line until between nine and twelve years later and to engage Russian concessionaries for stretches near the border. This example, too, illustrates that in the Near East the best Russia could hope to do was tag along limply behind her French ally.

The unsuccessful attempt to gain a place in the Ottoman debt administration was not St Petersburg's only attempt at financial equality, but other attempts were equally unfruitful. A plan which Sazonov had been pursuing since 1913 to have the Russo-Asian Bank buy up the Bank of Salonika with its far-flung chain of branches found no support. Paris did not wish to hand over branches of this bank in Constantinople, Smyrna and Syria to a Russian financial institution. Even the Russo-Asian Bank, which supposedly acted as St Petersburg's financial agent, refused the Foreign Minister's plan. Its directors let it be known that the Société générale de Paris, the chief shareholder in this 'Russian' bank, would not underwrite independent Russian business in the Orient. Instead, St Petersburg was encouraged to join in the operations of French and British financial groups that wanted to fuse the Bank of Salonika with the Turkish National Bank.[5]

---

3. See F. Ahmad, *The Young Turks: The Committee of Union and Progress in Turkish Politics 1908–1914* (N.Y., 1969).

4. For Russian policies toward Turkey before 1914 see: M. Hiller, *Krisenregion Nahost. Russische Orientpolitik im Zeitalter des Imperialismus 1900–1914* (Frankfurt, 1985).

5. *IB* I/4, nos. 21–2 *passim*. The French share of capital in the Russo-Asian Bank was about 65 per cent before 1914, cf. Girault, *Emprunts*, p. 513.

It becomes clear again and again that St Petersburg's financial policies in the Near East, were accepted at best as subservient to Russia's creditors. St Petersburg often made merely symbolic contributions to the international loans which the large powers arranged with the highly indebted Balkan states. When the oriental railways were internationalised after the second Balkan war, Russia was again more of a spectator than an actor. St Petersburg's financial role could not be any greater than the credit which international finance chose to make available to the financially dependent Russian Empire.

This marginal financial role could not be offset by trade with Turkey and the Balkan states.[6] Despite Russia's proximity even mercantile trade with Turkey remained extremely limited. Great Britain, Austria-Hungary and Germany dominated in this domain, followed by France. Russia was generally sixth, though occasionally fifth. Approximately 6 to 7 per cent of Turkey's imports and 4 per cent of her exports were channelled through Russian firms. Although most Russian wares (especially alcohol, cotton goods and sugar) were shipped to Turkey by way of Odessa, Russia's share of shipping to and from the Ottoman Empire never surpassed 10 per cent in tonnage or value. As a result of these modest statistics, St Petersburg considered creating a trading company shortly before the war which would have operated along the lines of the Italian Società Commerciale d'Oriente. In addition, any private person interested in acquiring a concession in Turkey could be sure of St Petersburg's undivided attention. However, no noteworthy initiatives resulted from such efforts by 1914.

As in the Balkans, Russia's prewar policy in the Near East was greatly hampered by the financial and commercial impotence of the Empire. Not even a few limited areas could be penetrated economically, and St Petersburg was repeatedly made to feel dependent on the strategy of its British and French allies. The latter often demonstrated a great lack of sensitivity in dealing with fundamental Russian interests. While St Petersburg strove mightily to bring its neglected Black Sea fleet up to the level of the Turkish fleet, English shipyards were building dreadnoughts for the Porte with the help of French financing. Their projected date of delivery in the summer of 1914 upset the Russian military almost as much as the prospect of seeing Liman von Sanders in the service of Turkey. St Petersburg

6. I owe the following information to M. Hiller.

could never count on a blank cheque from London and Paris for its policies in the Straits. The art of diplomacy was therefore all that remained for defending Russian interests in the Near East.[7] However, the task of preserving a balance between the fractious states in the Balkans without damaging relations with the Porte remained as difficult as ever. Even the self-interested sympathy which Serbia and Montenegro showed the Russian Empire was no reason for undiminished pleasure. King Nicholas was obsessed with weapons and monetary gifts and his dangerous capriciousness during the Scutari crisis had shown how easily partnership with these ambitious fellow-believers could develop into a burden.

One must keep these circumstances in mind in order to see how traditionally St Petersburg responded in a zone of conflict in which Russian nationalism devoted utmost interest. On the periphery of the Empire in Central and East Asia, Russia was able to imitate the ways and means of modern imperialism with some degree of success; in the Near East, however, she remained remarkably 'premodern'. There is no doubt that this was a consequence of the lack of competitiveness of Russian imperialism. In the Near East more than in the internal colonies, Persia or northern Manchuria, the difficulties engendered by Russia's backwardness once more came to the fore. Although Russia's interest in the Straits could doubtless be justified on economic grounds, as an attempt to secure her most important maritime route for exports, economics alone cannot explain the astonishing fixation which both Russian policy-makers and the public showed for this region.

Russia's 'historic responsibilities' and 'sacred obligations' in the Near East were constantly evoked. It was not the profit motive which lay hidden behind these phrases but an irrational sense of threat, the causes of which have already been discussed at length.[8] These fears fed on Russia's internal disorders: the crisis of identity of the upper classes, the structural damage caused by socioeconomic change, and the political weakness of a pseudo-constitutional regime which failed to satisfy either the rising bourgeoisie or traditional, decaying 'society'. Fear of revolution also played a part — the vague premonition that the plunge into chaos was near and could not be stopped.

Russian nationalism deflected these fears outward, projected them onto ancient enemies and directed them towards traditional

7. Cf. chap. 12.
8. Cf. chap. 13.

desires with the capacity to make Russian hearts beat faster: the sight of the Patriarchal cross on St Sophia; the destruction of the German *Drang nach Osten*; and the vision of Russia's Slavic brothers grouped around her in wide-eyed admiration. Compared with this, little enthusiasm could be stirred up by the prospects Russian imperialism offered of immense development along the Asian periphery, in the internal colonies and in adequately secured zones of influence. The 'educated classes' were not attracted by visions of the future which saw the colonisation of huge eastern territories as the engine of permanent modernisation. These areas seemed more a kind of exotic appendage than a vital part of the Russian cause. Emotional nationalism conceived of Russia as a European power, and these regions could offer little to satisfy such feelings. Certainly they could not serve as a substitute for everything which seemed to demand Russia's attention from Constantinople to the Adriatic.

Abbreviations

AHR	*American Historical Review*
APSR	*American Political Science Review*
ASEER	*American Slavic and East European Review*
ASS	*Archiv für Sozialwissenschaft u. Sozialpolitik*
BH	*Baltische Hefte*
BM	*Berliner Monatshefte*
CEH	*Central European History*
CEHE	*Cambridge Economic History of Europe*
CGAOR	*Tsentral'nyi Gosudarstvennyi Arkhiv Oktyabr'skoi Revolyutsii*
CMRS	*Cahiers du monde russe et soviétique*
CSP	*Canadian Slavonic Papers*
CSS	*Canadian Slavic Studies*
DDF	*Documents diplomatiques français*
EcHR	*Economic History Review*
EHR	*English Historical Review*
FE	*Frantsuzskii Ezhegodnik*
FOG	*Forschungen zur osteuropäischen Geschichte*
GuG	*Geschichte und Gesellschaft*
GP	*Die Große Politik der Europäischen Kabinette*
HGR	*Handbuch der Geschichte Rußlands*
HSS	*Harvard Slavic Studies*
HZ	*Historische Zeitschrift*
IA	*Istoricheskii arkhiv*
IB	*Die internationalen Beziehungen im Zeitalter des Imperialismus*
IM	*Istorik-marksist*
IRSH	*International Review of Social History*
ISSSR	*Istoriya SSSR*
IZ	*Istoricheskie zapiski*
JCEA	*Journal of Central European Affairs*
JCH	*Journal of Contemporary History*
JEH	*Journal of Economic History*
JGO	*Jahrbücher für Geschichte Osteuropas*

347

Abbreviations

JfWG	*Jahrbuch für Wirtschaftsgeschichte*
JGSLE	*Jahrbuch für Geschichte der sozialistischen Länder Europas*
JMH	*Journal of Modern History*
JNS	*Jahrbücher für Nationalökonomie u. Statistik*
KA	*Krasnyi arkhiv*
LW	*Lenin, Werke. 4. Auflage.* (Berlin, GDR)
MGM	*Militärgeschichtliche Mitteilungen*
NNI	*Novaya i noveishaya istoriya*
ODR	*Obshchestvennoe dvizhenie v Rossii*
ÖOH	*Österreichische Osthefte*
PJ	*Preußische Jahrbücher*
PR	*Polish Review*
PSS	Lenin, *Polnoe sobranie sochinenii*
QJE	*Quarterly Journal of Economics*
RSI	*Rivista storica italiana*
RR	*Russian Review*
SDG	*Sowjetsystem u. Demokratische Gesellschaft*
SEER	*Slavonic and East European Review*
Sowi	*Sozialwissenschaftliche Information für Unterricht u. Studium*
SR	*Slavic Review*
SS	*Soviet Studies*
VIst	*Voprosy istorii*
VLU	*Vestnik Leningradskogo Universiteta*
VMU-Ist	*Vestnik Moskovskogo Universiteta. Seriya Istoriya*
VSWG	*Viertelschrift für Sozial- u. Wirtschaftsgeschichte*
WZ	*Wissenschaftliche Zeitschrift*
ZfG	*Zeitschrift für Geschichtswissenschaft*
ZfO	*Zeitschrift für Ostforschung*
ZOG	*Zeitschrift für Osteuropäische Geschichte*

Bibliography

Adler, C.C., 'The "Revolutionary Situation" 1859–1861', *CSS* 3 (1969), pp. 383–99

Ado, V.I., 'Berlinskii kongress 1878 g. i. pomeshchiche'e-burzhuaznoe obshchestvennoe mnenie Rossii', *IZ* 69 (1961), pp. 101–41

___, 'Vystuplenie I.S. Aksakova protiv Berlinskogo kongressa 1878 g. i otkliki na nego v Rossii i Bolgari', *ISSSR* (1962/6), pp. 125–39

Ahmad, F., *The Young Turks: The Committee of Union and Progress in Turkish Politics 1908–1914* (New York, 1969)

Akhundov, V. Yu., *Monopolisticheskii kapital v dorevolyutsionnoi bakin-skoi neftyanoi promyshlennosti* (Moscow, 1959)

Albertini, R. v., *Europäische Kolonialherrschaft 1880–1940* (Zurich, 1976)

Allen, W.E.D., and Muratoff, P. *Caucasian Battlefields. A History of the Wars on the Turko-Caucasian Border 1828–1921* (Cambridge, 1953)

Allworth, E. (ed.), *Central Asia. A Century of Russian Rule* (New York, 1967)

Altrichter, H., *Konstitutionalismus und Imperialismus. Der Reichstag und die deutsch-russischen Beziehungen, 1890–1914* (Frankfurt, 1977)

Ambler, E., *Russian Journalism and Politics 1861–1881. The Career of Aleksei Suvorin* (Detroit, 1972)

Amburger, E., *Geschichte der Behördenorganisation Rußlands von Peter dem Großen bis 1917* (Leiden, 1966)

Aminov, A.M., *A. Kh. Babakhodzhaev, Ekonomicheskie i politicheskie posledstviya prisoedineniya Srednei Azii k Rossii* (Tashkent, 1966)

Anan'ich, B.V., *Rossiya i mezhdunarodnyi kapital, 1897–1914. Ocherki istorii finansovykh otnoshenii* (Leningrad, 1970)

___, *Rossiiskoe samoderzhavie i vyvoz kapitalov 1895–1914 gg. (po mate-rialam Uchetno-ssudnogo banka Persii)* (Leningrad, 1975)

___, 'Vneshnie zaimy i dumskii vopros 1906–1907 gg.', *IZ* 81 (1968), pp. 199–215

Anan'ich, N.I., 'K istorii otmeny podushnoi podati v Rossii', *IZ* 94 (1974), pp. 183–212

Anderson, M.S., *The Eastern Question 1774–1923. A Study in Interna-tional Relations* (London, 1966)

Andrew, C., *Théophile Delcassé and the Making of the Entente Cordiale*,

1898 to 1905 (London, 1968)

Anfimov, A.M., *Krupnoe pomeshchich'e khozyaistvo evropeiskoi Rossii (Konets XIX–nachalo XX veka)* (Moscow, 1969)

Anwar, K.M., *Russia and Central Asia. A Study in Diplomacy 1857–1879* (Peshawar, 1969)

Anweiler, O., *Die Rätebewegung in Rußland 1905–1921* (Leiden, 1958)

Aretin, K.O. von, and W. Conze (eds.), *Deutschland und Rußland im Zeitalter des Kapitalismus 1871–1914* (Wiesbaden, 1977)

Aronson, I.M., 'The Attitudes of Russian Officials in the 1880s toward Jewish Assimilation', *SR* 34 (1975), pp. 1–18

——, 'Russian Bureaucratic Attitudes toward Jews 1881–1894', PhD thesis, Northwestern Univ., 1973

Arutyunyan, G.S., *Iranskaya revolyutsiya 1905–1911 gg. i bolsheviki Zakavkaz'ya* (Erevan, 1956)

Arutyunov, G.A., *Rabochee dvizhenie v Rossii v period novogo revolyutsionnogo pod"ema 1910–1914 gg.* (Moscow, 1975)

——, *Rabochee dvizhenie v Zakavkaz'e v period novogo revolyutsionnogo pod"ema 1910–1914 gg.* (Moscow and Baku, 1963)

Askew, W.C., 'Russian Military Strength on the Eve of the Franco-Prussian War', *SEER* 30 (1951–52), pp. 185–205

Astafyev, A.I., *Russko-germanskie diplomaticheskie otnosheniya 1905–1911 gg.* (Moscow, 1972)

Atlas Aziatskoi Rossii. Izd. Pereselencheskogo upravleniya (St Petersburg, 1914)

Avantyury russkogo tsarizma v Bolgarii. Sbornik dokumentov (Moscow, 1935)

Avetyan, A.S., *Germanskii imperializm na Blizhnem Vostoke. Kolonial'naya politika germanskogo imperializma i missiya Limana fon Sandersa* (Moscow, 1966)

Avrekh, A. Ya., *Tsarizm i tret'eiyunskaya sistema* (Moscow, 1966)

——, 'Russkii absolyutizm i ego rol' v utverzhdenii kapitalizma v Rossii', *ISSSR* (1968/2), pp. 82–104

——, *Stolypin i Tret'ya Duma* (Moscow, 1968)

Bachmann, J.E., 'Recent Soviet Historiography on Russian Revolutionary Populism', *SR* 29 (1970), pp. 591–612

Balmuth, D., 'Origins of the Russian Press Reform of 1865', *SEER* 47 (1969), pp. 369–88

Barkai, H., 'The Macro-Economics of Tsarist Russia in the Industrialization Era', *JEH* 33 (1973), pp. 339–72

Bater, J.H., *St. Petersburg: Industrialization and Change* (London, 1975)

Baumgart, W., *Der Friede von Paris 1856. Studien zum Verhältnis von Kriegführung, Politik und Friedenbewahrung* (Moscow, 1972)

Bazylow, L., *Ostatnie lata Rosji carskiej. Rządy Stołypina* (Warsaw, 1972)

——, *Polityka wewnętrzna caratu i ruchy społeczne w Rosji na początku XX wieku* (Warsaw, 1966)

___, 'Zagadka 1 sentyabrya 1911 g', *VIst* (1975/7), pp. 115–27

Becker, S., *Russia's Protectorates in Central Asia. Bukhara and Khiva 1865–1924* (Cambridge, Mass., 1968)

Belokonskii, I.P., *Zemstvo i konstitutsiya* (Moscow, 1910)

Belyaev, N.I., *Russko-turetskaya voina 1877–1878 gg.* (Moscow, 1956)

Bensidoun, S., *L'agitation paysanne en Russie de 1881 à 1902* (Paris, 1975)

Benson, S., 'The Conservative Liberalism of Boris Chicherin', *FOG* 21 (1975), pp. 17–114

Berghahn, V.R., *Rüstung und Machtpolitik. Zur Anatomie des 'Kalten Krieges' vor 1914* (Düsseldorf, 1973)

___, *Der Tirpitz-Plan. Genesis und Verfall einer innenpolitischen Krisen- strategie unter Wilhelm II* (Düsseldorf, 1971)

Bermanskii, K.L., 'Konstitutsionnye proekty tsarstvovaniya Aleksandra II', *Vestnik prava* (1905/9), pp. 223–91

Besançon, A., *Education et société en Russie dans le second tiers du XIX siècle* (Paris, 1974)

Beskrovnyi, L.G., and Narochnitskii, A.L., 'K istorii vneshnei politiki Rossii na Dal'nem Vostoke v XIX v.', *VIst* (1974/6), pp. 14–36

Beskrovnyi, L.G., *Russkaya armiya i flot v XIX veke. Voenno- ekonomicheskii potentsial Rossii* (Moscow, 1973)

Bestuzhev, I.V., 'Bor'ba v Rossii po voprosam vneshnei politiki nakanune pervoi mirovoi voiny (1910–1914)', *IZ* 75 (1965), pp. 44–85

___, *Bor'ba v Rossii po voprosam vneshnei politiki 1906–1910* (Moscow, 1961)

Beyrau, D., 'Agrarstruktur und Bauernprotest. Zu den Determinanten der russischen Agrarreform von 1861', *VSWG* 64 (1977), pp. 179–236

___, *Russische Orientpolitik und die Entstehung des deutschen Kaiserreiches, 1866–1870/71* (Wiesbaden, 1974)

___, *Militär und Gesellschaft im vorrevolutionären Rußland* (Cologne, 1984)

Birth, E., *Die Oktobristen (1905–1913). Zielvorstellung und Struktur* (Stutt- gart, 1974)

Black, C.E., *The Establishment of Constitutional Government in Bulgaria* (Princeton, 1943; 2nd ed. 1970)

___ (ed.), *The Transformation of Russian Society* (Cambridge, Mass., 1960)

Black, C.E., et al., *The Modernization of Japan and Russia. A Comparative Study* (New York, 1975)

Blackwell, W.L., *The Beginnings of Russian Industrialization 1800–1860* (Princeton, 1968)

Bondarevskii, G.L., *Angliiskaya politika i mezhdunarodnye otnosheniya v basseine Persidskogo zaliva* (Moscow, 1968)

___, *Bagdadskaya doroga i proniknovenie germanskogo imperializma na Blizhnii Vostok, 1888–1903* (Tashkent, 1955)

Bonwetsch, B., 'Das ausländische Kapital in Rußland. Bemerkungen zum

351

Forschungsstand', *JGO* 22 (1974), pp. 412–25

——, 'Handelspolitik und Industrialisierung. Zur außenwirtschaftlichen Abhängigkeit Rußlands', in D. Geyer (ed.), *Wirtschaft und Gesellschaft im vorrevolutionären Rußland* (Cologne, 1975), pp. 277–99

——, *Kriegsallianz u. Wirtschaftsinteressen. Rußland in den Wirtschaftsplänen Englands und Frankreichs 1914–1917* (Düsseldorf, 1973)

——, 'Oktoberrevolution. Legitimationsprobleme der sowjetischen Geschichtswissenschaft', *PVS* 17 (1976), pp. 149–85

Borovoi, S. Ya., *Kredit i banki Rossii (seredina XVII veka — 1861 g.)* (Moscow, 1958)

Borzunov, V.F., 'Istoriya sozdaniya Transsibirskoi zheleznodorozhnoi magistrali XIX — nachala XX veka', unpubl. Cond. diss., Moscow, 1972

——, *Proletariat Sibiri i Dal'nego Vostoka nakanune pervoi russkoi revolyutsii (po materialam stroitel'stva Transsibirskoi magistrali, 1891–1904 gg.)* (Moscow, 1965)

Bovykin, V.I., 'Banki i voennnaya promyshlennost' Rossii nakanune pervoi morovoi voiny', *IZ* 64 (1959), pp. 82–135

——, *Iz istorii vozniknoveniya pervoi mirovoi voiny. Otnosheniya Rossii i Frantsii v 1912–1914 gg.* (Moscow, 1961)

——, *Ocherki istorii vneshnei politiki Rossii. Konets XIX v.–1917 g.* (Moscow, 1960)

——, 'O nekotorykh voprosakh izucheniya inostrannogo kapitala v Rossii', *Ob osobennostyakh imperializma v Rossii* (Moscow, 1963), pp. 250–313

——, *Zarozhdenie finansovogo kapitala v Rossii* (Moscow, 1967)

——, *Formirovanie finansovogo kapitala v Rossii: Konets XIX v.–1908 g.* (Moscow, 1984)

Brennan, W.H., 'The Russian Foreign Ministry and the Alliance with Germany', *Russ. History* 1 (1974), pp. 18–30

Brown, M.B., *The Economics of Imperialism* (London, 1974)

Bukovetskii, A.I. (ed.), *Materialy po denezhnoi reforme 1895–1897 gg.* (Petrograd, 1922), vol. 1

——, '"Svobodnaya nalichnost'" i zolotoi zapas tsarskogo pravitel'stva v konets XIX–nachale XX veka', *Monopolii i inostrannyi kapital v Rossii* (Leningrad, 1962), pp. 359–76

'Bulanzhizm i tsarskaya diplomatiya', *KA* 72 (1935), pp. 51–109

Bush, B.C., *Britain and the Persian Gulf 1894–1914* (Berkeley, 1967)

Byrnes, R.F., *Pobedonostsev. His Life and Thought* (Bloomington, Ind., 1968)

Cagolov, N.A., *Ocherki russkoi ekonomicheskoi mysli perioda padeniya krepostnogo prava* (Moscow, 1956)

Cameron, R.E., *France and the Economic Conquest of Europe 1860–1914. Conquests of Peace and Seeds of War* (Chicago, 1961, 1965²)

——, *French Foreign Investment 1850–1880* (Chicago, 1955)

Campion, L.K., 'Behind the Modern Drang nach Osten. Baltic Emigrés and

Russophobia in 19th-Century Germany', unpubl. PhD thesis, Blooming-ton, Ind., 1966

Carlgren, W.M., *Iswolsky and Aehrenthal vor der bosnischen Annexions-krise. Russische und österreichisch-ungarische Balkanpolitik 1906–1908* (Uppsala, 1955)

Carrère d'Encausse, H., *Réforme et révolution chez les musulmans de l'Empire russe: Bukhara 1867–1924* (Paris, 1966)

Chang Chung-tung, *China's Response to the Open Door, 1898–1906* (Mi-chigan, 1973)

Chermenskii, E.D., *Burzhuaziya i tsarizm v pervoi russkoi revolyutsii* (Moscow, 1970²)

___, *IV Gosudarstvennaya duma i sverzhenie tsarizma v Rossii* (Moscow, 1976)

Cherniavsky, M., *Tsar and People. Studies in Russian Myth* (New Haven, 1961)

Chernov, S.L., 'K voprosu o San-Stefanovskom dogovore 1878 g.', *ISSSR* (1975/4), pp. 133–47.

Chernukha, V.G., *Krest'yanskii vopros v pravitel'stvennoi politike Rossii (60–70-e gody XIX v.)* (Leningrad, 1972)

___, 'Vazhnoe svidetel'stvo o vneshnepoliticheskom aspekte pol'skogo vosstaniya 1863 g.', *Issledovaniya po otechestvennomu istochnikovede-niyu* (Moscow, 1964), pp. 217–20

Chertan, E.E., *Russko-rumynskie otnosheniya, 1859–1863 gg.* (Kishinev, 1968)

Chevigny, H., *Russian America. The Great Alaskan Venture 1741–1867* (London, 1967)

Chicherin, B., *O narodnom predstavitel'stve* (Moscow, 1866)

Chien, F.F., *The Opening of Korea, 1876–1885* (The Shoe String Press, 1967)

Chmielewski, E., *The Polish Question in the Russian State Duma* (Knox-ville, Tenn., 1970)

___, 'Stolypin and the Russian Ministerial Crisis of 1909', *CSS* 6 (1967), pp. 1–38

___, 'Stolypin's Last Crisis', *CSS* 3 (1964), pp. 95–126

Conroy, H., *The Japanese Seizure of Korea, 1869–1910,* (Philadelphia, 1960)

Conroy, M.S., *Peter A. Stolypin* (Boulder, Col., 1976)

Coquin, F.X., *La Sibérie. Peuplement et immigration paysanne au dix-neuvième siècle* (Paris, 1969)

Costello, D.R., 'Prime Minister Kokovtsov and the Duma. A Study in the Disintegration of the Tsarist Regime 1911–1914', PhD thesis, Univ. of Virginia, 1970

Crampton, R.J., 'The Decline of the Concert of Europe in the Balkans 1913–1914', *SEER* 52 (1974), pp. 393–419

Crean, E.M., 'The Governor-Generalship of Turkestan under K.P. von

Kaufmann, 1867–1882', PhD thesis, Yale, 1970

Crisp, O., 'French Investment in Russian Joint-Stock Companies 1894–1914', *Business History* 2 (1960), pp. 75–90

——, 'Russia', in R.E. Cameron (ed.), *Banking in the Early Stages of Industrialization* (New York, 1967), pp. 183–238

——, 'Russian Financial Policy and the Gold Standard at the End of the 19th Century', *EcHR* 6 (1953), pp. 156–72

——, 'The Russian Liberals and the 1906 Anglo-French Loan to Russia', *SEER* 39 (1960), pp. 497–511

——, 'The Russo-Chinese Bank', *SEER* 127 (1974), pp. 197–212

——, *Studies in Russian Economy before 1914* (London, 1976)

Dallin, D.J., *The Rise of Russia in Asia* (New Haven, 1949)

Davidovich, A.M., *Samoderzhavie v epokhu imperializma. Klassovaya sushchnost' i evolyutsiya absolyutizma v Rossii* (Moscow, 1975)

Derenkovskii, G.M., 'Franko-russkaya morskaya konventsiya 1912 g. i anglo-russkie peregovory nakanune pervoi mirovoi voiny', *IZ* 29 (1949), pp. 80–122

Derenkovskii, G.M., Ivanov, A.E., et al., 'Osnovnye itogi izucheniya istorii pervoi russkoi revolyutsii za poslednie dvadtsat' let', *ISSSR* (1975/5), pp. 42–60

Diestelmeier, F., *Soziale Angst: Konservative Reaktionen auf liberale Reformpolitik in Rußland unter Alexander II. (1855–1866)* (Frankfurt, 1985)

Dyakin, V.S., *Germanskie kapitaly v Rossii. Elektroindustriya i elektricheskii transport* (Leningrad, 1971)

——, 'K otsenke russko-germanskogo torgovogo dogovora 1904 g.', in *Problemy istorii mezhdunarodnykh otnoshenii* (Leningrad, 1972), pp. 156–73

——, *Russkaya burzhuaziya i tsarizm v gody pervoi mirovoi voiny, 1914–1917* (Leningrad, 1967)

Doctorow, G.S., 'The Fundamental State Law of 23 April 1906', *RR* 35 (1976), pp. 33–52

——, 'The Government Program of 17 October 1905', *RR* 34 (1975), pp. 123–36

Dorpalen, A., 'Tsar Alexander III and the Boulanger Crisis in France', *JMH* 23 (1951), pp. 122–36

Drummond, I.M., 'The Russian Gold Standard 1897–1914', *JEH* 36 (1976), pp. 663–88

Dubrovskii, S.M., *Stolypinskaya zemel'naya reforma* (Moscow, 1963³)

Dziewanowski, M.K., 'The Russian Revolution of 1904–05 and the Marxist Movement in Poland', *JCEA* 12 (1953), pp. 259–75

Edelman, R., 'The Russian Nationalist Party and the Political Crisis of 1909', *RR* 34 (1975), pp. 22–54

——, *Gentry Politics on the Eve of the Russian Revolution. The Nationalist*

Party 1907–1917 (New Brunswick, 1980)

Efremov, P.N., *Vneshnyaya politika Rossii 1907–1914 gg.* (Moscow, 1961)

Ekmecic', M., *Der Aufstand in Bosnien, 1875–1878* (Graz, 1974), vol. 1–2.

Emelyakh, L.I., 'Krest'yanskoe dvizhenie v Poltavskoi i Khar'kovskoi guberniyakh v 1902, g.', *IZ* 38 (1951), pp. 154–75

Emmons, T., 'The Peasant and Emancipation', in W.S. Vucinich (ed.), *The Peasant in Nineteenth-Century Russia* (Stanford, 1968), pp. 41–71

——, *The Russian Landed Gentry and the Peasant Emancipation of 1861* (Cambridge, Mass., 1968)

——, *The Formation of Political Parties and the First National Elections in Russia* (Cambridge, Mass., 1983)

Etner, M.L., *Russo-Persian Commercial Relations, 1828–1914* (Gainesville, Flo., 1965)

Erdmann, A. v., 'Nikolaj Karlovič Giers, russischer Außenminister 1882–1895'. *ZOG* 9 (1935), pp. 481–540

Erman, L.K., *Intelligentsia v pervoi russkoi revolyutsii* (Moscow, 1966)

Fadeyev, A.V., *Rossiya i Kavkaz pervoi treti XIX v.* (Moscow, 1960)

Fainberg, E.Ya., *Russko-yaponskie otnosheniya 1697–1875 gg.* (Moscow, 1960)

Feoktistov, E.M., *Vospominaniya. Za kulisami politiki i literatury, 1848–1896* (Leningrad, 1929; republished Cambridge, 1975)

Ferenczi, C., *Außenpolitik und Öffentlichkeit in Rußland 1906–1912* (Husum, 1982)

——, 'Nationalismus und Neoslawismus in Rußland vor dem Ersten Weltkrieg', *FOG* 34 (1984), pp. 7–127

Field, D., 'The Myths of the Tsar', in Field, *Rebels in the Name of the Tsar* (Boston, 1976), pp. 1–30

——, *The End of Serfdom. Nobility and Bureaucracy in Russia, 1855–1861* (Cambridge, Mass., 1976)

Fischer, A., *Russische Sozialdemokratie und bewaffneter Aufstand im Jahre 1905* (Wiesbaden, 1967)

Fischer, F., *Der Krieg der Illusionen* (Düsseldorf, 1969)

Fischer, G., *Russian Liberalism From Gentry to Intelligentsia* (Cambridge, Mass., 1958)

Fleischhacker, H., *Russische Antworten auf die polnische Frage 1795–1917* (Munich, 1941)

Fleischhauer, E., *Bismarcks Rußlandpolitik im Jahrzent vor der Reichsgründung und ihre Darstellung in der sowjetischen Historiographie* (Cologne, 1976)

Frank V., and Schüle, E., 'Graf Pavel Andreevič Šuvalov, russischer Botschafter in Berlin, 1885–1894', *ZOG* 7 (1933), pp. 525–59

Freeze, G., 'A National Liberation Movement and the Shift in Russian Liberalism, 1901–1903', *SR* 28 (1969), pp. 81–91

Fröhlich, K., *The Emergence of Russian Constitutionalism 1900–1904* (The

Hague, 1981)

Galai, S., 'The Impact of War on the Russian Liberals 1904–1905', *Government and Opposition* 1 (1965), pp. 85–109
——, *The Liberation Movement in Russia 1900–1905* (Cambridge, 1973)
——, 'The Role of the Union of Unions in the Russian Revolution of 1905', *JGO* 24 (1976), pp. 512–28
Galuzo, P.G., 'Das Kolonialsystem des russischen Imperialismus am Vorabend der Oktoberrevolution', *ZfG* 15 (1967), pp. 997–1014
——, *Turkestan — koloniya. Ocherk istorii Turkestana ot zavoevaniya russkimi do revolyutsii 1917 g.* (Moscow, 1929)
Garmiza, V., *Podgotovka zemskoi reformy 1864 g.* (Moscow, 1957)
—— (ed.), 'Predlozheniya i proekty P.A. Valueva po voprosam vnutrennei politiki (1862–1866) gg.', *IA* (1958/1), pp. 138–53
Garvy, G., 'The Financial Manifesto of the St. Petersburg Soviet 1905', *IRSH* 20 (1975), pp. 16–32
Gavlin, M.L., 'Rol' tsentra i okrain Rossiiskoi imperii v formirovanii krupnoi moskovskoi burzhuazii v poreformennyi period', *IZ* 92 (1973), pp. 336–55
Gefter, M.Ya., 'K istorii toplivno-metallicheskogo goloda v Rossii nakanune pervoi mirovoi voiny', *IA* (1951/6), pp. 49–80
Gerasimova, Yu.I., *Iz istorii russkoi pechati v period revolyutsionnoi situatsii kontsa 1850-kh–nachala 1860-kh godov* (Moscow, 1974)
Gerschenkron, A., 'Agrarian Policies and Industrialization: Russia 1861–1917', *CEHE* (1966), vol. 6, pp. 706–800
——, *Continuity in History and Other Essays* (Cambridge, Mass., 1968)
——, 'Criticism from Afar: A Reply', *SS* 25 (1973), pp. 170–95
——, 'The Early Phases of Industrialization in Russia: Afterthoughts and Counter-thoughts', in W.W. Rostow (ed.), *The Economics of Take-off into Sustained Growth* (New York, 1963), pp. 152–4
——, *Economic Backwardness in Historical Perspective* (Cambridge, Mass., 1962)
——, *Europe in the Russian Mirror* (New York, 1970)
Gerus, O.W., 'The Reformed State Council 1905–1917. A Phase in Russian Constitutionalism', PhD thesis, Toronto, 1970
Geyer, D., *Lenin in der russischen Sozialdemokratie 1890–1903* (Cologne, 1962)
——, *The Russian Revolution: Historical Problems and Perspectives* (Leamington Spa, 1987)
—— 'Rußland als Problem der vergleichenden Imperialismusforschung', *Das Vergangene und die Geschichte. Fs. f.R. Wittram* Göttingen, 1973), pp. 337–68
—— (ed.), *Wirtschaft und Gesellschaft im vorrevolutionären Rußland* (Cologne, 1975)
Giertz, H., 'Die außenpolitische Position Miljukovs am Vorabend u.

während der bosnischen Krise', *JGSLE* 18/2 (1974), pp. 77–113

Gindin, I.F., 'D.I. Mendelev o razvitii promyshlennosti v Rossii', *VIst* (1976/9), pp. 210–15

——, *Gosudarstvennyi bank i ekonomicheskaya politika tsarkogo pravitel'stva (1861 do 1892 gg.)* (Moscow, 1960)

——, 'Moskovskie banki v period imperializma', *IZ* 58 (1956), pp. 38–106

——, 'O nekotorykh osobennostyakh ekonomicheskoi i sotsial'noi struktury rossiiskogo kapitalizma v nachale XX v.', *ISSR* (1966/3), pp. 48–66

——, 'Russkaya burzhuaziya v period kapitalizma, ee razvitie i osobennosti', *ISSSR* (1963/2), pp. 57–80, (1963/3), pp. 37–60

——, *Russkie kommercheskie banki. Iz istorii finansovogo kapitala v Rossii* (Moscow, 1948)

Girault, R., *Emprunts russes et investissements français en Russie 1887–1914* (Paris, 1969)

Girault (Zhiro), R., 'Finansy i politika vo franko-russkikh otnosheniyakh 1887–1889 gg.', *FE* (1967), pp. 136–58

Gleason, A., *European and Moscovite. Ivan Kirevsky and the Origins of Slavophilism* (Cambridge, Mass., 1972)

Goehrke, C., 'Geographische Grundlagen der russischen Geschichte', *JGO* 18 (1970), pp. 161–204

——, 'Die geographischen Gegebenheiten Rußlands in ihrem historischen Beziehungsgeflecht', *Handbuch der Geschichte Rußlands*, Bd., 1, Lfg. 1 (Stuttgart, 1976), pp. 8–72

Gollwitzer, H., *Europe in the Age of Imperialism 1880–1914* (N 1969)

——, *Die gelbe Gefahr. Geschichte eines Schlagworts. Studien zum imperialistischen Denken* (Göttingen, 1962)

——, *Geschichte des weltpolitischen Denkens*, vols. 1, 2 (Göttingen, 1972, 1982)

Goryushkin, L.M., *Agrarnye otnosheniya v Sibiri perioda imperializma, 1900–1917 gg.* (Novosibirsk, 1976)

——, 'Razvitie kapitalizma v shir' i kharakter agrarno-kapitalisticheskoi evolyutsii v Rossii perioda imperializma', *ISSSR* (1974/2), pp. 49–70

——, *Sibirskoe krest'yanstvo na rubezhe dvukh vekov, konets XIX–nachalo XX* (Novosibirsk, 1967)

Graves, R.L., *Russia and Persia and the Defence of India, 1884–1892* (London, 1959)

Gregory, P., and Sailors, J.W., 'Russian Monetary Policy and Industrialization 1861–1913', *JEH* 36 (1976), pp. 836–51

——, *Russian National Income 1885–1913* (Cambridge, Mass., 1982)

Grigortsevich, S.S., *Dal'nevostochnaya politika imperialisticheskikh derzhav v 1906–1917 gg.* (Tomsk, 1965)

Grüning, I., *Die russische öffentliche Meinung u. ihre Stellung zu den Großmächten, 1878–1894* (Berlin, 1929)

Guchkov, A.I., *Rechi po voprosam gosudarstvennoi oborony i ob obshchei politike, 1908–17 gg.* (Petrograd, 1917)

Bibliography

Guliev, A.N., *Bakinskii proletariat v gody novogo revolyutsionnogo pod″ema* (Baku, 1963)
Guroff, G., 'The State and Industrialization in Russian Economic Thought 1909–1914', PhD thesis, Princeton Univ., 1970

Hagen, M., 'Die Deutschbalten in der III. Duma. Zwischen nationalem Abwehrkampf, Autonomiestreben und Klassenkampf', *ZfO* 23 (1974), pp. 577–97
——, 'Der russische "Bonapartismus" nach 1906. Genese und Problematik eines Leitbegriffs in der sowjetischen Geschichtswissenschaft', *JGO* 24 (1976), pp. 369–93
——, *Die Entfaltung politischer Öffentlichkeit in Rußland 1906–1914* (Wiesbaden, 1982)
Haimson, L.H., 'The Problem of Social Stability in Urban Russia 1905–1917', *Slavic Review* 23 (1964), pp. 619–42; 24 (1965), pp. 1–22
—— (ed.), *The Politics of Rural Russia, 1905–1914* (Bloomington, Ind., 1979)
Hallgarten, G.W.F., *Imperialismus vor 1914* (Munich, 1963), vols. 1–2
Hallmann, H. (ed.), *Geschichte und Problematik des deutschrussischen Rückversicherungsvertrags von 1887* (Darmstadt, 1968)
Hammer, M., *L'entente des trois empereurs: Recherches sur les méthodes et l'orientation de la politique extérieure russe entre 1879 et 1881* (Berne, 1973)
Hansen, J., *L'Ambassade à Paris du Baron de Mohrenheim 1884–1898* (Paris, 1907)
Hartl, J.H., *Die Interessenvertretungen der Industriellen in Rußland 1905 bis 1914* (Vienna, 1978)
Haumann, H., *Kapitalismus im zaristischen Staat 1906–1917. Organisationsformen, Machtverhältnisse u. Leistungsbilanz im Industrialisierungsprozeß* (Königstein, 1980)
Hayit, B., *Turkestan zwischen Rußland und China* (Amsterdam, 1971)
Haywood, R.M., *The Beginning of Railway Development in Russia in the Reign of Nicholas I, 1835–1842* (Durham, N. C., 1969)
Hegarty, T., 'Student Movements in Russian Universities, 1855–1861', PhD thesis, Harvard, 1965
Hehn, H.v., *Die baltische Frage zur Zeit Alexanders III. in den Äußerungen der deutschen Öffentlichkeit* (Marburg, 1953)
Heilbronner, Ä.H., 'P.Kh. von Schwanebach and the Dissolution of the First Two Dumas', *CSP* 11 (1969), pp. 31–55
——, 'The Russian Plague of 1878–1879', *SR* 21 (1962), pp. 89–112
Helmreich, E.C., *The Diplomacy of the Balkan Wars 1912–1913* (Cambridge, Mass., 1938)
Hildebrand, K., 'Imperialismus, Wettrüsten u. Kriegsausbruch 1914', *NPL* 20 (1975), pp. 160–94, 339–64
Hildermeier, M., *Die Sozialrevolutionäre Partei Rußlands 1900–1914* (Cologne, 1978)

___, 'Sozialer Wandel im städtischen Rußland in der zweiten Hälfte des 19. Jhs.', *JGO* 25 (1977), pp. 525–66

Hiller, M., *Krisenregion Nahost. Russische Orientpolitik im Zeitalter des Imperialismus, 1900–1914* (Frankfurt, 1985)

Hillgruber, A., *Bismarcks Außenpolitik* (Freiburg, 1972)

___, 'Riezlers Theorie des kalkulierten Risikos und Bethmann Hollwegs politische Konzeption in der Julikrise 1914', in W. Schieder (ed.), *Erster Weltkrieg. Ursachen, Entstehung u. Kriegsziele* (Cologne, 1969, pp. 240–55

Hink, H., *Bismarck's Pressepolitik in der bulgarischen Krise und der Zusammenbruch seiner Regierungspresse 1885–1890* (Frankfurt, 1977)

Hodgson, J.H., 'Finland's Position in the Russian Empire 1905–1910', *JCEA* 20 (1960), pp. 158–73

Hoetzsch, O., 'Russisch-Turkestan und die Tendenzen der russischen Kolonialpolitik', *Schmollers Jb.* 37 (1913), pp. 903–41, 1427–73

___, *Rußland. Eine Einführung auf Grund seiner Geschichte von 1904–1912* (Berlin, 1913)

___, *Rußland in Asien. Geschichte einer Expansion* (Stuttgart, 1966)

Hoffmann, H., 'Die Politik der Mächte in der Endphase der Kaukasuskriege', *JGO* 17 (1969), pp. 215–58

___, 'Das Problem einer Seeblockade Kaukasiens nach dem Pariser Frieden von 1856', *FOG* 11 (1966), pp. 130–75

Holzer, G.S., 'German Electrical Industry in Russia: From Economic Entrepreneurship to Political Activism, 1890–1918', PhD thesis, Univ. of Nebraska, 1970

Hölzle, E., *Der Geheimnisverrat und der Kriegsausbruch 1914* (Göttingen, 1973)

___, *Die Selbstentmachtung Europas. Das Experiment des Friedens vor und im Ersten Weltkrieg* (Göttingen, 1975)

Hopwood, D., *The Russian Presence in Syria and Palestine 1843–1914. Church and Politics in the Near East* (Oxford, 1969)

Hosking, G.A., *The Russian Constitutional Experiment. Government and Duma 1906–1914* (Oxford, 1973)

Hosoya Chihrio, 'Japan and Russia', in J.W. Morley (ed.), *Japan's Foreign Policy 1868–1941. A Research Guide* (New York, 1974)

Hsü, I.C., *The Ili Crisis. A Study in Sino-Russian Diplomacy, 1871–1881* (Oxford, 1965)

___, *The Rise of Modern China* (Oxford, 1975)

Hünigen, G., *Nikolaj Pavlovič Ignat'ev und die russische Balkanpolitik, 1875–1878* (Göttingen, 1968)

Hunt, M.H., *Frontier Defense and the Open Door. Manchuria in Chinese–American Relations 1895–1911* (New Haven, 1973)

Hutchinson, J.F., 'The Octobrists and the Future of Imperial Russia as a Great Power', *SEER* 50 (1972), pp. 220–37

Huttenbach, H.R., 'The Origins of Russian Imperialism', in T. Hunczak

Bibliography

(ed.), *Russian Imperialism from Ivan the Great to the Revolution* (New Brunswick, N.J., 1974), pp. 18–44

Hutton, L.T., 'The Reform of City Government in Russia, 1860–1870', PhD thesis, Univ. of Illinois, 1972

Ignatyev, A.I., *Russko-angliiskie otnosheniya nakanune pervoi mirovoi voiny* (Moscow, 1962)

Die Internationalen Beziehungen im Zeitalter des Imperialismus. Dokumente a. d. Archiven d. Zarischen u. d. Provisorischen Regierung 1878–1898, ed. M.N. Pokroswki: German version ed. O. Hoetzsch, Reihe I (Bd. 1–5), III (Bd. 1–2) (Berlin, 1931–43)

Isakov, G.S., *Ostzeiskii vopros v russkoi pechati 1860-kh godov* (Moscow, 1961)

Ischchanian, B., *Die ausländischen Elemente in der russischen Volkswirtschaft* (Berlin, 1913)

Istoriya pervoi mirovoi voiny 1914–1918, vols. 1–2 (Moscow, 1975)

Istoriya SSSR s drevneishikh vremen do Velikoi Oktyabr'skoi sotsialisticheskoi revolyutsii, vol. 5: *Razvitie kapitalizma i pod"em revolyutsionnogo dvizheniya v poreformennoi Rossii*, vol. 6: *Rossiya v period imperializma 1900–1917 gg.* (Moscow, 1968)

Itenberg, B.S., *Dvizhenie revolyutsionnogo narodnichestva. Narodnicheskie kruzhki i khozhdenie v narod v 70-kh godakh XIX v.* (Moscow, 1965)

Ivanov, L.M., 'O soslovno-klassovoi strukture gorodov kapitalisticheskoi Rossii', *Problemy sotsial'no-ekonomicheskoi istorii* (Moscow, 1971), pp. 312–340

Ivanov, M.S., *Iranskaya revolyutsiya 1905–1911 gg.* (Moscow, 1957)

[Izvolskii] Iswolsky, A., *Au service de la Russie. Correspondence diplomatique* (Paris, 1937), vol. 1

[Izvolskii], *Der diplomatische Schriftwechsel Iswolskis 1911–1914*, ed. F. Stieve (Berlin, 1925), vols. 1–4

[Izvolskii, A.P.], *The Memoirs of Alexander Isvolsky* (London, 1920)

Jablonowski, H., 'Die Stellungnahme der russischen Parteien zur Außenpolitik der Regierung von der russisch–englischen Verständigung bis zum Ersten Weltkrieg', *FOG* 5 (1957), pp. 60–92

Jakobs, P., *Das Werden des französisch–russischen Zweibundes 1890–1894* (Wiesbaden, 1968)

Jakovlev, A.F., *Ekonomicheskie krizisy v Rossii* (Moscow, 1955)

Jeismann, K.-E., *Das Problem des Präventivkrieges im europäischen Staatensystem mit bes. Blick auf die Bismarckzeit* (Freiburg, 1957)

Jevalich, B., 'British Means of Offence against Russia in the 19th Century', *Russian History* 1 (1974), pp. 119–35

——, *The Ottoman Empire, The Great Powers and the Straits Question, 1870–1887* (Bloomington, Ind., 1973)

——, *Russia and the Rumanian National Cause, 1858–1859* (Bloomington, Ind., 1959)

——, (ed.), *Rußland 1852–1871. Aus den Berichten der Bayrischen Gesandtschaft in St. Petersburg* (Wiesbaden, 1963)

——, 'Russo-Bulgarian Relations, 1892–1896', *JMH* 24 (1952), pp. 341–51

——, *St Petersburg and Moscow. Tsarist and Soviet Foreign Policy, 1814–1974* (Bloomington, Ind., 1974)

Jelavich, C., and B. (eds.), *Russia in the East 1876–1880* (Leiden, 1959)

Jelavich, C., *Tsarist Russia and Balkan Nationalism. Russian Influence in the Internal Affairs of Bulgaria and Serbia, 1879–1886* (Berkeley, 1958)

Kabuzan, V.M., *Narodonaselenie v Rossii v XVIII–pervoi polovine XIX v.* (Moscow, 1963)

Kachk, J., *Die Krise der feudalen Landwirtschaft in Estland* (Tallinn, 1969)

Kahan, A., 'Government Policies and the Industrialization of Russia', *JEH* 27 (1967), pp. 460–77

Kaiser, F.B., *Die russische Justizreform von 1864* (Leiden, 1972)

Kalinychev, F.I. (ed.), *Gosudarstvennaya duma v Rossii v dokumentakh i materialakh* (Moscow, 1957)

Kastelyanskii, A.I. (ed.), *Formy natsional'nogo dvizheniya v sovremennykh gosudarstvakh. Avstro-Vengriya, Rossiya, Germaniya* (St Petersburg, 1910), pp. 277–653

Katz, M., *M.N. Katkov. A Political Biography 1818–1887* (The Hague, 1966)

Kazemzadeh, F., 'Russian Imperialism and Persian Railways', *HSS* 4 (1957), pp. 355–73

——, *Russia and Britain in Persia, 1864–1914. A Study in Imperialism* (New Haven, 1968)

——, 'Russia and the Middle East', in I.J. Lederer (ed.), *Russian Foreign Policy. Essays in Historical Perspective* (New Haven, 1966³), pp. 489–552

Keep, J., *The Rise of Social Democracy in Russia* (Oxford, 1963)

Kennan, G.F., *The Decline of Bismarck's European Order. Franco–Russian Relations, 1875–1890* (Princeton, N.J., 1979)

Khalfin, N. A., 'O dvizheshchikh motivakh politiki Rossii v Srednei Azii (60–70e gody XIX v.)', *ISSSR* (1972/4), pp. 128–35

——, *Politika Rossii v Srednei Azii 1857–1868 gg.* (Moscow, 1960)

——, *Prisoedinenie Srednei Azii k Rossii (60–90e gody XIX v.)* (Moscow, 1965)

——, *Rossiya i khanstva Srednei Azii (pervaya polovina XIX v.)* (Moscow, 1974)

Kheyfets, M.I., *Vtoraya revolyutsionnaya situatsiya v Rossii (konets 70-kh–nachalo 80-kh godov XIX v.). Krizis pravitel'stvennoi politiki* (Moscow, 1963)

Khokhlov, A.N., 'Vopros o voennoi pomoshchi Rossii Kitayu v kontse 50-kh–nachale 60-kh godov XIX v.', *Strany Dal'nego Vostoka i Yugo-*

Bibliography

Vostochnoi Azii (Moscow, 1967)

Khromov, P.A., *Ekonomicheskoe razvitie Rossii v XIX–XX vekakh, 1800–1917* (Moscow, 1950)

Khvostov, V.M., *Diplomatiya v novoe vremya 1871–1914* (Moscow, 1963) = *Istoriya diplomatii 2*

——, 'Problemy zakhvata Bosfora v 90-kh godakh XIX v.', *IM* 20 (1930), pp. 100–29

Kieniewicz, S., *The Emancipation of the Polish Peasantry* (London, 1969)

——, *Powstanie styczniowe* (Warsaw, 1972)

Kinyapina, N.S., 'Bor'ba Rossii za otmenu ogranichitel'nykh uslovy Parizhskogo dogovora 1856 g.', *VIst* (1972/8), pp. 35–51

——, *Politika samoderzhaviya v oblasti promyshlennosti (20–50-e gody XIX v.)* (Moscow, 1968)

——, 'Srednyaya Aziya vo vneshnepoliticheskikh planakh tsarizma (50–80-e gody XIX v.)', *VIst* (1974/2), pp. 36–51

——, *Vneshnyaya politika Rossii vtoroi poloviny XIX veka* (Moscow, 1974)

Kipp, J.W., 'Consequences of Defeat: Modernizing the Russian Navy, 1856–1863', *JGO* 20 (1972), pp. 210–25

Kirchner, W., 'The Industrialization of Russia and the Siemens Firm 1853–1890', *JGO* 22 (1974), pp. 321–57

Kislinsky, N.A., *Nasha zheleznodorozhnaya politika po dokumentam Arkhiva Komiteta ministrov* (St Petersburg, 1901), vols. 1–3

Knorring, N., *General Michail Dm. Skobelev* (Paris, 1939, 1940), 2 vols.

Knutson, G.D., 'Peter Valuev: A Conservative's Approach and Reactions to the Reforms of Alexander II', PhD thesis, Univ. of Kansas, 1970

Koberdowa, I., *Wielki książę Konstanty w Warszawie 1862–1863* (Warsaw, 1963)

Kofos, E., *Greece and the Near Eastern Crisis, 1875–1878* (Salonika, 1975)

Kokovtsov, V.M., *Iz moego proshlogo. Vospominaniya 1903–1919 gg.* (Paris, 1933), vols. 1–2

Königslöw, J. v., *Ferdinand von Bulgarien. Vom Beginn der Thronkandidatur bis zur Anerkennung durch die Großmächte, 1886–1896* (Munich, 1970)

Korelin, A.P., 'Dvoryanstvo v poreformennoi Rossii (1861–1904 gg.)', *IZ* 87 (1971), pp. 91–173

——, 'Krakh ideologii "politseiskogo sotsializma" v tsarskoi Rossii', *IZ* 92 (1973), pp. 109–52

——, 'Rossiiskoe dvoryanstvo i ego soslovnaya organizatsiya 1861–1905', *ISSSR* (1971/5), pp. 56–81

——, 'Russkii "politseiskii sotsializm" ',*VIst* (1968/10), pp. 41–58

Korhonen, K., *Autonomous Finland in the Political Thought of 19th-Century Russia* (Turku, 1967)

Koroleva, N.G., 'Reforma Soveta Ministrov Rossii v 1905 g.', *Sovetskie arkhivy* (1972/1), pp. 85–8

Kostyushko, I.I., *Krest'yanskaya reforma 1864 goda v Tsarstve Pol'skom* (Moscow, 1962)

Koval'chenko, I.D., 'Sootnoshenie krest'yanskogo i pomeshchichego kho-zyaistva v zemledel'cheskom proizvodstve kapitalisticheskoi Rossii', *Problemy sotsial'no-ekonomicheskoi istorii Rossii* (Moscow, 1971), pp. 171–94

—, and Milov, L.V., *Veserossiiskii agrarnyi rynok. XVIII–nachalo XX veka. Opyt kolichestvennogo analiza* (Moscow, 1974)

Koz'menko, I.V., 'Iz istorii bolgarskogo opolcheniya', *Slavyanskii sbornik* (Moscow, 1948)

—, 'Russkoe obshchestvo i aprel'skoe bolgarskoe vosstanie', *VIst* (1945/5), p. 95–108

Krausnick, H., 'Holsteins großes Spiel im Frühjahr 1887', *Geschichte und Gegenwartsbewußtsein. Fs. f. H. Rothfels* (Göttingen, 1963), pp. 357–427

—, 'Rückversicherungsvertrag und Optionsproblem 1887–1890', *Geschichtliche Kräfte und Entscheidungen. Fs. f. O. Becker* (Wiesbaden, 1954), pp. 210–32

Krest'yanskoe dvizhenie v Rossii. Sbornik dokumentov, 1857–1861 (Moscow, 1963)

Krivoshein, K.A., *A.V. Krivoshein (1857–1921). Ego znachenie v istorii Rossii nachala XX veka* (Paris, 1973)

Krupinski, K., *Rußland und Japan. Ihre Beziehungen bis zum Frieden von Portsmouth* (Königsberg, 1940)

Krusius-Ahrenberg, L., *Der Durchbruch des Nationalismus und Liberalismus im politischen Leben Finnlands 1856 bis 1863* (Helsinki, 1934)

Kumpf-Korfes, S., *Bismarcks 'Draht nach Rußland'. Zum Problem der sozialökonomischen Hintergründe der russisch-deutschen Entfremdung im Zeitraum von 1878 bis 1894* (Berlin, GDR, 1968)

[Kuropatkin, A.N.], *General Kuropatkin. Memoiren. Die Lehren des Russisch-Japanischen Krieges* (Berlin, 1909)

Kutakov, L.N., *Portsmutskii mirnyi dogovor* (Moscow, 1961)

Lambsdorff, G. Graf v., *Die Militärbevollmächtigten Wilhelms II. am Zarenhofe 1904 bis 1914* (Berlin, 1937)

[Lamzdorf, V.N.], *Dnevnik V.N. Lamzdorfa 1891–1892*, ed. F.A. Rotshtein (Moscow/Leningrad, 1934)

—, *Dnevnik V.N. Lamzdorfa 1886–1890*, ed. F.A. Rotshtein (Moscow/Leningrad, 1926). Excerpts in German translation in: *BM* 9 (1931), pp. 158–77

Langer, W.L., *The Franco-Russian Alliance 1890–1894* (Cambridge, Mass., 1929)

Laue, Th. v., 'A Secret Memorandum of Sergei Witte on the Industrialization of Imperial Russia', *JMH* 26 (1954), pp. 60–74

—, 'Problems of Modernization', in I.J. Lederer (ed.), *Russian Foreign Policy. Essays in Historical Perspective* (New Haven, 1962, 1966[3]), pp. 69–108

—, *Sergei Witte and the Industrialization of Russia* (New York, 1963)

Laverychev, V. Ya., *Krupnaya burzhuaziya v poreformennoi Rossii 1861–1900* (Moscow, 1974)

——, *Po tu storonu barrikad. (Iz istorii bor'by moskovskoi burzhuazii s revolyutsiei)* (Moscow, 1967)

Lemke, H., 'Großbritannien und die deutsch–russischen Verhandlung über Persien und die Bagdadbahn nach der Zusammenkunft in Potsdam (1910/11)', *JGSLE* 18/2 (1974), pp. 115–45

——, 'Industrielle Revolution und Durchsetzung des Kapitalismus in Rußland', in P. Hoffmann and H. Lemke (eds.), *Genesis und Entwicklung des Kapitalismus in Rußland* (Berlin, GDR, 1973), pp. 213–40

Lemke, M., *Ocherki po istorii russkoi tsenzury i zhurnalistiki XIX stoletiya* (St Petersburg, 1904)

Lenin, V.I., *Polnoe sobranie sochinenii* (5th ed., Moscow, 1958–65), vols. 1–55

Lensen, G.A., *Korea and Manchuria Between Russia and Japan 1895–1904* (Tallahassee, Flo., 1966)

——, *Russia's Japan Expedition of 1852 to 1855* (Gainesville, Flo., 1955)

——, *The Russian Push toward Japan: Russo-Japanese Relations 1697–1875* (Princeton, 1959)

——, *The Russo-Chinese War* (Tallahassee, 1967)

Leontovitsch, V., *Geschichte des Liberalismus in Rußland* (Frankfurt, 1974²)

Leslie, R.F., *Reform and Insurrection in Russian Poland, 1856–1865* (London, 1963)

Levin, A., 'June 3, 1907: Action and Reaction', *Essays in Russian History* (Hamden, Conn., 1964), pp. 233–73

——, 'P.A. Stolypin: A Political Re-appraisal', *JMH* 37 (1965), pp. 445–63

——, *The Second Duma* (New Haven, 1940)

——, *The Third Duma. Election and Profile* (Hamden, Conn., 1973)

Levin, S.M., 'Krymskaya voina i russkoe obshchestvo' in Levin, *Ocherki po istorii russkoi obshchestvennoi mysli. Vtoraya polovina XIX – nachalo XX v.* (Leningrad, 1974)

Lieven, D.C.B., *Russia and the Origins of the First World War* (London, 1983)

Lincoln, W.B., 'The Making of a New Polish Policy. N.A. Milyutin and the Polish Question 1861–1863', *PR* 15 (1970), pp. 54–66

Linke, H.G., *Das zarische Rußland und der Erste Weltkrieg. Diplomatie und Kriegsziele 1914–1917* (Munich, 1982)

Liszkowski, U., 'Zur Aktualisierung der Stereotype "Die deutsche Gefahr" im russischen Neoslawismus', in *Rußland und Deutschland. Fs. für G. v. Rauch* (Stuttgart, 1974), pp. 278–94

——, *Zwischen Liberalismus und Imperialismus. Die zaristische Außenpolitik vor dem ersten Weltkrieg im Urteil Miljukovs und der Kadettenpartei 1905–1914* (Stuttgart, 1974)

Lyakhovskii, V.M., 'Zheleznodorozhnye perevozki i razvitie rynka. K istorii Ryazansko-Kozlovskoi dorogi 1860–70-e gody', *VMU-Ist* (1963/4), pp. 34–51

Löhr, B., *Die 'Zukunft Rußlands'. Perspektiven russischer Wirtschaftsentwicklung und deutsch-russische Wirtschaftsbeziehungen vor dem Ersten Weltkrieg* (Wiesbaden, 1985)

Long, J.W., 'The Economics of the Franco-Russian Alliance 1904–1906', PhD thesis, Univ. of Wisconsin, 1968

——, 'French Attempts at Constitutional Reform in Russia', *JGO* 23 (1975), pp. 496–503

——, 'Organized Protests against the 1906 Russian Loan', *CMRS* 13 (1972), pp. 24–39

——, 'Russian Manipulation of the French Press', *SR* 31 (1972), pp. 343–54

Löwe, H.-D., *Antisemitismus u. reaktionäre Utopie. Russischer Konservativismus im Kampf gegen den Wandel von Staat und Gesellschaft, 1890–1917* (Hamburg, 1978)

Lowe, P., *Great Britain and Japan 1911–1915. A Study of British Far Eastern Policy* (London, 1969)

Luft, P., 'Strategische Interessen und Anleihepolitik Rußlands in Iran', *GuG* 1 (1975), pp. 506–38

Lukashevich, S., *Ivan Aksakov 1823–1886. A Study in Russian Thought and Politics* (Cambridge, Mass., 1965)

Łukawski, Z., *Koło Polskie w rosyjskiej dumie państwowej w latach 1906–1909* (Wrocław, 1967)

Luntinen, P., *The Baltic Question, 1903–08* (Helsinki, 1975)

McKay, J.P., *Pioneers for Profit. Foreign Entrepreneurship and Russian Industrialization, 1885–1913* (Chicago, 1970)

MacKenzie, D., 'Kaufman of Turkestan: An Assessment of His Administration, 1867–1881', *SR* 26 (1967), pp. 265–85

——, *The Lion of Tashkent. The Career of General M.G. Cherniaev* (Athens, 1974)

——, *The Serbs and Russian Panslavism, 1875–1878* (Ithaca, 1967)

——, 'Turkestan's Significance to Russia 1850–1917', *RR* 33 (1973), pp. 167–88

MacMaster, R.E., *Danilevsky: A Russian Totalitarian Philosopher* (Cambridge, Mass., 1967)

Mai, J., *Das deutsche Kapital in Rußland, 1850–1894* (Berlin, GDR, 1970

Maisky, B. Yu., 'Stolypinshchina i konets Stolypina', *VIst* (1966/1), pp. 134–44 (2), pp. 123–40

Malozemoff, A., *Russian Far Eastern Policy 1881–1904* (Berkeley, 1958)

Manfred, A.Z., *Obrazovanie russko-frantsuzskogo soyuza* (Moscow, 1975)

——, 'Oformlenie russko-frantsuzskogo soyuza', *NNI* (1976), pp. 114–32

——, *Vneshnyaya politika Frantsii 1871–1891 godov* (Moscow, 1952)

Manfred, K., 'Frankreich u. die polnische Frage zur Zeit der französisch-russischen Allianz 1891–1914', *FOG* 21 (1975), pp. 115–332

Bibliography

Marinov, V.A., *Rossiya i Yaponiya pered pervoi mirovoi voinoi (1905–1914 gody). Ocherki istorii otnoshenii* (Moscow, 1974)

Markert, W., 'Die deutsch–russischen Beziehungen am Vorabend des Ersten Weltkrieges', in Markert, *Osteuropa u. die abendländische Welt* (Göttingen, 1966), pp. 166–86, 212–21

Martiny, A., *Parlament, Staatshaushalt und Finanzen in Rußland. Der Einfluß der Duma auf die russische Finanz- und Haushaltspolitik 1907–1914* (Bochum, 1977)

Martynenko, A.K., *Russko-bolgarskie otnosheniya 1894–1902 gg.* (Kiev, 1967)

Materialy po istorii franko-russkikh otnoshenii za 1910–1914 gg. (Moscow, 1922)

McCormick, T.J., *China Market. America's Quest for Informal Empire 1893–1901* (Chicago, 1967)

Medlicott, W.N., *The Congress of Berlin and After. A Diplomatic History of the New Eastern Peace Settlement 1878–1880* (London, 1963²)

Megrian, L.D., 'Tiflis During the Revolution of 1905', PhD thesis, Univ. of California/Berkeley, 1968

Mehlinger, H.D., and Thompson, J.M., *Count Witte and the Tsarist Government in the 1905 Revolution* (Bloomington, Ind., 1972)

Meininger, T.A., *Ignatiev and the Establishment of the Bulgarian Exarchate, 1864 to 1872: A Study in Personal Diplomacy* (Madison, 1970)

Melville, R., and Schröder, H.J. (eds.), *Der Berliner Kongreß. Die Politik der Großmächte und die Probleme der Modernisierung in Südosteuropa* (Wiesbaden, 1982)

Menashe, L., 'Alexander Guchkov and the Origins of the Octobrist Party: The Russian Bourgeoisie in Politics', PhD thesis, New York Univ., 1966

——, 'A Liberal with Spurs: Alexander Guchkov. A Russian Bourgeois in Politics', *RR* 26 (1967), pp. 38–53 (= chap. 3 of the unpubl. thesis)

Mendel'son, L., *Ekonomicheskie krizisy i tsikly XIX v.* (Moscow, 1949)

——, *Teoriya i istoriya ekonomicheskikh krizisov i tsiklov* (vols. 1 and 2, Moscow, 1959; vol. 3, Moscow, 1964)

Meng, S.M., *The Tsungli Yamen. Its Organization and Functions* (Cambridge, Mass., 1962)

Metzer, J., 'Railroad Development and Market Integration: The Case of Tsarist Russia', *JEH* 34 (1974), pp. 529–49

——, 'Railroads in Tsarist Russia: Direct Gains and Implications', *Explorations in Economic History* 13 (1976), pp. 85–111

——, 'Some Aspects of Railroad Development in Tsarist Russia', PhD thesis, Univ. of Chicago, 1972

Meyer, K., 'Rußland u. die Gründung des Deutschen Reiches', *Jb. f. d. Gesch. Mittel- u. Ostdeutschlands* 22 (1973), pp. 176–95

Migulin, P.P., *Voina i nashi finansy* (Khar'kov, 1905)

Milyukov, P.N., *Balkanskii vopros i politika A.P. Izvol'skogo* (St Petersburg, 1910)

___, *Vospominaniya, 1859–1917* (New York, 1955), vols. 1–2

[Milyutin, D.A], *Dnevnik D.A. Milyutina* (Moscow, 1947–50), vols. 1–4

Miller, F.A., *Dimitrii Miliutin and the Reform Era in Russia* (Nashville, Tenn., 1968)

Miller, J.M. Jr., 'The Concert of Europe in the First Balkan War, 1912–1913', PhD thesis, Clark Univ., 1969

Mommsen, W.J., *Imperialismustheorien* (Göttingen, 1977)

___, (ed.), *Moderner Imperialismus*, (Stuttgart, 1971)

___, *Das Zeitalter des Imperialismus* (Frankfurt, 1969)

Monopolii i inostrannyi kapital v Rossii (Moscow, 1962)

Monopolisticheskii kapital v neftyanoi promyshlennosti Rossii 1883–1914 gg. Sb. dokumentov i materialov, eds. M.Ya. Gefter et al. (Moscow, 1961)

Moore, B., *Social Origins of Dictatorship and Democracy* (Boston, 1966)

Morill, D.L., 'Nicholas II and the Call for the First Hague Conference', *JMH* 46 (1974), pp. 296–313

Morison, J.D., 'Katkov and Panslavism', *SEER* 46 (1968), pp. 422–41

Moritz, A., *Das Problem des Präventivkrieges in der deutschen Politik während der ersten Marokko-Krise* (Berne, 1974)

Morley, J.W. (ed.), *Japan's Foreign Policy 1868–1941. A Research Guide* (New York, 1974)

Morozov, G.P., 'Russko-frantsuzskie otnosheniya vo vremya voennoi trevogi 1887 g.', *FE* (1959), pp. 248–81

Morris, P., 'The Russians in Central Asia, 1870–1887', *SEER* 53 (1975), pp. 521–38

Mosse, W.E., 'England and the Polish Insurrection of 1863', *EHR* 71 (1956), pp. 28–55

___, *The Rise and Fall of the Crimean System 1855–1871. The Story of a Peace Settlement* (London, 1963)

Mukhin, A.A., *Rabochie Sibiri v epokhu kapitalizma, 1861–1917 gg.* (Moscow, 1972)

Müller-Link, H., *Industrialisierung und Außenpolitik. Preußen–Deutschland und das Zarenreich, 1860–1890* (Göttingen, 1977)

Narochnitskaya, L.I., *Rossiya i voiny Prussii v 60-kh godakh XIX v. za ob"edinenie Germanii "sverkhu"* (Moscow, 1960)

Narochnitskii, A.L., *Kolonial'naya politika kapitalisticheskikh derzhav na Dal'nem Vostoke, 1860–1895* (Moscow, 1956)

___, 'Velikie derzhavy i Serbiya v 1914 g.', *VIst* (1976/4), pp. 22–32

Naujoks, E., *Bismarcks auswärtige Pressepolitik und die Reichsgründung* (Wiesbaden, 1968)

Neiman, L., 'Franko-russkie otnosheniya vo vremya bosniiskogo krizisa 1908–1909', *FE* (1958), pp. 375–406

Neiman, L.A., 'Franko-russkie otnosheniya vo vremya marokkanskogo krizisa 1911 goda', *EF* (1969), pp. 65–91

Nifontov, A.S., 'Statistika urozhaev v Rossii v XIX v.', *IZ* 81 (1968), pp. 216–58

——, *Zernovoe proizvodstvo Rossii vo vtoroi polovine XIX veka* (Moscow, 1974)

Nikitenko, A.V., *Moya povest' o samom sebe. Zapiski i dnevnik, 1804–1877 gg.* (St Petersburg, 1905²), vols. 1–3

Nikitin, S.A., 'Russkoe obshchestvo i natsional'no-osvoboditel'naya bor'ba yuzhnykh slavyan v 1875–1876 gg.', *Obshchestvenno-politicheskie i kulturnye svyazi narodov SSSR i Yugoslavii. Sbornik statei* (Moscow, 1957), pp. 3–77

——, *Slavyanskie komitety v Rossii 1858–1876 gg.* (Moscow, 1960)

Nish, I.N., *Alliance in Decline. A Study in Anglo-Japanese Relations 1908–1923* (London, 1972)

——, *The Anglo-Japanese Alliance. The Diplomacy of the Two Island Empires 1894–1907* (London, 1966)

Nolde, B., *L'alliance franco-russe. Les origins du système diplomatique d'avant la guerre* (Paris, 1936)

Nolde, B.A., *Die Petersburger Mission Bismarcks 1859–1862* (Leipzig, 1936)

Nötzold, J., *Wirtschafspolitische Alternativen der Entwicklung Rußlands in der Ära Witte und Stolypin* (Munich, 1966)

Novotny, A., *Quellen und Studien zur Geschichte des Berliner Kongresses 1878* (Vienna, 1957), vol. 1

'Novye materialy o Gaagskoi mirnoi konferentsii 1899 g.', *KA* 50/51 (1932), pp. 64–96, 54/55 (1932), pp. 49–79

Ob osobennostyakh imperializma v Rossii (Moscow, 1963)

Okun, S.B., *Rossiisko-amerikanskaya kompaniya* (Moscow, 1939)

Ol' P.V., *Inostrannye kapitaly v Rossii* (Petrograd, 1922)

Olegina, I.N., 'Kapitalisticheskaya i sotsialisticheskaya industrializatsiya v traktovke A. Gershenkrona', *ISSSR* (1971/2), pp. 181–202

Opisanie russko-turetskoi voiny 1877–1878 gg. na Balkanskom poluostrove (St Petersburg, 1901–1913), 9 vols., 6 suppl. vols.

Oppel, B.F., 'The Waning of a Traditional Alliance. Russia and Germany after the Portsmouth Peace Conference', *CEH* 5 (1972), pp. 318–29

'*Organizovannyi kapitalizm*'. *Diskussiya v Komakademii* (Moscow, 1930)

Osobennosti agrarnogo stroya Rossii v period imperializma (Moscow, 1962)

Osvobozhdenie Bolgarii ot turetskogo iga, eds. S.A. Nikitin et al. (Moscow, 1961–67), vols. 1–3

Pares, B. 'Alexander Guchkov', *SEER* 15 (1936), pp. 121–34

Pavlovich, M., 'Vneshnyaya politika i russko-yaponskaya voina', *ODR* 2/1 (St Petersburg, 1909), pp. 1–32

Pershin, A., *Agrarnaya revolyutsiya v Rossii*, vol. 1: *Ot reformy k revolyutsii* (Moscow, 1966)

Pesda, J.L., 'Bunge and Russian Economic Development, 1881–1886', PhD thesis, Kent State Univ., 1971

Pétoux, P., 'L'ombre de Pougačev', in R. Portal (ed.), *Le statut de paysans libérés du servage, 1861–1961* (Paris, 1963), pp. 128–52

Petrovich, M.B., *The Emergence of Russian Panslavism 1856–1870* (New York, 1956)

Pfalzgraf, K., 'Die Politisierung und Radikalisierung des Problems Rußland und Europa bei N.J. Danilevsky', *FOG* 1 (1953), pp. 55–204

Picht, U., *Pogodin und die Slavische Frage* (Stuttgart, 1969)

Pierce, R., *Russian Central Asia 1867–1917. A Study in Colonial Rule* (Berkeley, 1960)

Pinchuk, B.C., *The Octobrists in the Third Duma 1907–1912* (Seattle, 1974)

Pintner, W., *Russian Economic Policy under Nicholas I* (Cornell, 1967)

Pipes, R., 'Domestic Politics and Foreign Affairs', in I.J. Lederer (ed.), *Russian Foreign Policy. Essays in Historical Perspective* (New Haven, 1966³), pp. 145–70

___, *Struve. Liberal on the Left, 1870–1905* (Cambridge, Mass., 1970)

Pisarev, Yu.A., 'Vosstanie v Bosnii i Gertsegovine i evropeiskie derzhavy (1875–1878)', *NNI* (1976/2), pp. 48–58

Pistohlkors, G. v., *Ritterschaftliche Reformpolitik zwischen Russifizierung und Revolution* (Göttingen, 1978)

___, '"Russifizierung" u. die Grundlagen der baltischen Russophobie', *ZfO* 25 (1976), pp. 618–31

Plass, J.B., *England zwischen Rußland und Deutschland. Der Persische Golf in der britischen Vorkriegspolitik, 1899–1907* (Hamburg, 1966)

[Pobedonostsev, K.P.], *K.P. Pobedonostsev i ego korrespondenty. Pisma i zapiski*, vol. I/1 (Moscow, 1923), pp. 233f.

___, *Pisma Pobedonostseva k Aleksandru III* (Moscow, 1925), vol. 2

Pogrebinskii, A.P., *Gosudarstvennye finansy tsarskoi Rossii v epokhu imperializma* (Moscow, 1968)

___, *Ocherki istorii finansov dorevolyutsionnoi Rossii* (Moscow, 1954)

Poidevin, R., *Les relations économiques et financières entre la France et l'Allemagne de 1898 à 1914* (Paris, 1969)

Pokrovskii, S.A., *Vneshnyaya torgovlya i vneshnyaya torgovaya politika Rossii* (Moscow, 1947)

Poletika, N.P., *Vozniknovenie pervoi mirovoi voiny (iyul'skii krizis 1914 g.)* (Moscow, 1964)

Polivanov, A.A., *Iz dnevnikov i vospominanii po dolzhnosti voennogo ministra i ego pomoshchnika 1907–1916* (Moscow, 1924), vol. 1

[Polovtsov, A.A.], *Dnevnik gosudarstvennogo sekretarya A.A. Polovtsova*, vol. 1: 1883–1886; vol. 2: 1886–1892, ed. P.A. Zayonchkovskii (Moscow, 1966)

___, 'Iz dnevnika A.A. Polovtsova (1895–1900 gg.)', *KA* 46 (1931), pp. 110–32

Popov, A., 'Anglo-russkoe soglashenie o razdele Kitaya 1899 g.', *KA* 25

(1927), pp. 111–34

Popov, A.L., 'Iz istorii zavoevaniya Srednei Azii', *IZ* 9 (1940), pp. 198–242

Portal, R., 'Industriels Moscovites: le secteur cotonnier (1861–1914)', *CMRS* 4 (1963), pp. 5–46

——, 'Die russische Industrie am Vorabend der Bauernbefreiung', in D. Geyer (ed.), *Wirtschaft und Gesellschaft im vorrevolutionären Rußland* (Cologne, 1975), pp. 133–63

Pospielovsky, D., *Russian Police Trade Unionism* (London, 1971)

Potanin, V.V., 'Tarif 1857 g. i. tamozhennaya politika Rossii 1856–1860 gg.', *VLU* 20/4 (1965), pp. 48–56

Preyer, W.D., *Die russische Agrarreform* (Jena, 1914)

Price, D.C., *Russia and the Roots of the Chinese Revolution 1896–1911* (Cambridge, Mass., 1974)

Price, E.B., *The Russo-Japanese Treaties of 1907–1916 Concerning Manchuria and Mongolia* (Baltimore, 1933)

Purges, J.G., and D.A. West (eds.), *War and Society in Nineteenth Century Russia* (Toronto, 1972)

Pyziur, E., 'Bismarck's Appraisal of Russian Liberalism as Prussian Envoy in St. Petersburg', *CSP* 10 (1968), pp. 298–311

Quested, R.K.I., *The Expansion of Russia in East Asia 1857–1860* (Kuala Lumpur), 1968

Rabinovich, G.Kh., *Krupnaya burzhuaziya i monopolisticheskii kapital v ekonomike Sibiri kontsa XIX – nachala XX v.* (Tomsk, 1975)

Raffalovitch [Rafalovič], A., *L'abominable vénalité de la presse.... D'après des archives russes, 1897–1917* (Paris, 1931)

Ramotowska, F., *Rząd carski wobec manifestacij patriotycznych w kro'lestwie polskim w latach 1860–1862* (Warsaw, 1971)

Rauch, G. v., *Rußland. Staatliche Einheit u. nationale Vielfalt* (Munich, 1953)

Rautenberg, H.-W., *Der polnische Aufstand von 1863 u. die europäische Politik im Spiegel der deutschen Diplomatie u. der öffentlichen Meinung* (Wiesbaden, 1979)

Rawson, D.C., 'The Union of the Russian People 1905–1907. A Study of the Russian Right', PhD thesis, Univ. of Washington, 1971

[Reutern, M.v.], *Die finanzielle Sanierung Rußlands nach der Katastrophe des Krimkrieges 1862–1878 unter dem Finanzminister von Reutern* (Berlin, 1914)

Revolyutsionnaya situatsiya v Rossii, 1859–1861 gg. (Moscow, 1960–74), 6 vols.

Revolyutsionnoe dvizhenie v Rossii vesnoi i letom 1905 g. (vol. 1: Moscow, 1957; vol. 2: Moscow, 1961)

Revolyutsionnoe narodnichestvo 70-kh godov XIX v. (vol. 1: Moscow, 1964; vol. 2: Moscow/Leningrad, 1965)

Revunenko, V.G., *Pol'skoe vosstanie i evropeiskaya diplomatiya* (Moscow, 1957)

Rexheuser, R., *Dumawahlen und lokale Gesellschaft. Studien zur Sozialgeschichte der russischen Rechten vor 1917* (Cologne, 1980)

Rhinlander, L.H., 'Russia's Imperial Policy: The Administration of the Caucasus in the First Half of the 19th Century', *CSP* 17 (1975), pp. 218–35

Rhyne, G.N., 'The Constitutional Democratic Party from its Origins Through the First State Duma', PhD thesis, Univ. of North Carolina, 1968

Riasanovsky, N.V., 'Asia Through Russian Eyes', in W.S. Vucinich (ed.), *Russia and Asia. Essays of the Influence of Russia on the Asian Peoples* (Stanford, 1972), pp. 3–29, 369–75

___, *Nicholas I and Official Nationality in Russia, 1825–1855* (Berkeley, 1967²)

Rieber, A.J., 'Alexander II. A Revisionist View', *JMH* 43 (1971), pp. 42–58

___, 'The Formation of La Grande Société des Chemins de Fer Russes', *JGO* 21 (1973), pp. 375–91

___ (ed.), *The Politics of Autocracy. Letters of Alexander II to Prince A.I. Bariatinsky, 1857–1864* (Paris, 1966)

___, *Merchants and Entrepreneurs in Imperial Russia* (Chapel Hill, 1982)

Riha, T., *A Russian European. Paul Miliukov in Russian Politics* (Notre Dame, 1968)

Ritchie, G.B., 'The Asiatic Department During the Reign of Alexander II, 1855–1881', PhD thesis, Columbia Univ., New York, 1975

Robbins, G.B. Jr., *The Famine in Russia 1891–1892: The Imperial Government Responds to a Crisis* (New York, 1975)

Rogger, H., 'The Beilis Case: Anti-Semitism and Politics in the Reign of Nicholas II', *SR* 25 (1966), pp. 615–29

___, 'The Formation of the Russian Right 1900–1906', *CSS* 3 (1964), pp. 66–94

___, 'Government, Jews, Peasants and Land in Post-Emancipation Russia', *CMRS* 17 (1976), pp. 5–25, 171–211

___, 'The Jewish Policy of Late Tsarism. A Reappraisal', *The Wiener Library Bull.* 25 (1971), pp. 42–51

___, 'National Consciousness in 18th-Century Russia' (Cambridge, Mass., 1960)

___, 'Russia in 1914', in *1914: The Coming of the First World War* (New York, 1966), pp. 229–53

___, 'Russian Ministers and the Jewish Question, 1881–1917', *CSS* 8 (1975), pp. 15–76

___, 'Was there a Russian Fascism? The Union of the Russian People', *JMH* 36 (1964), pp. 398–415

___, *Russia in the Age of Modernisation and Revolution, 1881–1917* (London, 1983)

Romanov, B.A. (ed.), 'Konets russko-yaponskoi voiny', *KA* 28 (1928), pp. 182–204

—, *Ocherki diplomaticheskoi istorii russko-yapanskoi voiny 1895–1907 gg.* (Moscow Leningrad, 1947, 1955²)

—, *Rossiya v Man'zhurii (1892–1906). Ocherki po istorii vneshnei politiki samoderzhaviya v epokhu imperializma* (Leningrad, 1929); English transl. as *Russia in Manchuria* (Ann Arbor, 1952)

—, (ed.), *Russkie finansy i evropeiskaya birzha 1904–1906* (Moscow, 1926)

Roosa, R.A., 'The Association of Industry and Trade 1906–1914', PhD thesis, Columbia Univ., 1967

—, 'Russian Industrialists and "State Socialism" 1906–1914', *SS* 23 (1972), pp. 395–417

—, 'Russian Industrialists Look to the Future. Thoughts on Economic Development 1906–1914', *Essays in Russian and Soviet History* (Leiden, 1963), pp. 189–208

—, 'Russian Industrialists, Politics and Labor Reform in 1905', *Russian History* 2 (1975), pp. 124–48

—, 'Workers' Insurance and the Role of the Industrialists in the Period of the Third State Duma', *RR* 34 (1975), pp. 410–52

Ropponen, R., *Die Kraft Rußlands. Wie beurteilte die politische und militärische Führung der europäischen Großmächte in der Zeit von 1905 bis 1914 die Kraft Rußlands?* (Helsinki, 1968)

Rosenberg, H., *Die Weltwirtschaftskrise 1857–1859* (Stuttgart, 1934, Göttingen, 1974²)

Roseveare, I.M., 'From Reform to Rebellion: A. Wielopolski and the Polish Question 1861-1863', *CSS* 3 (1969), pp. 263–85

Rostow, W.W. (ed.), *The Economics of Take-off into Sustained Growth* (London, 1963)

—, 'Kondratieff, Schumpeter and Kuznets', in 'Trend-Periods Revisted', *JEH* 35 (1975), pp. 417–53

—, *The Stages of Economic Growth. A Non-Communist Manifesto* (Cambridge, 1960)

Rowland, R.H., 'Urban In-Migration in Late-19th-Century Russia', PhD thesis, Columbia Univ., 1971

Rozental, E.M., *Diplomaticheskaya istoriya russko-frantsuzskogo soyuza nachala XX v.* (Moscow, 1960)

Rozhkova, M.K., *Ekonomicheskie svyazi Rossii so Srednei Aziei 40–60-kh godov XIX v.* (Moscow, 1963)

Rudd, C.A., 'The Russian Empire's New Censorship Law of 1865', *CSS* 3 (1969), pp. 235–45

Russko-yaponskaya voina 1904–1905 gg. Rabota Voenno-istoricheskoi kommissii po opisaniyu russko-yaponskoi voiny (St Petersburg, 1910) 9 vols.

Russko-kitaiskie otnosheniya 1689–1916. Ofitsial'nye dokumenty (Moscow, 1958)

Rutkowski, E.R. v., 'General Skobelew, die Krise des Jahres 1882 und die

Anfänge der militärischen Vereinbarungen zwischen Österreich-Ungarn und Deutschland', *Ostdeutsche Wissenschaft* 10 (1963), pp. 81–151

Rybachenok, I.S., 'Raznoglasiya v pravyashchikh krugakh o napravlenii vneshnei politiki v 1886–87 gg.', *VMU-Ist* (1973/5), pp. 78–87

Rybakov, Yu. Ya., *Promyshlennaya statistika Rossii XIX v. Istochnikovedcheskoe issledovanie* (Moscow, 1976)

Sablinsky, W., *The Road to Bloody Sunday* (Princeton, 1976)

Sadykov, A.S., *Ekonomicheskie svyazi Khivy s Rossiei vo vtoroi polovine XIX – nachale XX vv.* (Tashkent, 1965)

Sagratyan, A.T., *Istoriya zheleznykh dorog Zakavkaz'ya 1856–1921 gg.* (Erevan, 1970)

Samarin, Yu., *Okrainy Rossii*, ser. 1: *Russkoe Baltiiskoe pomore*, Vyp. 1 (Prague, 1868) — in *Sochineniya*, vol. 9 (1898)

Sarkisyanz, E., *Geschichte der orientalischen Völker Rußlands bis 1917* (Munich, 1961)

——, 'Russian Conquest in Central Asia. Transformation and Acculturation', in W.S. Vucinich (ed.), *Russia and Asia. Essays on the Influence of Russia on the Asian Peoples* (Stanford, Cal., 1972), pp. 248–88

——, 'Russian Imperialism Reconsidered', in T. Hunczak (ed.), *Russian Imperialism from Ivan the Great to the Revolution* (New Brunswick, NJ 1974), pp. 45–81

Sasonoff [Sazonov], S.D., *Sechs, schwere Jahre* (Berlin, 1927)

Sbornik dogovorov Rossii s drugimi gosudarstvami, 1856–1917 (Moscow, 1952)

Sbornik materialov po russko-turetskoi voine 1877–1878 gg. na Balkanskom poluostrove (St Petersburg, 1898–1911), 97 vols.

Scheibert, P., *Die russische Agrarreform von 1861. Ihre Probleme und der Stand ihrer Erforschung* (Cologne, 1973)

Schlarp, K.H., *Ursachen und Entstehung des Ersten Weltkrieges im Lichte der sowjetischen Geschichtsschreibung* (Hamburg, 1971)

Schlingensiepen, G.H., *Der Strukturwandel des baltischen Adels in der Zeit vor dem Ersten Weltkrieg* (Marburg, 1959)

Schlözer, K. v., *Petersburger Briefe 1857–1862* (Stuttgart, 1921)

Schmidt, V., *Die deutsche Eisenbahnpolitik in Shantung, 1898–1914. Ein Beitrag zur Geschichte des deutschen Imperialismus in China* (Wiesbaden, 1976)

Schramm, G., 'Militarisierung u. Demokratisierung. Typen der Massenintegration im ersten Weltkrieg', *Francia* 3 (1975), pp. 476–97

——, 'Die russische Armee als politischer Faktor vor der Februarrevolution (1914–1917)', *MGM* 18 (1975), pp. 33–62

Schrecker, J.E., *Imperialism and Chinese Nationalism. Germany in Shantung* (Cambridge, Mass., 1971)

Schröder, H.C., *Sozialistische Imperialismusdeutung* (Göttingen, 1973)

Schroeder, P.W., *Austria, Great Britain and the Crimean War. The De-*

struction of the European Concert (Ithaca, 1972)

Schüle, E., *Rußland und Frankreich vom Ausgang des Krimkrieges bis zum italienischen Krieg, 1856–1859* (Berlin, 1935)

Schulze-Gaevernitz, G. v., 'Der russische Nationalismus und seine wirtschaftlichen Träger', *PJ* 75 (1894), pp. 1–31, 337–64, 496–528

——, *Volkswirtschaftliche Studien aus Rußland* (Leipzig, 1899)

Schwarz, S.M., *The Russian Revolution of 1905* (Chicago, 1967)

[Schweinitz, H.L. v.], *Denkwürdigkeiten des Botschafters General von Schweinitz* (Berlin, 1927)

——, *Briefwechsel des Botschafters General von Schweinitz* (Berlin, 1928)

Seletskii, V.N., 'Obrazovanie partii progressistov. K voprosam o politicheskoi konsolidatsii russkoi burzhuazii', *VMU-Ist* (1970/5) pp. 33–48

Senkevich, I.G., *Rossiya i kritskoe vosstanie, 1866–1869 gg.* (Moscow, 1970)

Shannon, R.T., *Gladstone and the Bulgarian Agitation 1876* (Hamden, Conn., 1975²)

Shatsillo, K.F., 'Inostrannyi kapital i voenno-morskie programmy Rossii nakanune pervoi mirovoi voiny', *IZ* 69 (1961), pp. 73–100

——, 'O disproportsii v razvitii vooruzhennykh sil Rossii nakanune pervoi mirovoi voiny', *IZ* 83 (1969), pp. 123–36

——, 'Razvitie vooruzhennykh sil Rossii nakanune pervoi mirovoi voiny. Voennye i voenno-morskie programmy tsarskogo pravitel'stva v 1906–1914 gg.' avtoref. diss., Moscow, 1968

——, *Rossiya pered pervoi mirovoi voinoi. Vooruzhennye sily tsarizma v 1905–1914 gg.* (Moscow, 1974)

——, *Russkii imperializm i razvitie flota nakanune pervoi mirovoi voiny (1906–1914 gg.)* (Moscow, 1968)

Shepelev, L.E., *Aktsionernye kompanii v Rossii* (Leningrad, 1973)

Shneerson, L.M., *Avstro-prusskaya voina i diplomatiya velikikh evropeiskikh derzhav* (Minsk, 1962)

——, *Franko-prusskaya voina. Iz istorii russko-prusskikh i russko frantsuzskikh otnoshenii v 1867–1871* (Minsk, 1976)

Sidel'nikov, S.I., 'Sovetskaya i bolgarskaya istoriografiya Aprel'skogo vosstaniya 1876 g. v Bolgarii', *VIst* (1976/4), pp. 49–71

Sidel'nikov, S.M., *Obrazovanie i deyatelnost' Pervoi Gosudarstvennoi Dumy* (Moscow, 1962)

——, 'Zemel'no-krest'yanskaya politika samoderzhaviya v preddumskii period', *ISSSR* (1976/4), pp. 124–35

Sidorov, A.L. (ed.) 'Denezhnoe obrashchenie i finansovoe polozhenie Rossii (1904–1907 gg.)', *IA* (1956/3), pp. 88–123

——, 'Finansovoe polozhenie tsarskogo samoderzhaviya v period russko-yaponskoi voiny i pervoi russkoi revolyutsii', *IA* (1955/2), pp. 120–49

——, *Finansovoe polozhenie Rossii v gody pervoi mirovoi voiny* (Moscow, 1960)

——, 'Iz istorii podgotovki tsarizma k pervoi mirovoi voine', *IA* (1962/2), pp. 132–55

___, 'Konversii vneshnikh zaimov Rossii v 1888–1890 gg.', *IA* (1959/3), pp. 99–125

___, 'V.I. Lenin o russkom voenno-feodal'nom imperializme', *Ob osobennostyakh imperializma v Rossii* (Moscow, 1963), pp. 11–52

Silin, A.S., *Ekspansiya germanskogo imperializma na Blizhnem Vostoke nakanune pervoi mirovoi voiny 1908–1914* (Moscow, 1976)

Simmonds, G.W., 'The Congress of the Representatives of the Nobles' Associations 1906–1916. A Case Study in Russian Conservatism', PhD thesis, Columbia Univ., 1964

Simonova, M.S., *Agrarnaya politika samoderzhaviya v nachale XX v.* (Moscow, 1975)

___, 'Otmena krugovoi poruki', *IZ* 83 (1969), pp. 159–95

___, 'Politika tsarizma v krest'yanskom voprose nakanune revolyutsii 1905–1907 gg.', *IZ* 75 (1965), pp. 212–42

Simpson, J.Y., *The Saburov Memoirs or Bismarck and Russia* (Cambridge, 1929)

Sinel, A., *The Classroom and the Chancellery: State Educational Reform in Russia under Count Dmitry Tolstoi* (Cambridge, Mass., 1973)

Skazkin, S.D., *Konets avstro-russko-germanskogo soyuza. Issledovanie po istorii russko-germanskikh i russko-avstriiskikh otnoshenii v svyazi s vostochnym voprosom v 80-e gody XIX stoletiya* (Moscow, 1928, 1974²)

Skerpan, A.A., 'The Russian National Economy and Emancipation', in A.D. Ferguson and A. Levin (eds.), *Essays in Russian History* (Hamden, Conn., 1964), pp. 161–229

Sklyarov, L.F., *Pereselenie i zemleustroistvo v Sibiri v gody stolypinskoi agrarnoi reformy* (Leningrad, 1962)

Sladkovskii, M.I., *Istoriya torgovo-ekonomicheskikh otnoshenii narodov Rossii s Kitaem (do 1917 g.)* (Moscow, 1974)

___, 'Otnosheniya mezhdu Rossiei i Kitaem v seredine XIX v.', *NNI* (1975/3), pp. 55–64

Slavyanskii sbornik. Slavyanskii vopros i russkoe obshchestvo v 1867–1878 godakh (Moscow, 1948)

Snow, G.E., 'The Kokovtsov Commission: An Abortive Attempt at Labor Reform in Russia in 1905', *SR* 31 (1972), pp. 780–96

___, 'The Peterhof Conference of 1905 and the Creation of the Bulygin Duma', *Russian History* 2 (1975), pp. 149–62

___, 'Vladimir Kokovtsov. A Case Study of an Imperial Bureaucrat 1904–1906', PhD thesis, Indiana Univ., 1976

Snytko, T., 'Iz istorii narodnogo dvizheniya v Rossii v podderzhku bor'by yuzhnykh slavyan za svoyu nezavisimost' v 1875–1876 gg.', *Obshchestvenno-politicheskie i kulturnye svyazi narodov SSSR i Yugoslavii. Sbornik statei* (Moscow, 1957), pp. 78–106

Sobolev, M.N., *Istoriya russko-germanskogo torgovogo dogovora* (Petrograd, 1915)

Solov'ev, Yu.B., 'Franko-russkii soyuz v ego finansovom aspekte (1895–1900 gg.)', *FE* (1961), pp. 162–206

——, 'Pravitel'stvo i politika ukrepleniya klassovykh pozitsii dvoryanstva v kontse XIX veka', *Vnutrennyaya politika tsarizma (seredina XVI–nachalo XX v.)* (Leningrad, 1967), pp. 239–80

——, 'Protivorechiya v pravyashchem lagere Rossii po voprosu ob inostrannykh kapitalakh v gody pervogo promyshlennogo pod"ema', *Iz istorii imperializma v Rossii* (Moscow, 1959), pp. 371–88

——, 'Samoderzhavie i dvoryanskii vopros v kontse XIX veka', *IZ* 88 (1971), pp. 150–209

——, *Samoderzhavie i dvoryanstvo v kontse XIX v.* (Leningrad, 1973)

Solovyeva, A.M., *Zheleznodorozhnyi transport Rossii vo vtoroi polovine XIX v.* (Moscow, 1975)

Sontag, J.P., 'Tsarist Debts and Tsarist Foreign Policy', *SR*27 (1968), pp. 529–41

Spring, D.W., 'The Trans-Persian Railway Project and Anglo-Russian Relations, 1909 to 1912', *SEER* 54 (1976), pp. 60–82

Stadelbauer, J., *Bahnbau und kulturgeographischer Wandel in Turkmenien. Einflüsse der Eisenbahn auf Raumstruktur, Wirtschaftsentwicklung und Verkehrsintegration in einem Grenzgebiet des russischen Machtbereichs* (Berlin, 1973)

Starr, S.F., *Decentralization and Self-Government in Russia, 1830–1870* (Princeton, 1972)

Stavrou, T.G., *Russian Interests in Palestine 1882–1914. A Study of Religious and Educational Enterprise* (Thessaloniki, 1963)

Stein, H.P., 'Der Offizier des russischen Heeres zwischen Reform und Revolution', *FOG* 13 (1967), pp. 59-83

Steinberg, J., 'Germany and the Russo-Japanese War', *AHR* 75 (1970) pp. 1965–86

Steinmann, F., and Hurwicz, E. *Konstantin Petrowitsch Pobedonoszew. Der Staatsmann der Reaktion unter Alexander III* (Königsberg, 1933)

Stelnik, B. Ya., *Bakinskii proletariat v gody reaktsii 1907–1911 gg.* (Baku, 1969)

Stepanyan, S., *Armeniya v politike imperialisticheskoi Germanii (konets XIX – nachalo XX v.)* (Erevan, 1975)

Stephan, J.J., *The Kuril Islands. Russo-Japanese Frontiers in the Pacific* (London, 1975)

Strong, J.W., 'The Ignat'ev Mission to Khiva and Bukhara in 1858', *CSP* 17 (1975), pp. 236–59

Strumilin, S.G., 'Promyshlennye krizisy v Rossii 1847–1907 gg.', in idem, *Ocherki ekonomicheskoi istorii Rossii i SSSR* (Moscow, 1966), pp. 424–58

Struve, P., 'Velikaya Rossiya. Iz razmyshlenii o russkoi revolyutsii' (first published in: *Russkaya Mysl'* 1908, p. 1) in idem, *Patriotitsa. Politika, kultura, religiya, sotsializm. Sbornik statei za pyat' let (1905–1911 gg.)* (St. Petersburg, 1911), pp. 73–96

Suchomlinow, W.A., *Erinnerungen* (Berlin, 1924)

Sumner, B.H., *Russia and the Balkans, 1870–1880* (Oxford, 1937, 1962²)
___, 'Tsardom and Imperialism in the Far East and Middle East 1880–1914', *Proceedings of the British Academy 1941* (London, 1942)
Suvorov, V.A., *Istoriko-ekonomicheskii ocherk razvitiya Turkestana. Po materialam zheleznodorozhnogo stroitel'stva v 1880–1917 gg.* (Tashkent, 1962)

Tang, P.S.H., *Russian and Soviet Policy in Manchuria and Outer Mongolia 1911 to 1931* (Durham, N.C., 1959)
Tarnovskii [Tarnovskij], K., 'Eshche raz o "srashchivanii" i "podchinenii"', *Ob osobennostyakh imperializma v Rossii* (Moscow, 1963), pp. 419–38
___, 'Problemy agrarnoi istorii Rossii perioda imperializma v sovetskoi istoriografii', *Problemy sotsial'no-ekonomicheskoi istorii Rossii* (Moscow, 1971), pp. 246–311
___, *Sovetskaya istoriografiya rossiiskogo imperializma* (Moscow, 1964)
Tatishchev, S.S., *Imperator Aleksandr II. Ego zhizn i tsarstvovanie* (St Petersburg, 1903)
Taube, M.A., *Der großen Katastrophe entgegen. Die russische Politik der Vorkriegszeit und das Ende des Zarenreiches (1904–1917). Erinnerungen* (Berlin, 1929)
Taylor, G.R., *The Transportation Revolution 1815–1860* (New York, 1962)
Thaden, E.C., *Conservative Nationalism in 19th-Century Russia* (Seattle, 1964)
___, *Russia and the Balkan Alliance of 1912* (Pennsylvania, 1965)
___, 'Samarin's "Okrainy Rossii" and Official Policy in the Baltic Provinces', *RR* 33 (1974), pp. 405–15
Tikhomirov, M.N., *Prisoedinenie Merva k Rossii* (Moscow, 1960)
Tikhonov, B.V., 'Pereselencheskaya politika tsarskogo pravitel'stva v 1892–1897 godakh', *ISSSR* (1977/1), pp. 109–20
Tillet, L., *The Great Friendship. Soviet Historians on the Non-Russian Nationalities* (Chapel Hill, N.C., 1969)
Tkachenko, P.S., *Revolyutsionnaya narodnicheskaya organizatsiya "Zemlya i Volya" v 1876–1879 gg.* (Moscow, 1961)
Tobien, A. v., *Die livländische Ritterschaft in ihrem Verhältnis zum Zarismus und russischen Nationalismus* (Riga, 1925), vol. 1
Tolf, R.W., *The Russian Rockefellers. The Saga of the Nobel Family and the Russian Oil Industry* (Stanford, 1976)
Treadgold, D.W., *The Great Siberian Migration. Government and Peasant in Resettlement from Emancipation to the First World War* (Princeton, 1957)
___, 'Russian Expansion in the Light of Turner's Study of the American Frontier', *Agricultural History* 26 (1952)
Tukhtametov, T.G., *Rossiya i Khiva v kontse XIX – nachale XX v. Pobeda Khorezmskoi narodnoi revolyutsii* (Moscow, 1969)

___, *Russko-bukharskie otnosheniya v kontse XIX – nachale XX v.* (Tashkent, 1966)

Tupolev, B.M., *Ekspansiya germanskogo imperializma v Yugo-Vostochnoi Evrope v kontse XIX – nachale XX veka* (Moscow, 1970)

Tupper, H., *To the Great Ocean. Siberia and the Trans-Siberian Railway* (London, 1965)

Tvardovskaya, V.A., 'Ideolog samoderzhaviya v period krizisa "verkhov" na rubezhe 70–80-kh godov XIX v.', *IZ* 91 (1973), pp. 217–66

Ulunyan, A.A., *Bolgarskii narod i russko-turetskaya voina 1877–1878 gg.* (Moscow, 1971)

Vaisberg, I.D., 'Sovet ob"edinennogo dvoryanstva i ego vliyanie na politiku samoderzhaviya 1906–1914' (Moscow, cand. diss. MGU, 1956)

Vainshtein, A.L., *Narodnoe bogatstvo i narodnokhozyaistvennoe nakoplenie predrevolyutsionnoi Rossii* (Moscow, 1960)

Valliant, R.B., 'Japan and the Trans-Siberian Railroad 1885–1905', PhD thesis, Univ. of Hawaii, 1974

Valuyev, P.A. *Dnevnik 1877–1884* (Petrograd, 1919)

___, *Dnevnik P.A. Valueva*, vol.1: 1861–1864; vol.2: 1865–1876, ed. P.A. Zayonchkovskii (Moscow, 1961)

Velikaya reforma (1861–1911). Russkoe obshchestvo i krest'yanskii vopros v proshlom i nastoyashchem (Moscow, 1911), 6 vols.

Venturi, F., 'L'immagine di Garibaldi in Russia all'epoca della liberazione dei servi', *Rassegna storica toscana 1960*, p. 307ff.

___, 'Problemi del populismo russo', *RSI* 83 (1971), pp. 314–84

___, *The Roots of Revolution* (London, 1960)

Vinogradov, K.B., *Bosniiskii krizis 1908–1909 gg. — prolog pervoi mirovoi voiny* (Leningrad, 1964)

Vinogradov, V.N., *Rossiyai ob"edinenie rumynskikh knyazhestv* (Moscow, 1961)

Vitkind, N. Ya., *Bibliografiya po Srednei Azii. Ukazatel' literatury po kolonial'noi politike tsarizma v Srednei Azii* (Moscow, 1929; republ. Cambridge, 1972)

[Vitte, S.Yu.], 'Dokladnaya zapiska Vitte Nikolayu II (1900)', *IM* (1935/2–3), pp. 130–9

___, *Erzwungene Aufklärungen aus Anlaß des Berichtes des Generaladjutanten Kuropatkin über den Krieg mit Japan* (Vienna, 1911)

___, *Vorlesungen über Volks- und Staatswirtschaft (1901/02)* (Stuttgart, 1913), 2 vols.

___, *Vospominaniya*, vols. 1–3. ed. A.L. Sidorov (Moscow, 1960)

___, 'Vsepoddaneishii doklad ministra finansov S.Yu. Vitte Nikolayu II', *Materialy po istorii SSSR* (Moscow, 1959), vol. 6, pp. 173–222

Vnutrennyaya politika tsarizma (seredina XVI–nachalo XX v.) (Leningrad, 1967)

Vogel, B., *Deutsche Rußlandpolitik. Das Scheitern der deutschen Weltpolitik unter Bülow, 1900–1906* (Düsseldorf, 1973)

Volk, S.S., *Narodnaya volya, 1879–1882 gg.* (Moscow, 1966)

Volobuev, P.V., 'Iz istorii monopolizatsii neftyanoi promyshlennosti dorevolyutsionnoi Rossii', *IZ* 52 (1955), pp. 80–111

Voprosy istorii kapitalisticheskoi v Rossii. Problema mnogoukladnosti (Sverdlovsk, 1972)

Vosstanie 1863 g. i. russko-pol'skie revolyutsionnye svyazi 60-kh godov (Moscow, 1960)

Vovchik, A.V., *Politika tsarizma po rabochemu voprosu v predrevolyutsionnyi period 1895–1904* (Lemberg, 1964)

Vucinich, W.S. (ed.), *Russia and Asia. Essays on the Influence of Russia on the Asian People* (Stanford, 1972)

——, *Serbia between East and West, 1903–1908* (Stanford, 1954)

Vyshny, P., *Neo-Slavism and the Czechs 1898–1914* (Cambridge, 1977)

Waller, B., *Bismarck at the Crossroads. The Reorientation of German Foreign Policy after the Congress of Berlin 1878–1880* (London, 1974)

Walsh, W.B., 'The Composition of the Dumas', *RR* 8 (1949), pp. 111–16

Walter, D., *The Short Victorious War. The Russo-Japanese Conflict 1904–05* (London, 1973)

Wehler, H.-V., 'Bismarcks späte Rußlandpolitik 1879–1890', in idem, *Krisenherde des Kaiserreiches 1871–1918* (Göttingen, 1970), pp. 163–80

——, *Bismarck und der Imperialismus* (Cologne, 1969, 1973³, 1976⁴)

——, (ed.), *Imperialismus* (Cologne, 1970)

——, 'Sozialdarwinismus im expandierenden Interventionsstaat', in *Deutschland in der Weltpolitik des 19. u. 20. Jhs. Fs. f. F. Fischer* (Düsseldorf, 1973), pp. 133–42

Wernecke, K., *Der Wille zur Weltgeltung. Außenpolitik und Öffentlichkeit am Vorabend des Ersten Weltkrieges* (Düsseldorf, 1969)

White, J.A., *The Diplomacy of the Russo-Japanese War* (Princeton, 1964)

Whitman, J., 'Turkestan Cotton in Imperial Russia', *ASEER* 15 (1956), pp. 190–205

Wieczynski, J.L., 'Toward a Frontier Theory of Early Russian History', *RR* 33 (1974), pp. 294–95

Wierzchowski, M., *Sprawy Polski w III i IV dumie pan'stwowej* (Warsaw, 1966)

Wildman, A.K., *The Making of a Workers' Revolution. Russian Social Democracy 1891–1903* (Chicago, 1967)

Williams, W.A., *American-Russian Relations, 1781–1947* (New York, 1952)

——, (ed.), *Organisierter Kapitalismus. Voraussetzungen u. Anfänge* (Göttingen, 1974)

Witt, P., *Die Finanzpolitik des Deutschen Reiches, 1903–1913* (Lübeck, 1970)

Wittram, R., *Baltische Geschichte* (Munich, 1954)

Bibliography

—, 'Bismarcks Rußlandpolitik nach der Reichsgründung', in *Rußland, Europa und der deutsche Osten* (Munich, 1960), pp. 161–84

—, 'Das russische Imperium u. sein Gestaltwandel', *HZ* 187 (1959), pp. 568–93

—, 'Die russisch-nationalen Tendenzen der achtziger Jahre im Spiegel der österreichisch-ungarischen Berichte aus St. Petersburg', in Wittram, *Das Nationale als europäisches Problem* (Göttingen, 1954), pp. 183–213

Wittschewsky, V., *Rußlands Handels-, Zoll-, und Industriepolitik von Peter dem Großen bis auf die Gegenwart* (Berlin, 1905)

Wolters, M., *Außenpolitische Fragen vor der vierten Duma* (Hamburg, 1969)

Wortman, R., 'Koshelev, Samarin and Cherkassky and the Fate of Liberal Slavophilism', *SR* 21 (1962), pp. 261–79

Yaney, G., *The Urge to Mobilize: Agrarian Reform in Russia* (Urbana, Ill., 1982)

Young, L.K., *British Policy in China 1895–1902* (Oxford, 1969)

Young, M.B., *The Rhetoric of Empire. American China Policy, 1895–1901* (Cambridge, Mass., 1968)

Zabriskie, E.H., *American-Russian Rivalry in the Far East. A Study in Diplomacy and Power Politics, 1895–1914* (Philadelphia, 1946)

Zakharova, L.G., 'Krizis samoderzhaviya nakanune revolyutsii 1905 g.', *VIst* (1972/8), pp. 119–40

—, 'Otechestvennaya istoriografiya o podgotovke krest'yanskoi reformy', *ISSSR* (1976/4), pp. 54–76

—, 'Pravitel'stvennaya programma otmeny krepostnogo prava', *ISSSR* (1975/2), pp. 22–47

—, *Zemskaya kontrreforma 1890 g.* (Moscow, 1968)

Zakher, Ya. M., 'Konstantinopol' i prolivy', *KA* 6 (1924), pp. 48–76, *KA* 7 (1924), pp. 32–54

Zayonchkovskii, A., *Podgotovka Rossii k mirovoi voine v mezhdunarodnom otnoshenii* (Leningrad, 1926)

—, *Podgotovka Rossii k imperialisticheskoi voine. Ocherki voennoi podgotovki i pervonachal'nykh planov* (Moscow, 1926)

Zayonchkovskii, P.A., *Krizis samoderzhaviya na rubezhe 1870–1880 godov* (Moscow, 1964)

—, *Rossiiskoe samoderzhavie v kontse XIX st. Politicheskaya reaktsiya 80-kh–nachala 90-kh godov* (Moscow, 1970)

—, *Samoderzhavie i russkaya armiya na rubezhe XIX–XX stolety* (Moscow, 1973)

—, *Voennye reformy 1860–1870 godov v Rossii* (Moscow, 1952)

Zalyshkin, M.M., *Vneshnyaya politika Rumynii i rumyno-russkie otnosheniya 1875–1876* (Moscow, 1974)

Zeil, W., 'Der Neoslawismus', *JGSLE* 19/2 (1975), pp. 29–56

Zelnik, R.E., *Labor and Society in Tsarist Russia. The Factory Workers of St. Petersburg 1855–1870* (Stanford, 1970)

Zhidkov, G.P., *Kabinetskoe zemlevladenie (1747–1917 gg.)* (Novosibirsk, 1973)

Zilli, V., *La rivoluzione russa del 1905. La formazione dei partiti politici 1881–1904* (Naples, 1963)

Zimmerman, J.E., 'Between Revolution and Reaction: The Russian Constitutional Democratic Party (1905–1907), PhD thesis, Columbia Univ., 1967

Zolotov, V.A., *Khlebnyi eksport Rossii cherez porty Chernogo i Azovskogo moryei v 60–90e gody XIX v.* (Rostov, 1966)

Zuckermann, S., *Der Warenaustausch zwischen Rußland und Deutschland* (Berlin, 1915)

Zürrer, W., *Die Nahostpolitik Frankreichs und Rußlands 1891–1898* (Wiesbaden, 1970)

Zyzniewski, S.J., 'The Futile Compromise Reconsidered. Wielopolski and Russian Policy in the Congress Kingdom 1861–1863', *AHR* 70 (1965), pp. 395–412

___, 'Milyutin and the Polish Question', *HSS* 4 (1957), pp. 237–48

Index

383

Index